PENNY JUNOR

HOME TRUTHS

Life around my father

HarperCollins*Publishers*

HarperCollins*Publishers*
77–85 Fulham Palace Road,
Hammersmith, London W6 8JB

www.fireandwater.com

This paperback edition 2003
1 3 5 7 9 8 6 4 2

First published in Great Britain by
HarperCollins*Publishers* 2002

Copyright © Penny Junor 2002

The Author asserts the moral right to
be identified as the author of this work

ISBN 0 00 710214 3

Set in Sabon by
Rowland Phototypesetting Ltd,
Bury St Edmunds, Suffolk

Printed in Great Britain by
Clay Ltd, St Ives plc

Penny Junor is a writer and broadcaster. She is the author of previous best-selling biographies of both the Prince and the Princess of Wales, and two British Prime Ministers. For many years she presented *The Travel Show* on BBC2, and Channel 4's consumer programme *4 What It's Worth*. She is married with four children and lives in Wiltshire.

Reviews for *Home Truths*:

'. . . a painfully honest memoir of an almost wholly dysfunctional family'

'genuinely moving'   ANTHONY HOWARD, *Sunday Times*

'an unfailingly readable mixture of biography and self-analysis, often anguished, but punctuated by some very funny anecdotes . . . This is an eloquent and heartfelt epitaph'
                            ARNOLD KEMP, *Observer*

'a fascinating read . . . full of good stories and shafts of insight'
                            Sunday Telegraph

'[a] well-written rollercoaster of a book'
                            PETER MCKAY, *Daily Mail*

'Reading this book we are privy to the Big Fight – between good and evil in a man's soul. It is such an honest book that his daughter does not leave us with any sentimental optimism about which was victorious. What she captures so poignantly is the loveability of an outwardly unlovely person.'
                            A N WILSON, *Oldie*

'Penny's brave and searing biography'
                            SELINA SCOTT, *Evening Standard*

'. . . her remarkable memoir of life with father . . .'
                            ALAN WATKINS, *Spectator*

For Pam

The author and publisher are grateful to the following for permission to use their copyright material:

Text
Tom Utley review © the *Literary Review*; Lord Beaverbrook letters © Lord Beaverbrook; Roderick Junor letters © Suzy Junor; Lord Rothermere; *Evening Standard*, *Mail on Sunday* and *Daily Mail* articles © Associated Newspapers; *Observer* review © Alan Watkins; 'Relative Values' article © Danny Danziger; *Independent on Sunday* profile © Lynn Barber; Alan Watkins review © the *Spectator*; all *Daily Express* and *Sunday Express* articles reproduced by kind permission of Express Newspapers.

Photographs
The following photographs are © Express Syndication: Picture Section One: page 4, Lord Beaverbrook and son. Picture Section Two: page 9, JJ at desk; page 10, JJ with colleagues; page 11, JJ and Penny Junor in front of Express building; page 14, JJ with Mrs Thatcher; JJ and family at his investiture. Photograph of JJ with Selina Scott, page 12, reproduced courtesy of Grampian Television.

John Junor caricature reproduced by kind permission of Trog; Bill Martin cartoon reproduced by kind permission of Penny Hart.

All other photographs are from the author's personal collection.

Contents

Acknowledgements

This is an extremely personal book, and I am painfully aware that in writing about my memories of my father and my immediate family, I am inevitably invading the privacy of other relatives whose paths crossed ours and whose memories may be very different from my own. I am particularly aware of the sensibilities of my sister-in-law, Suzy Junor; but my brother's story is inextricably part of my father's and as such could not be ignored. I am grateful to her for reading the manuscript and allowing me to reproduce letters Roderick wrote as a child. I salute her fortitude; also that of her son, Rod, who is a remarkable human being and a credit to both his parents.

But, while much of the book has come from personal memories, a huge amount has come from my father's colleagues, family, friends, lovers and acquaintances, who have been enormously generous with their time and with their memories – some of which were funny, some shocking, some painful. I could have filled this book several times over with their stories about my father but, in the interests of keeping it portable, many have had to fall by the wayside. I am nevertheless very grateful to everyone I spoke to and have many happy memories of our meetings. In particular I would like to thank Jimmy Kinlay, who was not only hugely helpful but who additionally read and checked the manuscript for me. But many thanks also to the following for their help: Arthur Brittenden, Sally Brompton, Andrew Cameron, Ian Chapman, John S. Clark, Ray Cobb, Monty Court, Susan Crosland, Jane Crow, Paul Dacre, Peter Dacre, Max

Davidson, Christian Davies, The Rt Hon Lord Deedes, Lewis de Fries, Nigel Dempster, Michael Dove, Ken Duxbury, Robert Edwards, Mark Elsdon-Dew, Colin Emson, Robin Esser, Dickie Gay, Tom Gordon, the late William Gordon, Paul Halloran, Penny Hart, Clive Hirschhorn, Jonathan Holborow, Alan Hoby, Catherine Howatson, Richard Ingrams, Ian Irvine, Frank Johnson, Jean and Robin Johnston, Muir Junor, Roderick Kennedy, Alfred Lee, Nick Low, Graham Lord, David and Dorothy Macdonald, Mary McKenzie, Henrietta Mackay, Peter McKay, Sam Maclean, Murdoch MacLennan, Henry Macrory, The Rt Hon John Major, Lady Olga Maitland, Cliff Michelmore, Dr Stanley and Kathleen Miller, James Mossop, Ewen Murray, Dr Iain Murray-Lyon, Michael Murphy, Robin Oakley, Hugh Paterson, H. W. Reid, Tim Satchell, Selina Scott, The Rt Hon the Lord St John of Fawsley, Stewart Steven, Lord Stevens, Iain Stewart, Eric Sykes, The Rt Hon the Baroness Thatcher, Michael Thornton, Michael Toner, Peter Tory, Tom Utley, Leslie Vanter, Alan Watkins, Michael Watts, Maureen Whitelaw, Andrew Wilson, Charles Wilson, Susie Winter, Helga Zitcer.

I am also very grateful to the following people for their generosity in allowing me to reproduce material to which they hold the copyright: Lord Beaverbrook, for letters and memos written by his grandfather to my father, Lord Rothermere for a letter from his father to mine, Lynn Barber, Danny Danziger and Alan Watkins for extracts from articles they wrote, Penny Hart for the wonderful cartoon drawn by her late husband, Bill Martin, and Trog for his masterly caricature of my father. My thanks also to the following for organising permission for me to use various articles and columns: Paul Dacre, Editor-in-Chief of Associated Newspapers, Maninder Gill at Express Newspapers, Stuart Reid at the *Spectator*, and Nancy Sladek at the *Literary Review*.

Special thanks also to *Private Eye* for allowing me to roam through back issues in the comfort of the office, and to Steve Torrington, Group Library Editor at Associated Newspapers, for digging out copies of my father's columns.

But without Val Hudson, friend, confidante and Publishing Director at HarperCollins, this book would have made *War and Peace* look like a short story. She is nothing short of a genius and guided me with extraordinary skill and sensitivity – and if ever the world of publishing palled, would make an excellent therapist! Huge, huge thanks to her. Also to Monica Chakraverty, Senior Editor, whose hard work, skill, patience, good humour and attention to detail can only be marvelled at. She has been a complete joy to work with and I am indebted to her. Others at HarperCollins who deserve special mention and many thanks are Joanne Wilson, Zoe Mayne, Simon Dowson-Collins, Rhiannon James, Fiona McIntosh, Rachel Smyth, Digby Smith, Jim Blades and Sarah Ereira. And as always I owe very great thanks to my agent Jane Turnbull, a trusted and invaluable sounding board and friend.

And no list of names to thank would be complete without those of my family – James, Sam, Alex, Jack and Peta, who have lived with me, my father and this book for a very long time – and to Mary Wakefield, who sat up all night reading the original, unexpurgated version!

Foreword

I have written this book for all sorts of reasons, including the fact that some years before he died I promised my father I would. When I had finished writing it, one of his closest friends asked me whether I had been nice about him. I didn't know how to reply. What I have been is brutally honest, and some people may find that shocking. I have talked about things that some people might say should never have been talked about – ever. But I wrote them because, difficult as he was to love, I loved him and I wanted, after all these years, to understand what made him such an impossible, destructive yet delightful man, and I couldn't do that without exploring his demons. Besides, he was never afraid to write the truth and he would not have expected me to write any differently.

John Junor was a legendary figure in the world of newspapers. He was Editor of the *Sunday Express* for thirty-two years from 1953 to 1986. For many of those years that newspaper was to be found on the breakfast table of over four million people each Sunday morning. He wrote a controversial current affairs column for twenty-two years, which was required reading for most of Britain's politicians and decision makers. He was a charming, charismatic man; he was also a bully, a sentimentalist and a control freak – as men who wield that degree of power often are – but he was a brilliant newspaperman. He had a feel for his readers, which was second to none, and a loyalty to his staff that was unmatched in Fleet Street.

He had written memoirs of his own. *Listening for a Midnight Tram* was a wonderfully evocative title, and it was a very good, gossipy read, but apart from some early memories of his childhood in Glasgow the book told you next to nothing about him. I was not the only one to be disappointed. I wanted to know what made him tick, what he felt about the things he had done in his life: his highs, his lows, his loves, his hates, his regrets.

So I wanted to write this book to fill in the gaps, and to see if I could find an explanation for why he was the way he was, and why he was so destructive towards my mother. For a long time I thought he was the only father who behaved as he did, but I now realise that, while my experiences may have been specific, they were not unique, and that ours was not the only family caught in the maelstrom that surrounds such a man. Like so many big, powerful characters, their success comes at a high price. The price he paid for that success was his family – the one thing, apart from newspapers, he really cared about.

I knew my father well and I saw him often, and I thought there would be no real surprises, but I was wrong. There were surprises that have dramatically altered my opinion of him. Maybe that is why he wanted to me write this book, so that, looking through the diaries, the papers, the letters and the unpublished novels he left for me, painfully linking together the pieces of his life, I would understand.

When he wrote his memoirs, most of the critics were unkind – so unkind that Tom Utley, who worked for my father in the last years of his editorship, felt moved to put pen to paper, and for the first and only time in his life volunteered to write a book review. This is what he wrote in the *Literary Review*.

Few, I think, would dream of calling him a nice man. As an Editor he was a tyrant – pig-headed, often monstrously unreasonable and full of barmy theories about politics and politicians . . . For those of us young enough or thick-skinned enough to endure a great deal of bullying, sentimental encouragement and humiliation, life under his command was tremendous fun. I quickly became, and remain, a devoted fan. But his memoirs are not really about him. And nobody could get any idea from reading them of the fact that they are the work of a columnist of genius and the last of the giants of old Fleet Street ... Others have been very sniffy about Junor's interest in the rich and famous. But I cannot think of a much better qualification for a journalist ... and if he appears to be more interested in his subjects' personality quirks than in their place in history, well, so are most of his readers. But John Junor, the sage of Auchtermuchty and the man who is constantly having to urge Alice to pass the sick bag, is quite as great a man in his way as the people he writes about, courts and lunches. I would rather read a book about him than this one by him.

Well, Tom, here it is.

CHAPTER ONE

A Shopping Trip

I can't remember when I stopped calling my father 'Daddy'. But I can remember when I stopped trusting him. I can only have been five or six. We went off on our own in the car together, a pale blue Ford Consul, which he had bought new in April 1953. We were going shopping. I can still remember the feeling as the car scrunched and bumped its way down the flinty drive, sitting alongside my father on the bench seat in the front, leaning forward with my arms on the dashboard, excited and nervous at the same time. Nervous, because I hated being alone with him, but excited because he was an exciting man to be with. Nothing was humdrum around my father. Every day, every outing, every game, everything he ever did, saw, knew, or ate was special. It was the best. He had a curiosity for everything that went on around him, an enthusiasm for those things he could control, and an optimism that was completely inexhaustible.

I loved him, of course, but it was never as simple as that. He wasn't like other people's fathers. One minute he would be sloppily sentimental and demand kisses and hugs, and the next he would be bad-tempered and shout at everyone, particularly my mother. I didn't like either extreme. But the real reason I didn't like being on my own with him was because, so often when we were alone, he would lecture me. I am sure there were other subjects, but the only one I remember was the evils of sex. I think he was trying to ensure that I would not grow up to be promiscuous, but he began aversion therapy well before I was aware of a life beyond dolls and make-believe, and I found the whole thing very alarming.

1

If there was a lecture on this occasion I don't remember it, but I do remember us both tucking into the sweets before we were halfway down the drive. They were little round orange-flavoured boiled sweets that were individually wrapped in orange Cellophane that you had to untwist to open. My father loved sweets and always kept a supply in his car, and for a while these were his favourite. Travel Sweets, in a round tin, were another. He also loved shopping. Shopping was an obsession, as much, I think, for the opportunity to speak to shopkeepers as for the pleasure of buying. They were his readers, they were representative of the man in the street, and finding out what they thought about life gave him a good feel for what the country thought. He liked small shops, which were run by the owner, and would be loyal to them.

As a child, what I liked best about shopping with him was that he always bought me something. That day he bought me some apples. Now, there was an ongoing needle match between my parents about apples. My mother liked and bought green apples. My father liked and bought red apples and used to rub them on his chest to make them shine, behaviour which my mother, who was very correct in her manners, couldn't abide. I was piggy in the middle, caught between the two, not wanting to hurt either parent by favouring either colour. It was the story of my life in microcosm.

So there we were out shopping together. My father was in a good mood, which was not always the case, and we were having a good time. These were the occasions when I felt sublimely happy in his company and wished it would go on forever. Sadly it never did.

'Just you sink your teeth into that,' he said, as he watched me take a juicy red apple, which he encouraged me to buff up on my jumper first. 'Isn't that a wonderful apple? Isn't it the best apple you've ever tasted?' 'Yes,' I said, basking in his approval. 'It's absolutely delicious.'

A satisfied grin came over his face, which at the time I was too young to recognise. Later I was to know it only too well. No sooner had we arrived home than he sprang from the car bearing the bag full of gleaming rosy fruit, and announced triumphantly to my mother that I had told him I really preferred red apples after all – I had just been saying I liked the green ones to please her.

2

My devastation was total. In my desire to please him I had been tricked into betraying my mother. It was a painful lesson and, although I always longed to, I never really trusted him again. The idea of confiding in him and opening up to him emotionally was very seductive and, time and again throughout my life, I came close, desperately wanting a relationship that could never really be. The sad thing is that I am certain he, too, wanted the sort of relationship I longed for, but he couldn't prevent himself from spoiling it – from using a confidence to his advantage to score a point in one way or another at a later date.

My father scared me. Not because he was violent – he only spanked me twice that I can remember, and he never hit my mother – but he was moody and unpredictable, and could be very cruel. In a good mood he could be the most charming, entertaining, amusing, generous man on earth, and I adored him. In a bad mood he could be vicious and say the most hurtful things. And there would be no apparent rhyme or reason for either, at least none that I, as a child, could discern. He might go to bed in a good mood and at breakfast the next morning lose his temper because the butter was the wrong temperature or his toast was not how he liked it. The evenings were just as unpredictable. There would be no knowing how he would be when he came home from the office at night. The only certainty was that his foul moods cast a blight on the entire household.

CHAPTER TWO

Midnight Tram

When I was quite small, we spent a family holiday in Glen Clova and, on the way there, stopped in Glasgow briefly and went to visit one of my father's elderly aunts – the only one I ever met. She lived in a forsaken, blackened tenement building, the like of which, with my comfortable Home Counties upbringing, I had never seen. We walked through a doorway and into a dark, dank, stinking stairwell with worn stone stairs and grime on the walls. We climbed to the second floor, then in through another door to a gloomy one-roomed flat that Aunt Ellen, a tiny, hunched figure with big, loving hugs, called home.

My father began life in just such a run-down tenement as this. It was in Shannon Street, in a working-class district of Glasgow called Maryhill. He was born John Donald Brown Junor, on 15 January 1919. There were two rooms for a family of five and no indoor sanitation. His mother was forty-two when she gave birth to him. She had lost twins that were stillborn some years before, making him the youngest, by ten years, of three boys. Sandy, his father – short for Alexander – worked for the Glasgow Steel Roofing Company and, soon after my father was born, became Works Manager, a post he held for over thirty years. There was very little money in the family, and Sandy never had a bank account, but he was always employed – unusual in those depressed post-war days, when so many men were on the dole. So, compared to some, they must have considered themselves well off.

JJ very seldom spoke about his childhood, and it is hard to know how poor they really were, but he was later obsessed by what people wore, by outward appearance, and he talked about the shame of children he knew being sent to school with worn and ragged clothes, even underclothes. He was horrified that I dressed my children in clothes from Oxfam when they were small and we had very little money, and later in the 1980s when they chose to wear ripped jeans and torn T-shirts.

I never knew Sandy: he died when I was three, and I don't remember ever meeting him, although diaries suggest that I was taken to see him when I was just a few months old. He must have had a hard life with precious little respite, and it certainly seems as though he got nothing out of family life. He was born in 1880 in the Black Isle, in the Highlands of Scotland, where his father was a farm manager. At eight, his mother died and at thirteen he was sent off to look for work in Glasgow by his father who had married again. He found a job at the steelworks and stayed there for the rest of his working life, growing progressively deafer as a result of the constant noise. Maggie, my grandmother, was his second wife; his first wife, a domestic servant, died in childbirth a year after their marriage, leaving him a widower at twenty-five.

Less than a year later he married Margaret Dickie; and if he had been looking for a soft, sympathetic creature to soothe his cares he had picked the wrong woman. She was three years older than him, short, solid and as tough as old boots, with great ambition for her offspring. As my father said, if she had devoted a bit more time to her husband and a little less to pushing her sons ever upwards, his father's life would have been different. As it was, Sandy lived for his work and for Friday nights – payday. Each week, having handed over the weekly housekeeping allowance to Maggie, which she made sure he did, he would take the remaining few shillings to the pub and get drunk.

JJ said that he hated Friday nights, hated the shouting, the rowing, and what he called 'the cursing monster' that his father became when he arrived home from the pub. His cousin Tom Gordon, who lived with the family as a paying guest while he was at secondary school in Glasgow, and was two years younger than JJ, remembers no such thing. He questions the ugly, drunken scenes that JJ talked about. Sandy spent the evening in the pub, he doesn't deny, but says he was never a fighting drunk. According to Tom, 'Sandy would arrive home in a happy and jolly mood, singing his favourite little ditty, "Uncle Sandy met a pie man on the promenade". Tom rather liked him and remembers no 'cursing monster'. Having weaved his way home, Sandy would take himself off to the kitchen 'recess', the bunk bed built into the wall where he and Maggie slept. There he would stay for the rest of the weekend, fortifying himself from time to time with bottles of beer. But on Monday morning he would be up and off to work without fail, and back to his mild-mannered self.

He was a tall, gentle, tactile man, with a deep, sonorous voice, which JJ inherited, who said little and, with the exception of Friday nights, kept his head down. Yet, for some reason, my father felt no affection for him at all. He also admitted that he never had a real conversation with his father, saying that the deafness Sandy suffered as a result of his job made communication difficult. At the steelworks by all accounts – and people whose fathers used to work for Sandy have come forward to tell me this – he was decent, hardworking and much respected by his workforce as a skilled craftsman and a fair manager. But at home he was evidently low in the pecking order.

If my father dreaded Friday nights because of the drunken rows, the experience didn't stop him behaving in much the same way in his own marriage, years later. One of my abiding memories from a childhood of emotional ups and downs was of my father and mother shouting at one another. In the evenings it was usually fuelled by alcohol, and it always started by JJ saying something unkind, or reacting angrily to some perfectly innocent question or innocuous remark. But, unlike his father, JJ's drinking was not confined to one night of the week. Apart from a couple of bouts of illness, he drank just about every day, usually at lunchtime and then again in the evening. Drink either made him soppy and sentimental or belligerent, depending upon whom he was with.

JJ must have despised his father's milder characteristics, too, because throughout his life JJ denigrated mild-mannered men, particularly those who had capable wives. He was also very rude about men with moustaches, which his father had. He despised men who wore hats (his father wore a bowler and a brown, soft felt hat) and he condemned pipe smokers; his father, it was no surprise to discover, smoked a pipe.

His mother was a different matter. JJ adored her and credited her, never his father, with having given him the education that allowed him to escape the poverty of Glasgow in the 1930s. Like many Scottish matriarchs of the time, she recognised that education was the route to success and was utterly determined to get her three sons into university. She drove them remorselessly and, when their cousins or friends were out messing about or kicking a football after school, more often than not, they would be studying. Tough as this regime must have been, the results were remarkable. Bill, the eldest, became the headmaster of a large secondary school in Glasgow by his early twenties, Tom became a highly successful GP, with a practice in the North of Scotland in his early twenties, and JJ went south and became the youngest and longest-serving Editor of the *Sunday Express*, which for many years was one of the most successful national Sunday newspapers in the country.

All found success, but at what a cost? Bill became an alcoholic and had to give up teaching long before he should have. He never married and spent much of his life in a home for alcoholics in Dumfries. Tom, whose wife died tragically, leaving him with two young children, became a depressive alcoholic and died at the age of fifty-six from an accidental overdose of barbiturates. And my father, while making a huge success of his professional life, was a deeply flawed character, who never, I fear, found true happiness or real friendship.

Maggie, by the time I knew her, looked like the granny in the famous Giles cartoons, utterly spherical with little round glasses, and ropes of beads around her neck. She would come to visit for a couple of weeks every summer – visits that my mother dreaded as a result of having lived with her when she and my father were first married. By the time I knew her she was in her late seventies and obviously a shadow of her former ferocious self. She would sit knitting woollen socks all day on four thin little needles, which I found mesmerising. And all I ever remember her saying was, 'Oh dear, oh dear, oh dear,' in a strong Glaswegian accent, as though the worst was always imminent.

She came from a family of nine children, all but two of whom married. Thomas Dickie, their father, was a schoolmaster who taught for thirty years at a little village school in Kershopefoot, near Newcastleton, in the Borders, where you could stand with one foot in Scotland and the other in England. There were glowing tributes in the local press when Thomas retired, about his prowess in the schoolroom, but he was equally well known in the local pub. Like most members of the Dickie family, he had a serious weakness for whisky. He drove a horse and cart and was famous for having trained his horse to come to the door of the pub when he whistled at the end of an evening. He would then have to navigate the path to the door of the schoolhouse on foot, and his children used to delight in tying string across the way to trip him up as he lurched drunkenly home.

After Thomas retired in 1914, he and his wife, Janet, went to live with their two unmarried children, Ina and John – another very heavy drinker – in a large flat at 100 Buccleuch Street in Glasgow. JJ never knew the schoolhouse in Kershopefoot, but he knew both grandparents because, every Sunday night, the family used to congregate at Buccleuch Street to play cards, chat and eat Aunt Ina's soup. JJ never spoke to me about his grandparents, but he did once give me a copy of a local newspaper cutting that he must have either come across or been sent, from 1930, which was a tribute to his grandfather on his eighty-second birthday, and described his life as a schoolmaster. Thomas had died later that year, when JJ was fourteen, and Janet died three years after him. JJ's numerous cousins remember their Grandpa Dickie as a cantankerous old so and so, and the residual memory of their grandmother was of the archetypal matriarch, sitting in a chair, presiding officiously over the comings and goings of her family.

Thomas Dickie had set up all his children in business: Ina had a greengrocer's shop, Ellen had a sweet shop, Tom was a wine merchant, Robert was a blacksmith, and Mary, Agnes, Bessie and Maggie all had dairies selling milk and groceries, the equivalent of the English corner shop. John, the youngest, was the only one without a business of some sort: he was a clerk at one of the gasworks in Glasgow.

Of all the sisters, Maggie was the toughest, the most determined and, I would guess, the least maternal. She cared about her sons passionately, but more in terms of what they could make of themselves than as the rounded, happy human beings they might grow into – but then maybe that is a luxury of the moneyed middle classes. Also, in the evenings, when the children were home and Sandy was back from a hard day's work, when they could have been together, shared a meal and talked to one another, Maggie was out, indulging an obsession. For, while several of her siblings became alcoholics like their father, her weakness was whist. She played almost every night of her adult life. There were whist drives all over Glasgow at that time and, no matter how far afield, she would take the train or bus or tram, sometimes a combination of all three, to get her evening fix – often not returning until nearly midnight when the last tram stopped.

As a small boy, JJ would lie awake waiting for the sound of her key in the door, unable to sleep until he knew she was safely home. She was a good player and often came home with the evening's first prize, which might be a bag of groceries, but it didn't make for a happy home life. There were no family meals, or entertaining; there was always plenty of food in the flat, but it was mostly soups and mutton pies, to which the children would have to help themselves. Green vegetables were unheard of.

The family moved from Shannon Street when JJ was five. He had just one memory of that first home, which haunted him all his life. He remembered as a toddler being held out of the window by some unidentified young woman, and being terrified he was going to be dropped into the street below. He would tell the story with a mixture of fear and anger, as though it had happened yesterday, and I often wondered whether his fundamental dislike of women had something to do with this incident.

Another early memory that had a profound effect on him was spending his fifth birthday in an isolation hospital suffering from diphtheria and scarlet fever, which he had caught from his brothers. Diphtheria was a very serious disease in those days, a lot of people died from it and, as a small boy, alone, cut off from his family, he was terrified. He never forgot the smell of the place, and throughout his life had a real horror of illness and hospitals. He hated being anywhere near them, even as a visitor, and, although I went into hospital a number of times during my childhood, I don't remember him ever coming to visit me. The only time he did was when I was grown up and had just had my second baby – he brought the first one in to see his new brother.

By the time JJ was released from the isolation hospital, the family had moved house. They were living in a semi-detached council house at 82 Walnut Road in Springburn, which, with five rooms – three up and two down – and a garden, was little short of paradise. That was not the only change. JJ began school for the first time, at Elmbank Public School, and Maggie took over a new dairy, round the corner in Hawthorn Street.

JJ's brother Bill was twelve years older than him, and Tom ten years older, so to all intents and purposes my father was brought up as an only child. Being so much the youngest, he was Maggie's favourite and, although she was a tough woman in many respects, she was also hugely sentimental, as only the Scots can be. I suspect 'No' was not a word she used very frequently with her youngest born.

One of the bonuses in writing about my father has been discovering relatives I scarcely knew existed. Last year I drove up to the northeast coast of England to meet a complete stranger, yet he looked and spoke like a combination of my father and my uncle Bill. Sitting at the table in the back room of his small semi-detached home in Redcar, I felt an extraordinary sense of belonging. The eighty-year-old with twinkling eyes has now become a firm friend and I wish I had known him earlier. As boys, he and my father had spent every school holiday together.

Tom Gordon was a cousin and, while he sought out fading photographs, he told me about their boyhood. He grew up in Turnberry, the Ayrshire village of golfing fame, where his father was the local blacksmith and his mother – Maggie's sister – ran the village shop and post office. Tom was a surveyor and, when JJ bought our house in 1958, he asked him to come and advise on the cesspit; he never did have any shame about asking for free professional advice from friends and relatives. Apart from that, their contact for the last fifty years or so was minimal.

Tom's elder brother, Bill, never left Turnberry, and his sister, Netta, took over the shop from their mother, but she died some years ago. After meeting Tom, I went to see Bill and his wife, who lived just over the road from the shop. He had worked as head groundsman at the famous Turnberry Hotel, but sadly he died not long after I met him.

There had been fourteen first cousins in all. Many of them are no longer alive, but I found another in Tunbridge Wells. Dickie Gay practises as a chiropodist in the front room of his house and, in between tending the toes of the celebrated, has become an expert on the family's history. Between the three of them, I learned more about my father's family and his childhood in Glasgow than I had ever known from him.

Despite his brothers being so much older, JJ's was not a lonely childhood. He frequently saw his aunts, uncles, cousins and friends. Sometimes he and a cousin would go to the cinema together, or go to watch the local football team, Partick Thistle, play on a Saturday afternoon. JJ was mad about football till the day he died and, from those early days of his childhood, he always harboured an ambition to score a goal between goalposts that had a net; but he never, ever did. When he played the game as a boy, it was mostly with a small, cheap ball on the streets. On the rare occasions when he played with a real football on a real football pitch, the surface was made of ash and cinders, not grass, and although there were goalposts, there was never a net behind the goalposts.

JJ's holidays were spent in the country. The day after school ended for the summer holidays, he would be packed off to stay with one of Maggie's relatives. This was no hardship: he loved it. His Uncle Robert and Aunt Mary were in Bo'ness on the Firth of Forth, and had a son called Tom. Aunt Bessie and her husband, Archie Macdonald, lived at Garelochhead in Dunbartonshire, with children Catherine and Robert. They had eight cart horses used for pulling vans for the family dairy business, as well as hens and turkeys. Aunt Agnes, married to Peter Gay, lived in Bearsden with their sons Bill and Dickie. Aunt Ellen lived in Partick with her husband Tom Adamson and son Wallace. And Aunt Mary and husband William Gordon and their children Bill, Tom and Netta lived by the sea in Turnberry.

But the place he loved best of all was Turnberry. Mary was his favourite aunt, and some of the happiest days of his childhood were spent there. Mary must have had a phenomenal capacity for work, as well as a heart of gold. For, in addition to looking after her family and running the shop, she regularly had up to eleven extra guests to feed and house. The cousins didn't often visit together, because there was quite an age range, but it was not unknown for the entire clan to descend, sometimes with their parents, and grandparents. And of all the sisters, it was Mary who looked after old Grandpa Dickie in his dying days.

JJ would travel the forty-seven miles from Glasgow to Turnberry on the bus. The fare was 3s. 6d., and, up to the age of fifteen, JJ was sick without fail about ten miles short of his destination. At the age of fifteen, he claims to have been sufficiently distracted by pretty girls on the bus to forget all about it, although I am not sure he ever truly got over his travel sickness – and it is something he handed down to me.

Bill Gordon, his brother Tom and JJ were good friends. A treat when they had enough money was to go to the little playhouse in Girvan, five miles away, which had travelling companies at the weekends. Sometimes Bill Gay, another cousin, would join them. They would sit in the front row and take the mickey out of the dancing girls, or suck oranges noisily in an attempt to put them off. Sometimes they would go from Girvan up to the theatre in Paisley and take a box, but they were no better behaved there. One night, fixing the trio with a hard stare, one of the comedians said: 'There's many a bad egg in a box.' JJ was never a hugely enthusiastic theatre-goer in later life, but he loved variety. He used to take me to the Players' Theatre under Charing Cross station, which put on old-fashioned music hall shows with great character actors like Clive Dunn performing; and he loved that as much as I did. It must have taken him back to his childhood.

At night, after the show, he and his cousins would lie awake in

bed discussing the finer attributes of the chorus girls. They used to
sleep in a couple of huts in the garden, and in a converted shed that
was normally used as a tearoom. Mary was a good cook, particularly at baking, and there was always plenty to eat. Potatoes grew
in the garden and there were hens to provide eggs. In return, the
cousins had to work for their keep. They would deliver her freshly
baked bread and rolls and bags of groceries to customers, or do the
newspaper rounds. It was a small village and there was no other
shop, so Mary played a very important part in the local community
and she was always the first to help anyone in trouble.

Turnberry's biggest claim to fame, then as now, was the golf. It
boasted two championship courses and a vast, luxury hotel, which
sat in beautifully manicured grounds, overlooking one of the courses
and the sea. It attracted some of the wealthiest people in the country
and, as soon as my father was strong enough to carry a set of golf
clubs, at about the age of eleven, he, like his cousins, used to caddy
for the hotel guests. This brought him into contact with people like
the Mackintosh family, who had made a fortune out of toffees, and
the Salmons of Lyon's Corner House fame. He was caddying one
day for Pat Salmon, one of the daughters of the family, when she
sliced a ball into the whin bushes. JJ clambered after it, and Pat
followed, protesting flirtatiously that he was too young to take her
into the bushes.

It was not unusual to caddy two rounds a day, earning 2s. 6d.
a round, plus a tip if they were lucky. At the end of the day, the
boys would play a few holes themselves. JJ loved golf and played
it almost every week of his life, although he was never as good as
one might have expected, given his early immersion. But maybe he
was picking up more about the people he caddied for than the game
itself. At night, he would hang around the grounds of the hotel
until the orchestra struck up, then he would press his face against
the ballroom windows and watch the elegantly dressed men and
women enjoying a lifestyle that was not only entirely alien to him,
but also totally out of the reach of anyone he knew.

He would often talk about this during my childhood, explaining
that he wasn't envious as he looked in; he simply wanted to join
them. And with his irrepressible optimism, which I only saw waver

in the last year of his life, he never for one moment doubted that one day he would. Back home in Glasgow, he would put out the lights and listen to late-night dance music on the wireless from top hotels like the Savoy and the Dorchester – the Savoy's bandleader, Carrol Gibbons, was his idol – and dream happily of what lay ahead.

I don't imagine his mother suffered from doubt either. A gypsy once told her fortune: 'You have three sons,' she said, 'two of them have done well but your third will outstrip both of them and will become famous. You will be very proud of him.' By that time Bill was already a headmaster, Tom had qualified as a doctor – despite his father's wishes that he should follow him into the steelworks – and JJ was a schoolboy.

By now, the family had moved to 91 Oban Drive in Maryhill, where they rented a small second floor flat for £32 per year. They had sacrificed space for a rather better address. It had a smart stained-glass front door, which led into a little entrance hall off which were two small bedrooms, a small bathroom and a minute kitchen. There was a black solid-fuel range in the kitchen, and the bunk bed where his parents slept. At the front, with a view over Maryhill, was an all-purpose living-cum-dining room. The advantage of Oban Drive was that it was closer to JJ's new school, and education was the key to his escape.

CHAPTER THREE

The Gift of Education

JJ was proud of his Scottish origins, but kept none of the friends from his boyhood and, despite the closeness of his cousins, he saw next to nothing of them once he moved away. Their names became little more than signatures on greetings cards at Christmas. As for his father's side of the family, I never heard him even mention a single name. He took us all to visit Dingwall and the Black Isle once when I was very young, and we saw the names of our ancestors on headstones in the churchyard. We had even knocked on a door and found a family of Junors inside, who must have been related I suppose, but my father never once referred to his paternal grand-father or a single aunt, uncle or Junor cousin. I didn't even know if there were any – and stupidly, in retrospect, I never thought to ask.

My father's boyhood friends did not even send Christmas cards. I had no names to go on, and a trip to Glasgow turned up nothing. So I wrote to the *Glasgow Herald* and asked for help. I wanted friends and I hoped to turn up a relative or two from his father's side of the family. The newspaper published an article about me and, although no Junor responded, I heard from several people who remembered him from school and university, including John Clark, better known as Jack, who was his best friend in the fourth and fifth year.

Two of the secondary schools in Glasgow had names that could be easily confused. North Kelvinside Secondary, or NKS, was the state co-educational school where my father went in 1931, and

Kelvinside Academy was the posh fee-paying school, where the toffs in the neighbourhood went. NKS was huge: it had two thousand pupils when my father was there, with about thirty-six children to a class, but it had a good reputation and was highly respected. Nevertheless, it was not unknown for old boys from NKS to drop the 'North' when needing to impress in later years, and Jack Clark thought JJ might have been the type to blur the distinction; he was very ambitious, even then.

But I would be surprised if he ever did. He never pretended to be something he was not. He was very comfortable with his Home Counties life in England amongst the middle classes, but he never tried to affect a smart English accent or deny his working-class roots. He was not ashamed of his humble origins; on the contrary, I think he was extremely proud of them. After lunching with Lord Montagu, years later, he wrote in his diary, 'Edward Montagu lunches with me at the Reform. He is a nasty bit of work and makes me thank God I was born a plebeian.'

JJ always maintained that the Scottish educational system was the best in the world, but after the depression of the 1920s most children in Glasgow left school at fourteen and failed to finish their education, even though it was free. Their families simply could not afford to keep them at school when they could have been out earning a living. JJ knew that his parents had made great sacrifices to put him and his brothers through university. He regarded education as the most precious gift a parent could give any child.

Jack and my father hung around together. They went to the pictures and, on at least one occasion, saw the main feature in one cinema, then ran all the way to another cinema to watch the main feature there too. Sometimes they met up with other friends in tearooms and cafés, not that there was any coffee worth drinking in those days. What they drank was usually Camp coffee, concentrated, syrupy stuff that came in a bottle.

Despite JJ being as close to Jack as he was to anyone at that time, Jack was never invited to Oban Drive, and knew nothing about his family or his home life. Their interest in girls was a common theme, but they did little more than talk and fantasise. Neither would have dared do much more, even at the age of sixteen or seventeen. As Jack Clark says, 'We were both under the domination of "The Scottish Mother",' and going out with a girl would have been quite out of the question. The only real opportunities for meeting girls were at school dances and meetings – particularly the rambling club – but it was innocent stuff. JJ had crushes on various girls, including one in Girvan whom he met while at Turnberry, and another in Carlisle, but he had no girlfriend while he was at school, and studying was still very much a priority.

His English teacher, Hugh Paterson, often spoke of JJ as having been his prize pupil; and many years later JJ wrote in his column that Hugh Paterson had been a source of inspiration to him. But he was not a regular contributor to the school magazine, although he did have a poem published in the Christmas issue in 1932. It was called *Parody on 'Seafever'*, which was a poem by John Masefield – and the 'Tally' was one of the many cafés in Glasgow run by Italian immigrants, renowned for their ice cream.

> *I must go down to the 'Tally's' again, to that lovely little shop,*
> *And all I ask is ginger beer and a luscious lolly-pop,*
> *And hot peas, and vinegar, and a dash of H.P. Sauce,*
> *And a knife and fork to eat them with, while the Tally counts*
>   *his loss.*
>
> *I must go down to the 'Tally's' again for a lovely cup of tea,*
> *With a large pie, and a warm pie, it is excellent for me,*
> *And all I ask is plenty more of the macaroni hash,*
> *And a sweet girl, with a sweet face, and tons of ready cash.*
>
> *I must go down to the 'Tally's' again to taste the 'Tally's' ice,*
> *To the lemonade and chocolate, of which I've had 'suffice';*
> *And all I ask is a cheery smile from a laughing fellow diner,*
> *And another drink of Tony's pop, for there surely is no finer.*

After school JJ went on to read English literature at university, but he never had any pretensions about his writing, nor I think any great love of literature. The works he was familiar with, and quoted liberally because he did have the most incredible memory (and why,

why didn't he pass that on to me too?), were those he read at university. He read very few books by the time I was growing up, claiming that he read so much in the course of his work that reading was no longer a pleasure; although his diaries from the early 1950s suggest that it once had been. Many were the evenings he would enjoy settling down with a detective story by the fire. But he would never give books as presents and, as a rule, hated being given them, but then he was never a very gracious receiver of presents, and a very difficult person to buy for because anything he wanted he immediately went out and bought himself. I remember only one exception, when I gave him a second-hand, leather-bound copy of Rupert Brooke's poetry, which he treasured.

What JJ nurtured from his early days was an interest in politics and journalism and, as a schoolboy, he had ideas about a career in both. At the age of sixteen, during the summer of 1935, he wrote to the *People's Journal*, Scotland's national weekly paper, asking for a job. They had no vacancy, but I wonder what his future would have been if they had taken him on, a year before he was due to go to university, or whether his mother knew he had applied for a job. He also took the Board of Trade eyesight test and was offered a cadetship with Anchor Line to join the *SS Elysia*, which he turned down. Instead, he went to work in a bank for three months to earn some money between school and university. The bank manager predicted he wouldn't be there long. 'He's brilliant,' he said, 'he's wasted in the bank.' And for a while JJ and his cousin Tom Gordon also had jobs in the theatre, playing extras in a courtroom drama called *Laughter in Court*, starring Yvonne Arnaud, Diana Sheridan and Jack Knight.

As a teenager, JJ would talk politics with his Uncle Peter, over Aunt Ina's soup at Buccleuch Street on a Sunday night. Peter worked as Chief Clerk at the Glasgow Corporation Gasworks, and their discussions were so heated that on one occasion Peter stormed out. But it was at Glasgow University in 1936 that politics became a serious passion for JJ, and something for which he discovered he had a real talent. Politically, it was a very exciting and uncertain time, with the outbreak of civil war in Spain, and Hitler and Mussolini flexing their muscles across Europe. Emotions at Glasgow, as in most universities, were running high. JJ was violently anti-Fascist, anti-Franco and, above all, anti-Hitler. But the political society he joined at Glasgow was not a left-wing one – he didn't like the Socialists any more than he liked the Conservatives. He joined instead the Liberal Club. One or two of his more sceptical cousins thought it was a canny choice, born more out of a desire to be noticed in a very under-subscribed club than a genuine statement of his political beliefs. But it was very typical of my father to go against the flow. And while he veered slightly to the right of Genghis Khan in his later years, he never lost his disdain for either the Tory establishment or card-carrying Socialists.

It was true that there were not many members of the Liberal Club, so few in fact that he was immediately appointed Assistant Secretary. That said, he did a great deal to persuade others to join. He had a great gift for public speaking, both in Union debates and on public platforms, and he became a well-known figure on the campus. When he became President, two years later, the Liberal Club had one of the biggest memberships among the political societies in the university and, in the autumn of 1938, he and his friends successfully ran an election campaign to appoint the parliamentary leader of the Liberal party, Sir Archibald Sinclair, as the new Rector.

Suddenly JJ found himself being treated as a celebrity by Liberals all over Scotland, and invitations to attend conferences and make speeches came thick and fast. There was a crucial by-election in 1939 in Kincardine and West Aberdeenshire, where he was brought in to keep audiences entertained until the Liberal candidate arrived. One night he was on the platform for two hours until he was relieved. He found the experience incredibly exciting.

JJ accepted another invitation that was even more exciting. It was from Lady Glen-Coats, the newly selected prospective Liberal candidate for Orkney and Shetland. She was forty, half-French and fabulously rich, a member of the Coats cotton-thread family. She invited JJ, as President of the Glasgow University Liberal Club, and his opposite number in Edinburgh to go to Orkney and Shetland with her during the summer vacation of 1938, to tour the constituency and make speeches on her behalf. All their hotel expenses were to be paid and each was given a cheque for £30 for any incidental expenses they might incur. At that time, JJ had never seen such a large amount of money and it's highly unlikely that any member of his family had either.

The trip opened his eyes to a whole new way of life – the life he had glimpsed through the ballroom windows at Turnberry, and it focused his ambition for the future. They stayed in first-class hotels, ate local lobster and spoke to packed meetings every night. People walked from miles around to sit in village schoolhouses and hear them speak, and they were a highly intelligent electorate. It was a fantastic experience, and JJ had never enjoyed himself more.

With the start of the new term he was back to reality in Oban Drive, but it was not the end of the relationship with Lady Glen-Coats. I don't know whether there was ever anything physical between them, but she was an attractive, vivacious woman, who had once been a model for the society painter Sir John Lavery. She must have been rather exotic. Her husband had pots of money and very little else; he was much older than she was, a shy, diffident character with a pronounced stammer who, according to my father, was also extraordinarily naïve. In typical fashion, JJ doubted whether the couple had ever had sex. Their home in Ayrshire, on the banks of the River Doon, was run by a small army of servants and gardeners, and JJ was invited to spend weekends there. On his first night he felt as though he had been transported into fairyland – until he returned to his room after dinner to find that a valet had unpacked his battered cardboard suitcase. There, to his horror, displayed on the dressing-table were his pitiful belongings: one tatty toothbrush, one tube of toothpaste and a Woolworth's safety razor.

The next summer Lady Glen-Coats invited him to spend the long vacation working as her private secretary. The job paid handsomely – £4 a week, plus a car – and it opened up a whole new range of contacts. Through her, JJ met a number of leading Scottish journalists; he joined the Press Club, where he and his cousin Tom Gordon would go and play bridge; and he wrote the occasional political article, one of which was accepted by the Glasgow *Evening Times*.

On 4 July, Lady Glen-Coats took him as her escort to the American Society Independence Ball and Banquet at the Dorchester Hotel in London. He must have been in seventh heaven, rubbing shoulders with some of the greatest names in British and American society, including the Duke of Kent and the American Ambassador, Joseph Kennedy. After a sumptuous six-course meal they danced to the very music that he had spent years listening to on the wireless in his room in Oban Drive. After years of dreaming, he was there in person, dancing with one of the richest women in Scotland, secure in the belief that this was just the beginning.

In July, Lady Glen-Coats also took him on a trip to Berlin. They travelled by ship from Hull and, as they sailed up the River Weser to Bremen, passing pleasure boats all the way, JJ came to a sight that made the hair on the back of his neck stand up. Field after field lay stacked with grey warplanes. The atmosphere in Berlin was electric, and they awoke the first morning to the sound of a military band parading down Unter den Linden, led by an officer on a white horse. Just before leaving Glasgow, JJ had read an article explaining that one could always tell when the Germans were on the point of war: military bands started to parade through the streets led by officers on white chargers.

Panic rising, he rushed to the *Daily Telegraph*'s Berlin office to consult with their correspondent, Michael Nairn, whom he had met the day before. Nairn was packing, and stopped long enough to say, 'If I were you I'd get the hell out of here. The balloon is about to go up.' JJ dashed back to the hotel to tell Lady Glen-Coats, and two hours later they were in a train on the way to the Dutch border, passing trains heading for Berlin, packed with German soldiers. They arrived back in London on 1 September, just two days before Neville Chamberlain announced that Britain was at war with Germany.

CHAPTER FOUR

The War – a Lucky Escape

How JJ survived the war I will never know. He was a menace with anything mechanical. I remember the day I took my brand new, shiny green Renault 4 to show it to him, and found him giving his brand new, shiny red tractor-mower a spin. The smiles of greeting on both of our faces froze as it became obvious he didn't know how to stop the thing, and with a sickening crunch he ploughed into the driver's door, behind which I sat transfixed with horror. He had more lawn mowers than the average garden centre, but thankfully he usually found someone else to use them. Yet during the first few years of the war, he was let loose on aeroplanes – although if he hadn't been, he would never have met my mother.

He signed up first of all for the navy. Within a week of Chamberlain's announcement, he discovered that liners on the Clyde were being converted into armed merchant-cruisers, and there were a few vacancies for midshipmen. A friend had wangled himself a commission and, upon hearing this, JJ applied for one himself. The friend was assigned to HMS *Forfar*, and JJ became Midshipman RNR (T124) on board HMS *Canton*, soon to go on northern patrol in the Denmark Straits.

The friend was a young man called Ronnie Mackay whom he had met at university. He lived in the next street, but because of the social differences between them – Ronnie's father was a lawyer and he had been to the fee-paying Kelvinside Academy – they had never met before. At university, where there were no such barriers, they became close friends.

My father was always a very lucky man, and it was never more in evidence than during the war. The *Forfar* was torpedoed that first winter and Ronnie was among the dead; he was nineteen years old. Shortly before his death, he wrote to JJ from the ship, excited by the prospect of the two of them meeting up again.

My Dear John

Thank you kindly. Your news is very pleasant to the ears. As a matter of fact I believe that it is not impossible but that we'll meet in a certain port in the South of England ere long. I hear you may be coming here, and if you do I hope the Gods are kind enough to keep us here until you come, for we will paint that town red. Imagine, John, if after all we were to be fairly near each other.

If you see a snotty called Ross Warden (RNVR) over at Whitefield Road please give him my very best regards, and tell him I'll be writing.

By the way, John, you'll notice that I have my typewriter with me. Well I'd advise you to take yours too, but be careful how you break the ice. For example if you go up to somebody right away and say you can type you'll just get a Hell of a lot of extra work. But if you gradually let it leak out that you can type, you can, my good man, cash in on it. You may for example be comfortably sleeping in the cipher department when you might have been keeping a bloody cold watch on the bridge. Not that I've got Hellish much out of it so far.

Although I've been actively on 'Service' for but a few weeks, John, I might be able to help you quite a bit, and if there is anything I can do please let me know. Also don't hesitate to call the folks, for Dad knows a fair amount about our uniforms and etiquette, etc, as he was a Lieut. RNVR in the last war, although he never got much farther afield than Stornoway and these places. Further he knows pretty well all the steps his last born took in this war.

*If you see Stuart thank him for his note, and please give my
kindest regards to everyone, and write again soon.*
Ever Yours
Ronald

Ronnie was the first of many close friends JJ lost during the next
five years. Yet, time and again, he himself escaped by a whisker.
His first ship, the *Canton*, ran into a reef off the west coast of
Scotland that ripped a hole 125 feet long in her hull. The holds
flooded with water, two-and-a-half feet deep, but by some miracle
the bulkhead held and they were able to creep astern for three days
to the safety of the Clyde.

His second ship, HMS *Salopian*, was torpedoed – immediately
after JJ had applied for transfer to the Fleet Air Arm – ironically
because he wanted to see more action; and during his training as a
pilot his diary is littered with entries like 'Flying very badly', 'Got
lost. Landed at Bramcote aerodrome', 'Almost crashed with Tom
Wells'. At one stage during the advanced training, a chief instructor
from headquarters came to assess the recruits and picked JJ to fly
with. Once safely back on the ground he asked what JJ had done
in civilian life. He explained he had been a student. 'Oh,' said the
instructor, 'I thought you might have been a bus driver.'

But the luckiest escape of all was in Canada in 1941, where he
was sent to complete his training. He was flying from an airfield at
Kingston, Ontario, and one night went up in a Fairey Battle to
practise circuits and landings round the airstrip – a simple night-
flying exercise. The date happened to be 13 April – not good for a
man as superstitious as he was. His diary recorded: 'All one had to
do was to take off, climb on zero by the directional gyro to 500
feet, turn left on to zero nine zero, then on to one eight zero, then
on to two seven zero, turn left again and there were the lights of
the runway waiting to meet you.'

That night his gyro failed to unlock and, by the time he realised,
he was lost. There was no moon, no stars and not a single light to
be seen beneath him, nothing but impenetrable blackness waiting
to meet him. He knew that Lake Ontario had been to the left when
he took off, one hundred miles long, thirty miles wide. Towards

the right, there was a dense forest of trees 150 feet high. He had no radio, no 'Mae West' lifejacket and no inflatable dinghy. He had a parachute and petrol for precisely two hours and forty-seven minutes.

For two hours and thirty minutes, in mounting panic, he flew in circles trying to find the airfield, going over his options. He could either parachute into the unknown or stay with the plane when it crashed. He knew he was going to stay with the plane. 'Partly because I was shit scared. Partly because I knew that if I bailed out the chances of being hit by the tailplane were high. I also knew that my chances of survival were almost zero.' So he prayed. And suddenly, as if in answer to his prayer, he saw two lights – one red, one green – about a thousand feet below. They were the lights of another aeroplane on the same circuit from the same aerodrome. He followed it down and landed and, as he parked the aircraft, his engine spluttered and died from lack of petrol. He didn't tell a soul what had happened.

This incident, plus one other, gave my father a completely unshakable belief in the existence of God and of predestination. It didn't turn him into a churchgoer: he only ever went to church at Christmas, and he held the Church of England and its leaders in utter contempt because of their lack of moral leadership. But in his view the church had nothing whatever to do with God. God was the creator of all things bright and beautiful, and God understood human frailty and was all-forgiving. But it was not a subject he ever discussed or debated; he wouldn't discuss or debate anything remotely philosophical and simply became angry if anyone attempted to question him.

The second incident to convince JJ that God not only existed but had a purpose for him, happened in December of the same year. He was on his way from Trinidad, where he had been training, to Liverpool via New York, in a Norwegian freighter. The ship was heavily laden with six thousand tons of sugar for Britain, and crept along in a convoy doing no more than four knots. Five days out of New York, at 11 p.m., the convoy was attacked by a pack of German U-boats. The Norwegian crew climbed into one-piece rubber survival suits, with whistle, torch and knife attached. He and his three fellow passengers went up on deck in their greatcoats and strapped on their Mae Wests, in which they would have had no chance of survival in the freezing December Atlantic. All around them ships were exploding and bursting into flames. JJ prayed and said that suddenly he became quite calm and knew that everything was going to be all right. For him it was, and when the attack was over they all went below deck into the warmth of the saloon and hungrily ate a huge plate of ham sandwiches that the ship's cook happened to have put out just before the attack for the late-night comfort of passengers.

But although he survived, he arrived in Liverpool on a bitter morning in January, to discover that he had lost three of his closest friends. He and the three friends that died had met as trainees. They had been through the thrills and dangers of flying together, lived through air raids and the terrors of war. They had spent their free time and their leaves together, played bridge, partied and painted the town red. He was closer to those three, as a result, than he had been to anyone before – and, sadly, he never made such close friends again. One of them, a New Zealander, flew into a 'stuffed cloud' – a mountain obscured by cloud – near Oban, and was buried in the churchyard there. Twenty-odd years later, on a family holiday in Scotland, JJ took me and my brother to visit his grave. He then wrote to tell his friend's elderly mother in Auckland how beautifully the grave was kept, planted with red roses that were in flower when we were there. His mother wrote back, clearly touched; I found her letter amongst my father's papers.

It was shortly before he went off to Canada that JJ met my mother. They were training at Elmdon over Christmas 1940, and there was a New Year's Eve party, to which one of their instructors, George Welsh, a flight lieutenant in the RAF, had brought his seventeen-year-old daughter, Pamela. She was stunning: tall and slim, with high cheekbones, big blue eyes and wavy, golden blonde hair cascading down her back. JJ, aged twenty-one, had never met anyone so beautiful or so poised and was immediately smitten. At midnight he found himself standing next to her during the singing of 'Auld Lang Syne', and announced, rather drunkenly, 'I am going to marry you.'

The entry in his diary for Wednesday 1 January 1941 reads:

*00.01 hrs saw me meet and kiss Pamela Welsh. Was very
drunk. Bill W. had passed out. Meeting Pamela augurs a grand
year.*

Monday 6
*Kept wondering how to see Pam. Had a drink with Higgins,
CFI and Welsh after Armstrong ceremony.*

Friday 17
*CO's party in George, Solihull. F/Lt Welsh invites me to visit
him at 18 Ladbrooke Road.*

Monday 20
*Went to visit Welshes. Took Len Morgan with me. Pam
loaned me a torch.*

Wednesday 22
*With Graham Irvine took back Pam's torch. Kissed her
goodbye and got further loan of torch. Also got photograph.*

The next day, Pamela left for Newcastle, where she had a wartime
job as a fire-watcher, and a few weeks later JJ set sail for Canada.
But he kept her photo by him, and on his return from Trinidad in
January 1942 they became engaged. JJ was never very handsome,
but he had charm and charisma and, throughout his life, women
found him irresistible. He flirted with and flattered them, and wooed
them with his deep, warm, sonorous voice. He was tall, slim, dark
and in uniform. Pam fell madly in love with him and they married
on 21 April at Gosforth, where her father was stationed. He was
twenty-three, she was nineteen.

Their backgrounds could not have been more different. Pam was
a complete innocent, who had been brought up in a comfortable,
middle-class, Roman Catholic family, sheltered from the depri-
vations and family strains that JJ had known for most of his life.
George, her father, whom I didn't meet until I was in my teens, was
a handsome adventurer, whom Pam hero-worshipped. He had run
away from school at the age of seventeen and lied about his age in

order to fly in the First World War, where he had been awarded a DFC. Aeroplanes were his passion. His father, like generations of Welshes before him, was a doctor with a family practice in the Northumberland village of Felton. They had a big house there beside a trout river, which had been in the family for more than a hundred years, and Pam's grandfather had had one of the very first motor-cars, which she had remembered riding in as a child. Like most RAF families, they had led rather a peripatetic life. She was the eldest of three and had been educated at the girls' convent in Bedford and was intending to go to art school when the outbreak of war scuppered her plans. She was then only sixteen.

Doris, her elegant, cultured, violin-playing mother, was rather snobbish and, had she known about JJ's background, I suspect she would have been very much against the match; but it was wartime, one man in uniform looked as dashing and eligible as the next, and the Scottish accent made him completely classless. Even Pam was unaware of his background until after they were married, when he took her to Scotland to meet his parents.

They were married in a Catholic church, which normally insists that any children of a mixed marriage, such as theirs, be brought up in the Roman Catholic faith. Characteristically, JJ refused to agree to any such thing. As a result, my brother and I were never christened and were both loosely brought up in the Church of England, although JJ himself was a Scottish Presbyterian. I often used to go to Roman Catholic services with my mother, however, to keep her company, just as I went to the Anglican church with my father on Christmas Day for the same reason. Every time he went he would put several twenty-pound notes into the collection, as if to make up for his absence for the rest of the year.

As they made their vows, Pam wearing a simple suit, JJ in uni-form, neither of them could have been happier. They were passion-ately in love, completely and utterly besotted with one another. And as he slipped the platinum wedding band on to her finger, promising to love, honour and cherish her, and to be faithful to her 'till death us do part', no promise was easier to make; he didn't just love her, he worshipped her. She was pure, perfect and he couldn't believe his luck. It's all there in the diaries that he wrote during the early years of their marriage, and in the letters she wrote to him in the early 1950s, which he kept. There are precious few, but there is absolutely no doubt that at that time Pam was desperately, delightfully, deliciously in love with him too. JJ's cousin, Tom Gordon, says there was no doubt about it. Pam stayed in Oban Drive periodically during the war, when JJ was stationed elsewhere, and Tom was also living in the flat. 'We talked a lot and went often to the cinema. She loved and adored him.'

JJ's mother was another matter. Pam, in her sheltered nineteen years, had never encountered anyone like Maggie before and was completely horrified when JJ took her home to meet his family. His eldest brother, Bill, was still living at home, and had a serious drink problem. He used to get so drunk at school during the day that the boys would take it in turns to walk him home, and he was finally asked to resign. It was a tragedy. Bill was a kind, gentle, non-confrontational character – quite unlike his two brothers – and in his youth had been Captain of Glasgow University Golf Team and fanatical about football and cricket. He was sensitive and softly spoken, with a scar on his top lip that bore witness to active service in North Africa during the war. He never married and I had always assumed that, if he'd lived in a different time, he might have been gay. Apart from drink and cigarettes, which he virtually chain-smoked, there seemed to me to be no joy in his life whatsoever. What I now know is that, long ago, he had been secretly in love with his brother Tom's wife.

Tom had married his childhood sweetheart, Jean Maclean, who was his best friend, Sam's, younger sister. He had met her at school, when they were seventeen and fifteen years old respectively, and thereafter Tom spent more of his time in the Maclean household with Sam and Jean's family than he did in his own. Unlike his own mother, Mrs Maclean was a good cook. Maggie was insanely jealous and would stand in the street outside the Macleans', near Charing Cross, shouting at Tom, calling him all sorts of names and complaining about how badly he was treating his poor old mother. Tom had never been particularly fond of his mother, preferring his father, and this did nothing to improve matters.

Tom and Jean were married in North Kelvinside Church in 1935, and there was a big reception afterwards. My parents' wedding was very austere by comparison, but then it was wartime. None of JJ's family was there, and only Pam's immediate family – her parents, her brother Peter and sister Helen. Then, after a brief visit to Glasgow to meet the relatives, they went to Tarbert on Loch Fyne for a few days before he had to get back to active service. JJ wrote a note on a postcard of the view.

Darling, I love you a hell of a lot. I'm going to miss you a hell of a lot. Remember always the perfect peace and beauty of this haven in the hills and know that no matter how far you are from here, I want you to be happy always.

They began married life with nothing and, after their first month together, had precisely one pound between them – a crisp, new one-pound note. JJ made Pam smear it with lipstick, then they put it into a little tapestry purse, and vowed never to spend it. Neither of them ever did. Throughout the war they lived on his Fleet Air Arm pay and at the end of each month usually had a few shillings left. But since most of his fellow officers came from middle-class families with plenty of money to spend, it can't have been easy keeping up. One of the other officers once asked my father how much money, if he were put to it, could he raise? Not wanting to appear poverty-stricken, JJ exaggerated wildly. 'About a hundred,' he said. His friend looked interested. 'A hundred thousand pounds?'
'No, a hundred pounds.'

Money never interested my mother in the slightest. With her background, she had more money as a child growing up than JJ had ever had, and although she suddenly found herself having to stretch even the most meagre wartime rations, it was not an issue for her; but I suspect it was for my father. I think knowing that he was unable to provide for her as well as her father had done irked him. It also irked him that she so demonstrably adored her father – even though JJ was in no doubt that she adored him too.

Shortly after their marriage, Pam's family moved to a house in the country near Horsham in Sussex, and when Pam and JJ first came to live in the South, they went to live with them. By this time,

Pam was pregnant with my brother. Living with in-laws is never easy, but it was the beginning of serious difficulties between my parents and possibly the first inkling Pam had of the future that lay ahead. In later years, JJ would say his in-laws were boring and stupid – a lack of intellect was his greatest put-down of anyone – and he'd accuse them of sponging off him on the rare occasions that they came to stay. But I think what troubled him far more than their brainpower, or anything else, was Pam's love for them and the closeness she shared with her family. Sadly for Pam, it was a closeness that had to endure years of separation. In 1947, her parents left England for Kenya. She missed them enormously, and could have done with their support in troubled times, but it had the benefit of keeping them at arm's length from my father.

JJ insisted that Pam should have the baby in Scotland rather than Sussex. He jokingly explained to the voters of Dundee East a few years later that he had done so 'because I could not accept the possibility that one day my son might play football for England'. I don't think he ever had any ambitions for Roderick to play professional football – and if he did they were sadly disappointed as my brother's only real sporting prowess was on the tennis court. He wanted his son to be a true Scot, I don't doubt, but I suspect he also wanted to get Pam away from her family and establish ownership. And so she was sent away to Aberdeen on her own to stay with Tom and his wife, who lived in Skene where Tom practised as the local GP. It was an experience that scarred her for the rest of her life.

My brother was born on 19 September 1944, and given the names Roderick Robin Macgregor. The name was a compromise. Pam wanted to call him Christopher Robin but JJ wouldn't hear of it; he wanted a Scottish name for his son, although throughout his childhood he was actually known as Tink, short for Stinker. By the end of his life, wild horses would not have persuaded my father to live in Scotland, but he believed until the day he died that the Scots were fundamentally superior in every way to the English.

My mother profoundly disagreed. Removed from the succour and reassuring presence of her family, my mother found childbirth painful and frightening and, although she was delighted with

Roderick, the whole episode was deeply traumatic, and responsible in part, I imagine, for what became in later life an illogical but intense hatred of Scotland and all things Scottish.

CHAPTER FIVE

Fleet Street

Having transferred to the Fleet Air Arm, JJ discovered that flying terrified him and, as he was the first to admit, he was never destined to be a flying hero. His log book repeatedly records his ability as a pilot as 'Below the average' or 'Unsuited to night flying'. And for the rest of his life he had great admiration and affection for anyone who had flown. But at the beginning of 1944 he had a stroke of luck, which probably saved his life.

He was stationed at a naval air station in Burscough, Lancashire, and one night there was a particularly good mess party. Full of good drink, he found himself suggesting to his Station Commander that they should have a station magazine. The following morning, having entirely forgotten about his bright idea, he was summoned to see the Commander and told to go ahead. When the magazine finally came out, a copy was sent to the Admiralty in London, where by an extraordinary coincidence – not to say luck – Admiral Sir Denis Boyd, the Fifth Sea Lord and Commander of the Fleet Air Arm, was planning a service magazine. He had invited Alan Herbert, a famous writer, to be Editor, but wanted a young pilot who knew something about the Fleet Air Arm to be his assistant. JJ was summoned to London to be interviewed by the Fifth Sea Lord himself.

He duly presented himself in the Admiral's office in Lower Regent Street, where he was greeted by a secretary, who disappeared through a connecting door to tell the Admiral that he had arrived. At that moment an air raid warning sounded. London was under heavy attack from doodlebugs and, as he sat there in splendid isolation, JJ marvelled at the courage of the Fifth Sea Lord, sitting in the next-door office, carrying on quietly with his work, unfazed by the danger. After a very long while the door opened and in walked the secretary. 'Good God!' he said, 'are you still here? I had forgotten about you. We've been in the air raid shelter for the last half hour.'

JJ came away with the job of Editor and never flew again. Alan Herbert had turned the job down, and the Fifth Sea Lord simply handed the whole thing over to my father. It was another extraordinary stroke of luck. He called the magazine *Flight Deck* and it turned out to be a huge success. In the final issue, in January 1946, he wrote a tongue-in-cheek farewell piece explaining how the magazine had been put together.

> The idea was that the magazine should have as much life-saving information as possible but at the same time should be made palatable by a leavening of humour. An Air Branch type (and here we modestly drop the editorial 'we') was appointed as Editor. He was obviously the outstanding candidate having had more rejection slips from the Editors of *Lilliput*, *Strand* and *Titbits* than had all the rest of the Branch put together.
>
> ... That first issue was a nightmare business ... We sat back to await comment and – we hoped – congratulation. There was hardly what might have been called an avalanche of comment. To be truthful there were three letters in the first three weeks. Of these the Assistant Editor (bless his soul) had written two. The third was terse and to the point. In three lines the writer gave an adequate outline of our history from birth. In a final crushing couplet he gave brief directions for our future ...

The success of *Flight Deck* enabled JJ to get a toe into Fleet Street. From the moment he took the job he was working in London, in an Admiralty attic, and at the end of the day would go to the Press Club where he made a number of good friends, some of whom contributed to the magazine. He also began moonlighting, quite illegally, as a subeditor for an Australian news agency, Australia Associated Press. His task was to condense stories from the British newspapers and send them over the wire to Sydney. Thus when *Flight Deck* disappeared and he was demobilised, he had a job to go to and was taken on to the staff of the *Sydney Sun*.

Journalism wasn't JJ's first choice of career: politics was, and I often wonder what would have happened if he had won the seat in Parliament that he craved. His first try was in July 1945, while still Editor of *Flight Deck*. He stood as the Liberal candidate in Kincardine and West Aberdeenshire, the constituency where, as a student, he had campaigned so vigorously for the Liberal candidate in 1939. For three weeks leading up to the general election he took the platform in his own right. They were the most exhilarating three weeks of his life, travelling tirelessly from one meeting to another, knocking on doors, visiting factories and talking to people in the street, while Pam, carrying Tink in her arms, trailed in his wake. He lost to the Conservative candidate, but it was close, 642 votes, and, at twenty-six, he narrowly missed becoming the youngest MP in the House of Commons. Disappointed, he returned south to bide his time for an opportunity to try again.

It came in the autumn of 1947 with a by-election in East Edinburgh. Once again he was selected as Liberal candidate, once again he took Pam and Tink to help canvass. 'Mr John Junor . . . started his campaign tonight with a fighting speech,' reported the *News Chronicle*. '"I have not come here to be the token candidate for a lost cause," he said. "I have come here to fight and win."'

The press called him, 'a precocious youngster . . . fighting with all the zeal of a Crusader'. But it was not enough. Not even the eloquence of his old friend, Sir Archibald Sinclair, who came to speak in his support, was enough. JJ polled just 3379 votes, and Labour held the seat with 16,906. Labour won three by-elections that week, and the Liberals did badly in all three. As the *Bulletin* commented:

For the Liberals the lesson is wholly discouraging. They had a particularly able candidate in East Edinburgh, but he lost his deposit . . . Undoubtedly there are a great many intelligent people in both Scotland and England who would like to see a Liberal revival. But there is not the faintest sign that such a revival is on the way.

Disappointed yet again, but personally exonerated, JJ went back to the *Sydney Sun* – to discover he was out of a job. His boss was an affable drunk called Gordon Gilmour, who wrote an eponymous London Diary for the paper. Only the truth was, he didn't write the column at all: JJ wrote it while Gilmour languished in the pub. But one can only assume that JJ can't have been doing it particularly well because, when the Editor in Sydney woke up to what was going on, he sent someone over to London, who sacked the pair of them.

So, two weeks before Christmas, JJ found himself with a wife and three-year-old son to support, no job and no house. He had left the Fleet Air Arm with wealth beyond his wildest dreams – £99. 15s. – in the bank, his gratuity for six years of war service. A payoff from the *Sydney Sun* brought his capital up to nearly £400, but it was of little consolation. The lease on a furnished house he and Pam had taken was at an end and they had been negotiating for a new one; but, with no job, he could get no reference, and the house fell through. There was no alternative but to move into a hotel – the Bury's Court Hotel in the Surrey village of Leigh – for £4.50 a week each and half price for my brother.

JJ's only hope lay in a letter he had written to the Editor of the *Daily Express*, the famous Arthur Christiansen, asking for a job. Fleet Street was a magical place for aspiring journalists in those days, the *Daily Express* was the most successful and exciting newspaper, with correspondents and stringers stationed all over the world, and no expense spared in bringing its readers the best, the fullest and most up-to-the-minute stories. Christiansen was widely regarded as the greatest Editor of his day. Every young journalist dreamed of working for him, and for his proprietor, the legendary multimillionaire press baron, Lord Beaverbrook.

Beaverbrook was a small man with huge charisma, and entirely self-made. He was the son of a strict Scottish Presbyterian minister, one of ten children, born and brought up in New Brunswick in Canada. By the age of thirty, William Max Aitken, as he then was

– he was given a peerage in 1917, and took the name Beaverbrook after the town where he was born – had made a fortune for himself as a financier. But he had worked as a journalist on the way up and owned a magazine, and already knew the power of the press. He came to England in 1910, leaving behind him a brewing scandal over a cement deal, and decided to settle and, with his contacts and his fortune, he was soon a Tory MP. He was a fervent imperialist, and a passionate believer in tariff reform; and he set about acquiring a newspaper as a means of promoting his political convictions. In 1916 he managed to buy the *Daily Express*, two years later he founded the *Sunday Express*, and in 1923 he bought the *Evening Standard* by outsmarting the Berry brothers, owners of the *Telegraph*.

He was an eccentric. Some thought him a genius, a truly great man, and loved him deeply; others thought him downright evil. He could be tyrannical, brutal, cruel, and selfish; he was bigoted and homophobic and disliked black people; at the same time he could be enormously kind and considerate. But, for all his eccentricities and prejudices, there was no disputing his brilliance as a newspaper-man. His instincts were unerring, and his passion for journalism all-consuming.

But he had plenty of critics. A Royal Commission was set up by the Labour government to investigate his newspapers. He was accused of running them as personal fiefdoms, allowing his Editors no freedom, and of using his newspapers as his own personal mouth-piece. He was also said to operate a secret blacklist of people who were never to be mentioned in his newspapers – names like Sir Thomas Beecham, Emperor Haile Selassie, Paul Robeson and Noel Coward – all banned for political or personal reasons.

Nevertheless, in the drab years after the war, Express Newspapers was the most successful and most talked about newspaper group in Fleet Street. JJ was hugely flattering in his letter to Christiansen, a device he perfected over the years, and the Editor saw him, and immediately offered him a job as a reporter at eighteen guineas a week. It was less than he had been paid by the *Sydney Sun* but, as he later said of that day, 'it was as if I had suddenly been plucked from the middle of an Atlantic storm'. He had just turned twenty-nine.

Fleet Street at that time was a village, with its own pubs, its own restaurants, even its own parish church – St Bride's, built by Sir Christopher Wren – and its own heroes and giants. JJ felt he had joined a very special world and he loved it, he loved the buzz, loved the gossip, loved the sense of community, and he loved the excitement and urgency of newspapers, the smells, the noise and the atmosphere. He felt at home and among friends, and he never lost his enthusiasm for any of it.

The *Express* was selling over four million copies a day, it had an intelligent readership and was highly thought of. It was a broadsheet, like every newspaper at that time, but it was bright all the way through, well subbed, well written, classless, newsy and snappy – Beaverbrook insisted upon at least twenty-two stories on the front page. The *Sunday Express* was slightly different, and this was the paper in the group that Beaverbrook used most as his personal platform. It had found a winning formula from which it never wavered: right-wing tub-thumping by its distinguished and long-serving Editor, John Gordon; a patriotic adventure serial, often about the recent war, benign gossip about well-known people; malicious gossip about socialist politicians in the Cross-Bencher column; a Giles cartoon; and comprehensive sports coverage. The *Evening Standard* was the one paper that Beaverbrook's friends read and was allowed to be more sophisticated and therefore less profitable.

Beaverbrook was almost seventy when JJ joined the *Express*. His colourful and controversial days of active politics were over. He had served in the Cabinet in both world wars, he had been on close terms with Bonar Law, Northcliffe, Churchill, Lloyd George and Roosevelt, he was widely credited with having made possible the victorious Battle of Britain, he had negotiated with Stalin while German troops advanced on Moscow – and he had a mixed reputation. Some admired him for his part in winning the Second World War, and saw him as a journalistic genius. Others thought he was a pre-war appeaser, a malign influence on Churchill, a self-aggrandising newspaper proprietor and a corrupter of young journalists. His best years may have been past, but he was certainly no spent force.

Their first meeting was in Beaverbrook's London home on the

eighth floor of Arlington House in Piccadilly. Beaverbrook was about to go to Canada, and JJ's name had been put forward as a possible companion. He had been at the *Express* for just fourteen weeks. The note in his diary says, 'Arrived for interview – cool, calm and more or less collected. Tripped over phone wire! B non-committal.' The following day he wrote, 'Spent day wondering when decision would come. Was fairly sure I had made good impression but when Robertson [E. J. Robertson, Chairman of Beaverbrook Newspapers] rang at 5 p.m. it was to say – no go. I shall prove to B he was very, very wrong.' Beaverbrook took a younger journalist from the *Evening Standard* instead.

JJ's genius was not apparent from the start. His first story made the front page, but he wasn't pleased with it. 'Can and will do better', he told his diary. A little later he was sent down to Dover to cover two events: the arrival of the Olympic Torch, en route to the Olympic Games at Wembley Stadium, and the arrival of an Italian cross-Channel swimmer. Believing the Channel swim to be a straightforward affair, he filed a straightforward report of what he saw. The Olympic Torch story, however, provided him with much more scope, for as the runner stepped on to British soil, the perpetual flame went out, and one John Junor stepped forward and relit it with his cigarette lighter. It made a great story, but his heroics counted for little when the next day's *Daily Mail* had a brilliant exposé of the Italian cross-Channel swimmer, who turned out to have been a complete charlatan.

Hard news was never JJ's forte, but politics was a subject he understood and loved, and Christiansen swiftly put him onto reporting by-elections, where he was much more successful. It was his political writing above all that won him favour with Beaver-brook. Christiansen was a tubby little man with eyes that twinkled behind gold-rimmed spectacles, and a great capacity to enthuse and inspire his editorial staff. He was a natural showman and, according to JJ, would conduct his editorial conferences, 'As if he were Master of Ceremonies on a glittering Palladium stage,' before repairing to the bar at Poppins, a pub in Poppins Court round the corner, where he held court surrounded by his acolytes. JJ never did this when he became an Editor, but he did learn a lot from Christiansen, including the use of a notice board outside his office. Every day his secretary would put up a bulletin with his views on the previous day's paper. He administered praise and criticism in equal measures.

One day in his bulletin, Christiansen announced that he wanted to start a new column on current affairs and called for volunteers and for suggestions as to what it should contain. JJ volunteered immediately and wrote a long memorandum describing what he would put in his column if he were given the job. He wasn't. It went instead to James Cameron, but was abandoned after only a few weeks, although Cameron went on to a long and distinguished career. Looking back, it amused JJ to ponder on what might have happened had he written for Christiansen the same sort of column he was to write for the *Sunday Express* many years later – whether his, too, would have been killed after a few weeks.

As it was, he was soon writing Cross-Bencher, a highly influential political column for the *Sunday Express*. Initially he was asked to do it as holiday cover for three weeks, and that first week he was at a complete loss. He had no idea what to write about. He had never been to the Lobby of the House of Commons, where political writers have briefings and spend most of their week. And apart from the people he had stood against and met during elections and by-elections, he had no political contacts.

But he knew this was a great opportunity. 'This new job may mean the opening of gates to new and exciting fields' he told his diary. And he was saved by a typical stroke of luck. Charles Wintour, a colleague on the *Evening Standard*, showed him a booklet, issued by the Transport and General Workers' Union, which listed the amount of money the union paid in grants to MPs. He began his first column on 18 August 1948:

Where do the pennies raised by political levy on £5-a-week trade unionists go? Into the job of safeguarding the incomes of Socialist MPs.

For the cheapest way of becoming an MP is to be born with a Socialist spoon in the mouth.

And the cheapest way of remaining an MP is to stick the spoon into the trade union jam . . .

Beaverbrook regarded Cross-Bencher as his own personal voice, and it was the one area of the *Sunday Express* over which he allowed John Gordon, the Editor, no control. He didn't trust Gordon's political judgement, so it was Max Aitken, his son, officially the paper's Manager, to whom JJ reported and delivered the column.

Max was a dashing figure, nine years older than my father, tall, dark, handsome and a magnet for beautiful women. He was a war hero, an outstandingly brave and effective fighter pilot who had learned to fly at Cambridge and signed up for active service as soon as he could; he had flown in the Battle of Britain, and been awarded the DFC and DSO. JJ liked him but, for all his bravery, he was a shadow of his father. He had no real interest in newspapers. His passion was yachting and he bought himself a lovely house on the waterside at Cowes with private mooring to which he escaped at every opportunity, surrounding himself there with wealthy, like-minded, fast-living friends.

It was to Max that JJ delivered his first Cross-Bencher column. 'Max saw it and liked it . . . And finally the Old Man – his reactions unknown – yet,' JJ's diary records. The next day: 'And the Old Man liked it!!! Only the most minor of corrections. Congratulated by Max.' Then: 'The Beaver approves. And that applies, it appears, to me too. Got a handy little tax-free rise.'

The next week Max warned him to stand by on Sunday for a visit to 'the Beaver'. His father was arriving back in England and wanted to see JJ at Cherkley, his country estate near Leatherhead in Surrey. 'Old Man due back at 1 p.m. . . . . Heaven help us. Heaven has obliged. Max rings to say Old Man liked the column.' And then a memo to himself, 'The Old Man no doubt has a lot to offer me, but I too have much to offer him. We should meet as equals.'

They met for two hours in the library at Cherkley: 'He called me a new and notable name in Fleet Street,' he recorded. 'Old Man went off to Canada. Sorry in a way to see him go. He really is a genius.' Beaverbrook had begun by being complimentary about the column, then moved on to discuss politics, and, when he couldn't find a particular newspaper he was looking for, suddenly barked 'Get me Wednesday's *News Chronicle*.' JJ immediately jumped to his feet, but it was Max that Beaverbrook had been addressing, who scurried off down the corridor in search of the missing title. JJ loved this story – he was fascinated by the relationship between father and son. 'Here was Max Aitken, DSO, DFC,' he would say, 'one of the great war heroes, handsome beyond measure, chased by every gorgeous-looking girl in London, acting like a frightened little boy in front of his father. That is precisely what he was. He so adored that father and Beaverbrook adored him, although he would speak about him disparagingly and often treat him with contempt. Deep down there was a deep love, and Max tried so desperately and, so often, unsuccessfully to imitate his father.' Ironically, anyone commenting twenty or thirty years later might have said much the same about the relationship between JJ and his own son.

He never went back to his old job and, although most weeks he sweated blood over it, often staying up until 2 or 3 a.m. – with Pam sitting up alongside him while he worked – the column was going well. Even so, he was still writing himself stiffening notes in his diary. 'Be more assertive. You know your worth. Make other people realise it.'

CHAPTER SIX

Happy Families

It was a Friday, the day before Christmas Eve, and JJ had been writing Cross-Bencher for four months. He had finished the column and dashed out at lunchtime to buy Tink a present, his very first bicycle. He came back to find the office in turmoil. Max Aitken had been frantically trying to get hold of him. Beaverbrook wanted to see him right away at Cherkley. He was to take the train to Leatherhead where a car would meet him.

He thought that this could only mean one thing, that Beaverbrook hadn't liked his column, and would make him do it again. He made his way to Cherkley in a fury. When he arrived Beaverbrook said nothing about the column, but invited him to jump into the passenger seat of his car, a little Hillman Minx, and took him off on a tour of the estate. Beaverbrook stopped the car at three houses, two unoccupied, the third with a little old lady *in situ*. At each of the houses they got out and, with no explanation, had a look around. JJ's temper was beginning to boil. If he was going to have to rewrite the column, there was little enough time before Christmas without wasting it on a drive round the countryside. Unusually, he held his tongue.

Back at the big house, Beaverbrook finally spoke, but it was not to criticise his work. Instead, he beamed at JJ. 'Would you like one of those houses?' he said. 'Which one would you like? You can have it rent free and you can have it whenever you like.'

Flabbergasted, my father said he would like the first house. 'Good,' said Beaverbrook. 'Bring your wife over on Sunday so that she can see it.' My mother in fact chose the third of the houses they had been shown, a brick and flint semi-detached house called Garden Cottage, which was home to them for the next ten years. 'Pam and I go to Cherkley. Sherry in sunshine. Beaver thinks Pam is wonderful. Rang me at night to tell me so.' A few days later: 'Called to Arlington 2.30 p.m. Old Man in excellent mood. "Goodbye boys," he says and off go Max and I like a couple of school kids.'

The family moved into Garden Cottage on 8 January 1949. 'Moved – or rather Pam did the moving. But how nice to go back to our own house and our furniture. Old Man rang in morning.' The next day, 'Settling in rapidly. Tink had wonderful day racing cars. He definitely likes the place.' And the day after, 'Max invited us to tea.' The next weekend, 'Shooting with Tink. Bacon and eggs. Walking and wooding. Delightful.' Then, 'A full and happy day. Sawed wood till my arm ached. Cinema with Pam in evening. Lovely.' One day he went out and bought a shotgun to add to his arsenal of one airgun. 'Frightful extravagance. Bought sixteen-bore gun. What a day. Five-and-a-half hours marching in search of game. Tink and Pam adorable. Took Pam to see *Johnny Belinda*.' Most of the time he shot at clays, or even an old tin plate, but he was never the best shot – as he was the first to acknowledge. 'Sunshine after lunch and we go shooting. What lucky rabbits to have me at the other end of the gun.'

My earliest memories are of Garden Cottage, of seeing my mother laughing happily with friends, or wrestling to tame the tangled garden; my father cooking potatoes on a camp fire – what we did before anyone thought of barbecues, I suppose – and putting them straight on to the fire unwrapped, which meant they came out black, coated with ash and totally inedible; and Tink playing with his electric train set, and building weird-shaped cars and aeroplanes with Meccano. It was about the most glorious place a child could grow up in, completely and utterly safe. It sat in splendid isolation at the top of a walled garden, where Christmas trees were grown. On one side it backed onto acres of woodland and on the other to Mickleham Downs, with miles of grassy tracks and gallops. You could go for days without seeing another human being, just birds and wild animals, and complete silence. It was idyllic.

I was born at 5.25 a.m. on Wednesday 6 October 1949, delivered by our family doctor, Alan Everett, at a nursing home in Leatherhead. I never asked why I wasn't born in Scotland, but I am sure Pam was relieved to be allowed to stay at home. My mother hadn't wanted to have another baby. After her experience with my brother five years before, she vowed never to do it again; but she was persuaded by a friend and neighbour, with a son the same age as Tink, that she must. JJ was becoming so obsessed with him, that he was in danger of being completely spoilt. And so I came into the world. I don't know if it did the trick: JJ ended up spoiling us both I suspect, but Roderick was always very special to him.

JJ treated Tink more like a friend and confidant than a child and, by the time I was old enough to notice such things, it was clear to me that my brother was well above my mother and me in the family pecking order. I never once remember my mother taking precedence over Tink. If we were all travelling in the car together, my father would drive and my brother was the one who sat in the front beside him. My mother and I went in the back, where I was invariably carsick. On long journeys I used to lie snuggled under her arm with my head on her chest listening to her heartbeat, or else I would sleep with my head in her lap. She was soft and warm and safe.

I even remember that JJ would not allow Pam to let Tink see her naked; he said he didn't want her to spoil his pleasure at seeing a young girl's body for the first time. JJ never let me see him naked either, but not for the same reason I'm sure. If ever I walked in on him in the bath, which he hated, he would protect his modesty with a flannel. I would be mesmerised by his floating flannel; how come I couldn't get my flannel to float? I tried again and again. It was years before I realised what kept his aloft.

Shortly after I was born, a nurse arrived to help out, but she didn't last the week. JJ described her as 'slightly uppish' at first sight, 'pretty grim, never smiles' by the second day and, by day four, he had sacked her. Tink meanwhile had taken to his bed with a streptococcal throat, which meant that Pam and I had to stay in the nursing home until he was no longer infectious. So it was ten days before we finally came home – to a rapturous welcome. JJ was thrilled to have Pam back, 'Wonderful, wonderful to be together again,' he wrote.

JJ brought Tink in to see me hours after my birth, and it was the beginning of a very special relationship between us. He was five, and my father told him that I was a present for him. From that day forward he was immensely affectionate and protective towards me. He never hurt me, never fought with me, I don't even remember us having a cross word as children. I never stopped being his little sister, but he let me be with him and he taught me things, showed me how things worked, let me play with his toys, and sometimes even let me hang around when he had friends for the day. We had no secrets from one another and, later, when our home became a battleground, we were there for each other. Life at that time would have been very tough without him.

For some time we had au pairs, who looked after us both. The only one I remember was a pretty German girl called Mekki, who gave me some little hedgehog figures on skis. If I am honest, I remember the hedgehogs better than Mekki, but then they were with me for longer. Otherwise Bob Young used to look after us. He was the head gardener and, like most of the estate staff, he lived in the Stable Yard at the bottom of our drive.

Bob was hugely tall and thin with big ears and a large wart on his nose – not unlike Roald Dahl's *BFG* – and one of the nicest, gentlest, men I've ever known.

Bob Young had a wife, Edie, who worked as a cleaner at Cherkley, and three children, Margaret, John and Angela. Their house was a second home to my brother and me. John and Tink were good friends, and so were Angela and I. Margaret was married to a teddy boy with Brylcreemed hair, and they lived in a council flat in Dorking, so I didn't see her very often, but she was a source of endless fascination to me. I was fascinated by the entire household: how they spoke, how they ate, what they ate, how they lived – it was all so different from mine. It was a terrible shock when Bob dropped down dead with a heart attack; he can't have been much more than fifty-five. I had never encountered death before. The family kept him in a coffin in the front room before the funeral, and then a fleet of black cars arrived and a whole lot of serious-looking men in black suits took him away.

Soon after I was born, Beaverbrook offered us the second half of Garden Cottage, which gave us two staircases, four bedrooms, two bathrooms, and two sitting rooms – one with a small black-and-white television in it, bought for the Queen's coronation in 1953, when all the estate workers came up to watch the pageantry. The one in the other half of the cottage was a smart one for visitors, with a white carpet and a gramophone that was scarcely ever used. Neither of my parents was musical. The first record I remember being played in the house was Max Bygraves' 'Gilly Gilly Ossenfeffer Katzenellen Bogen by the Sea'. That was about as cultured as we got. We also had the soundtracks from musicals like *South Pacific* and *Oklahoma!*, which Pam and JJ had been to see in London. But there was no classical music in the house and no opera. Neither of them could stand it. What my mother liked best was calypso, but she was virtually tone deaf, and my father liked sentimental Scottish ballads.

My parents did lots of socialising in those days. People came to the house most weekends or my parents went out: drinks, coffee, lunch, dinner, even for coffee and brandy after dinner, or they went to parties or the theatre in London, and on Monday nights it was the cinema. Their friends were a mixture of local professionals, with a high concentration of doctors – JJ was a great hypochondriac and befriended doctors shamelessly – and journalists and politicians from London. Manny Shinwell, George Wigg, Harold Wilson, and Richard Crossman were all friends. Michael Foot, who had once worked on the *Evening Standard*, had a weekend cottage on the estate, and would come over for a drink every now and again; he was often a fellow dinner guest at Cherkley too.

With guests, we ate in the dining room, which had a cheetah-skin rug on the floor that had been shot by Pam's father in Kenya, and mounted on green felt. Its head was stuffed and raised and people were always tripping over it, but it was never moved. The rest of the time we ate in the kitchen, where there was a black Rayburn stove that burned day and night. It was the only warm room in the house. There were a couple of open fires, but otherwise, with no central heating, the only other form of heat was paraffin. Pam went round lighting the heaters every night, and for the first few years there was no electricity in the house either, so she also lit oil lamps. I imagine my father's lifelong love of oil lamps must have been nostalgia for these happy, early days when he so relished family life.

Every evening before going to bed, Pam would make porridge for breakfast and leave it in the bottom oven overnight. And first thing every morning she would stoke up the Rayburn with anthracite and empty the ashes outside. She was always the practical one in their marriage, and the one who did the physical work around the house and garden, she was the one who did the decorating, never JJ. He was completely useless: he knew nothing about car engines, nothing about fuses or DIY and was very happy in his ignorance. It was probably just as well, as he was incredibly clumsy. His fingers were like great spatulas and quite unsuited to any kind of finesse. Even opening a carton of cream could end in disaster, and often did.

Pam had impeccable manners and, although she was not strict in any other way, she did care how Tink and I spoke and how we behaved at table. We learned more by example than instruction, but we were in no doubt about what was, and was not, acceptable. We were not allowed to hold our knife and fork like pencils, or to wave them around while we talked. We had to put them together in the centre of the plate when we had finished eating, with the fork lying prongs down, and we were never, ever allowed to put our knives in our mouths, or pick anything up with our fingers. Milk had to go into a jug, and butter into a butter dish, no bottles or wrappers on the table. We were not allowed to say 'pardon', it had to be 'I beg your pardon' or 'excuse me', and we could never put our elbows on the table or speak with our mouths full.

JJ had obviously grown up with very different eating habits but, in general, he adopted her conventions, although there were one or two exceptions which I think irked her – and polishing apples on his chest was definitely one of them. He also picked up chops and chicken bones and ate them in his fingers, biting into them as one imagines Henry VIII did, and he had a curious way of eating oranges, which was also pretty grizzly to watch. He would cut them in two and bite into each half, scraping and slurping with his teeth, while juice dribbled down his chin.

On dark, blustery winter's nights, the woods at the back of the house, so benign by day, could be scary. Just outside my bedroom, there was a large studded door with a huge, old-fashioned key, the sort you found in fairy tales, which opened onto a little bridge that led straight onto a grassy track and into the woods. Goldilocks would have found it irresistible. At night I would lie awake in my bed and imagine creatures coming through the door into my room, but the woods were not malevolent and I don't remember ever having any nightmares about them.

What I did have nightmares about, recurrently, was falling down one of the staircases at Garden Cottage. I have no idea what sparked them off, I have no memory of a real fall, yet again and again I would be falling steeply, into nothingness, and I would wake up just as I was about to hit the bottom. I could never stop the dream, never wake up halfway down. It was terrifying, I absolutely hated it, and I have hated the sensation of losing my stomach ever since. I have never been able to go on big dippers, and bad turbulence on an aircraft is hell. Even now I have the dream from time to time, and it is still the staircase at Garden Cottage.

Occasionally JJ would tell me bedtime stories, although he wasn't often around at my bedtime. When he did, he would always make them up. I don't remember him ever reading to me from a book; all his stories came out of his head, made up as he went along, and usually about a little girl with plaits, which would be me. One, which always haunted me, was the story of a little girl with a dog, which ran into the back of a furniture removal van. The little girl ran into the back of the lorry after him and before she could say 'Jack Robinson', the driver had closed the doors and they were speeding off along the road. I can't remember how the story ended, except that I have a vivid picture of the lorry parked on the grassy track outside our house. I gave removal lorries a very wide berth after that.

The wood was a magical place and Tink and I used to play there a lot. There were wonderful, tall beech trees and great oaks and some of the oldest yew trees in southern England. They looked so pretty with the sunshine dappling through the leaves in the spring, or heavy with snow in winter. The wood's character changed with every season. And it was bristling with wildlife: badgers, foxes, deer, squirrels, rabbits and a huge variety of birds. And on the ground, there were giant snails, which at some time in the past had been brought over from France and now roamed the area. I even think there was the odd red squirrel in the early days, before they were entirely decimated by grey squirrels. Tink used to shoot the grey ones with an airgun, and earned himself some pocket money in the process. The government paid sixpence a tail in an effort to stop the imported grey squirrels wiping out the indigenous population.

One day Tink accidentally shot a jay, which turned out to be a mother with a nest full of chicks. Realising they would die if he left them, he climbed the tree and took the chicks home to rear them in the house. They lived in a shoebox and we fed them with bread and water out of a pipette until they grew into big healthy birds. By this time they were entirely tame and strutted about the house creating mayhem. They never showed any inclination to fly further than the fruit cage, where they systematically stripped it of every sort of red, ripe and luscious berry they could find. They were full of character and extraordinarily inquisitive. I can't remember what happened to them all, but I do remember there being a series of disasters culminating in the last remaining bird being drowned in the loo, having slipped on the hard plastic seat and finding itself unable to get out. There was much wailing in the house that night, and accusations about who had been stupid enough to leave the loo lid up, but I suspect my mother, who was particularly fond of raspberries, was secretly delighted.

Next to the fruit cage was a grass tennis court that we made. It wasn't exactly All England specification: it was on an angle of about 20 degrees, and with no proper netting around the outside, and the rabbits were a bit of a problem, but at least with that slope it did drain well. So most weekends during the summer friends would come and play tennis – sometimes until quite late in the evenings. I would lie in bed in my brother's room which overlooked the court, with the window wide open, listening to the sound of balls being thwacked, and the shrieks and laughter. Afterwards they would sit outside drinking and chattering beneath the window. I am sure it rained some weekends, but I don't remember the rain.

Every afternoon Pam and I used to walk down a steep and stony unmade-up road to the village of Mickleham to meet Tink from his nursery school. It was called the William IV Hill, named after the pub at the bottom, where JJ went for a pint with Bob Young from time to time. One day we must have been late and Tink had already set off for home. We found him walking towards us with another small boy in tow. 'This is William,' he announced proudly. 'He's coming to tea.' William, sadly, was not very forthcoming about any other names he might have, where he lived or what his phone number was, but all was well in the end and William became an inseparable friend for many years.

Garden Cottage was rent free, but Beaverbrook extracted his pound of flesh in return for the privilege of living there. When he was in England, my father was on call day and night, seven days a week, and spent almost as much time at the big house as he did with us. Every weekend during those periods, he would be telephoned and invited to lunch, and because no Beaverbrook employee ever left his company until he had been dismissed, he would often end up staying for dinner too. It was never dull, his fellow guests were invariably fascinating people, but Beaverbrook had no respect for JJ's free time and gave no thought to the effect his demands might have on the family.

One Sunday, some friends were bringing their children over for a game of cricket on the little pitch we had made behind the Stable Yard. I don't think what we played ever resembled cricket but we had a lot of fun. Beaverbrook rang about an hour before our friends were due to arrive to ask my father to walk with him. Reluctantly he agreed, as he always had to. They walked in the direction of our cottage and as they drew near they heard laughter and the sound of a bat and ball. Beaverbrook asked what was going on. JJ explained. 'You should have told me,' said Beaverbrook at once. 'Just walk back with me and then you can go home.' JJ's gratitude was short-lived. Back at the house the Old Man wanted to go through the day's paper with him, then wanted my father to have a quick look at a film he planned to show his dinner guests on the screen in his private cinema to make sure it was suitable. By the time he got away it was 8 o'clock, and he was lucky to have escaped so early.

CHAPTER SEVEN

Beaverbrook

It's hard to judge size or distances from the past. When I was at prep school, there was a huge climbing frame, which only the really brave played on. The bars were so big you couldn't close your hand around them to grip properly, and the top was miles above the ground – one girl dropped from the top and broke her leg. It was the scariest thing in the whole district, yet I went back once when I had grown up and was convinced that they must have changed my climbing frame for a puny, little one. So my memory of Garden Cottage is probably wildly inaccurate too. It seemed a very long way from the big, solid, grey stone house that was Cherkley, where Beaverbrook lived, but it was probably not much more than a mile.

I never went inside the big house, although I saw it through the trees often, and I only ever once met Lord Beaverbrook. I was playing with my friend Angela in the yard outside her house when this tanned and wizened figure appeared wearing a brown felt hat and wielding a walking stick. He asked who we were, and when we told him, he announced that he was Lord Beaverbrook. Then he dug into his pocket and pulled out some coins and gave us half a crown each.

Despite this being our only meeting, I grew up with Beaverbrook. His influence over my life was all-pervasive. He was always on the phone to the house, and when he wasn't on the phone, my father would be talking about him, and when he wasn't talking about him, he was with him, summoned at a moment's notice, irrespective of family commitments. I know we were not unique. The mega-rich and mega-powerful often have no consideration for their employees' private lives. But Beaverbrook's presence in our lives had a more sinister effect too.

I don't know whether my father consciously modelled himself on the Old Man, but he displayed an uncanny number of his characteristics, which if his early diaries are anything to go by, were not evident when he was a young man. They suggest a far gentler character than the man he became, and his cousin Tom Gordon confirms this. He finds it hard to believe that the John he knew as a boy became so difficult. But, for ten years, JJ lived in Beaverbrook's house, for ten years he was at his beck and call, he was guest, companion, sparring partner – but always employee – and Beaverbrook was, without question, the biggest single influence in his life. He spent hour after hour after hour with him, listened to him, watched him and learned from him. JJ admired him greatly. The Old Man was a bewitching character, his mind was razor sharp, his judgement superb, but he was a bully and could be devastatingly cruel.

Beaverbrook spent much of his year abroad, no doubt for tax reasons, but wherever he was in the world, he was in touch, either by memo, dictating at length into a machine that was always by him, or by telephone. When he was in England it was not unusual for my father to see him every single day and to speak on the phone three or four times a day. And, although it irked him sometimes to be dragged up to Cherkley on a Sunday for lunch, and be kept until 8 or 9 p.m., or to be summoned when he got home in the evening, he loved being one of the chosen few.

When Beaverbrook was in London, they walked together almost every day, mostly in St James's or Green Park, but it could be anywhere. As they walked, 'the Beaver' would quiz him closely about the day's news and what possible leaders or leader-page articles could be written. JJ had to have read every newspaper thoroughly by the time they met – as he knew Beaverbrook would have done – and already formulated some ideas to put forward. It was a training that JJ never forgot: he read every newspaper, every day thereafter for the rest of his life. All the papers were delivered to the house and he started to read them over breakfast, finishing them off on the journey to London; and no one could talk to him while he did so. He would repeatedly tell me that I would never be any good as a journalist unless I did the same. I knew he was right, but I simply didn't have time. I had a house, a husband and children to look after, as well as trying to earn a living, and there weren't enough hours in the day. He wasn't interested in excuses, he dismissed any attempt to explain.

He and Beaverbrook shared a number of characteristics. They were both easily bored and fiercely intolerant of bores and fools. Both were moody and took no trouble to disguise it; both could be very childish and petulant; neither did things they didn't want to do, both had an enormous disregard of the Establishment and a contempt for privilege. They were both quirky about their diet. They were both bullies, and both could be cruel. And their attitude to women was very similar. Beaverbrook loved beautiful women and had many in his life, but they were expected to keep their mouths shut, particularly at the dinner table, unless they had something interesting to say. In JJ's view, few women said anything worth hearing, and unless they were good-looking, or would sleep with him, he had no interest in them at all.

I suspect Beaverbrook was the father JJ wished he had had; he was the complete antithesis of poor, kind, henpecked Sandy. He provoked in my father the full gamut of emotional reactions and challenges but, fundamentally, JJ loved him. He would say of him that he was quite the most remarkable man he'd ever met. No one could match him for quickness of brain and breadth of knowledge. His reading was encyclopaedic and, with the possible exception of sport, there was virtually no subject of which he did not have a deep understanding.

Beaverbrook invited his favourite journalists to his villa at Cap d'Ail in the South of France. JJ's first visit was in July 1949. Beaverbrook telephoned one morning to ask him and said 'bring your wife'. Being seven months pregnant with me, Pam was unable to fly, and so JJ went on his own. 'I write this in mid-air over France', he recorded in his diary, 'with Old Man's whisky by my side and some Cognac inside. 8.50 p.m. I see the Mediterranean for first time.' He wrote to Pam the next day.

Darlingest

I had a quite terrific trip. On the London to Paris plane they served us with ice cream and biscuits. Then we left Paris at 6 p.m. and began the trip to Nice. At 7.50 p.m. they served us with a meal in a cardboard box. Jolly nice too. Then about 8.25, when it was getting quite dark, we arrived over the Mediterranean and landed at Nice in starlight.

A car was waiting and off I set for here where the Old Man let me have ten minutes for sandwiches and a half bottle of wine before getting down to work. I got to bed at 12, limp and exhausted. And now I'm at work again on next week's column. He is bathing just now, and that's about the only reason I can sneak five minutes off to write to you.

I've got a jolly nice bedroom with a bathroom attached. But it's terribly hot and I have to sleep under a mosquito net.

Angel, I love you, and love you and just love you. I hope you are missing me terribly, 'cos I'm missing you most awfully.

I suppose I had better get back to the typewriter.

Darlingest, promise you belong to me for all time. I just could not live without you. Take care of yourself, precious angel. And tell Tink his best friend sends him lots and lots of love and kisses.

I adore you, you lovely, lovely, lovely woman.

All my love and kisses, darlingest

Johnny

PS See you Monday. What a wonderful thought.

And to his diary he wrote, 'Instead [of lunch at the Ivy] I work, I swim in the Mediterranean. I walk to Monte Carlo. And I sit out on the patio looking at the stars and listening to the classics. From where I write I can see the Italian coast. And the summer house in which I work was where *Private Lives* was produced.'

La Capponcina was an imposing property, set on the hillside

above Monte Carlo, that Beaverbrook had bought in 1939. He decamped there with his staff every summer: Raymond the valet, Mead the butler, plus nurses and secretaries. Raymond would collect visitors in the Rolls-Royce, one of many cars Beaverbrook would have out there. Some visitors, his high society friends, were invited for pleasure, others to work, but they enjoyed the hospitality of the house either way, and even employees joined Beaverbrook and his guests for dinner each night. The garden was his pride and joy. There was a walled rose garden, where he picked and dead-headed the roses, a blue verbena lawn, on which no one was allowed to tread, on pain of 'being hanged from the highest tower in Monte Carlo', and a swimming pool, which he swam in every morning. There were cloisters, a fountain, and a veranda running along the front of the house, where they sat shaded by vine and wisteria growing overhead.

JJ had never been to the South of France before and had never enjoyed such luxury, but it was not until the dinner guests had gone home on the Sunday night that he realised why he had been invited. The Duke and Duchess of Windsor were amongst the guests, and JJ found the seating had been so arranged that he had no one to talk to but the Duchess. Beaverbrook, it transpired, had bought her memoirs, which an American journalist was ghosting. The two were not getting along, and he was afraid that if they had a serious falling out the memoirs might never be completed. He wanted to see whether she and JJ liked one another, so that if the worst came to the worst, he could be brought in to take over the ghosting. They ate at a refectory table set out under the stars, and got along famously, but fortunately his services were never needed. He remained a great fan, and said of her that she had the great gift of making a man feel as if, at that moment, he were the only man in her life. He wrote in his diary, 'He is charming, and simple. She is radiant, mature and quite lovely. She allowed me to do the talking, even prompted me to, and she seemed fascinated by whatever I had to say.'

JJ rose quickly under Beaverbrook's tutelage, but he was never a lackey. His diaries show that they had not been living at Garden Cottage for long before he and Pam were house-hunting. Whether it was because he disliked being beholden to the Old Man, and found it trying to be living on his doorstep and perpetually on call, I don't know. I suspect he was keen to own a house of his own as an insurance against falling out with his benefactor. When they argued, as they frequently did, he must have felt very vulnerable. Just one week after moving into the house he recorded in his diary, 'Stormy session with Old Man.' The next day, which happened to be his thirtieth birthday, 'Old Man sent cryptic note with column. I spent most of day rewriting. Not at all bad I thought. Beaver visited Pam. 'Twas poor way to spend birthday.'

Beaverbrook's reaction to the column was all-important – and often seemed to be dictated by his mood; and Beaverbrook's mood in turn dictated my father's. When things were going badly we all suffered. In April 1949, Beaverbrook arrived back in England by boat. 'Old Man's boat late. Max stranded at Southampton. And me with my little typewriter brushing up my efforts and keeping my fingers crossed. Called to Cherkley 7.30 p.m.'

The next day Beaverbrook was back at the big house again. 'Old Man as alert and vigorous as ever. I seem to be in favour. But what a morning's work putting his ideas into effect. Not so bad a column when finished.' Then a private thought to himself, 'How funny to have Max and I again running round like scalded cats. He runs even faster than I do.' A couple of weeks later he was in trouble again. 'Old Man comes back from Somerset [where he had a farm] in fire-eating mood. I'm the fire.' Again, on a Friday, 'Wrote fine column in evening', but by Saturday, 'had fine column duly massacred by Old Man in afternoon. Felt very bitter at having to be author of fifth-rate column.'

Most of Beaverbrook's acolytes were frightened of him. Some would literally shake with fear when they were sent for, and most did their utmost to agree with everything he said. I don't think JJ was ever frightened of him, and if he disagreed with something, or didn't like the way he was being treated, he said so. 'Old Man rings at 10.30,' he recorded in his diary in February 1950, 'and I tell him to go to hell. Then I recant and give him Bercat's Bevin story – for Ministry of Labour. He rings later to tell me I can have the house next door.' A month later, 'Cherkley at 10. Old Man asks if I'm losing enthusiasm. I reply, "Not as long as *Express* does not become Tory mouthpiece." We walk in sunshine.'

Not long afterwards they were in the South of France for a month together. 'I sulk all day with Beaver. Walk with Billy. Then in evening rapprochement with Old Man who takes me with him in car to Monte Carlo.' Another guest during that month was an old and loyal friend of Beaverbrook called Brigadier Michael Wardell. JJ makes a note, 'I tell Wardell I've just seen Beaver in bed, fast asleep and with a look of innocent, blissful happiness on his face. Said Wardell, "He must be dreaming he is flogging someone!"'

In the midst of all this, JJ was still toying with politics. In 1949 he was adopted as the Liberal candidate for Dundee and, when I was two-and-a-half weeks old, I was taken up north for his adoption meeting, but it ended in disappointment. At the general election in February 1950, despite a brilliant start to his campaign, he was forced to back out of the contest to allow a straight fight between the Tory and the sitting Labour candidate, John Strachey. The only consolation was a promise he extracted that if the Tories failed to capture the seat, he would have a clear run at it at the next election. 'Tories accepted our agreement,' he wrote. 'What a sad day. It becomes sadder as events – and party anger – unfolds.' The next day was only salvaged by a football match: 'Dundee v Preston only bright spot in hellish day.'

Eighteen months later JJ was back. The Tory candidate had failed to oust Strachey, who was now Secretary of State for War, so in the general election of 1951 he made one final attempt to be an MP. The third candidate was a Communist, Dave Bowman, a Glaswegian train driver, who went on to become General Secretary of the NUR and a good friend. It was a tough fight, which JJ relished, and once again his powers of oratory, and sheer hard work, won him plaudits from the press, but he too failed to unseat Strachey. It was close. He lost by 33,000 votes to 36,000.

He returned to Fleet Street to an ultimatum from Beaverbrook. Did he want to go on playing around with politics or did he want to make himself a career in journalism with all the treasures that journalism could provide? 'If it's politics,' said Beaverbrook, 'you will reach the highest echelon. But if it is journalism, I will put on your head a golden crown.' JJ had no choice. He had a wife and two children. He had no financial resources and was a member of a political party that appeared to have no hope of ever winning a seat in Parliament. He opted for journalism.

For the previous ten months he had been back at the *Daily Express*, as Chief Leader Writer and Assistant Editor, working once again with Arthur Christiansen who, like John Gordon, was jealous of his relationship with Beaverbrook. 'The Beaver' was well aware of this, and he would taunt Christiansen. He would go for days without phoning him and then phone JJ instead and ask him to pass on messages about how the newspaper should be conducted. It was cruel, but then Beaverbrook could be cruel. He seemed to take delight in humiliating people or putting them through physical discomfort.

In the South of France, JJ wrote in his diary, 'Beaver makes nurse go into sea with a rope tied round her waist. I hold other end. She screams with fear and cold. Beaver laughs.' At Cherkley, there was a heated swimming pool that Beaverbrook used to swim in every morning, and at one time it had been the duty of George Malcolm Thompson, a colleague on the *Express*, to tell Beaverbrook what was in the newspapers each morning. Thompson hated swimming, as Beaverbrook well knew, yet he took great pleasure in forcing him into the water. One day as he emerged from the pool, blue and shivering, Beaverbrook said, 'Good, isn't it, Thompson?' 'I like it very much, sir,' he replied. 'If only I didn't find that I had to micturate every time I enter the pool.' He was never asked to swim in the pool again.

When my father told stories of Beaverbrook's cruelty, it was never to condemn him; it was always with a kind of sneaking admiration. He would often recount the day Christiansen was replaced. Christiansen had suffered a heart attack while staying with Beaverbrook in the South of France, and had returned to the office to find a new Editor *in situ*. Beaverbrook showed Christiansen to the lift. 'Sorry to see you going down,' he said.

A favourite maxim of Beaverbrook's was, 'If you walk over a man once, you can walk over him again any time you want to.' JJ adopted it as his own. He determined that no one would ever walk over him, and prided himself that no one ever had. Time and time again, like Beaverbrook, he walked over people who were too polite or ill equipped to stand up for themselves.

One of my father's great journalistic principles was that he would never write something in which he did not believe, and never allow himself to be compromised by either friendship or favours. Although he was a Liberal, he had no difficulty in working for Beaverbrook because, as he saw it, his newspapers were basically on the side of good. But there were occasions when he couldn't stomach the line Beaverbrook wanted to take. One such occasion was in April 1951, during the Korean War, when Beaverbrook wanted the paper to carry leaders supporting the American General Douglas MacArthur. JJ told Christiansen he couldn't write them. A policy meeting was called, and his views were supported by others at the meeting. 'So no comment appears on MacArthur – and thus I am saved from having to quit.' But a few days later Beaverbrook intervened.

Chris talks with Beaver at 11.30. Then message comes to me at Reform asking me to ring Beaver in S. of France immediately. I eventually get through to him at 1.30. He dictates a leader supporting MacArthur. I write it down and then give him my views. Back at office I type out his leader literally as he gave it to me and hand it to Chris under heading 'Notes from Lord Beaverbrook'. I sense Chris is furious that I haven't tried to make a good leader of it.

They clashed again in April 1952 when Beaverbrook allowed himself to be leant on by Churchill to stop the *Express* writing anti-Tory leaders. JJ wrote a special entry in his diary.

Churchill has been kicking up hell about Express *leaders – and their anti-Tory bias . . . Churchill has lunch with Beaver at Chartwell on Saturday April 5. Thereafter Beaver switches policy and becomes pro-government so as to lend Churchill his personal support. On April 8, he shoots down a leader of mine in which I criticise six-month delay in payment of increased Old Age Pensions. On Friday April 4, I have a leader analysing causes of Tory failure removed after Churchill invitation to Beaver is issued.*

Thus to April 9. Pickering, Robertson, Max and myself are summoned to Arlington. Beaver pontificating on need for a more pro-government policy. I ask some questions, surly questions. Does this mean we no longer attack government for failure to get out of GATT, for failure to cut down on British Council, for United Europe policy etc, etc.?

Beaver asks me to stay behind. Asks me 'Am I with him with my heart as well as my head? I say with neither if he gives up prosecution of Empire. I ask him if Tory price for our support is a worthwhile one. Angrily he demands if I am trying to insult him.

I assure him I am trying to do no such thing. But I point out we have Tories over a barrel and could use the chance to get some of our policies put into effect – GATT for example.

In the evening (after drinking champagne and brandy) I am summoned to Arlington at 10.20 p.m. Max leaves as I arrive. Beaver is there with shoe and sock off scratching his sole. Bracken is there too. After Bracken goes, Beaver gives me headlines for his broadcast. Stay there till 1.30.

A couple of weeks later, 'I write a leader on Egypt which I believe may annoy Beaver. I am convinced he is ready to rat over the Sudan issue. My tough leader will make ratting more difficult.' And again, on 5 May, 'I have excellent idea for a leader challenging American attempt to grab control of British Mediterranean fleet – but the Beaver is for appeasement. Am I developing a contempt for him I wonder?'

If he was, it didn't last. And Beaverbrook continued to show him favour with ever more responsibility. 8 September 1952, 'Beaver tells me he thinks I am the only tough man he has at his disposal on the *Express*. He obviously thinks Chris is too ready to crumble at first sign of trouble.' The next day, 'Beaver tells me I'm to edit paper two days a week. I blurt out that I want more money. He does not seem surprised and is very genial.' Two days later he had his rise, and by Friday, 'I am this day – and for this day alone – Editor of the *Express*. I write part of the leader column. Whole paper turns out magnificently.' But the following Monday, 'Chris starts to tear Saturday's paper to bits. I expected him to do this. He even puts a piece on the bulletin. I hope I remember this the next time I feel disposed to sympathise with him.'

Criticism didn't appear to dent JJ's confidence at all; there is not a single entry in several years of diaries where he admits to any kind of self-doubt. 'Another excellent column,' he was writing two days later. 'Chris told me yesterday's was best I had ever done. He is not far wrong either. I am in top form – but only as far as writing is concerned.' Next day, 'Have a brilliant idea on Bevan shot down by long range from Paris and I am furious. Nor do I hide my wrath at having to make do with a fourth-rate idea of the Old Man.'

At the end of April 1953 Beaverbrook made JJ Deputy Editor of the *Evening Standard*, which obviously cheered Christiansen. 'Chris becomes awfully friendly now that I am going,' he wrote. JJ enjoyed the *Evening Standard* and liked the Editor, Percy Elland. After just a week he was writing, 'Things are going very well on the *Standard* and for the first time I am really enjoying journalism. I really am working hard and I think results are beginning to come.' Then, 'I am getting on much better with the staff than any-one ever guessed I would. Newspaper looking first-rate.' He par-ticularly enjoyed it when Percy Elland was away and he edited the paper.

Then, in the early summer of 1954, while they were out walking at Cherkley, Beaverbrook told him that he was going to make him Editor of the *Sunday Express*, John Gordon had retired by this time and become Editor-in-Chief, although he was still writing a current affairs column, and Harold Keeble, who had been brought in to replace him, was proving to be wrong for the job. Their conversation was a secret between the two of them until the autumn but then, true to his word, Beaverbrook shunted Keeble to the *Daily Express* as Associate Editor and, on 21 September, JJ became Editor of the

Sunday Express at the age of thirty-five. The golden crown had been placed on his head, and there it sat for the next thirty-two years.

CHAPTER EIGHT

Where Once Was Love

I once asked one of my children's friends what his father did. The little boy, who can't have been more than three or four, thought for a very long time, then he said, 'He climbs a ladder in the bathroom, and changes the light bulb.' If anyone had asked me when I was the same age what my father did for a living, I could have told them instantly. The *Sunday Express* took over our lives. Every night my father would come home, bolt his supper, pour himself a whisky, then sit for the rest of the evening with a purple pencil in his hand, surrounded by damp page proofs, reading and marking material for the coming week's paper. No one was allowed to talk.

The other factor that dominated our lives was his illness. Newspaper journalism is a stressful business. Every day you start afresh, finding news, checking facts, coaxing sources, thinking of fresh ideas, new approaches, then writing good, compelling copy, which the Editor likes; all of this while the clock ticks inexorably towards edition time when the paper goes to press, and if you haven't quite finished, or are waiting for just one more phone call, it's too late, the page has gone and a blank white space gives testament to your failure.

When JJ was writing the Cross-Bencher column, there had been the nagging fear of having no stories by the end of the week. When he was writing leaders – a job normally done by a team of writers – he was on his own for many months. So not only did he have to come up with two if not three ideas every day, he had to write them all and to a tight deadline. In addition, there were the sundry articles that Beaverbrook would suddenly suggest, which he would have to sit down and write in the Old Man's presence. But the greatest stress must have been Beaverbrook himself, which no other journalist suffered to the same extent because no other journalist lived on his estate as we did. There were his daily, relentless demands, the walks, the summons to Arlington or Cherkley, the lunches, the dinners, the need to be on top of the news and the personalities in the news, on top of politics and political gossip. JJ could never fully relax, not even when Beaverbrook was out of the country, and the pressure took its toll.

Something had to give, and what went first was his health, and what followed was his marriage. He developed a massive duodenal ulcer, which gave him excruciating and almost constant pain. His diaries are littered with references to feeling unwell and the state of his tummy. 1953 began badly. 'Pam, Tink (his first time up at midnight) and I see the New Year in. My tummy, I regret to report, is in most unseasonable mood.' 2 January. 'I hesitate over going to town at all but eventually wobble into office about 4 p.m. and stage a remarkable recovery. Could it have been assisted by receipt of a friendly message from Beaver?'

'The Beaver' was the real problem; JJ knew that he had no time for people who were ill, and there would be no chance of promotion if he confessed to any kind of infirmity. And so he kept it to himself, and miraculously fooled everyone. He ate whatever food Beaverbrook presented him with, however rich or unsuitable for his condition. And when Beaverbrook provided Champagne for him to drink at dinner, which is what he gave his guests at that time, although he himself drank whisky, JJ could not refuse, although the acidity practically crucified him. 'My tum has a good day,' he wrote in December 1952, 'and I come home whistling in the starlight.' But the next day, 'My tum is again bad and oh woe is me.' The next day, 'I take sandwiches and milk to the office and have my best lunch of the week. If I could do this every day I would be absolutely fine.' And on another day, 'Tum bad and quarrelsome.'

The pain made him exceedingly bad tempered and difficult to live with. I imagine he was putting on a brave face during the day, so that no one would guess he was ill, then taking it out on us when he came home. Brutally put, he sacrificed his family for the sake of his career; but what else was he to do? He needed to succeed in order to support his family, and maybe he thought his family would understand. I am sure my mother did understand to begin with, but the bad temper never stopped. Long after the pain was under control and the ulcer healed, he continued to lash out at her.

Five weeks after he became Editor of the *Sunday Express*, the ulcer haemorrhaged and he collapsed in the office in fear of his life. He took to his bed at Garden Cottage, 'feeling as weak as water', and read detective stories. A nurse arrived to look after him, 'a dear old soul called Miss Robertson who fusses around and does little or nothing', and JJ had dozens of visitors, including Max's glamorous new wife, Vi. Alan Everett, the genial, red-faced doctor, came to visit twice a day, and repeatedly tested his blood count. And Lord Beaverbrook arranged for his own Harley Street physician, 'the great Dan Davies' to visit who, to JJ's great relief, deemed surgery unnecessary.

Beaverbrook himself was in Canada at the time and sent a telegram immediately.

I am so sorry about your illness but it is the price youth pays for being too eager in the pursuit of fame. I speak with the voice of experience. Take your time. Convalescence is important. Beaverbrook.

Shortly afterwards a letter arrived:

Dear Junor
  I am so sorry to hear of your illness. I hope it isn't the result of too much 'brain' and that you will be well soon.
  You must not worry about the paper until you are over your illness. Then is the moment to go full speed ahead.
  You may want a period of convalescence. If your doctor so decides, I wish you would let me know.
  Yours sincerely
  Beaverbrook

At the height of JJ's illness, I was packed off to stay with friends in Dorking. Judy Clarke and I had begun at nursery school together and our parents had become friends. Her father, Ian, was a GP and therefore immediately attractive to JJ, and her mother, Marie, a fellow Scot, had been a nurse. It was the first time I had stayed away from home and everything was very strange. They lived in a three-story, semi-detached town house with a garden front and back and a dingy, dank, damp cellar. I slept in the spare room, which had a gas fire in the wall that burst into flame when a match was put to it – something I had never seen before, being used to paraffin – and every night Judy and I would get into bed, her woolly, brown toy poodle would jump on top, and Marie, her mother, would sit on the edge of the bed and sing:

> *Half a pound of tuppenny rice,*
> *Half a pound of treacle,*
> *That's the way the money goes,*
> *Pop goes the weasel.*

When Judy was in her own room and the lights were out I would lie in bed on my own, smelling the strange smells of other people's linen and listening to the strange sounds that are other people's houses. In the mornings, Marie would be downstairs in the kitchen humming merrily while she cooked bacon and fried bread for our breakfast. She even used to hum while she drove us to school, tapping the accelerator in time to the music, which played havoc with my incipient carsickness.

Marie was a warm, jolly woman, who would do anything for anyone, but I was always slightly alarmed by her briskness and efficiency, born no doubt from her years as a hospital matron. Even her hair was efficient. She had waist-length, black hair that she twisted into a ring on the top of her head, and it fascinated me to watch her do it. Everything about Marie fascinated me. She was everything my mother was not. She was the first big-breasted woman I had seen dressing, and what went on under her clothes was a revelation. Judy was an only child, after a series of miscarriages, which was sad for Marie. She should have had a whole dormitory to organise, cook for and sing to; but when her sister-in-law died, leaving two sons, she happily took them under her wing.

JJ was not allowed out of bed for over a week, and it was more than two-and-a-half weeks before his blood count had risen enough for him to be allowed downstairs. He recorded how Everett then started giving him liver injections, 'with a needle which has long lost any point it ever had. I suggest to him he buys a new one'. But he was soon feeling better than he had done for years and, having had little more than milk and sponge cake to eat for weeks, he soon declared himself 'as hungry as a horse' and was once more bursting with enthusiasm for life. As soon as he had been given the all clear by a specialist in London, he and Pam went to Brighton for a week's recuperation by the sea, and I was deposited once again with the Clarkes – this time minus a tooth. As JJ recorded faithfully in his diary for Friday 3 December 1954, 'Tuppence loses her first tooth and is very, very pleased with herself. Comes and wakes me up to show it to me.' My nickname was Tuppence, usually abbreviated to Tuppy – presumably on the grounds that tuppence was more valuable than a penny, and Penny was what every Penelope is called. JJ hated above all doing what other people did.

At much the same time as I lost my tooth, I stopped sucking my thumb. My routine was to suck the thumb of my right hand, preferably while holding a blanket, and twist a piece of hair on the top of my head with the other hand. The blanket was soft and safe and smelt of all that was good. I am sure, in reality, having had children with exactly the same penchant, that it smelt foul, which may explain why my mother did the one and only thing in my entire life that made me cry. While I was at school, she gave my blanket to the rag-and-bone man. This was a shabbily dressed old man with a flat hat and hardly any teeth, who went about with a horse and cart, shouting 'rags 'n' bones', in a sing-song voice that carried for miles. I assume he collected old clothes and bits of material, although heaven knows what for, and I shudder to think what sort of bones he was after, or what use he had for them. He would make his way up to Garden Cottage every six months or so and after he took my blanket away I developed a terror of the man.

My thumb-sucking came to an equally dramatic end. I was sitting on my mother's lap sucking my thumb and twirling my hair as usual while she read me a story. The book was *Struwwelpeter*, which describes itself as 'Merry Stories and Funny Pictures' but is, in fact, a collection of moralistic horror stories for children with terrifying illustrations. That night she read a story called 'The Tale of the Thumb-Sucker', which I have to reproduce in its entirety to get the full grizzly picture.

> One day Mamma said 'Conrad dear,
> I must go out and leave you here.
> But mind now, Conrad, what I say,
> Don't suck your thumb while I'm away.
> The great, tall tailor always comes
> To little boys who suck their thumbs;
> And ere they dream what he's about,
> He takes his great sharp scissors out,
> And cuts their thumbs clean off – and then,
> You know, they never grow again.'
>
> Mamma had scarcely turned her back,
> The thumb was in, Alack! Alack!
>
> The door flew open, in he ran,
> The great, long, red-legged scissor man.
> Oh! Children, see! The tailor's come
> And caught out little Suck-a-Thumb.
> Snip! Snap! Snip! The scissors go,
> And Conrrad cries out 'Oh! Oh! Oh!'
> Snip! Snap! Snip! They go so fast,
> That both his thumbs are off at last.
>
> Mamma comes home: there Conrad stands,
> and looks quite sad, and shows his hands;
> 'Ah!' said Mamma, 'I knew he'd come
> To naughty little Suck-a-Thumb.'

I don't think Pam read it with any ulterior motive at all, but the effect it had on me was electrifying. I had nightmares about the red-legged scissor man, and never, ever, put my thumb in my mouth again – although in times of stress I have to confess to twirling my hair, even today.

Six weeks after collapsing in his office, JJ was back at work, but Dan Davies warned him that he would have to stick to bland food indefinitely. Beaverbrook gave him further advice. Writing from his house at Nassau in the Bahamas,

> *My dear John*
> *I am glad of your recovery. I read in a paper today that boiled cabbage water is a sure relief for your complaint.*
> *And with good wishes and my regards to your wife*
> *Yours sincerely*
> *Beaverbrook*

I don't recall my father taking that advice, but he did listen to Dan Davies, and stuck to the diet he prescribed pretty faithfully for the rest of his life. I suspect it was the sort of food he preferred anyway, having had nothing very exotic during his childhood, but it allowed him to become a complete bore about the food he would eat. Everything had to be plainly cooked, with no sauces or flavourings, and casseroles had to be cooked with no onions, and most definitely with no garlic. He hated garlic with a passion and claimed to be so sensitive to its horrors that if a knife that had been used to chop garlic was then used in the preparation of his food, he could taste it, and would refuse to touch it.

The restaurants he ate in frequently came to know that he would want some variation of whatever was on their menu, and I am sure they cursed quietly; but my mother, who cooked for him every evening, was driven completely mad. She was a good and enthusiastic cook, and having to make and eat the sort of food he insisted upon – like boiled mince without so much as an onion or herb to cheer it up – was very disheartening. He also hated vegetables, with the exception of potatoes – again a reflection of his childhood, no doubt – and, since he was almost perpetually on a diet to keep his weight down, certainly in later years, he wouldn't eat potatoes either, or never more than a teaspoonful. The only thing that kept scurvy at bay, I presume, was his passion for melon, grapefruit and freshly squeezed orange juice which he drank every morning for breakfast with a kind of religious zeal.

Looking back, his illness was probably one of the major causes for his marriage to fall apart. My father always told me that they had ten very happy years together. I don't remember them, and grew up believing that my mother had never loved my father. She always told me that she married him out of pity. She had loved a boy called Derek who went away at the beginning of the war to India and married someone else and was then lost. It broke her heart, and when she met my father, she felt sorry for him because he was also very probably about to be killed. After their marriage she realised she had made a big mistake. I believed that sending her to Scotland to give birth to my brother, away from her family, was one of the more inhumane things he had done to her.

I believed it all and, having watched them together throughout my life, there was absolutely no reason to question any of it. But, going through JJ's papers after his death, I found letters from her. There are not many, but they were written as late as 1951, two years after my birth, seven years after Tink was born, and nine years into their marriage, which tell a very different story.

There is no doubt Pam was traumatised by the experience of giving birth to my brother, and that might well have coloured her memory of being sent up to Scotland but, given the warmth and strength of their relationship at that time, as their letters and photographs bear witness, I begin to doubt that she could have travelled there entirely against her will.

In the summer of 1951, JJ spent a month with Beaverbrook at Cap d'Ail and Pam missed him terribly. She wrote every day. This, on their wedding anniversary:

Darlingest,

Just imagine – I was really talking to you this morning and when I was talking to you it didn't feel at all as if you'd been away for years and years, but now again it does darling. Oh darling Johnny I love you so, I'm filled with longing for you, I positively ache for you, I want to feel your arms around me and the warmth of your face against mine. Oh darling I just love you and love you and love you.

I think this is a hell of a way to spend such a terribly important thing as our anniversary – I came in from the garden at ten past eight – it has been beautifully warm all day and as I was still warm I didn't light the fire and now at ten I'm freezing! For supper I had my eternal egg, and I look like nothing on earth in my green jumper and slacks and all curled up on the chair.

Darling little thing you're so terribly, terribly sweet – your cable was wonderful, I simply loved it, it was absolutely perfect and this afternoon I had a wonderful letter. Darlingest, I've had you for eight years and still all I want and all I ever want is you.

Oh darling, darling, darling I want you so, I need you so and I love you and love you and love you so.

All my love and all my kisses my darling wonderful one,
Pam

And then when she heard he was coming home:

Darlingest,

You're coming home on Monday – are you really coming home on Monday? I can't believe it, it's too wonderful. My heart already is beginning to behave most peculiarly. I can't imagine the condition I shall be in by the end of the week.

Wardell phoned me last night just as I was going to bed and told me – though I haven't had your letter yet. When I did go to bed I couldn't go to sleep for hours – it's too silly. Angel do you think I'll have grown, are you sure you'll still love me as much? You must, I couldn't bear it if you didn't.

Today we've had the most fantastic weather. It's been freezing cold with numerous hail showers. At tea time it got nearly as dark as night and we had to light the lamps – by five *it had recovered and was light again – at 6.15 I stuck Tink in the bath and grovelled on the floor collecting his Meccano and when I looked up, Gor blimey, the ground was white with snow and the most enormous snowflakes coming down fast and furiously and it snowed for about an hour.*

Darlingest adorable, I love you, I adore you, I worship you. Darling I am completely crazily head over heels in love with you – you silly old thing.

All my love and kisses my darling little love,
Pam

Finding these few, precious letters, and reading the diaries that JJ wrote at about the same time, was shattering.

My cousin, Jean – Tom's daughter – who is ten years older than me, says that Pam and JJ were the first couple she had ever seen who were obviously in love. We all went on holiday to Carolle in Normandy together in 1951. 'They were always very physical with each other, holding hands, hugging, very tactile and very much in love.' Jean was eleven on that holiday and her brother Muir was fifteen. Their mother Jean had died of cancer two years before after a medical blunder. Tom never entirely recovered.

Muir saw JJ as an ally, more like an older brother than an uncle. 'He was good fun to be with. He was full of enthusiasm and encouraged me, he said I could do anything, be anything.' Muir, like his father, became an alcoholic, and remembers that holiday as the time he first felt that alcohol was the answer to his problems. 'One night the grown-ups went to the casino and I went into a bistro and ordered brandy. It was a wonderful feeling, like the lights had come up on stage and the curtains opened and all my fear and anxiety subsided. JJ came back and said, 'You're pissed, we'd better not let your father see.'

I don't think I have any memory of the holiday at all, being only twenty months old, but my father told two stories about me so often that I feel as though I remember. In the evenings I was put to bed while everyone else went down to dinner. One night they were happily eating, when people in the dining room started to titter with laughter. It was not long before they discovered why. I had woken up and gone looking for them. Because of the warm night, I was stark naked, but fully confident that if I couldn't see people they wouldn't be able to see me. So there I was, this podgy little figure, tottering around the dining room with my hands held up over my face, peeping through the fingers, as I searched every table for some familiar faces. On a later occasion, I also caused a moment of parental panic that holiday by biting off and swallowing a piece of a glass from which I was drinking.

We never went on holiday with Tom and his family again. I next met Jean when I was twenty-five, and it was like looking in a mirror and seeing a familiar face that I had known all my life. We had grown up six hundred miles apart, with ten years between us, and yet it was like meeting a long-lost twin. We hadn't shared experiences; what we had shared was a maiden name and all that being a female Junor entailed.

For the next seven years we went on our own to Cornwall, but we were never alone for long. JJ always made friends on holiday, wherever we went, he attracted people like a magnet – everyone from local tradesmen to fellow holidaymakers that he might meet on the beach, on the golf course, in the pub, anywhere. He enjoyed having an entourage, and needed the stimulation that new people provided.

For the first few years we went to the Headlands Hotel in Portgaverne, a whitewashed building on the cliff top with wonderful views over the sea. Portgaverne itself was just down the hill, a small bay with a stony beach, where JJ used to take Tink to swim before breakfast. When the fishing boats came in, the noise of the seagulls wheeling and swooping overhead was deafening.

In the afternoons we used to sit outside a little café-cum-shop, and I would drink Vimto. Round the corner from Portgaverne was the more famous Port Isaac, with its steep narrow winding streets leading down to the bay, where the fishermen in yellow oilskins and waders used to spread out their nets to dry over upturned hulls, and the air was thick with the smell of fish. JJ befriended a number of the fishermen and year after year we used to go out mackerel fishing with a fisherman called Raymond in the early mornings. One year a huge basking shark came right alongside the boat, and lay there in the water beside us for what felt like hours. It was almost twice the size of our little boat. We all sat very still, even Raymond. He said it wouldn't have harmed us, but it could very easily have tipped us into the sea and we were a long way from land with not a life jacket between us.

After early morning fishing, we would drive to Daymer Bay, with its huge expanse of golden sand, or we'd go fishing for crabs with shrimping nets in the rock pools when the tide was out. JJ could never sit still, he always wanted to be moving from one activity to another and organising everyone to a strict timetable. Then we might go to Rock a little further along the coast, where we learned to sail with Ken Duxbury, a bronzed Adonis, who was the local heartthrob. JJ immediately signed him up to write about sailing on the *Sunday Express*, which he continued to do for thirty years. He ran a little sailing school in Rock and, despite the vagaries of the English summer, I never remember him wearing more than a skimpy pair of swimming trunks. Pam hated the water, but JJ, Tink and I all learned to sail with Ken in a little twelve-foot dinghy called *Louise*. He had a bigger one, a Wayfarer, called *Whisper*, and would endlessly sing, 'Every little breeze seems to whisper Louise,' as he dragged boats up and down the shore. He remembers my father going solo for the first time, sitting in the stern, his not inconsiderable weight nearly swamping the craft, drifting back with the flood tide towards Porthilly Point and quite petrified (though he'd *never* admit it) that he was bound for Wadebridge, eight miles up the creek, while the rest of the family ate the sandwiches in the dunes at Rock.

From Rock we might take the ferry across the estuary to Padstow, or we would go board-surfing at Polzeath and buy Kelley's Cornish ice cream from a van on the beach, which JJ with his sweet tooth loved. He said it was the best ice cream in the world, and he was quite a connoisseur of ice cream, as of all things. All the great Italian ice-cream makers who fled Mussolini went to Glasgow and set up milk bars, he would say. That was how his friend Charles Forte began.

Some of the people we met on holiday we would spend day and night with for the two or three weeks we were together, then never see them again. Other friendships lasted longer, like one forged in the summer of 1953. 'The sun shines brilliantly,' he recorded in his diary. 'Tink and I go for a pre-breakfast dip and meet a charming Irish doctor – Brendan Wyllie.' The Wyllies lived in Rolvenden, in Kent, and later that year we went to see them. On the way home we passed a sign by the side of the road saying 'Labrador puppies for sale' and, on the spur of the moment, which was one of the things I loved about my father, we stopped and bought one. He did everything on the spur of the moment, everything on instinct and gut feeling. Sometimes I think he lived to regret it, especially when he said things that a moment's reflection might have stopped him saying; but most of the time, his instincts were right.

The dog was a triumph. It was a yellow dog, with outsize feet and ears, and a soft, pale coat that was about three sizes too big for him, teeth like needles, and a tongue that left no millimetre of our faces unlicked. Tink and I spent the journey home taking it in turns to have him on our lap, and thinking of a name for him. By the time we reached Garden Cottage he had been christened Tio, short for Horatio Nelson, which must have been his kennel name. 'The puppy is delightful and sleeps with Pam and me – which is disconcerting,' wrote JJ. 'The children are fascinated by it and its kisses are eagerly sought.' My father doted on him, but Tio was a dog with a charmed existence. Being a male, he roamed and, judging by the phone calls we had inviting us to retrieve him, he travelled miles. He once ended up under the wheels of a Green Line bus on the A24 and on another occasion stole someone's Sunday joint from their kitchen table in a house in the village: both equally life-threatening.

That year JJ bought a new car and sold the old one, a little grey Morris Minor with a drop hood, which I loved. Aged three, I was devastated that it was going, and so JJ promised he would buy me one of my own when I was twenty-one. It was obviously quite an emotional parting for him too. 'I drive lovely FSA 84 to Kilburn and leave it looking dejected for some new owner,' he wrote in his diary. 'I get cheque for £400.' But by the next day he was feeling more cheerful. 'Take delivery at 2.30 of my new Consul and am as excited as a child. Get home at 3 a.m. and sidelights refuse to go off. Tink and Tuppence come out of bed to inspect it.'

Very gradually, JJ was moving up in the world. Having no rent to pay must have made life very much easier, but he was still nervous about spending money. 'I go to Savile Row and order myself two suits,' he wrote in February 1953. 'About the most daring thing I have ever done.' A year later, 'Look in at Simpson's and dither about buying a new coat. I really need one and would get one if I were not so chronically broke.' Two weeks later, 'Succumb to temptation – also to necessity – and buy a new overcoat.'

Pam was always thrifty, even in later years when they had more money. She filled the house with beautiful antiques, which she bought for peanuts in auction rooms and house sales, the irony being that what she bought because she couldn't afford anything else, subsequently became far more valuable than anything she might have bought if they'd had any money.

Despite JJ's passion for shopping, he was never a very big spender either. What he liked best were bargains. He shopped every single Monday without fail, buying fruit, bread, gadgets, garden machinery – anything that took his fancy and could be had for a knockdown price. He would rather buy a dozen rotten oranges than spend the same amount of money on six decent ones. His only real extravagance was a yacht, which he bought many years later. Money was a source of endless fascination to him – and worry. He kept meticulous accounts of his income and expenditure and never allowed himself to get into debt.

With the arrival of Tio, our summer occupation of the Headlands Hotel came to an end and we rented a house each summer thereafter in Daymer Bay. The dog came too, and he was no less adventurous off his own patch. One year we went on an outing to Padstow. We drove to Rock, left the car parked by the golf course, and took the ferry across the estuary in the usual way. We spent most of the day there, had lunch, had a swim and, during the course of it all, managed to lose Tio. Panic-stricken, we searched all over, calling his name, whistling, asking if anyone had seen him. The ferryman said he had seen a yellow Labrador earlier in the afternoon, which had climbed aboard the ferry. It had jumped ship several hundred yards short of the shore and he had last seen it swimming in the direction of Rock.

With our hearts in our mouths, we boarded the ferry ourselves and headed back across the estuary. Paw prints in the sand led from the beach to the car, and there were prints all over the car windows where he had obviously jumped up hoping to find someone inside, then tracks leading away again. They must have been made hours before, and he was nowhere to be seen. We called and called until we were hoarse, and asked everyone we came across if they had seen a dog but no one had.

Eventually, in despair, we gave up. By the time we reached the house we were renting, it was dark. We were full of gloom and recriminations, but suddenly as the car swung into the drive, there miraculously, caught in the headlights was one very dirty, very wet, very tired dog, sitting on the doormat. How he found his way back the three or four miles to a house he hardly knew remained a mystery, and one that fascinated my father.

CHAPTER NINE

The Editor

JJ made it clear to his staff on his first day in the Editor's chair that they could expect some changes, and they recognised straight away that they had a powerful Editor at the helm once more. Most of them were relieved, if a little nervous. 'It was rather like being back at school,' said one. 'You had to put your piece in like an essay, and he would read every note and paragraph of it.'

'I have seen most of the staff by now,' he wrote in his diary, 'and am quite favourably impressed. Lots of youngsters with real talent around.' He had no anxiety about taking on the job, no doubts about his ability, and no difficulty in telling people after that first Sunday's paper that he was unhappy. 'Tear Bernard Drew off a strip for having missed a story on Saturday night,' he wrote; and when his old friend Charles Wintour was making a hash of adapting a book for serialisation, he had no qualms about taking the job away from him and giving it to someone else.

He enjoyed the job from the outset. 'Editing a paper is a much more exciting job than being second in command,' he wrote. 'There's a zest in going to work when you are Number One.' The only problem was that John Gordon, who had become Editor-in-Chief, also enjoyed being Number One and was not willing to relinquish the position. It wasn't long before things came to a head. Max Aitken phoned Garden Cottage one evening in a fury. JJ had left the office at about 4.30 that afternoon to take us to Bertram Mills's circus at Olympia, as he did every year. Max wanted to know where he had been; the Chairman of the *Sunday Express*,

E. J. Robertson, had been trying to contact him. Was he not aware that the Chairman disliked the idea of a series JJ was planning to run, called 'How to make a Million'? JJ strongly suspected the Chairman had been put up to it by John Gordon, who was vocal in his criticism of JJ, and couldn't resist interfering. He rounded on Max. He had been given the job of editing the *Sunday Express*, he said, and if the management didn't have faith in his judgement then they should find someone else to do the job.

Nevertheless, it made for a very difficult relationship. The following day his diary entry read, 'We listen to a series of platitudes in Gordon's room. The chiefs of the Beaverbrook press have about as much guts as a cartload of rabbits.' A little later, 'Have a row with John Gordon and get sympathy but precious little support from Robertson. They are a weak and pretty unscrupulous bunch.' He told Beaverbrook about the trouble he was having with John Gordon but the Old Man was not prepared to intervene.

Beaverbrook telephoned the office every Saturday evening to find out what was going on. 'What's the news?' he asked one week. JJ excitedly told him they had the most brilliant scoop and he was intending to run it right across the front page. It was a picture of the Loch Ness monster – the scoop of all scoops – a perfect shot of a long-necked creature peering out of the mist straight at the lens. It was taken by two respectable, middle-class boys from Manchester. They had been camping on the shores of Loch Ness and, having taken the picture, had rushed into the Manchester office of the *Sunday Express* and handed over the camera with the film intact. There was no way the negative could have been tampered with. The picture was genuine, everyone agreed.

'Don't print it,' said Beaverbrook emphatically. JJ explained the provenance.

'I don't care,' he said. 'Don't print it.'

'But why not?' pleaded JJ.

'Because there is no such thing as the Loch Ness monster and, although I don't know how they did it, the picture just has to be a fake.'

Reluctantly JJ killed the picture. The boys were university students, it was a rag week stunt and, although the film hadn't been tampered with, the monster was a blow-up imitation. The *Sunday Express* and its Editor had come close to looking very foolish. JJ took the lesson to heart and when anyone claimed to have seen the Loch Ness monster thereafter, he would never let the *Sunday Express* touch the story; convinced by Beaverbrook, he would say, 'Because there's no such thing as the Loch Ness monster.'

Every week he had a memo from Beaverbrook – as did all his editors – dictated from wherever Beaverbrook was in the world, making it crystal clear that he read every page and was prepared to challenge every shortcoming. If he was abroad, Beaverbrook sent a recording of his dictation by airmail to his secretary for transcription. He would write about personal foibles, such as the use of long sentences, or the word 'throw' in relation to a party, both of which he disapproved. He would question JJ's decisions about what prominence was given to particular stories, he wanted to know how much various contributors were being paid, who wrote a particular unsigned piece, or whose fault it was that a news item was not picked up until the second or third edition, and if he thought a writer needed a change of job within the paper, he said so.

'I have been reading very extensively today, Mr Junor,' he wrote on 5 July 1956, 'so you must expect a great many comments.' They ran to five pages of single-spaced typing – about a newspaper that was only ten or, at most, fourteen pages long in those days.

On balance I think the paper is very fine. So you will forgive me if I pick out, having read so extensively, what I conceive to be the weaknesses . . . I would warn you not to take this as criticism at all, merely an old man giving advice to a young boy, comparative youth. I would warn you against the article that is written in an armchair in a comfortable library with a lot of books about. Compare with the material that a reporter can produce. The reporting article is the rich article. There again, the articles must have passion. Those writing according to order seldom show passion . . .

Every week JJ would painstakingly reply to these memos, point by point, sometimes admitting fault or failure, sometimes sticking to his guns.

> *What does Anne Scott-James means when she writes that the Queen has been to ten race meetings, often going on more than one day? Does she mean often going, I do not understand it . . . . I do not think the Queen is a fine rider, Mr Junor. You might like a controversy on that subject. I think she rides very badly . . . I do not see a great deal of reporting on the Anne Scott-James page.*

JJ's reply on the matter of Anne Scott-James:

> *A race meeting is usually spread over three days so when Anne Scott-James says that the Queen has been to ten race meetings often going on more than one day, it means that she may attend on two successive days or on two days out of three.*
>
> *I agree with your criticism of Anne Scott-James. The trouble is, I think, she has been trying too hard and has become a little stale. She is off on holiday for a fortnight and I am sure will return restored to her full brilliance.*

JJ was very loyal to his staff in the face of criticism from Beaverbrook, and was always keen to commend writers to him, particularly those he had hired himself. But about a year into his editorship, the two men had a serious falling out. One Sunday the paper ran a sensational story saying that Britain's supersonic fighter aeroplane, the Swift, was not, in fact, supersonic. Vickers, who made the aircraft, were unsurprisingly furious, but so was Beaverbrook. He wanted to know why he had not been consulted in advance. JJ said he had seen no reason to consult when he had satisfied himself the story was true. In future, he was told, a manager would sit in on his editorial conferences – meetings between the Editor and his department heads when possible stories were first discussed. JJ refused point blank; a manager, he knew, would present the staff with a conflict of loyalty, they wouldn't know who was running the show – Editor or manager. He was pressed to reconsider; he refused.

Finally, when Beaverbrook realised he was not going to get his way, he turned his back on my father and there followed the unhappiest months of his editorship. Beaverbrook stopped speaking to him. He didn't invite him for walks, didn't invite him to Cherkley, didn't telephone, he didn't even send him his weekly memos. They were all addressed to Max Aitken, and laden with criticism of the paper for him to pass on to the Editor.

Max, I want you to tell Junor ... I have heard that
Mountbatten story over and over and there is nothing new in
it and I don't think much of it ... I don't like name and
address withheld in the correspondence col. at all. ... The
Political Notes. You must have some more news in them. ... I
am tired of reading of McLeod being an expert Bridge player.
I suggest you develop some other virtue in that young man
now. Providing of course that you believe that a good Bridge
playing capacity is a virtue ...

JJ sent his usual replies, painstakingly and politely, if a little icily. But it was clear to him that Beaverbrook was trying to push him out of his job. He went to see Max and told him what he thought. Max didn't disagree, so JJ went home to Garden Cottage and told Pam to go straight out and start looking for a house of our own.

The next day Beaverbrook said he would see him at Arlington House. They walked in the park and Beaverbrook continued to criticise the paper. 'Why don't you let a manager come and sit at conference?' he said. JJ explained, and they continued to walk. At the end the Old Man cheered up. He said he thought things would go better on the *Sunday Express*; he still had faith in JJ. Now would he allow a manager into conference? JJ shook his head. 'He will regret losing me more than I regret losing him,' he told his diary that night.

But there was no parting. My father remained as Editor and, in time, normal relations were resumed. No manager ever sat in on editorial conferences, nor did we move house. It must have been a very unpleasant and nerve-racking time for him; and I wonder whether, if we had already had a house of our own, the story would have had a different outcome; JJ might have told the Old Man to get stuffed. Equally, had Beaverbrook known JJ was in a position to walk out, he might have been less childish.

I can't believe my father admired this behaviour but, in later years, he could be equally childish himself. If ever he was thwarted or caught out, or had a row with someone, he would send them to Coventry, as Beaverbrook had done. He could go for weeks without talking to someone: my mother, my brother and I were all victims at one time or another. And he fell out with an old golfing partner over an oozler (a bet for halving the eighteenth hole) and killed a friendship of over twenty years standing. They never spoke again.

Despite Beaverbrook's commenting on everything that my father did in the *Sunday Express*, when JJ found himself in real trouble, at the end of 1956, and looked to Beaverbrook for support, it was not forthcoming. It was during the Suez crisis, when petrol rationing was introduced in Britain because supplies couldn't get through the Suez Canal. JJ came across a circular, which had been sent to all political parties, making it quite clear that, although tradesmen and ordinary motorists would be severely restricted, there would be very lavish petrol rations for the political parties. He wrote the following piece, on 16 December, under the headline:

PRIVILEGE

Tomorrow a time of hardship starts for everyone. For everyone? Include the politicians out of that.

Petrol rationing will pass them by. They are to get prodigious supplementary allowances.

Isn't it fantastic?

The small baker, unable to carry out his rounds, may be pushed out of business. The one-man taxi company may founder. The parent who lives in the country may plead in vain for petrol to drive the kids to school.

But everywhere the tanks of the politicians will be brimming over.

What are MPs doing about this monstrous injustice? Are they clamouring for Fuel Minister Mr Aubrey Jones to treat politicians like the rest of the community?

If it were a question of company directors getting special preference you may be sure that the howls in Westminster would soon be heard from John o' Groats to Ebbw Vale. But now there is not a squeak of protest.

If politicians are more interested in privileges for themselves than in fair shares for all, let it swiftly be made plain to them that the public do not propose to tolerate it.

And let Mr Aubrey Jones know that, if he is so incapable of judging public feeling, he is not fit to hold political office for a moment longer.

MPs were enraged and JJ was summoned before the Committee of Privileges in the House of Commons. He was allowed no legal representation – though he was to be cross-examined by the Attorney General – and was given no advice. There followed not so much an interrogation as an inquisition by a group of men, each of whom JJ realised looking round the table, he had attacked at some time or another in Cross-Bencher. They were furious about a letter he had written the previous day to the Speaker of the House, in which he said, 'I regret that the leading article in the *Sunday Express* of December 16th has been misread and misunderstood by some Members of Parliament.'

He was not prepared to apologise for what he saw as a perfectly legitimate comment about the petrol crisis, and the more he was grilled, the testier he became with the result that, 'Having heard Mr Junor's evidence and having considered his demeanour while giving evidence' the Committee found him guilty of serious contempt. 'Mr Junor was given every opportunity to express his regret and to apologise for his conduct,' said the official report. 'He said he did not mean to be discourteous to the House of Commons or to bring it into disrepute and that if it had been interpreted as discourtesy, then he was sorry.' The Committee recommended to the House that, 'in view of the gravity of the contempt committed by Mr Junor, he should be severely reprimanded.'

And so he was. He was summoned to appear before the Bar of the House of Commons on 24 January 1957 'at a quarter-past three o'clock' – and became the last journalist of the twentieth century so to do. About eight or nine years later, I was in a school party being shown round the Houses of Parliament by Sir Harry Legge-Bourke, the father of a friend of mine. Upon reaching the Bar, unaware that I was in the group, he launched into a colourful reconstruction of the last time an offender had appeared before it, 'It was the Editor of the *Sunday Express*', he said, and went on to describe my father's ordeal, as he might have reminisced about a public hanging.

The night before JJ's appearance he had two phone calls at home from friends with conflicting advice. Dick Crossman urged him to use his time at the Bar of the House to speak out in favour of the freedom of the press and to tell the House of Commons to go to hell. Manny Shinwell told him to placate the House and say he was sorry. He took the advice of both of them. But the person from whom he would have appreciated some support that night was Lord Beaverbrook. There was no phone call, no message, no word. JJ suspected he was afraid of being called before the Bar himself.

When he arrived at the House of Commons he was taken into custody by a series of Serjeants-at-Arms, in traditional uniform, wearing black tights, with long silver swords. They were clearly excited by having a prisoner to break the tedium of their normal routine. This is part of the account he wrote of the experience at the time:

The task of actually escorting me belonged to the Serjeant-at-Arms himself, Major-General I. T. P. Hughes. Colonel Thorne [Deputy Serjeant-at-Arms] promptly and summarily ordered the Assistant Sergeant-at-Arms out of the room and proceeded with great and undisguised pleasure to explain the procedure to me.

He offered to rehearse the steps and bows with me. He

warned me not once but twice that after retreating backwards from the Speaker once I had completed my statement, I should be careful in my right about turn, since the Serjeant-at-Arms would also be making a right about turn at the same time and in view of the fact that he had a mace in his hand, I would be well advised to steer clear of him to allow him room for manoeuvre.

. . . I was hustled back to the lobby where the Serjeant-at-Arms met me with the mace. I then walked into the House with him. It was crammed to capacity. The only feeling I had was that no matter what happened I would show no trace of nervousness. Nor in any circumstances would I appear abject. I had always dreamed of making a maiden speech in the Commons. But I had never envisaged circumstances such as these.

I took a deep breath, pulled my shoulders back and said,

'I wish to express my sincere and unreserved apologies for any imputation or reflection which I may have caused upon the honour and integrity of members of this House of Commons in the article which I published in the *Sunday Express* on December 16.

'At no time did I intend to be discourteous to Parliament. My only aim was to focus attention on what I considered to be an injustice in the allocation of petrol – namely the allowance given to political parties in the constituencies.

'In my judgement these allowances were a proper and indeed an inescapable subject for comment in a free press. That was a view, which I held then and hold now. But I do regret deeply and sincerely that the manner in which I expressed myself should have been such as to have been a contempt of this House.

'I have nothing more to say, sir. I now leave myself in the hands of this House.'

And the House, which had listened to his statement in absolute silence, was left to decide whether he should be sent to the Tower of London.

After I had made my statement and had withdrawn from the House, I was taken back to the Serjeant-at-Arms' office where I was asked if there was anything I wanted.

Expecting a longish stay there, I replied, 'Yes, I would like a pot of tea, three rounds of toast and some cakes.'

But before he had time for tea and toast, word came through that the House had decided to accept his apology and take no further action. He emerged a hero. The *Yorkshire Post* reported, 'He made a favourable impression in all quarters of the House and not least among his colleagues in the Press Gallery. The House agreed at the end that its dignity had been maintained and sustained. Mr Junor withdrew without any loss of his and indeed seemed to have gained in stature.' Still Beaverbrook said nothing.

Beaverbrook's birthday was 25 May, and every year my father gave him a present. One year he bought him a pair of binoculars, which he stored in the drawer of his desk. He told Bob Edwards, who was newly arrived as his Deputy on the *Sunday Express*, that he must also buy a present, and showed him the binoculars with pride. 'That's real leather,' he said handing him the case. 'Smell it.' The next day he said that he had changed his mind about the binoculars. He was going to keep them for himself. 'Look what I'm giving him instead,' he said, and from the same drawer of his desk he produced a sheepdog whistle in a small leather box. It was the sort that was so high pitched it was inaudible to the human ear. 'Do you think he'll get the joke?' asked JJ. 'He's the shepherd, we're the sheep?'

Lost for ideas about what to give a millionaire, Bob Edwards went out and bought him a plastic birthday card for two shillings, which played a mediocre version of 'The London I Love'. He wrote a devoted message inside and delivered it to Arlington House. But bought no present.

The next morning Beaverbrook telephoned and asked Bob if he would like to go walking with an old man. Bob found him still opening presents. 'Junor sent me a whistle that didn't blow,' he said. 'I could have explained,' says Bob, 'but sensing that my chances of taking over the paper had measurably increased, I treacherously did not. After a moment or two's thought, Beaverbrook added, "The pea must have fallen out".'

Soon afterwards Bob had a letter thanking him for 'Your most original birthday card. I shall play it again and again. And with all good wishes, B.' JJ buzzed him on the intercom later that week. 'By the way, did the Old Man ever thank you for his birthday card?' 'No,' said Bob tactfully. 'He didn't thank me either,' said JJ.

In fact my father had been thanked – he was obviously being equally tactful.

My dear Junor
　　So very many thanks for this unique present.
　　I have discovered the secret after some manipulation. But the final solution was provided by the Prime Minister of Newfoundland. I shall use it for Paddy and also for Miss Rosenberg.
　　Yours sincerely
　　B

Paddy was the dog and Miss Rosenberg, Beaverbrook's secretary – 'delicious, delectable Jo' as JJ described her – who tended Beaverbrook's every need.

The binoculars stayed in JJ's office drawer where he put them to good use. One day the City Editor came in to talk about an idea, which clearly didn't enthral my father. As the man warmed to his theme, JJ pulled out the binoculars, raised them to his eyes, and looking out of the window, suddenly said, 'Do you know, Ted, with these binoculars I can see the pigeon shit on the roof of St Bride's church?'

CHAPTER TEN

A Home of Our Own

When I was about seven or eight, my teacher asked everyone in the class to write essays on what we wanted to be when we grew up. We were all horse-mad at the time and I don't think there was a single girl who wanted to be anything other than a riding instructor, myself included. Like most little girls of that age, we all wanted to conform to the group. I was no different; I wanted to conform just as much as everyone else, and I wanted my family to conform. The problem was they didn't.

My father wasn't like anyone else's. Other people's fathers were invisible and distant. If you went to their houses, they might say 'hello', but that would be it. Mine wanted to know everything about my friends; he interrogated them, and would tell them things about me, puffing me up, which I couldn't bear. He often used to come to collect me from school on Monday afternoons, and I dreaded it. I went to a small co-ed prep school in Dorking, called Stanway, which sat at the top of a short hedge-lined drive. There was room for a few cars to park in front of the house, and parents who arrived early to collect their children parked there. The others had to park in the road and walk up the drive.

JJ always arrived early. His car at that time was a huge, ostentatious, cream-coloured Armstrong Siddeley Star Sapphire. It looked like the sort of thing that ought to have wedding ribbons on the bonnet and been hired out by the day. When I came out of school with all my friends and saw that sitting in the drive, I wanted to die. They all had ordinary, boring cars, and that was what I longed for: anonymity. I insisted that JJ park it not just at the bottom of the drive but round the corner so that no one would see it belonged to me. Although what I really wanted was for him not to collect me at all – he was the only father who did.

At the onset of petrol rationing during the Suez crisis, the gas-guzzling Star Sapphire was put into mothballs and JJ bought a second-hand Austin 7, which was very economical on fuel. It was a black, ugly little car, so old it was virtually vintage. He was very pleased with it but, because it was different and stood out, it embarrassed me just as much as the big car. Again I implored him not to bring it up the drive to the front of the school but to park it around the corner and walk.

Just to put this into perspective . . . at one stage my mother was a problem too. She looked more like a big sister than a mother. She had long hair halfway down her back, and lived in slacks and jumpers. Most mothers in the 1950s wore skirts, stockings and high heels, and one Christmas I gave her a skirt and some red lipstick to try and make her look the part. I am pleased to say I grew out of that phase quite quickly and thereafter loved the fact that she was so different.

My attitude to my father was not so easily fixed. It was not just that he embarrassed me in front of my friends. The real problem was I felt embarrassed by his attention. He slobbered over me, particularly when he had had a few drinks, and demanded hugs and kisses. He would look at me with a soppy expression on his face, or – if I refused – a hurt expression. I couldn't bear it. Looking back, it seems churlish to have spurned his affection and praise – but the truth is that he smothered me with love, almost to the point of suffocation. He would always say how marvellous I looked or how clever I was and, worst of all, he would boast about me to his friends in my presence. He was fiercely competitive on my behalf. He needed to establish with the parents of my school friends that I was prettier and wittier at whatever I was doing, or that the marks I was getting were better than their daughters'. I was actually none of these things, which is perhaps why I hated it so much.

My mother demanded nothing and I loved her to bits. She never told me she loved me but she didn't need to. It could never have crossed my mind for an instant that she didn't because her every action and every word made it perfectly clear that I was as important to her as she was to me. I loved being with her because she was never sharp or disapproving, never stuffy, never cross. She was the easiest-going person I have ever known and quite the most selfless. She was always in a good mood, always fun to be with, always kind and, as I grew older, I confided as much in her as I did in my best friend. In many ways she was my best friend.

As a family, there was a clear division between the sexes. Although my father lavished me with his love, his interest in me was curiously superficial. He never asked my opinion about anything, never wanted to know how I felt or what I thought – and I think I had a lucky escape. My brother was the one whose opinions he wanted. Tink was his best friend, Tink was the one he took aside for serious talks, who was asked his views on current affairs and who was expected to read and appraise the *Sunday Express* each week – all at an age when he should have been looking for conkers or having fun with his mates. Not that he complained. Tink enjoyed the attention; it made him feel very grown-up and important, but it wasn't much of a childhood, and it made him horribly precocious and rather pompous.

When JJ faced his inquisition before the Committee for Privileges over petrol rationing, Tink, then twelve years old, sent him the following letter.

> *Dear Mr Junor,*
> *I would be very grateful if you would give me a detailed report on your happenings in the House of Commons on December the 18th.*
> *I greatly admire your courage, sir, and I also agree with your statements that you made in and out of the House.*
> *Yours sincerely,*
> *Roderick Junor*

I was seven and rather disinterested and, although I watched the news report on television the day JJ appeared before the Bar, Tink was entirely bound up in it. That night when JJ arrived home,

Tink was in tears. 'You gave in, Daddy,' he said. 'Why did you give in?'

I never noticed when I was a child that my brother was either precocious or pompous – it is our cousins, Jean and Muir, who bear witness to his behaviour when he was small. Tink was my hero and could do no wrong. I adored him and he adored me. We felt like twins, though born five years apart. We each had odd ears, one of mine matched one of his, as though we had been mixed up in the womb and come out with the wrong bits. There was even a synergy in the food we liked. He only liked the yolk of egg, I only liked the white; he ate the icing on Christmas cake, I ate the marzipan; he ate my tomatoes, I ate his lettuce. He called our mother 'Pam', but 'Mummy' if he was desperate. I called her 'Mummy', and only Pam when I was really desperate. At that time we both called JJ 'Daddy'.

In May 1958, we had a rude shock. Tink was sent away to boarding school four hundred miles from home, and our happy times together came to an end. I missed him terribly, missed having someone to talk to as I lay in bed at night, missed having an ally when times got tough. He began in the summer term, aged just over thirteen-and-a-half, having had some intensive coaching to get him through common entrance. My father said he was a late developer, which turned out to be true, as there was no doubt he was very bright. Pam had wanted him to go to Charterhouse, which was close at hand in Godalming, but JJ insisted that his son should have a Scottish education, so Tink was duly sent away to Fettes in Edinburgh, which he regarded as banishment. We all drove up to deliver him there in May 1958 with his trunk and all-important tuck box; and after looking round the school and meeting his housemaster, there was a stoic farewell. His first letter home must have been very reassuring to my parents.

Darling Mummy, Daddy and Penelope,
  My first night was wizard, the beds aren't bad and I slept like a bomb. Lights went out at 9.25. There are many nice boys. My form room is lower third, it seems quite good and I received my books today. For breakfast we had porridge or so

*called (it was foul) and then a miserable little egg. I was glad
to tuck in to my tuck box. Sorry for such a short note but I
haven't got much time.*

Having a wonderful time,
Love from Tink

He wrote every week without fail, cheerful, newsy letters, and never
betrayed how miserable he felt, four hundred miles from everything
he loved. He was playing a lot of golf, he had joined the school
cadet corps, he had climbed to the castle, he had come fourth in
Latin, and would appreciate some more tuck. And we all wrote
back and sent food parcels; my letters adorned with drawings of
horses, because by this time I thought of little else. It was an austere
school with a harsh regime and no creature comforts. That first
term when we all went up for sports day, Pam wrote her name in
the grime on the wall on one of the staircases. Five years later it
was still there.

Although he was away from home and the daily influence of JJ,
my brother's interest in his world continued unabated, and almost
every week he complimented JJ on the *Sunday Express* – something
he continued to do, every Sunday without fail, throughout his life.
He wrote, aged fifteen:

*I've just read the paper, and what a paper it is! Absolutely
terrific 3,500,000 copies being bought every week. No
wonder though, after reading it. Wonderful leader about
Britain's roads, it's about time something was said about
them.*

*Cross-Bencher was powerful stuff too. I found it very
interesting. Who did it this week?*

*John Gordon as usual brought up all the scandle [sic] of the
past few days, but very good scandle. Wonderful about the
Hemel Hempstead swindle. Let's hope it will wake people up a
little.*

*Yes, I must say after reading through that paper it's not
surprising at all that three and a half million copies are sold
every week of the year. Let's hope this figure will keep rising*

and by this time next year it will be up to four and a half
million. I wouldn't be surprised at all if it went up to four and
a half million, besides it jolly well deserves to.

Was the leader on our roads your idea? It really was terrific
and I agreed with every word of it.

Three months after Tink started Fettes, we left Garden Cottage and
moved away from Beaverbrook's rapacious clutches. After months
and months of house-hunting, Pam finally found us somewhere
to live. It was a five-bedroom period farmhouse, eight miles from
Dorking, which cost £6,000. It was the first property JJ had ever
owned – his parents had never owned a house – and he fell passion-
ately in love with it. He cherished the hope that it would stay in
the family through generations.

Wellpools Farm was set on its own along a country lane, with
outbuildings and stables and three acres of land. Some years later,
when the neighbouring farmer retired, he bought a further hundred
acres surrounding the property. The original part of the house dated
from the seventeenth century, and was very pretty. It was whitewashed brick with exposed timber beams, but in the nineteenth
century a wooden extension had been built, which looked a bit like
a railway signal box. This was the only part of the house with big
windows and high ceilings, and the only door frames that didn't
smack people over six feet tall. It was also without doubt, the coldest
part of the house, with the dining room downstairs, and above it
my brother's and my bedrooms. For many years we had no central
heating; we could see our breath on winter mornings, and there
would be ice on the inside of the window panes. Even with central
heating that part of the house was always freezing.

The kitchen was always the warmest room in the house, heated
by an Aga, which like the Rayburn at Garden Cottage ran on solid
fuel. Once again it fell to my mother to carry in the anthracite from
the coal house each morning, stoke the Aga and remove the ashes.
The diaries suggest that these were the sort of tasks my father might
have done in the early years, before I was born, because he talked
cheerfully about chopping wood and logging. He gardened at that
time, too, and clearly enjoyed domesticity, but I have no memory

of that. My memory is that he never did anything around the house or garden.

JJ now expected Pam to do everything, I think on the grounds that he did enough work editing the *Sunday Express*, and he would belittle the work she did in keeping house, and make no effort to help keep it clean. Once a week she polished the red tile floor in the entrance hall, and the wooden parquet flooring in the sitting room, and without fail JJ would walk straight in without attempting to wipe the mud off his feet, and ruin all her hard work. If she complained he would say, 'I didn't notice the floor had been polished.' He never praised her for anything, never admired anything, never thanked her. She did everything: she cooked, washed and cleaned and the house was always immaculate, bulbs were always replaced, dripping taps fixed, the sitting room fire laid, logs in the basket, clean and ironed shirts in the airing cupboard, and food on the table bang on time at every meal. Yet he always implied that she did nothing. If he was in a bad mood, he would criticise everything from a crease in his shirt to the temperature of the butter, and she would be responsible.

Pam was a very good homemaker. She had exquisite taste and a great eye for antiques. She filled the house with furniture she bought cheaply at auction, painted the walls magnolia, and chose furnishings that were in perfect keeping with the age and style of the house. Then, with the help of the octogenarian gardener we inherited with the house, she set about transforming the garden.

My parents always gave us separate presents for birthdays and Christmas. Pam's, because she had only what money JJ gave her as a housekeeping allowance, were usually very simple, and most often a book. His presents were always extravagant and showy and invariably made Pam's offering fade into insignificance. That first Christmas at Wellpools, he excelled himself. When I woke up on Christmas morning he told me to go outside and look in the stable. I rushed out with my heart in my mouth, and the cobwebby old stable that had been used to store junk and bits of garden machinery was transformed. And there, standing in a bed of golden straw, was a beautiful bay pony. The local farmer, George Spooner, a large, friendly, red-faced man, whose land abutted ours, had been in on the surprise. He had kept the pony at the farm and brought him up and left him in our stable very early that morning. I was almost sick with excitement: I had longed and longed for a pony of my own. I lived for my weekly riding lessons, I read nothing but horsy books, and knew the Observer Book of Breeds backwards. This Christmas morning my father had made all my dreams come true.

Brownie (as I called him, plumbing the great depths of my imagination) turned out to be a complete fiend. Within minutes of my taking him out of the stable, he had taken a bite out of my shoulder and very nearly kicked Tink. My father, who knew absolutely nothing about horses, took prompt action and whacked him repeatedly on the rump with a walking stick. This did nothing to calm the situation, although my shrieks for him to stop can't have helped either. Brownie threw his head up, snatching the reins out of my hands, rolled his eyes until they were almost all white, and set off at top speed down the garden. Between us we managed to round him up, but it was not a promising start, and didn't get much better. I soon decided that Brownie should live out in the paddock but he was impossible to catch. Every time I tried, I would take a carrot or a sugar lump. He would come up to me, take the goody and, before I had a chance to grab hold of his head collar, he would swing round and lash out with his hind legs, then go galloping off, hissing and snorting. As time passed, I became increasingly nervous, not to say downright terrified.

Chippy Gilbey, of Gilbey's Gin fame, who at that time was one of Pam and JJ's closest friends, heard the sorry tale over lunch one day. She had had horses all her life. 'What you need to do,' she said, coming to the rescue, 'is show him you're not afraid – let him know who's boss.' And so, after a rather good Sunday lunch, she offered to demonstrate. While we all kept safely behind the fence, she went out into the middle of the field. Brownie dutifully came over to her and took the sugar lump from her flattened hand. 'You see?' she said, turning to her audience, 'you just have to . . .' and before she could finish her sentence, the little brute had turned and kicked her smartly in the stomach. Chippy declared that Brownie was dangerous, and he was sent straight back to the horse dealer up the road, who must have seen JJ coming a mile off. This time

Chippy went too and found me something much more suitable.

Periwinkle, as I named the replacement, after the pretty blue flowers in a wild bit of the garden, might have been the model for Thelwell's cartoons, which ran in the *Sunday Express*. She was dappled grey, round and shaggy and with the sweetest temperament of any pony I have known before or since. I would sit in the field with her for hours, and she would nuzzle my face and hair. I could kiss her on the mouth and hug her round the neck, and not once did she attempt to bite or kick. For many years, she was my very, very best friend and confidante. But Perry turned out to be a bit of a dark horse. She seemed to be growing around the girth at rather an alarming rate, so once again we called on Chippy for advice. 'She's unfit,' spake our expert. 'All she needs is a bit more exercise. Trot her up and down the road twice a day.' So I duly stepped up the exercise, until one morning I went out into the field and found Perry nursing a brown and distinctly wobbly foal. I immediately wrote to my grandfather in Kenya, whom I had never seen, and told him the exciting news, 'My pony has had a fowl!' Pam wanted to call the foal Charles – JJ had a friend called Charles Foley – but JJ had a sense of humour failure and so we called it Cinquecenta instead.

That summer we had been to Italy, hence the name Cinquecenta. It was our first foreign holiday in years. The previous summer the weather in Cornwall had been awful, so JJ decided we would go abroad and be sure of some sunshine. So we drove in the Armstrong Siddeley Star Sapphire all the way through France and down the west coast of Italy to a picturesque little village by the sea called Fiascherino where we settled into a small family hotel. That afternoon we went on to the beach and the sand was so hot we couldn't walk on it in bare feet; that night we had dinner on the terrace, under the trailing jasmine and bougainvillea, and so it was for the next two days. The sun blazed, the sea was like a warm bath, and the evenings were scented and balmy. And then the weather broke and I think Italy had its worst August since records began. For three weeks it rained solidly, and tempers became severely tested as we shivered and sloshed around St Peter's Square, trudged up the leaning tower of Pisa, and bought endless souvenirs from dripping market stalls. It was quite a relief when the three weeks were up and we drove the car north to Genoa to board the *Braemar Castle* to sail back to England.

JJ loved being on a ship again and, in typical fashion, immediately befriended the Captain and senior members of the crew, which ensured that we were well looked after. It was the most wonderful experience. Time seemed to stand still on board, the real world suspended for a while. She was a splendid ship, one of the Union Castle fleet, on her way back from Africa, so most of the passengers had been at sea for weeks. There was a swimming pool on board, filled with sea water that slurped dangerously in rough weather, a games deck where we played deck quoits, and a special children's area with books and crayons and every conceivable game to play.

At night everyone dressed formally for dinner, which we frequently ate at the Captain's table; there were dances, and one night there was a fancy dress competition. I lived on a diet of Sea-Legs, which were no match for the weather in the Bay of Biscay, where I was so sick I couldn't even get out of my bunk; but it was on the *Braemar Castle* that I fell in love for the first time. Paul Rusham came from Kenya, was twelve years old and wonderfully good looking, with a black patch over one eye for reasons that I no longer remember. I was nine. We swam, we ran around the deck, we played quoits, and at night we went out to the deserted deck, and held hands under the stars. It was very romantic. On our last night together he wrote me a love letter and left it on my pillow. The next morning he asked if I'd found it. I rather shyly said I had. He asked, 'Do you know what the crosses on the bottom of the page are?' 'Yes,' I said, blushing. 'What? What are they?' he said, goading me to say the word, but I was so shy and so crippled with embarrassment that I simply turned beetroot and prayed for the ground to swallow me.

The following summer, in 1960, my mother went on holiday to Kenya to stay with her family. She had seen none of them since they left England in 1947 and, since they were all hopeless letter-writers, there had been very little contact. My grandfather had bought a farm near Nakuru in the west of the country, and indulged his passion for flying by teaching at the local club. Both Pam's brother and sister, Peter and Helen, who had emigrated with their parents, had married, and Helen had two young sons. But the family had lived through difficult times in Kenya. They were there during the notorious Mau-Mau in the 1950s when, for four years, Europeans were mercilessly attacked, raped and killed by terrorists from the Kikuyu tribe. My grandmother slept with a gun under her pillow and never got over the fear she lived with day and night that she and her family might be slaughtered at any moment. She hated Kenya thereafter and couldn't wait to get away, but George absolutely loved it and refused to leave until he lost everything he had after Independence in 1963.

While Pam was in Africa, I was dispatched to stay with the Clarkes again, and my father took my brother to the Canary Islands. I don't know whether JJ couldn't afford to send me to Kenya too, or if he was not prepared to let his children go and see Pam's family. He would never have gone himself. And so Pam went on her own, and completely and utterly fell in love with Africa. She came back full of stories and was lit up by seeing her family again; I don't remember seeing her so happy. JJ never paid for her to go again.

My father came back from the Canaries, complaining that he couldn't stand the heat of the place, and went straight to bed with another bleeding duodenal ulcer. Once again Beaverbrook wrote to him:

Dear John

Take plenty of time to recover and don't rush back to your office too soon.

You are having your wretched attack at the right time. For you will be fit and well for the entrance of the Sunday Telegraph *into the Fleet Street competition.*

I was told reliably that Brian Roberts, the very competent news editor, is going to the Sunday Telegraph. *That they have had 600 applicants for jobs. That their intention is to concentrate on news and to produce articles on the news, illustrated on a much bigger basis than anything which has been attempted in Sunday journalism so far.*

They look upon the supplement system of the Observer *and*
Sunday Times *unfavourably and they believe that the public is
tired of them.*

With all good wishes
Yours sincerely
Beaverbrook

The *Sunday Telegraph* did not cut across the *Sunday Express*
market. There were a lot of Sunday newspapers when JJ became
Editor – nine in all – but its main rival was the *Sunday Dispatch*,
owned by Lord Rothermere, which on the strength of soft-porn
serials, did rather well until Randolph Churchill started to call
Rothermere the Pornographer Royal. Rothermere told his Editor to
clean up the paper and, under pressure from the *Sunday Express*,
which was steadily increasing in circulation, it went downhill. After
a succession of failing Editors, it was finally bought by the *Sunday
Express* in 1961. The penultimate Editor was Wally Hayes. Beaverbrook telephoned my father at home to tell him about his appointment. 'I'm told he's very good,' he said. 'You're going to have to
be on your toes.'

JJ was furious. 'Well if he's better than me there's nothing I can
do about it. But if he's no better than the other Editors they have
had then he will go the same God-damned way as the rest of them.'
He did.

CHAPTER ELEVEN

Never Trust a Man with a Beard

Most of the people who worked for my father were with him for years and, having grown up with the *Sunday Express*, their names were almost as familiar to me as my own. But in most cases they were just names. Many of them are no longer around, sent to a premature grave in some cases by a combination of alcohol and stress. The remainder, I discovered, not only keep in touch with one another but meet on a regular basis, and stories about life around my father still dominate the conversation.

JJ had a remarkable gift for spotting talent. Some of the most successful names in British journalism began as his protégés or did a stint on the *Sunday Express*, and learnt their craft under his tutelage. Some wrote to him asking for jobs – and he saw everyone. Some submitted articles on spec, which he read because he read everything, and he would ask them in to see him. And some he found. The most bizarre of these has to have been Michael Watts, whom he overheard arguing the toss about pensions with a friend on the top of a double-decker bus in 1960. He followed him, found out who he was, invited him in for an interview and gave him a job on the spot without reading a single cutting. He did everything by instinct. He would decide within moments of meeting someone whether they would be right for the paper, and being right for the paper had as much to do with their personality and temperament as their track record. He employed people he liked – and if they were Scottish, so much the better – and he was always very anxious that they should like him.

My father's life and his routine were very disciplined; and he was a stickler for timekeeping in the office. He did the same thing every day. He always got up at 6.45 a.m. and listened to the *Today* programme on full volume – thus waking the rest of the household – while he shaved, bathed and cleaned his teeth and tongue, retching in the process. He had orange juice or a pink grapefruit, a boiled egg and two slices of cold toast for breakfast with strong continental coffee. He left the house at the same time every morning and drove at breakneck speed to Dorking Station, catching the train in the nick of time. When he arrived at Waterloo, he walked over Blackfriars Bridge, only ever taking a bus if it was pouring with rain. He arrived in the office bang on 10.00 a.m. – even when he had a chauffeur to drive him in later years – and he expected his staff to be in at 10.00 a.m. too.

He never had a cigarette before lunch, which made him very impatient for lunch and eager to get through it as fast as possible. He left the office at 6.00 p.m. – as did his staff if they were wise – took the number 4 bus to Waterloo Station, and caught the same train each night, arriving home at 7.45 p.m. without fail. His routine was like clockwork, timed to the minute, and woe betide my mother if she wasn't ready with breakfast or supper bang on the appointed hour. He had wine with supper and two large whiskies afterwards while he worked, and stopped only for the *News at Ten* and *Match of the Day*. The only exceptions were Fridays and Saturdays. On Friday, he spent the night in London, for reasons that I never entirely fathomed, and on Saturday, which was press night, he left the office at midnight. Sunday and Monday were his days off, when he played golf or went sailing, and did his compulsory shopping.

Peter McKay, who is one of the most colourful columnists in Fleet Street, now writing in the *Daily Mail*, was twenty-one when JJ wrote and asked him to come to London for an interview. It was 1964 and he was then working on a local paper in Aberdeen and had been very helpful to a reporter from the *Sunday Express*, who had put in a good word for him. My father gave him a job on the spot, and although he subsequently left the *Sunday Express* – a crime not forgiven most people – it was the start of a very special relationship that endured until my father's death thirty-three years later.

Peter could tease my father in a way that not many could get away with, and I can't think of anyone's company that my father enjoyed more. But at their first meeting, JJ was concerned about how Peter would look after himself in London. 'What are you going to do about your washing?' he said. 'What about your shirts?' Peter suggested a laundry. 'No, no, laundries are much too expensive. What you'll do is you'll send them home to your dear old mother and that would be very wrong. Why don't you buy these new nylon shirts, they are brilliant: you wash them and hang them up on a wire coat hanger and the next morning you can put them straight on without ironing them. I will advance you money.' He then buzzed the News Editor. 'I'm sending through Peter McKay. He's joining us from Scotland next week. Could you advance him £10 to buy shirts.' 'Certainly, John,' said the News Editor, betraying not the slightest surprise that someone he'd never heard of was joining the staff and that he had to give them £10 with which to buy shirts.

Clive Hirschhorn, who wrote show-business and theatre reviews for the *Sunday Express* for twenty-five years, was another of my father's favourites, but for three of those years he suddenly and inexplicably found himself out in the cold. Nothing he wrote or said or suggested was right, then just as suddenly as the frost had begun, he became the blue-eyed boy once more.

They first met after Clive had been sacked by the *Daily Mail*, two weeks before Christmas in 1964. Clive wrote to every editor in Fleet Street, and JJ was the only one who saw him. He asked Clive one question, 'So what went wrong?' Clive, who was twenty-five, explained that he seemed to have been a pawn in a vendetta between the *Mail*'s show-business writer and the Editor. 'That's fine,' JJ said, 'that's all I need to know.' And by way of a trial sent him off to interview Margot Fonteyn, the world-famous ballerina, with one proviso. 'I don't want you to talk about the ballet.'

The *Sunday Express* was a top newspaper in those days with a colossal circulation – Tink's prediction from Fettes that the figure would soar to 4.5 million was eerily accurate. No star turned down a request to be interviewed, and Clive had no difficulty arranging to meet Margot Fonteyn, but the interview was a disaster. Getting her to talk was like getting blood from a stone. He wrote the interview nevertheless and handed it in, but he knew that it hadn't worked, and imagined that would be the end of his association with the *Sunday Express*. The phone duly rang and it was Gordon Robinson, the Features Editor, saying that the piece hadn't worked, but the Editor realised she was probably the wrong subject. Why didn't he go and interview someone more voluble? Astonished to be getting a second chance, Clive discovered that Eartha Kitt and Laurence Harvey were both in town. Both gave him brilliant interviews and as a result he was taken on for three months on probation, at £30 a week. On his first day in the office, JJ called him in and told him he had liked the interviews but he was not to expect to see anything in the paper for at least three months. The very next Sunday JJ decided he didn't like an article Peter Dacre had done and ran the Eartha Kitt interview instead.

Clive was expected to produce a piece a week, so when his idol Tennessee Williams came to London to promote *The Night of the Iguana* two weeks later, he fixed a lunch at the Savoy. He didn't expect it to go far, knowing that Tennessee Williams was not quite right for the *Sunday Express*, but he duly handed in what he had written to my father. It was the end of the day, yet ten minutes later the office was abuzz. The Editor wanted to use the piece that Sunday, Clive was told. 'You say Tennessee Williams used to drink a quart of whisky a day. What sort of a quart is it? An imperial quart?' he was asked. 'The Editor wants to know.'

That Sunday, Clive opened the paper to find his interview had been given a full page. On Tuesday morning he was called in to see my father. He immediately thought he must have claimed too much in expenses. 'Have you seen the notice board outside my office, Clive?' asked JJ. 'Go and look then come back in here.' Again, terrified it was something to do with his expenses, he went to look at the board. 'Last week's *Sunday Express*,' it read. '1. Clive Hirschhorn's interview with Tennessee Williams was superb.' He went back into my father's office beaming. 'That was a great interview, Clive,' said JJ. 'You are now a fully fledged member of the *Sunday Express*, you are no longer on probation and your salary has gone up to £35.' 'This, after three weeks,' says Clive. 'I take my hat off to him.'

JJ looked upon his staff as a growing family. Tom Utley joined the paper in 1983, and is now a leader writer and columnist on the *Daily Telegraph*. He was twenty-four and had come from the *Financial Times*, where after two weeks he still had no idea who the Editor was. JJ was a stark contrast. 'Within three seconds of joining the *Sunday Express*, I knew who he was and his views on men with beards, men who drank white wine, his birthday and everything about him because he was so much talked about everywhere.

'I've met tyrannical editors galore, but not tyrannical and paternal at the same time, as he was. There was a slight feeling that he was head of the family, he stood up for us. He treated us all like school-boys, lavishing undeserved praise or undeserved abuse by turns and we all minded.' But, though JJ might bully, criticise and shout at them himself, he gave huge loyalty and he expected loyalty in return.

Alan Watkins was taken onto the *Sunday Express* by my father in 1959, on the strength of one article published in the *Socialist Commentary*, about JJ's Contempt of Parliament. JJ summoned him and said, 'You're a very lucky man. You can write and it's taken me fifteen years to get where you are now. I will offer you a job as a feature writer at £20 a week.' Alan was twenty-six, was quickly promoted to Cross-Bencher and was one of my father's favourites.

Alan left to join the *Spectator* four years later and JJ never forgave him. 'A long period elapsed before he spoke to me again. He was a very jealous editor and anybody who left the *Sunday Express* was guilty of some sort of treason, even if they went to the *Daily Express*. I knew it was going to be good experience working for him, but I didn't want to be a popular journalist. I wanted to succeed Henry Fairlie as political columnist of the *Spectator*. He was not at all pleased. He said Ian Gilmour [the owner at that time] would sell the *Spectator*, it was a failing concern and the Editor was a failed politician, I was making a big mistake and would regret this.'

There was a curious incident, soon after Alan left, which made matters worse. He wrote a book called *The Liberal Dilemma*, which his secretary at the *Sunday Express*, Pauline Elliot, had offered to type for him. One day JJ wandered into her office after lunch and found her busy at work. When he asked her what she was doing, she said she was typing Alan's book. 'Well that's got nothing to do with the *Sunday Express*,' said JJ, and sacked her on the spot. The office was shocked, and Colin Cross, another writer who had shared Pauline with Alan, was so incensed that he immediately handed in his resignation and went to work for the *Observer*. Whether my father intended his action as an example to others that there should be no private work done in office time on office equipment, or whether he did it to spite Alan, remains a mystery. Suffice it to say, he did nothing like it ever again.

Alan went on to become one of the most respected political columnists of his generation. He has a memory like a fox, a passion for personalities and gossip and he is a compelling storyteller. And he looks as though he might have taken root in El Vino's, the famous Fleet Street wine bar where journalists used to congregate before the newspaper industry was split up and relocated to office blocks across London. He ignored my father's advice long ago: 'Steer clear of El Vino,' JJ used to say. 'It rots the brain, you know. It's just a lot of journalists telling stories, and the stories go round and round and you never get any new ones, just exaggerated versions of the ones you heard yesterday.' There was a great deal of truth in this.

One day Alan was sitting on the bench that lined two walls of the Editor's office with his legs stretched out in front of him. JJ admired the shoes he was wearing and asked how much they cost. He was always fascinated by what people wore, and what they paid for what they wore. 'Just under £10,' said Alan. There followed an interrogation into his age, his salary and his financial commitments. 'So,' said my father. 'Earning £20 a week, with a wife and baby, and a mortgage, you spend half of that on a pair of shoes. You shouldn't: it's not fair to your wife and baby.'

Some time later Alan was wearing another new pair of shoes. He had seen a pair in the small ads and sent away for them. They cost £2 10s. JJ noticed at once and asked how much he had paid for them. 'You're just embarking on a career in Fleet Street,' he said. 'The sky's the limit. Let me give you a piece of advice. The biggest mistake that an ambitious young journalist can make is to buy cheap shoes.'

My mother used to say that my father said whatever suited him at the time. She was right, he did make pronouncements and the next day or the next week, would say something entirely contradictory, with the same emphatic conviction. If challenged he would simply deny that it had ever happened and, if cornered by too many witnesses, he would turn red in the face, fix you with burning eyes, and launch into a searing and personal attack, which left no one wanting to pursue the matter for a moment longer.

But there were some things he never changed his mind about, like men who wore hats or smoked pipes. 'Never trust a man with a beard,' he would also advise young journalists; 'Never sneer – no-one ever destroyed a man by sneering – go for the full frontal'; 'Always look forward and never back'; 'An ounce of emotion is worth a ton of fact'; 'You must believe everything that you write; you must be as sincere as you would be before a television camera.' These were the principles that guided his journalism and the writing of the people who worked for him – all principles that originated with Beaverbrook.

The result was that the ethos of the *Sunday Express* never changed during the years of his editorship. One of his greatest fans is Paul Dacre, who has been Editor of the *Daily Mail* for the last ten years, a paper that in some ways bears a remarkable similarity to the old *Sunday Express*, which is not entirely coincidental. His father, Peter, worked for JJ for thirty-two years, and the *Sunday Express* dominated Paul's childhood no less than it did mine – as did the vagaries of my father's mood.

'There would be moments of ecstasy when JJ liked a piece my father had written, and moments of gloom laced with alcohol when he didn't. He was a constant and forceful presence in our household. My father was a passionate and dedicated journalist and Sunday lunchtime was spent analysing Fleet Street, constantly talking about JJ, and about articles in the paper. He was passing on to me his love of journalism, and through it, a great deal of JJ. My father had a love-hate relationship with him: admiration, with the trooper's resentment of a heavy-handed boss occasionally.'

JJ's anger was deeply unnerving, and he would leave carnage in his wake, but it seldom lasted long. In the office, he would bawl people out if they made a mistake or failed to do what he wanted, and he would do it as and when he felt angry – he didn't wait until he could speak to someone in private. It could be in the middle of his editorial conference in front of colleagues, down the telephone, or one-to-one in his office. He had an intercom in his office, with which he could buzz all his heads of department and, at the flick of a switch, terrorise the editorial floor. It was open-plan but everyone knew at once whose buzzer had gone off by whoever jumped.

At 5.30 p.m. one afternoon, he was flipping through a copy of the *Evening Standard* on his desk when suddenly he buzzed his foreign Editor, Arthur Brittenden, wanting to know whether he had read a story about President de Gaulle in Sam White's column. Arthur said he hadn't.

'Arthur, what time is it?'

'I'm not with you, John, I don't understand.'

'I asked you a simple question, Arthur.'

'It's half past five, John.'

'Ah good, your watch agrees with mine. And what position do you hold on the *Sunday Express*, Arthur?'

'I don't understand what you're getting at.'

'I asked you a very simple question. What position do you hold?'

'Foreign Editor.'

'The Foreign Editor of the *Sunday Express* at 5.30 p.m. on a Friday afternoon has not read Sam White's column in the *Evening Standard*,' said JJ stonily. 'May I suggest, Arthur, that you read the work in question and pay particular attention to item three, and, after you've read it, give me a buzz, because there might be something there for your gifted correspondent in Paris.'

However alarming the methods he used to achieve it, the results were worth it. As Paul Dacre says, 'It was an unyieldingly professional newspaper, a unique product, a product that never forgot its readership in a way that so many newspapers these days have. Every sentence had to appeal to the reader; and JJ was legendary for reading every word of copy. I would often see my father's copy, with JJ's handwritten comments on it, in his briefcase. The ruthless observation of detail and unyielding precept that, "If I can't understand it, the reader won't understand it," and the view of the organic whole.

'There had to be balance in the paper, lots of happiness, a belief that you don't want to knock people down all the time. The *Sunday Express* had this formula for lifting people out of their lives, letting them escape through aspiration and dreams: always tell stories through human beings; have delayed intros to features – they set the scene – then come to the point; never begin a story in the past, always use the throw-away detail, "the house with the yellow door".

'It was an overall ethos: there was a passionate belief in the power of the interview and a basic integrity; not condescending towards the reader but not going down highfalutin routes that bore him to death. Those were tricks that had been honed by JJ, and introduced by JJ. He was a powerful influence on me, and I suppose, without overintellectualising it, I suspect an awful lot of *Sunday Express* ethos has shaped my understanding of newspapers.'

But since newspapers gave up their tenure of Fleet Street in the 1980s, the industry has changed. Nowadays, it's not too much of an exaggeration to say that stressed young men and women sipping cappuccinos at their work stations, screened off from their colleagues, can go for a whole day talking to no one. With e-mail zapping copy from the far corners of the country, many of the writers don't even need to go into the office. The papers that they write for are huge, their contact with their Editor is minimal, and the feedback on their work, in many cases, zero.

No one who worked for my father ever felt ignored. In addition to reading every last syllable they wrote – and leaving them in no doubt about what he thought of it – he had a marking system that everyone understood. He would see the top copy of everything that everyone wrote and would send it back to the author with one of the following: 'Mr X brilliant', 'Mr X excellent', 'Mr X very good', 'Mr X good', 'Mr X fair', 'Mr X', which meant okay it will do; and the bottom grades were 'Mr X a word please', and, the worst, 'Mr X words please'.

Cross-Bencher was at the House of Commons one afternoon when his secretary rang and said, 'I think you'd better come straight back to the office.' 'I said, "Why? What's he written?" And she said, "I don't know, it's a funny little squiggle and I think you should come back straight away." So I went all the way back to the office and there on my desk was my copy and he'd put alpha plus. It really did matter what he put, and other Editors don't understand how pathetic we all are, we're like actors, we just love praise. He understood that completely and was very generous with it, as he was with his abuse, but I remember the praise much more than the abuse. Very often he was right.'

The copy was not only graded, it was marked. He ringed every grammatical error: slang, split infinitives, non sequiturs, full stops where there should have been a semicolon. He even picked up a hanging participle once. 'You don't know what I mean, do you?' he said to his Literary Editor, Graham Lord, who was brought up in Rhodesia, and admitted ignorance. He then delivered a lecture, not only on the hanging participle – where you relate the second part of the sentence to the wrong noun, but also on the virtues of the Scottish education system. 'Of course I can't expect anything better from you, since you were educated at the Robert "Moogabby" School of English Literature.' His pronunciation made it all the funnier.

He read the copy as the reader would too. If there were any unanswered questions or missing details he would insist upon the writer finding out the answer before he would pass the piece. Alan Hoby, who was one of the most experienced sportswriters in Fleet Street was driven mad by this, like everyone else. 'When your copy had gone in, the dread buzzer would go and there would be some extraordinary, out of the way, thing he wanted to know. It's very difficult to ring busy people, to ask whether they had three brothers, or what their father was. But he was right, people liked to know these things.'

Not content with reading their copy when it came off the typewriter, he read it again in proof form after it had been typeset, and he would notice if a piece of punctuation he had changed on the top copy had not been properly set. Furthermore, he insisted on seeing and approving every cut or alteration on a proof.

But he was sensitive about interfering with copy. Before Alan Watkins became Cross-Bencher, he was writing features, 'Which in

Junor's words meant "Being reserve centre-forward in a first-division team," the first centre-forward being AJP Taylor. One of my tasks was to give him a selection on a Wednesday or Thursday of subjects I might like to write about. I would have three or four ideas, put them in to him, he would always choose the one involving the Royal Family – he was a great believer in articles on the Royal Family – I would write the piece, and on Friday he would say to me, "Alan, I just want to say this to you. There is only one word for that article you've written: brilliant. You know I wouldn't change a single comma if I were going to use it. But AJP has come up with this article, completely out of the blue, but he is under contract so we've got to use it." In fact Taylor never had an idea in his life, and would be enormously bullied by John – although I'd never know whether this performance was put on for my benefit. Taylor would be on the other end of the line in Oxford and John would say, "Alan I want this article to begin 'In August 1939 with the people on the beaches and the little children playing, Punch and Judy, sandcastles, then dark clouds over Europe.' Have you got that? I want lots of nostalgia about 1939," and Taylor would then write what Junor had told him to write.

'On those occasions when Taylor hadn't come up to scratch or he was on holiday, Junor would call me in and say, "We're going to use this piece, Alan. I'm sure you're very pleased. I've made these little alterations." He had marked the galley in ink and he said, "Do you agree with these?" I thought that showed enormous courtesy to someone in his late twenties. He was very good in that way. The idea of completely rewriting stuff which is what goes on nowadays would have been anathema to him.'

The paper had a definite formula, including a photograph of a pretty girl, usually a model or an actress, on the front page. There was nothing newsworthy about the picture, and no pretence in the caption that it was newsworthy. JJ selected the models, and considered it a perk of the job to take those he found particularly attractive out to lunch or dinner on a Friday night. Sandra Paul, who later married the Conservative MP Michael Howard, was a favourite, with whom he lunched and dined regularly for several years.

Every week there would be three leaders. One political, one financial maybe, and the third – relief after the fulminations of the first two – an uplifting story of human endeavour, or about the wonders of nature, or the joys of the seasons, or a little boy who'd saved his dog's life, or a dog who'd saved his little boy. And on the leader page each week would be an article written by either a leading Conservative politician or a distinguished historian like AJP Taylor.

But, like Beaverbrook, the part of the newspaper JJ cared about most was the political pages. He would say that the real point of the newspaper was the political message it conveyed. The rest, although no less important, was the icing on the cake, the sweetener to make the political pill more palatable. His political team, who generally wrote leaders as well, were recognised as his favourites and usually treated rather more gently than everyone else in the office.

Alan Watkins wrote Cross-Bencher for some years. One afternoon, he and a couple of colleagues were staggering down the corridor at about 4.30 p.m. – an hour-and-a-half late – after a very good lunch, when JJ stepped out of his office and caught them red-handed. 'Hello, John,' said Alan waving cheerily, 'everything all right?' JJ waited until they reached him and said in a menacing voice, 'If ever any of you gentlemen find the discipline of the *Sunday Express* no longer bearable you must come and tell me.'

Alan learnt a lot about handling JJ from watching what happened to his predecessor as Cross-Bencher, Wilfred Sendall. 'Wilfred would go down to the House, have a busy Thursday afternoon, then go back to the office and write his column until very late at night, then take a car home. The next morning at 10.00 a.m., Mac [the Cross-Bencher secretary] would type it out and, at 10.40 a.m., Wilfred would take it in to John, who would then tear it apart. He would never pass one of Wilfred's columns. "Ah, Wilfred," he would say, "I can see you've been fishing off the terrace and you've fished up a few used contraceptives, a dead cat and two tins. That's your catch. Now, Wilfred you must rewrite the column entirely. You must have sandwiches and Pepsi-Cola for your lunch, which Mac will bring you." Wilfred would then take it in at 3.30 p.m. or 4.00 p.m. and JJ would say, "That's fine but it needs a new tailpiece".

'I twigged early on that Wilfred's error was to give him time. So, when I came to do it, I wrote the column on the Tuesday afternoon, finished it off on Friday morning, gave it to Mac to type before lunch, but told her not to show it to anybody. Then I went out to lunch, had a few drinks in El Vino – I remember drinking Pomery in those days – with Peter Dacre and one or two others, then we'd go to Shortlands Salt Beef Bar in Fetter Lane, then on to Mooney's Irish pub for Gorgonzola and port; a fairly invigorating lunch. Then I'd get back at about 3.30 p.m. – the rule was you had to be back at 3 p.m. but I'd bend that a bit on a Friday. I'd take the column in to him and he'd say, "Not one of your best, Alan, but it'll have to do, it's too late to make any changes, but I think you'll have to use another tailpiece".'

JJ also took a great interest in sport and understood the importance of a strong sports section to the success of the *Sunday Express*. He was mad about football and golf and, to a lesser extent, tennis, and he brought in stars like Denis Compton, Dick Francis, and Danny Blanchflower to write for the paper, which despite the Sports Editor's misgivings over the latter, turned out to be a huge success. 'It annoyed me at the time, because he didn't discuss it,' says Leslie Vanter, who was Sports Editor for twenty-one years, 'he simply rang and said Blanchflower was starting next week. I'd only been in the job a couple of weeks. I didn't think it was a good idea, but I was completely wrong. He was a hell of an asset and had quite a following.'

JJ didn't interfere much in the sports pages, but he did suggest personalities to interview. Denis Law, a famous Manchester United and Scottish footballer, was one of his favourites. Alan Hoby was once dispatched to interview him and, at lunch, Law had asked for a glass of wine. 'When I put this in my story, the dread buzzer went. So I went in. "Wonderful piece Alan, but footballers do not drink white wine. Footballers have to train, Denis Law wouldn't have these marvellous reflexes if he drank wine." It was difficult to get a word in edgeways because he was always right. "What do you know about wine? You're a sports writer. Why did you put it in your copy? Denis Law's a footballer." "But he's a human being too," I said, and in the end it went through.'

The only people JJ really wanted interviewed in the *Sunday Express* were people he knew about, on the basis that if he didn't know about them then in all probability neither would his readers, and they would therefore not be interested. It made life tough for his writers. Peter Dacre, who for many years wrote Meeting People, once did an interview with the comedian Eric Sykes, written as though they were having a game of golf, which, given JJ's own enthusiasm for the sport, he thought he would love. Curiously, when he put his copy in to my father there was no reaction and JJ didn't use the piece, because he didn't know who Eric Sykes was. That Saturday night a Sunday paper called *Reynold's News*, came out with an article about Eric Sykes. 'Peter, didn't you do a piece on Eric Sykes?' said JJ. 'Let me see it,' and the next week it was in the paper. JJ and Eric then met and became close lunching and golfing friends. He called Eric a comic genius, and often went to see his shows and films, long after he had given up general theatre- and cinema-going.

During his first year on the paper, Clive Hirschhorn interviewed some big names, including Noël Coward, Vivien Leigh, P.G. Wodehouse, Sybil Burton, Richard Rodgers, the cartoonist Charles Adams and Barbra Streisand, but the only one that made it into the paper was P.G. Wodehouse. Years later it all became clear. 'I was going through some stockpiled copy in Gordon Robinson's office and came across my Streisand interview. And on it John had written, "Mr Robinson, I have never heard of this woman, have you?" And underneath Gordon had written, "No neither have I."'

My father knew exactly what he wanted from every piece that appeared in the *Sunday Express*. As Penny Hart, who worked as a reporter on the paper for twenty years says, 'He had a very sure instinct for our readers, as we did, because we were schooled by him to know exactly who we were writing for and what their opinions would be on anything. So we had a very close relationship. He always made us write to people if we got letters, a boring thing we did every week, but it was good. He was very reluctant and nervous to change things, he would always get people to put ideas up but never used any of them. The readers hated any change anyway. Once they left the crossword out inadvertently and we got about three million letters showering down. It was a very English paper, it reflected everything about the English, their love of animals, their independence, courage, and it was a good feedback for people.'

JJ had two golden rules. One, he would not allow the paper to break up marriages. 'Private fucking is private fucking,' he would say, and an illicit affair was strictly out of bounds, but once a couple had clearly made a decision to end the marriage, even privately, then he had no qualms about using whatever means were necessary to get the story for the *Sunday Express*. He loved gossip, loved stories of sexual adventure. The second golden rule was that there would be no stories about people who were gay. Graham Lord, who became the paper's Literary Editor in 1969, interviewed the American novelist James Baldwin, author of *Giovanni's Room* and *Another Country*. 'He was living in the South of France, but I interviewed him at the Savoy in London. JJ said "Go and do it" – he'd heard the name. So I came back and wrote this article about this very precious, very epicene black man. JJ called me in and said, "I never realised he was black." "Well all his books are about being black, that's what Baldwin's all about." "And he's homosexual as well. I don't think we'll be running this piece," and he never did.

'He did have this idea that the *Sunday Express* should be pristine, whiter than white with nothing that would offend children. The News Editor, Bob McWilliams would ask about everyone the reporters wrote about "Is he okay?" And if he was unmarried you had to try and work out why. I once wrote a story about a perfectly normal chap called Robert who liked to be known as Bobby, so I called him Bobby in the story. Bob McWilliams said, "You know Bobby is a suspect name, it's a queer's name. Is he queer? Well don't call him Bobby because JJ will kill the story." At least with JJ you always knew where you stood. He had firm opinions and stuck to them.'

Another subject on which he had firm opinions was travel, which Lewis de Fries wrote about for over twenty years. Travel had to be upbeat – negative pieces ended up on the spike; and he was very particular about the sort of food Lewis should mention in his pieces. He couldn't choose chicken from a menu 'because everyone in the

East End is eating chicken', nor could he have soup or ice cream, presumably because that was the working-class diet JJ grew up on. And if he was in Scotland he had to have porridge for breakfast. One week Lewis handed in his piece about a hotel in Scotland where he had eaten cereal for breakfast. JJ was on the buzzer straight away. 'Why didn't you have porridge?' Lewis said it wasn't on the menu. 'Nonsense, of course there was porridge, there's always porridge in Scotland.' And when Lewis insisted, he said, 'Well you ring them up and tell them to put porridge on the menu or they will not be in the *Sunday Express*.'

He had views about wine too. For the last seventeen years of his life, my father was almost more famous for a remark about wine than for any of his other achievements – but it has been frequently misquoted. Lewis de Fries was the one to whom the remark was originally made. JJ said to him one day, 'Lewis, you're writing much too much about white wine.'

'Really? What's the objection?'

'Only poofters drink white wine, Lewis.'

Although the saying became a legend, and I don't doubt he said it, I am sure my father didn't believe a word of it. He drank white wine at home frequently, particularly Muscadet, although he did drink far more red.

Years later, when JJ was knighted, Lewis Chester of the *Sunday Times* wanted to interview Lewis de Fries about JJ. He declined, thinking it wrong to talk about his Editor to another newspaper, but thought he should tell JJ he had been asked. 'Lewis,' JJ said, 'I don't give a fuck what you say about me to another newspaper. All publicity is good publicity and don't you forget it.' And so Lewis duly spoke to Chester and, in the course of the interview, told the story about the white wine.

Months later, my father had a blazing row with Lewis de Fries in the open-plan office, which subsequently appeared, word for word, in *Private Eye*. Assuming Lewis was responsible for this, JJ called him in and went bananas.

'I didn't give them the story,' said Lewis.

'Oh come on,' JJ said, 'who else would know these details?'

'John, you bawled me out in front of an open-plan office, it was within earshot of everyone. You know there are leaks in this office to *Private Eye* and it certainly isn't me.'

Lewis got very upset because JJ simply wouldn't believe him. That evening they met at the bus stop and Lewis tackled him again, 'Do you really imagine I would do that?' he asked.

'You weren't too fussy in telling everyone about the white wine, were you?' said my father.

'John, I took that as a sample of your humour, I did not believe you were being serious.'

'Oh yes,' said JJ acidly, 'my humour.'

When Jimmy Kinlay joined the staff as a subeditor early in 1960, JJ told him he should always remember that no one was ever sacked from the *Sunday Express*. At that time the paper carried a Bible quiz, of which Beaverbrook was particularly fond, written by a minister who sent it down the wire every week from Scotland. Kinlay's job was to mark it up, and send it down for typesetting. Sometimes the copy would be a bit scrambled. One day one of the questions was: "Who entered the lions' den?" to which the answer was, of course, Daniel. The word Daniel hadn't come through very clearly, so Jimmy wrote it in by hand, but the Linotype operator read it as David, and that was the name that appeared in the paper. That Sunday morning JJ was subjected to the wrath of Beaverbrook and, when he arrived in the office on Tuesday, incandescent with rage, he demanded to know who was responsible. Jimmy recalls that, in thirty years of knowing my father, he had never seen him so angry.

'He was striding up and down the floor of his office and he said, "I want you to give me ten reasons why I should not sack you on the spot." Fortunately I was more quick-witted in those days, and I said, "I can only think of one", and he stopped in his tracks and looked at me very strangely, and said, "What's that?" and I said, "It was just about a week ago you told me that no one ever gets sacked from the *Sunday Express*". And that completely floored him. The hands were going. "Don't ever do anything like that again," he said.'

JJ angry was a terrifying sight. He went completely puce in the face, his big shoulders came up around his ears, his chin went down, and he fixed the object of his rage with his pale blue eyes narrowed and deadly cold, and said whatever it took to crush them. He would gesticulate menacingly with his hands, palms outstretched working them in rhythm to his voice, which grew louder and more vitriolic as he warmed to his theme. Then he would screw one hand into a fist, and repeatedly thump the table with it, or slam it into his other open hand. His language could be appalling, not that he ever swore in front of me, but it was the personal nature of the attack that chilled more than the language he used – certainly at home. And if ever Pam or Tink or I tried to defend ourselves he would always bellow, 'Don't shout at me.'

His rage used to frighten me, it always frightened me, to the day he died, but I pretended it didn't. I became more combative the older I grew but I never lost the fear. I had watched my mother being gradually, painfully, broken by him, and, although she occasionally made the odd remark that touched a nerve, she was not in the same league as him. It wasn't in Pam's makeup to be unkind, and nothing in her sheltered upbringing had ever prepared her for the need to defend herself. She simply wasn't capable.

She would write down the things he said to her on little scraps of paper or backs of envelopes and keep them, and brood, and she might think of the perfect putdown half an hour later, but she never had the riposte at the time. Some of the things he said to her were so cruel, so devastating and so untrue that I wanted to hit him, beat him with my fists, so that he would begin to feel some fraction of the pain he inflicted. I wouldn't actually hit him, except once, but at times the blood seemed to be pounding inside my head, and I'd be so angry and upset I wouldn't know quite what I'd do, but knew I couldn't stand by and say nothing. I had to protect her. I was a tougher, nastier character than she; I could stand up to him better than she could.

Sometimes he would hold his hands up at me, as if in surrender, smile patronisingly and say, 'Yes, you're quite right, my little darling. Quite, quite right' – and I would want to hit him again! At other times he would say, 'You're marvellous. Come and give me a kiss.' He could swing from vicious to sentimental in the batting of an eye. I couldn't. I would be cross for hours. Like my mother,

I had a tendency to brood and, if I had been under fire one minute, I couldn't behave as though nothing had happened the next. One evening, in the wake of a row, he found me taking some clothes out of the airing cupboard, and tried to give me a hug and a kiss. I pulled back and said, 'Go away, get off me.' He pulled back and stood staring at me gravely through hooded eyes, swaying gently, his face etched with the pain of rejection. 'You'll be sorry one day,' he said. 'You'll miss me when I'm gone.'

It was rare, but not unknown, for his anger to last longer than a few minutes. Max Davidson, as a young subeditor, once made an error of judgement over a story that came in to the office when he was on his own at 2 a.m. one Sunday morning. It was in the early days of jumbo jets, and the first jumbo to fly from Seattle to Washington had made a botched landing. Although no one was hurt and there was no damage done, its wheels had touched an earth bank at the end of the runway. Instead of changing the front page and leading the newspaper with the story, he ran it on page one, but as a short.

'JJ thought this was a tremendous disaster. I had failed to see the significance of this story. Why had I done it? I said it was an error of judgement. Why had I not rung him at home? I didn't think it was worth disturbing him. He interrogated me for a whole week. Every day the buzzer would go, would I go in to see him, and he would say to me, "I want to examine the thought processes that made you do this." I said, "There were no thought processes whatsoever." He was so dramatic. He used to stand at his lectern and I would stand beside him like a naughty schoolboy. Or he would put his head in his hands at his desk and say, "I don't know how you could do a thing like this." Or if he was really angry, he had a fountain pen on his desk and he used to throw it at the carpet like a dart.'

Not everyone in his office could take it. Some he reduced to tears on occasion, and some he simply picked on and bullied. John Buchanan was a tall, bespectacled, mild-mannered man, who stayed with him for more than thirty years, yet JJ criticised him relentlessly, and called him a cunt with such regularity that he formed The Cunt Club – anyone who had been so called by the

Editor that week could wear a red-topped pin in their lapel.

One day my father was complaining to a colleague that no one could hear him down the new intercom system that had recently been installed. 'I'll show you what I mean,' he said, and pressed a switch on the box on his desk. John Buchanan's startled and tentative voice came through the loudspeaker.

'John, can you hear me?'

'I beg your pardon?'

'I said can you hear me?' bellowed JJ, his face reddening with anger.

'Yes, I think I can hear you.'

'Can you hear me properly?'

And without waiting for a reply, he cut him off. His colleague was in fits of laughter at the absurdity of the situation, but JJ failed to see what was funny.

He could laugh and did laugh, but never at himself. Other people's misfortunes had him in stitches, like the day a friend was seasick over the side of a boat into the teeth of a strong wind, and the whole lot blew back into his face. JJ could barely stand up he was laughing so much. I have to confess that my brother and I inherited exactly the same sort of humour, and the sound of someone sitting on a whoopee cushion was enough to crack us all up, although I like to think that I laugh at rather more than farts and banana skins today. But any joke that relied upon farce or irony or a play on words, left JJ cold.

He laughed at his own jokes, but he didn't often laugh at anyone else's – even when they were suitably lavatorial. He was quite capable of saying 'That's very funny' without the hint of a smile on his face. It was the same with cartoons. He thought Bill Martin was one of the best cartoonists in Fleet Street, but when he came to select the ones he wanted for the paper each week, he seldom laughed out loud. And once said with great seriousness, 'That is the funniest cartoon I've ever seen in my life.' Whereas his suggestion that the tail cone of a DC9, that blew off at 25,000 feet, might have been caused by someone in the lavatory kept him chuckling for days.

CHAPTER TWELVE

The Art of Lunch

Journalists coming into newspapers today have missed out on a way of life that can never be recreated – the only consolation is that their livers might last longer. The Fleet Street that JJ presided over is nothing like the industry today. The siege of Wapping in the mid 1980s, when Rupert Murdoch took on the unions, changed newspapers for ever. Post Wapping, proprietors were free at last to embrace the new technology, free to manage, free to make money. It was the end of decades of union supremacy, the stranglehold that had brought the industry to its knees time and time again, but it was also the end of a way of life and a culture that, for generations, had spawned great and colourful characters and nurtured huge talent. Post Wapping, Fleet Street disbanded, newspapers relocated, and journalists learned to spend their days staring at sterile computer screens. The vibrant village that JJ stepped into in 1948 had turned into a faceless, efficient metropolis.

No one in my father's day ever drank fizzy water or took less than a couple of hours for lunch. Drinking and long lunches were not abuses, they were an essential part of the information-gathering process, and JJ encouraged it, despite his warnings about recycled gossip at El Vino. Journalists from up and down the street met one another in one of a handful of pubs, all a stone's throw from their offices, and cross-fertilised news and views and came up with ideas that they could take back to their typewriters.

Before he became Editor, JJ would take guests to the Reform Club in Pall Mall, where he was a member. Later, when he had a more generous expense allowance, he took them to smart restaurants. But he was always careful of money, even Beaverbrook's, and he made sure his staff were too.

Arthur Brittenden, who went on to become an Editor himself, and a director of News International, remembers being firmly rapped over the knuckles by my father over his expenses. He joined the paper the year JJ became Editor and was told by the News Editor that he could have up to £20 per week in expenses, regardless of whether or not he spent that amount. One day JJ called him into his office and queried an item on his claim form, saying he found it hard to believe that Arthur had actually spent this money. The new recruit protested that he thought it wasn't necessary to have actually spent the money. 'If you were with Lord Beaverbrook,' said JJ, 'and he took his jacket off and then he went out of the room, would you put your hand into Lord Beaverbrook's jacket and take his wallet out and take a £5 note out of it before he came back into the room?' 'Don't be ridiculous,' said Brittenden, 'of course I wouldn't.' 'Well that's exactly what you're doing now with your expenses, you're picking Lord Beaverbrook's pocket.'

What JJ wanted was for his reporters to use their expenses properly. The idea of a dry lunch would have horrified him. One of the first pieces of advice he gave to all his young journalists was how to take people out to lunch – lunch being 'the way to get information out of people'. He had long perfected the art. JJ loved to lunch, but although he had an expense account and ate at some of the most expensive restaurants in London – making them serve everything plainly grilled with never any gravy or sauce – he had strict rules for minimising the damage.

'What you must do,' he would say, 'is always look very firmly at the set lunch and say, "Well I don't know about you, but this looks very good, I'm going for this," and don't ever give them a sniff of the à la carte. However, if there is no set menu, order, to begin with, avocado pear or melon or a bowl of soup. Your guest will not dare to order oysters or smoked salmon. Then go for a main course where the vegetables come with it. Vegetables in restaurants are scandalously over-priced. If no vegetables come with it, order one vegetable only. There is never any need to order potatoes.

Potatoes are fattening. There should be no need to order anything else. Now, wine: the basic rule is to have nothing to do with wine lists or wine waiters. Say in decided tones: "I'll have a bottle of the house, or the carafe, wine."'

This was not just advice for employees. He did the same when taking people to lunch himself, both privately and, when the *Sunday Express* was picking up the bill. Whenever we went out as a family, he would always say, 'Right, no one's having the à la carte. Is that clear?'

Arthur Brittenden was the first reporter JJ hired when he became Editor, and his account of their first lunch together is typical. They went to L'Escargot, one of JJ's favourite restaurants at that time.

'They made a great fuss of him as he went in and sat at his table – he always had the same table. I started to look at the menu and John said, "There's only one thing to eat here, melon and steak," and then he told me what I was going to drink. Years later, we were at the White Tower, it was my lunch, long after I'd left the *Sunday Express*, and George the owner, and I started discussing clarets – he knew the sort of wine I liked – when John cut in and said, "We will have the Othello." This was a Cypriot wine that George kept a few bottles of on a shelf, and as far as I am aware the only person who ever drank it was John. Of course he would tell you, you were a fool to spend money on these clarets because the Othello was just as good. It wasn't, it was disgusting.'

Another of JJ's favourite restaurants was the Terrazza Est in Chancery Lane, where an eager Italian called Luigi was manager. One Saturday evening, JJ collared three colleagues and invited them to have supper with him. As they drove up Fleet Street, he turned to them and said, 'Now this is not a huge slap-up meal, you understand, but they do a very good Welsh rarebit here and quite a good pasta. I might as well take your orders now.' When they arrived, he brushed off all attempts to greet and seat and hand out menus. 'I've got the order all ready, Luigi,' he said, 'just take it.' Sensing the frost around the table, he became more conciliatory, 'Of course we could have a dessert,' he said. 'I'm going to have the ice cream.'

I am sure that expensive London restaurants posed something of a dilemma for him. The Editor in him liked to impress his guests, and he enjoyed being treated like minor royalty by the restaurants he favoured – helped enormously by lavish tips; but the Presbyterian Scot in him disapproved of spending £10 or £15 on a piece of steak that he knew cost less than thirty per cent of that in the butcher's shop, or wine at £20 a bottle which he could have bought for £8. And because he shopped so much, he knew the price of everything – and, some might say, the value of nothing. As a result, he was a difficult and at times insufferably rude customer. He hated being fussed over, hated wine waiters pouring the wine, hated garnishes on his food, hated being kept waiting, hated being given a table that was not of his choosing, and invariably wanted something cooked differently from the way it appeared on the menu. It's a miracle he wasn't run through with a kitchen knife years ago.

But I think his behaviour in restaurants was also about control. He liked to be in control of everything and everyone. If he sat where a waiter suggested, the waiter was in charge; being awkward, making the chef cook something special, making the wine waiter abandon his training, making everyone nervous, reversed the dynamics and put him firmly in charge. And what better way of controlling his guests than buying them an expensive lunch and making them eat and drink what he chose?

He had a favourite table in every restaurant, usually by the door so he could watch everyone who came and went. One day there was a new waiter on duty at Arcadia in Kensington, who gave his table away to someone else. By the time JJ arrived, his guest was sitting at the table he'd been shown to, which was the mirror image of JJ's but on the other side of the door. JJ was furious. 'Get up from there,' he said, 'I'm not having that table.' The terrified head waiter, full of explanations and apologies, said he could have any other table in the restaurant he liked. He looked round and saw a big table beautifully laid up for eight people, and he said, "I'll have that."

Although most waiters must have wanted him broiled, there were some that thought the world of him. He knew them by name and would ask about themselves and their families, and remember the details. Each time he saw them he would ask how their son was, or what progress he was making at school, or how their wife's operation had gone. It wasn't just waiters: he did the same with shopkeepers, office drivers, anyone who came into regular contact with him. These were his readers and he had a genuine interest in learning about their lives and their preoccupations. And if ever there was an opportunity to offer help in some way, provided it was help he could give at one remove, he gave it.

One of his favourite restaurants for many years was Le Boulestin in Covent Garden, and there was a waiter there he had befriended, whose son had gone off to Leyton Orient, a small-time football club, as an apprentice. Telling him none of this, he summoned Alan Hoby over a weekend to go and interview the manager of Leyton Orient. When Alan said there was no real story because they hadn't done anything, JJ hit the roof. 'Haven't done anything?' he said. 'They've got a marvellous apprentice scheme, they help young players.' So Alan tried but failed to get hold of the manager, which made JJ even more livid. 'He thought I was refusing to do what the Editor wanted. "We can't have two prima donnas in this office," he said. What I didn't know and not even the omniscient, omnipotent JJ knew, was that the manager was about to be sacked. No wonder I couldn't get hold of him. But was I vindicated? Was I hell. I was in even bigger trouble.'

Another habit, when JJ took people to lunch, was to ply them with alcohol. He derived a curious pleasure out of watching others lose control. Despite his florid complexion, his own consumption when he was working was quite moderate in comparison with his Fleet Street colleagues at that time. He would take members of his staff out to lunch and continually top up their glass as they ate. Then, with coffee, he would insist they have a Grappa or a Calvados, which were his own favourites. He would then sit back and watch the consequences, and nothing amused him more than the sight of someone gradually losing the power of speech. He would literally shake with mirth.

Drink was an integral part of Fleet Street life in those days, and for many people on the *Sunday Express*, as on other newspapers, it was a serious problem, which destroyed their health, wealth, marriages and often all three. There was no stigma whatever attached to coming back from lunch in liquid form, and no danger of being sacked because of it. JJ was a tough boss, and tough about timekeeping, but as long as the work was done and was good – and some people appeared to write better with a few drinks inside them – he had no problem with it.

Alan Watkins liked a drink at lunchtime. He also liked a little snooze after his lunch and there was a bench in the Cross-Bencher office that might have been made for him. One afternoon Bernard Harris, another political writer with an office nearby, spotted Alan lying prone and dashed in to see my father, expressing grave concern for his colleague's welfare. 'What do you mean?' said JJ. 'He looked perfectly all right when I saw him this morning.' 'Well I don't think he's all right now because he's stretched out on the bench in the Cross-Bencher office.' 'Bernard, you are a shit,' said JJ. 'You know perfectly well that he's pissed. He'll be all right in half an hour when he wakes up.'

One Christmas, after a particularly good lunch, Jimmy Kinlay, by now the Features Editor, was dancing on top of the Deputy Editor's desk when JJ came out of his office and wanted to know what on earth was going on. Jimmy kept on dancing; and no one else offered any explanation. Finally he collared a reporter.

'What's Jim doing?' he asked.

'Well I think he's calling the faithful to prayer,' came the reply.

'Can someone get him down?'

'Not likely.'

And so he left them to it and went back into his office.

My father seldom did any serious drinking in Fleet Street himself, mostly, I suspect, because he didn't like losing control. The only night of the week he had a drink with colleagues was on a Saturday, when, once the first edition had been put to bed, he and his deputy, Victor Patrick, Jimmy Kinlay, and a few others would go to the Press Club and play snooker. And every Saturday, without fail, he had lunch with his leader writing team. For many years they went to the Cheshire Cheese in Fleet Street, the famous beef restaurant with sawdust on the floor where Samuel Johnson allegedly used to write in the eighteenth century. Every week he had the same thing: roast beef and mashed potatoes with a double Beaujolais, which he got through in forty-five minutes flat. He would leave the others

Above: The Dickie family. My grandmother (*second from left*) standing alongside her brothers and sisters with their parents. Thomas Dickie, a schoolmaster, had set up all his children in business.

Below: My father as a toddler on his mother's lap with, from left, his brothers Bill and Tom, and father Sandy.

Above: My father and Sandy in the garden of their council house in Walnut Road. It was one of JJ's greatest regrets that he never felt any affection for his father.

Left: In 1941 he had a lucky escape on board the SS *Thalassa*, attacked by U-boats in mid-Atlantic.

Below: His closest Fleet Air Arm friends were not so lucky. He lost them all in quick succession.

Right: 'I'm going to marry you,' JJ announced drunkenly on the night he met Pam. Fifteen months later he did. Pictured after their wedding in April 1942 in Gosforth. She was the daughter of his flying instructor.

Below: It was wartime, they were young, penniless and very much in love. At the end of their first month together, they had precisely one pound between them.

Left: The success of *Flight Deck* enabled my father to get a toe into Fleet Street.

Below: Canvassing as a Liberal candidate – one of three failed attempts to become a Member of Parliament.

Below: Lord Beaverbrook with his son Max Aitken, DFC DSO. JJ found their relationship fascinating.

Above: Garden Cottage – the house on Lord Beaverbrook's estate where we lived rent-free for ten years.

Left: My mother with my brother and me. She never looked or behaved like other mothers. As a child I was convinced she was a saint.

Right: Before I was born, Pam and JJ on the beach in Aberdeen with his brother Tom and family before tragedy struck. (*From left*) Jean, Tom, Pam, Tink, JJ and Muir.

Left: Roderick and me in about 1965 – at that time we couldn't have been closer.

Right: Roderick with the AC Cobra – one of a series of fast cars JJ drove – in the drive at Wellpools.

Below: The Polaroid photograph that JJ sent through the post on my seventeenth birthday, along with the keys.

Right: Roderick and Suzy on board *Outcast*. Suzy managed to look stylish wherever she was.

Right: A picture of me on the harbour wall in Anstruther, wearing the fox-fur coat my father gave me.

Below: James on the harbour wall on the same day – we took each other's photo. The telephone box from which he rang to ask JJ's permission to marry me was a few feet away.

Below: Roderick with JJ. He had been JJ's best friend all his life – an onerous role for a small boy.

Right: My father never had the patience to learn anything properly. On skis he was an accident waiting to happen.

Left: Relaxed and in a good mood, there was no better company – but it never lasted.

Right: At Walton Heath with Alex. Golf was a passion and so were his grandchildren.

drinking and go back to the office alone. In later years the leader writers' lunch moved to El Vino across the street, and he switched to a cheese sandwich, but otherwise the pattern remained the same.

It was very rare, even in the early days, for JJ to have lunch by himself. Lunch was the high spot of his day and he used it not just as an opportunity to meet famous, interesting and influential people, but as a valuable source of stories. Manny Shinwell, later Lord Shinwell, was a great friend at that time, and one of his best sources, as was his PPS George Wigg and a couple of Labour MPs with whom Wigg shared a flat. Manny was sixty-five and Secretary of State for War in the Labour government, when they first met in 1949, and already a legendary figure. For many years they lunched together every Friday and remained close friends. JJ once wrote in his diary, 'Lunch with Manny – dear old Manny. I think I like him best of all the politicians. If he were leader of a party I might even join it.' The feeling was obviously mutual. Despite having two ex-Prime Ministers at the lunch to celebrate Manny's one hundredth birthday in 1984, it was JJ he chose to have sitting beside him, and he requested that, when he died, JJ should be the one to give the address at his funeral.

Although my father's lunches were paid for by the company, he did actually use those lunches to entertain people who might give him stories. It was common practice in the newspaper business at that time, however, for people to claim for lunches they had never had. Expenses were viewed as a means of boosting their salary, and the amount claimed by *Express* journalists, who travelled first class and ate and drank lavishly, were the wonder of Fleet Street. It was a monumental racket. Even when I arrived on the *Evening Standard* in the 1970s, I was taken aside and it was explained how they worked. Everyone was allowed up to a certain amount a week in expenses, which was for taking contacts to lunch or buying them drinks, and also for taking taxis. If you didn't spend the entire amount, then you should claim for it anyway, and you simply made up names of contacts. You also submitted phoney receipts to back up the claim, and there were plenty of restaurants and wine bars around Fleet Street happy to hand out blank receipts. This was not dishonest, it was explained to me, it was a more tax-efficient way for the company to pay you more. But it was made equally clear that, if you were caught by the Editor or by management, you'd be out on your ear.

If there was one thing JJ would not tolerate it was dishonesty. Yet when, many years later, a chief leader writer was caught actively fiddling his expenses, far from condemning the man, JJ tried to save him. Ronnie Spark had been claiming double his allowance for a long time by means of adding a new figure after my father had signed his claim form each week. It was Jimmy Fitzpatrick, the General Manager, who spotted it and alerted JJ. The Chairman insisted he be sacked on the spot, but despite seeing the evidence for himself, JJ tried to intervene. He asked Michael Toner, who was Father of the Chapel of the NUJ, to plead Ronnie's cause with the Chairman. 'But Ronnie's not in the Chapel,' protested Michael. 'He would never give me the time of day.' He did go however. 'Why are you defending this crook?' said the Chairman. 'He's not even a member of the union. Junor's put you up to this, hasn't he?'

'The trouble is Ronnie Spark has got expensive tastes,' JJ would say, 'and he can't really afford to indulge them.' He blamed himself for this, for having persuaded him to fly to South Africa, where he developed a taste for the high life. Once he had the taste for it, he couldn't stop himself, and had to fiddle his expenses to pay for his newfound lifestyle. 'It has to be bollocks,' say colleagues, 'but this is what he seriously believed.' And when JJ realised he couldn't save him he rang Larry Lamb, then Editor of the *Sun*, and persuaded him to give Ronnie a job.

Ronnie Spark wasn't just fiddling his expenses. According to another colleague, he was helping himself to books that came in for review, which the Literary Editor put out every week for people to buy cheaply, the money for which went to charity. Ronnie was taking up to twenty hardbacks a week. When JJ was made aware of what was happening he said, 'You must let Ronnie take the books he wants. He's a very erudite man you know. He's very hard up and he has expensive tastes.'

For some reason that no one on the staff could fathom, JJ had a soft spot for Ronnie, although they say Ronnie never had a good word to say about JJ in return. He was the only member of staff who got away with leaving the office early. Mike Dove even composed a song about him, which they used to sing in the office:

> *Ronnie Spark,*
> *Home before dark,*
> *Gone by noon,*
> *Not a minute too soon.*

There was only one other person who was allowed to come and go as he pleased and that was Carl Giles, the cartoonist, who was a law unto himself, and much indulged. Giles was the genius who had been producing cartoons for both the *Daily Express* and *Sunday Express* since before JJ became Editor, and who was without doubt the group's most valuable asset. He used to work from his studio at home in Suffolk and send his drawings to London by train. Occasionally he visited the office and, if he wanted to go drinking at 5 o'clock in the afternoon, then someone senior would take him. One afternoon, he and JJ wandered into Poppins together, only to find two of his *Sunday Express* staff, Major Tim Carew and Brian Gardiner, both military historians, propping up the bar, well into an early evening snifter. The next morning he summoned Carew to his office and tore him off one hell of a strip, assuming, erroneously, that he had led the younger man astray. Major Carew, a distinguished soldier and holder of the Military Cross, lost his temper, said, 'I've shot better men than you,' and marched out, never to be seen again.

In the summer of 1963, it was my father who was on the point of marching out. I was at boarding school when I heard the news. I had begun boarding in the autumn of 1962 at a school he chose for me near Cranbrook in Kent, called Benenden. It was recommended by one of the doctor friends we had made on holiday one year. He and Pam had been to look round the school and meet the headmistress, Miss Betty Clarke.

I remember their return, although I am not sure whether Pam had more contempt for the headmistress or my father. During their meeting Miss Clarke had totally ignored my mother and spoken exclusively to my father, who, to hear Pam tell, sat in her thrall like one of the many dachshunds that followed her everywhere. She was a fiercely bright, but very shy, woman with no small talk, and her attention flattered him. He decided she had a great brain, and I was duly dispatched to Benenden, on the freezing, windswept, isolated but very beautiful Weald of Kent, where, to JJ's great delight, Princess Anne followed a year later. He felt that the Queen had vindicated him in his choice of school.

That summer's evening in 1963, my housemistress called me to the phone. A phone call was unusual. We kept in touch with our parents by letter in those days; the telephone was for emergencies. It was my father. He wanted me to know that he had resigned as Editor of the *Sunday Express*, and was ringing with the news lest I read about it in the newspapers. He explained what had happened and sounded, as he always did, in control of the situation. I was not to worry; everything would be all right.

He had resigned on a point of principle – a growing disenchantment with Harold Macmillan and the knowledge that, with a general election looming, Lord Beaverbrook would want his newspapers to support him. He was not prepared to. There was another issue that rankled. He had discovered that Beaverbrook had told Bob Pitman, one of JJ's protégés, that he wanted him to take over John Gordon's column as and when Gordon stopped writing it. JJ was furious that Beaverbrook should be planning the affairs of the *Sunday Express* without even bothering to consult him. But Macmillan was the principal trigger. He told Max Aitken how he felt, Max consulted Beaverbrook, and the message came back that if JJ didn't support Macmillan the *Sunday Express* would have to find a new Editor.

He had no alternative but to resign. That night, instead of going home, he found three colleagues still in the office and took them to the Old Bell for a drink. Leslie Vanter, the Sports Editor, was one of them, and remembers that my father was very shaken that Beaverbrook had accepted his resignation. Max Aitken, he said, had been imploring him not to resign, saying, 'He's an old man for God's sake, give in to him,' but JJ refused to budge. 'That's the end of my new boat,' he said mournfully. The atmosphere in the pub was like a wake, and one of the party suggested they go across the road to Poppins and cheer up. As they waited in the traffic to cross the road, JJ turned to Leslie and said, 'There's no need for you to worry, you know. You're coming with me. I'm going to the *Mail* and you're coming as Sports Editor.' Leslie asked what the *Mail*'s existing Sports Editor was going to say about that. 'Oh he'll go', he said, 'you're coming.'

It was agreed that JJ would continue working for six months and train an Editor-elect during that period, namely Arthur Brittenden, who was then editing the *Daily Express* in Manchester. It was also agreed that he would continue to do his best to promote the welfare of the *Sunday Express*. 'This I do with a full heart, for my one aim is to leave the *Sunday Express* in an even stronger position than it is in now,' he wrote to Beaverbrook. 'In turn, during that period, my authority and dignity as Editor will in no way be diminished.'

Two weeks later, he became aware that the office lawyer, who habitually sat behind him on the Back Bench on Saturday nights to read the proofs and give legal advice, kept taking the proofs away. JJ asked what was going on, and discovered, from a deeply embarrassed lawyer, that an equally embarrassed Edward Pickering, a former Editor of the *Daily Express*, had been brought in by Lord Beaverbrook. He had asked Pickering to look at the proofs to ensure that nothing went into the newspaper of which he would disapprove.

JJ was livid. He rang the Chairman and told him that he had entered into an agreement with goodwill for six months in return for certain guarantees. Those guarantees were being entirely vitiated. If Pickering were not told to get out of the building immediately, then he would play dirty too. He would leave the building himself, and take the cream of the *Sunday Express* staff with him – confident that they would follow. Pickering was on his way within fifteen minutes, and the remainder of the six months were trouble free.

Bob Edwards was editing the *Daily Express* by this time and Beaverbrook invited him to Arlington House and offered him a cigar. 'Lady Dunn was there [the widow of his oldest friend James Dunn] so I knew something was afoot that wasn't going to do me any harm. He said, "Tell me, Bob, who should be Editor of the *Sunday Express*?" He indicated he had asked Max's opinion and I knew who he would have suggested – Derek Marks – and he would have been a disaster. [Marks was then Deputy Editor of the *Evening Standard*.] So I thought I'd play a little game and said, "I'd be very reluctant to give my opinion. Max Aitken has given his and if I suggest someone different it's not going to please Max, is it, and I have difficulties in that direction." I was stirring it up. And he said "Balls! Who should be Editor of the *Sunday Express*?" And I said, "There's only one Editor of the *Sunday Express* and that's John Junor, and he's got to go on being it." He was very pleased with that answer and it was the right answer.' It didn't stop him appointing Derek Marks, however. Three weeks before the six months were up, Max Aitken told Brittenden that he would not become Editor after all, it would go to Marks.

The job offers for JJ during those six months did not come thick and fast. The *Daily Mail* did not beat a path to his door. He wrote to Lord Rothermere asking for a job and was invited to tea, over which they discussed the Tory leadership. JJ discovered Rothermere was, 'so ignorant and so arrogant and so unaware of what was happening in politics that he refused to believe anything other than what he thought he knew'. There was an invitation to become an interviewer for *Panorama* and, two months before he was due to leave, Lord Beaverbrook suggested that once he had left the *Sunday Express* he might continue to write a column for it.

But he was saved by events. Days before his time was up, he was standing in his bathroom shaving, listening to the *Today* programme on Radio 4, at full volume as ever, when he heard a news item that changed his future. Macmillan was being admitted to hospital for a prostate operation. JJ knew he would have to resign as Prime Minister.

'Beaverbrook absolutely rejoiced,' recalls Bob Edwards. 'He rejoiced to me. He rang up JJ and said, "We're saved, we're saved. You don't have to resign now, do you John?" John jumped into a car and was driven to Cherkley and they immediately agreed any disagreement between the two of them no longer existed, they embraced and John came back.' Derek Marks on hearing the news that he was no longer going to be Editor of the *Sunday Express* simply said, 'Oh fuck it.'

He wrote to me:

> *My darling, darling Tuppy,*
> *Just a very short letter to tell you that thanks to Mr*
> *Macmillan's resignation, we are still in business. And still in a*
> *job.*
> *Mummy and I had dinner with Lord B. last night and*
> *buried the hatchet. Pleased? I jolly well am.*
> *Write soon – and have fun.*
> *Lots and lots of love and kisses*
> *Daddy*

The crisis was over, both men's pride remained intact, and the invitations to dine with Beaverbrook were resumed. He was often there twice a week, but instead of the great dinner parties of the past, he was now the only guest. And now at dinner, instead of the champagne that Beaverbrook had previously insisted JJ drink, he was given claret – a whole bottle of Château Latour 1953, to himself. That Christmas Beaverbrook gave him a case of it as a present.

What JJ had not known when he resigned was that Beaverbrook had cancer of the prostate. In future, he would dine alone with Beaverbrook and the ex-Lady Dunn, Marcia Christoforides, who was now Beaverbrook's wife. She had been left a huge fortune by James Dunn, a Canadian industrialist, and it tickled Beaverbrook that she was not only thirty years younger than him, but she was also richer than him – she hadn't married him for his money. They were married for just one year, but she had been his constant companion for much longer, and cheered his final years.

On 25 May 1964, Beaverbrook's fellow Canadian Roy Thomson organised a banquet for him at the Dorchester to celebrate his eighty-fifth birthday. He was by now a very sick man, in constant pain and virtually confined to a wheelchair. Yet the evening was a triumph, and he stood up and made a speech with such vigour and charm that it brought tears of pride to my father's eyes.

'The man who is not true to himself is no journalist,' he said. 'He must show courage, independence and initiative. He must also, I believe, be a man of optimism. He has no business to be a pedlar of gloom and despondency. He must be a respecter of persons, but able to deal with the highest and the lowest on the same basis, which is regard for the public interest and a determination to get at the facts. I take more pride in my experience as a journalist than any other experience I have had in my long and varied life.

'It is time for me to become an apprentice once more. I am not certain in which direction, but somewhere, sometime, soon . . .'

That night a documentary about Beaverbrook, in which JJ had taken part, was shown on television. Beaverbrook saw it himself later in the week from his bed at Cherkley. He telephoned my father to say, 'I have seen the television programme. Thank you very much indeed, John, for all the kind things you said about me.' Three days later he was dead.

CHAPTER THIRTEEN

Love Affair with France

JJ's biggest fear during those months before Macmillan's resignation was that if he didn't get another job quickly, he wouldn't be able to afford the boat he had on order. As it was she arrived in early 1964, and changed all of our lives. We learned to say 'sheet' instead of rope, and 'port' and 'starboard' instead of left and right, to tie the right knots and refer to the boat as 'she'. She was a twenty-eight-foot Fairey Fisherman, which he had first seen at the Boat Show, the perfect vessel for a beginner with a very imperfect crew. She looked like a lifeboat, built more for safety than style, which was just as well since my father was no safer on the sea than he had been in the air.

JJ had taken navigation lessons at night school, with a dentist friend he had met skiing one year, called David Macdonald, who shared the boat until he bought one of his own. But my father was not what one might describe as a practical man; in fact he was decidedly ham-fisted and accident-prone. But he did at least know his limitations and would invariably invite friends to come sailing with him to help. He called the boat *Maggie D* after his mother, who died the year before, and kept her on dry land at the Fairey Marina on the River Hamble in Hampshire.

His mother had died of a heart attack in February 1963 at the age of eighty-five. She had been living in a nursing home for the last months of her life, which she hated, and would implore visitors to take her home. I was at school at the time of her death and there was never any suggestion that I, nor my brother or mother, might go to the funeral. But there was another absence that JJ took grave exception to. His brother Tom, who had never entirely forgiven his mother for her hostility towards his wife Jean, failed to make the journey to Glasgow to bury his mother, and sent his son-in-law instead. He had been suffering from depression for years and he said he couldn't face a crowd of people, so stayed in Aberdeen. But my father was never good at listening to excuses, or even under-standing other people's problems. He was appalled and, in typical fashion, refused to speak to his brother. Two years later Tom was dead from an overdose of barbiturates – and, to the best of my knowledge, there was never any reconciliation between the two of them before he died.

Not long after Maggie's death, JJ's eldest brother, Bill, who had long been struggling with alcoholism, gave up the flat in Oban Drive and went to live at Crichton Royal, a hospital in Dumfries, which specialised in alcohol addiction. He arrived as a patient, but ended up working for the hospital in the office. And every summer when he came to spend his fortnight's holiday with us at Wellpools, JJ would take him sailing.

Maggie D would be parked in a huge cradle on wheels, and getting in and out of the water was almost as entertaining as the sailing. The cradle would be towed to the ramp at the water's edge and then driven into the sea until it floated. Coming back, was not quite so easy. We had to aim for the cradle, which required a lot of flapping, shouting and bad temper. There would be brief moments of calm during a day's sailing, when we were safely moored somewhere, usually over a bottle of red wine, cold chicken and Scotch eggs that Pam had made for lunch, but the getting to and from that safe haven in the River Beaulieu, or at Cowes on the Isle of Wight, was always fraught.

JJ would stand at the wheel, bellowing instructions, and using nautical terms than none of us understood. It was not long before Pam opted out of sailing altogether. Every week she dutifully made him a picnic, and found his sailing jacket and all the other bits and pieces he needed for the day, which he could never find in the flap of trying to get away from the house in time so as not to miss the tide. It was with a sigh of relief that she would watch his car shoot out of the drive in a swirl of gravel, and roar off down the road.

JJ drove everywhere at top speed, mostly I think as a way of letting off steam. If he was in a bad mood or had just had a row with someone, he would drive even faster, throwing the car into corners and braking and accelerating violently. He had a succession of fast cars – after the Armstrong Siddeley he had at least four Aston Martins, an AC Cobra, a couple of Jensens, and several Lotuses before moving on to Range Rovers in the 1980s – and he drove each and every one of them to the limit.

Before I went away to school, he would drive me in to Stanway, my prep school in Dorking, every morning – we had an Aston Martin DB6 at that time. Every morning, we would meet a red E-Type Jaguar, which he would race the eight miles along narrow, windy roads, each car trying to overtake the other. I don't know who the man was or where he lived, and to the best of my knowledge neither did JJ. He certainly never spoke to him, and they didn't even smile or wave; they just battled to be in front.

Bill, who lived a very quiet existence up in Dumfries, used to be terrified by JJ's driving, as JJ well knew, and he took a sadistic pleasure in scaring him. Bill was a gentle soul and didn't often speak up for himself, so I used to try and intervene and stop my father being quite so beastly. It didn't always work. One Sunday the three of us were driving down to the boat for a day's sailing. We reached Dorking in record time, after screeching round the little country lanes, and JJ stopped to fill up with petrol. Breakfast had not gone well and he was already in a filthy mood. Bill was shaking with fear. He was a chain-smoker but JJ wouldn't allow him to smoke until he had had his first cigarette of the day after lunch. I don't think it was just the speed that frightened him – his brother frightened him – and he didn't much care for a day on the boat either, but was never given any choice in the matter. When JJ got back into the car, I asked whether he would mind driving a little more slowly because Bill and I were a bit nervous. 'Certainly,' he said icily. 'Is this slow enough for you?' and proceeded to drive the seventy-odd miles down to the Hamble at 20 mph the whole way.

By the time my father bought *Maggie D*, I was at boarding school and Tink was at university so he and I could only sail during the holidays. But from March to October, JJ sailed every Sunday or Monday religiously, taking friends, neighbours, members of his staff on the *Sunday Express*, anyone who could be useful on board the boat and was prepared to be shouted at in return for a good lunch. The drive was nearly two hours each way, and as with everything he did, it became a ritual. He left the house at the same time every morning, wanted the same thing – cold chicken and Scotch eggs – for lunch, and week after week he broke his journey at the same place in Bishop's Waltham to do some shopping on the way down. Then, week after week, on the way home he would stop at an old manor house in Chawton, the village where Jane Austen was born. The lady of the manor, JJ discovered, had fallen on hard times, and did teas and sold fruit cake and free-range eggs to keep body and soul together. So every week he stopped to spend money with her, and bought more eggs and fruitcakes than we could ever eat, or even give away. And on the journey home he listened to *Sing Something Simple*, which was his favourite radio programme. He went whatever the weather, rain or shine, or howling gale, and every year thereafter his summer holidays were spent on the boat, tied against the harbour wall in a little Normandy fishing village called Barfleur.

He found Barfleur by chance and fell in love with it. He loved the lighthouse on the rocks, the square Norman church with the bells that summoned the faithful, the lifeboat house with its chute into the sea, and the fishing boats that jostled alongside him on the harbour wall. And he loved the people. There was Edouard Boissard, the great moustachioed former captain of the lifeboat, who ended up in a wheelchair with both legs amputated; Pierre Lamache, the one-legged fisherman with his fearsome wife and house full of caged songbirds; Gerard Theuriau and his sexy blonde wife Françoise, who came from Paris every August with their children; very formal, upright Colonel Quinet and his wife, who had retired from the army to a house in the High Street; and their son, Michel, who became a doctor that JJ was able to consult over a bowl of moules marinière.

He also loved the shops and the shopkeepers. There was Monsieur Duval, the ironmonger; Claudette in the bakery where he went to buy bread every morning; and Monsieur Gosselin, the grocer in neighbouring St Vaast, who had a particularly fine selection of cheap wine. He loved the restaurants, the old-fashioned Hotel Moderne where we ate at night, and the Café de France on the quayside where he drank strong coffee and pastis. And he loved the sea. Every morning before breakfast he would swim, no matter what the weather, no matter how icy the water; and he would get out after thirty seconds saying how marvellous it had been. Swimming was perhaps not the best term for what my father did in the water. He would flail about on his back, blowing like a whale, or make the motions of a front crawl with his head high above the water, face pinched tight, and head turning to left and right with every tortured stroke.

He made dozens of friends in Barfleur, most of them French. They were mostly younger than he was – throughout his life he attracted young men, generally preferring their company to that of his contemporaries – and pretty, flirtatious girls. He took them sailing, or entertained them on the boat. In the mornings he played tennis with them on the windswept municipal court, or played golf, then they would sit outside the Café de France for drinks before lunch. Lunch was usually on board, he would then have a quick sleep and, in the afternoons, he would go to the beach, swim and play ball games. *Maggie D* became a focal point of the town, and everyone passing along the quayside would shout 'Bonjour Monsieur Jean' as they passed. Pierre Lamache would drop in fresh fish from his early morning catch, which my father would cook for lunch, and in the evenings, a crowd would get together for dinner, and wherever they had eaten, be it in someone's house or a restaurant, everyone would come back to the boat for a nightcap. M. Gosselin's wine, and whisky, which he bought in bulk from the bonded warehouse in Cherbourg, flowed generously and Monsieur Jean was king of all he surveyed.

For much of the time JJ was on his own in Barfleur, or with Tink in the early days, while Pam and I would be in Spain. The arrival of the *Maggie D* coincided with Pam's brother and sister leaving Kenya and settling in the South of Spain and, when JJ went to France, Pam and I went there. They settled in a small village called

Fuengirola, where the two families set up a water sports business. Today Fuengirola is a hideous sprawl of high-rise concrete with a six-lane highway running through it, but in the early 1960s, when package holidays were just beginning, it was a typical, sleepy, fishing village with pretty whitewashed bungalows lining the shore, fishing boats hauled up onto the beach, and nets spread out to dry. It was almost entirely populated by small, wizened old women in black widows' weeds. But all that rapidly changed, and in just a few years the beaches were covered in bronzed bikini-clad bodies, there were bars, clubs, hotels and restaurants, and you could hardly hear above the noise of cement mixers and cranes on the construction sites.

We went there for about a month every summer and it was bliss, but I usually spent a week or so in Barfleur as well. Pam came once or twice in the early years too but she didn't enjoy it at all and in the end stayed away. JJ seldom sailed while he was there. The boat served as rather spartan living accommodation, but for all the damp and discomfort, and the loo that required a degree in engineering to operate, I used to love lying in my bunk at night listening to the noise of the rigging tap-tapping against the mast and the water gently lapping against the hull.

August was party time in Barfleur, and one of the high spots of the season was a regatta, which the whole town came out to see. There were buntings out and horns blowing and a great deal of noise and excitement. Every year JJ entered the yacht race, and every year he won it, which enhanced both his love for the town and his celebrity status within it. He won it by virtue of having the largest engine. There was nothing in the rules specifically forbidding their use, and so JJ shamelessly powered his way past every other yacht in the race, returning year after year to a hero's welcome. And year after year he proudly collected his cup, amidst grand ceremony, from the Mayor. It was many years before the rules were amended – JJ was on to his second boat by then, a thirty-two foot, six-berth Hillyard that he called *Outcast* – and when the rules were changed he stopped entering the race. He was miffed; he didn't have the patience to sail the course, and could see no point in doing it if he wasn't going to win.

My father's love affair with Barfleur lasted thirty-five years. Eventually he bought himself a small house there, and when his sailing days were over, he stayed in the house for his three weeks in August. When he first told me he was planning to buy one, I had visions of something old and picturesque, set on its own in some romantic spot, overlooking the sea. Instead it was a terraced house in the town, overlooking neither the sea nor the harbour – unless you craned your neck from the dormer window in the attic, which he did, saying the while, 'Isn't that a marvellous view?' But on the plus side it was three minutes walk from both the harbour and the beach, and very close to the shops.

Years later, JJ would say to Peter McKay: 'How much do you think I bought that house for?'

'I've no idea,' said Peter.

'£17,000,' said JJ. 'Guess how much it's worth now?'

'£100,000?' asked Peter.

'No.'

'£150,000?'

'No. £17,000 – they don't go up in price there.'

JJ loved the house with a passion, and talked about retiring there one day. I had my reservations. It had an outside loo in the court-yard, a decidedly odd bath in the kitchen, no heating, no garden; and a couple of years after he bought it, a nightclub opened up opposite, so the noise at night was deafening. For the first week of August the noise was deafening all day too. It was the week of the fair, a travelling fair that installed itself at the harbour end of the town, with dodgems and rides, helter-skelters and merry-go-rounds, motorbikes and shooting arcades, coconut shies and stalls, and candyfloss, popcorn, and roasting chickens. It was my father's idea of heaven – and every year we rode the rides, threw balls and hoops, drove the dodgems, and bought candyfloss.

JJ loved sticky things like candyfloss. Food of all sorts made up an important part of his holiday, as did shopping. Every morning he went out to the boulangerie to buy bread, croissants and pain au chocolat for breakfast, on an old bicycle he had bought to keep at the house. We ate it on the little table in the courtyard at the back, alongside the privy with the washing line overhead, where the trunks from his early morning swim hung to dry. He would also squeeze oranges for juice and make strong, bitter coffee, which we drank in big French cups.

We were on holiday, there was no hurry, no trains to catch, no deadlines to meet: it should have been relaxed, and for the first day or so it very often would be, but JJ couldn't keep it up and life in Barfleur was just as tense as it was at home. No one was allowed to do things in their own time, or worse still, do nothing. The day was spent watching the clock and speeding from one activity to the next, which was how JJ always spent his leisure time. Everything had to be done at the appointed hour and for the appointed length of time, irrespective of the weather. But of all the timings, lunch was the most crucial. Nothing made him more thunderous than to have to wait for lunch, or to eat with people who took a long time to finish. He made no attempt to disguise his irritation, even when a guest of his French friends. It was the same at home, or indeed wherever he was in the world, for the simple reason that he was desperate for his first cigarette of the day. His self-imposed discipline of never smoking before lunch had nothing to do with health: he didn't believe that smoking killed you – that was scaremongering propaganda – and he thought that non-smokers were by and large tremendous bores. I think it was a way of taking the moral high ground, to prove that he was in control of his craving, unlike my mother who took great pleasure in having her first cigarette with her breakfast coffee. But denying himself did nothing to diminish JJ's craving, of course, it just made him extremely bad-tempered and, as a result, lunch was always taken at a spanking pace so he could finally light up that first cigarette.

The highlight of his day in Barfleur was dinner, when holding court in one of his favourite restaurants surrounded by his French friends, he would be more relaxed than anywhere. Part of the attraction of Normandy for JJ was the simplicity of the cooking, which suited his delicate stomach, but also the cost. Repeatedly he would write about the food he ate on holiday, chastising the British for being so overpriced – although no one else who went to Normandy ever seemed to be able to find the cheap menus he did.

The menu in a Normandy restaurant was the most expensive available. To start, there was luscious lobster.

Then came a choice of sole or steak, pommes frites, salad, a magnificent cheese board, crusty fresh bread and mounds of butter and a mouth-watering gateau. The service was impeccable.

And the price? £7.50 a head. For everything. Including tax and service.

And that was the deluxe menu.

For less than £3 in the same restaurant a Frenchman can eat like a prince on, for example, moules marinière, coq au vin and scrumptious apple tart.

How do the French do it when the cost of basic food is higher than in Britain?

I don't know. I just wish some British restaurateurs could spend their own holidays in Normandy discovering the secret.

Barfleur was the one place where he was never bored; and where his friendships remained more or less stable. His tolerance for the French was far greater than his tolerance for his friends at home. He put it down to the language barrier. He spoke very passable French, and enjoyed practising it, but he was probably never fluent enough to fully understand or be fully understood. If he had been, or if he had been with these people for longer than three weeks at a stretch, he knew he would have been bored silly. As it was, they were dear friends who welcomed him and his abundant hospitality year after year with open arms.

I never took the boat across to France with my father: neither my stomach nor my nerve was up to it. Even the best of sailors tended to heave in the heavy seas they met most years in the English Channel, because JJ didn't wait until the weather was right. He set sail without fail on the Saturday night of the weekend before his holiday started. He would take the boat over to France, install it against the harbour wall in Barfleur, then travel home that afternoon as a foot passenger on the ferry to Portsmouth, and a week later travel out with his car, so that he was mobile during his holiday.

He never let bad forecasts or weather warnings deter him from anything. Time and again, with snow lying deep on the ground and the roads impassable, JJ would set off for the office or the golf course, or into Dorking to do his weekly shopping. Radio announcements warning people not to travel unless their journey was absolutely essential, only enhanced the challenge, and he never came unstuck: he had the luck of the devil. He always made it up hills where other cars had foundered, always made it through floods, and always arrived in France in one piece.

One year, however, the trip very nearly ended in disaster. He had taken Vic Patrick, Peter Vane and Bill Martin, all colleagues from the *Sunday Express*, and the four of them set out sometime after midnight. They had driven down from London, having put the paper to bed. The boat was never short of alcohol, the bilges were lined with wine and whisky, and after they had all had a few drinks, which would not have been their first of the evening, JJ went below deck to sleep, leaving the others on watch. All three of them continued to drink steadily through the night and were all very drunk when they hit heavy seas. Peter Vane had the helm but was feeling so seasick he had to hand over to Bill Martin. Bill then lit a cigar – about the most nauseous smell for someone already about to heave – and when Peter caught a whiff of the smoke he went berserk and came after Bill with every intention of killing him. There followed a hair-raising chase all round the deck of the boat, with Bill in very real fear for his life, until Peter caught his foot on a stanchion and fell flat on his face, which brought him to his senses.

The only trip of any length I made with JJ was when we sailed from Barfleur to the Channel Island of Alderney early one morning. As we approached the island, notorious for treacherous rocks that surround it, we hit dense fog, and went round and round in circles for several hours, while JJ slept soundly below deck. Pierre Lamache, at the helm, the one-legged fisherman, whom JJ insisted was such an expert sailor he had never used a compass or chart in his life, could be heard quietly asking in French, if anyone had the direction finder.

CHAPTER FOURTEEN

Stranger than Fiction

My father wrote two novels in his life, neither of which was published. One was an intriguing whodunit, written in the 1940s, called *Murder in the Mews*, which must have been rejected. The other was the story of a love affair, which he wrote in the 1960s. It is the untitled story of a forty-two-year-old newspaper editor who is found out in his adulterous relationship with a nineteen-year-old model. This book was not fiction.

I knew he had written the novel, but I had never seen it. No one had. He kept it locked in the bottom drawer of his desk, insisting it was too sexy for anyone to see. A more likely explanation is it was too revealing. As I turned the pages of the manuscript, I realised that this was a chillingly accurate account of a story I knew from my childhood, a story that effectively brought about the end to my parent's marriage.

Curtis was in a filthy mood as he flung the E-type into top gear.

How the hell, he asked himself, had he ever let himself in for this?

When he had first been invited, the date had been so far ahead that there was no reasonable excuse for refusing. So he had accepted while making the mental reservation that he would ring up nearer the time and invent some reason for abandoning the trip. It nearly always worked. It hadn't made him the most popular man in Fleet Street but so what? If you were the editor of a national newspaper then popularity mattered a lot less than if you merely hoped to be an editor. You only had to crawl on the way up.

He looked across for a second at the man in the passenger seat.

Bennett was a bore. Paunchy, fifty-fivish, a retired Admiral with a plump red face, badly fitting false teeth and an irritating habit of talking to you as if you were an able seaman who had forgotten to shave.

But this morning he seemed strangely diffident, reflected Curtis as he scudded the Jag into a left-hand bend at 75 miles per hour.

'Johnny,' said Bennett, 'I think I ought to tell you that we will have a couple of passengers on board today. A couple of girls. I meant to tell you on the telephone but I wasn't sure if they were coming until last night. And it would have been a little embarrassing telephoning in front of Mabel.'

God, the old bastard, thought Curtis. Mabel, who looked like a plate of rice pudding, squashed flat after thirty years of marriage to Bennett, certainly would have been embarrassed.

'That's all right, Bob,' he said easily – 'Who are they?'

'They're a mother and daughter. I'm more or less a godfather to the child. She's only nineteen and just started as a model. Spends most of her time fighting off the advances of dirty old men in advertising agencies. The mother is the widow of an old friend of mine who was killed in the Med. In 1945. I've more or less kept an eye on them ever since.

'Look,' he continued defensively. 'I can rely on your discretion on this, can't I? There's nothing in it. But Mabel is so damned touchy. Besides we had to have someone to cook and wash up in the galley. I would have asked your wife but I know she doesn't like sailing.'

That's for sure, thought Curtis bitterly. Judith doesn't like doing anything. Especially with me.'

On the way home Curtis suggests they stop for dinner together in a restaurant.

It was nearly eleven o'clock when Curtis announced that he was going to bring the E-type round from the courtyard.

'I'll come and help you,' said the girl impulsively.

In the darkness of the courtyard he slipped into the driving seat and pretended an inability to find his headlight switch. The girl stuck her head through the window.

'There it is,' she said.

He turned his head towards hers and gently pulled her towards him.

She looked at him, hesitated for a second and then he felt her sweet tongue searching the back of his throat.

'Ring me tomorrow,' she whispered. 'But not before six.'

He drove home singing all the way.

Curtis and Gail, the girl's name, go on to have an affair.

I remember my father's affair with the model vividly. She was the elder sister of one of Roderick's girlfriends. He had some very pretty girlfriends in his youth, but the most memorable was Anita Fisher, known as Nini. He can't have been more than seventeen when he knew her, and they were both still at school, but she was far and away my favourite. Her father had died when she was a child and she lived in London with her mother and nineteen-year-old sister.

Her sister's name was Zandra, but she was known as Zaza. She was a Lucie Clayton model, tall, slim and very beautiful. She had shoulder-length, white-blonde hair as Nini did, but she wore heavy make-up and was far more sophisticated than her little sister. I remember her being very flirtatious with my father, and he with her, but that was nothing exceptional, he flirted with every good-looking woman, and plenty of good-looking women flirted with him.

When I discovered, some years later, that they had had an affair I was disgusted. I had always assumed that it happened because of Roderick's friendship with Nini. Zaza and her mother came to Wellpools on a couple of occasions, and it seemed logical to suppose that this was how and where she and JJ first met, and their affair began. What I didn't know until I read JJ's novel was that it had nothing to do with Roderick. Roderick had never previously met

Nini, nor would have done. The reason the Fishers came to Wellpools was because JJ was secretly having an affair with Zaza, and wanted to show off his house to her, and presumably his wife and family too. So he arranged for my mother to cook lunch for his lover and to play the gracious hostess – just as Curtis did in the novel. I would like to think that this twist was pure fiction, but the details of the affair in the novel so closely mirror real life that I have to believe they are largely true.

In the novel, Curtis met Gail and her mother sailing. I wondered whether that was how JJ met Zaza and her mother. If so, I knew it must have been in the summer of 1961. I racked my brain as to which friend he might have been sailing with, but the clue was in the novel and, by checking it alongside his office appointments diary for 1961, the facts sprang out at me. Curtis and the girl are in a casino. 'They gambled for only a few minutes. She insisted on putting her francs on Number 10 since that was the day they first met.' I looked through the diary at all the tenths of the months. Bingo. Monday 10 July 'Sailing with Ben Bolt. Dinner Admiral Bolt, Mrs Erskine and Miss Fisher.' The entries were always slightly cryptic because it was his office diary, which his secretary saw and wrote appointments in.

Admiral Ben Bolt was the father of a great prep school friend of mine called Sarah Bolt – I was a bridesmaid to one of her elder sisters – and he had a yacht called *Ariadne*, which he kept on the Solent. Fellow guests that day were obviously Betty and Zaza Fisher, and they had stopped and had dinner together on the way home.

It was the beginning of a real-life and extremely dangerous affair, conducted mostly in a service flat in Fetter Lane, provided for my father by Beaverbrook Newspapers. It was in a block called Clifford's Inn and, for as long as I can remember, JJ habitually spent Friday nights there. Zaza had a key. JJ, like his character in the book, Johnny Curtis, was forty-two. Zaza, like her literary counterpart, Gail, was nineteen, and with her looks could have had any man she chose. It seems bizarre that she went for someone twenty-three years older and slightly running to fat. But he was at the height of his power as an Editor, at the helm of a hugely successful newspaper, he drove a powerful, expensive car – an Aston Martin, in fact, not an E-type; he would never have had a Jaguar, calling them 'Jew boy's Bentleys' – and he had enormous charm when he turned it on, and charisma. All of that must have seemed attractive to a rather naive nineteen-year-old that had grown up without a father. I expect he also promised to put her on the front page of the *Sunday Express*, and turn her into a star.

Meetings with Zaza are recorded in his office diary, but so too are meetings with her mother. This is the first point where fact and fiction diverge. Curtis invites Gail to come with him to Monte Carlo. His proprietor wants him to fly there to try and persuade an eighty-five-year-old novelist to sell his memoirs to the Sunday paper. She is keen to come, so he takes Gail's mother to lunch on one occasion to persuade her to allow her daughter to go with him. The mother agrees, and believes throughout the affair what she is told, that there is nothing sexual in their relationship.

In January 1962, Beaverbrook asked JJ to go to Monte Carlo to try and persuade the octogenarian Somerset Maugham to sell his autobiography for serialisation in the *Sunday Express*. But that was six months after he and Zaza first met. My guess is he took Zaza with him, and probably on other trips too, but I find it hard to believe that he needed quite so many lunches alone with Betty to persuade her to let him. He clearly liked her company and she was an attractive woman of forty-five. Whether mother and daughter were aware, I don't know. I do know that for a long time my mother was blissfully unaware, and the visitors' book at Wellpools, which was only sporadically used, records that she entertained them both on at least two occasions. They came to a Christmas party in 1961 and dinner, ironically, on April Fools' Day.

In the novel, Curtis has two daughters, Jane and Sally, and it is the younger one, Sally, who becomes best friends with Gail's younger sister, Anna. In reality it was my brother who became friends with the younger sister, not me. In the novel Sally and Anna find love letters from Curtis in Gail's bedroom, which they show to Judith.

I never knew how Pam found the love letters she took to her lawyer, but I know she had quite a collection. She was unlikely to have found them at Wellpools. He would have conducted the affair from his office. It's inconceivable that he would have brought them home and if he had they would have been locked up in his desk along with his bank statements, which he never let her see, and everything else. I assume, therefore, that what happened in the novel is what happened in real life. It was Roderick and Nini who found the letters. I know that Roderick challenged my father. 'Yes,' he said, 'I am sleeping with Zaza, what's the problem?' When Pam saw the letters, she went straight to a divorce lawyer in Reigate. Through him, she hired a private detective to watch the flat in Fetter Lane and, armed with conclusive evidence of his adultery, told him she intended to file for divorce.

JJ was the one who broke the news to me. Pam, he said, no longer loved him and planned to divorce him, but he didn't tell me why. With tears running down his face, he said how bitterly unhappy he was and how he loved her more than anything and wanted to be with her more than anything, but he knew he could say some terrible things at times, he was not a good husband and she was unable to forgive him.

I was twelve. I hated the perpetual fighting, I hated the drunken confrontations, and the vicious things he said to Pam – all the things that made me hide under the bedcovers at night or run out of the house and cling, sobbing, to my pony's neck. But divorce frightened me, divorce split families in half – I had seen what happened to my friends. And I hated seeing my father cry. I challenged Pam. How could she do this? Why? And I pleaded with her to stop, pleaded with her not to go through with it. It was some years before she told me why she had filed for divorce. I had no idea at the time that it was because he had been sleeping with Zaza.

When confronted with his adultery in the novel, Curtis turns the tables on Judith.

'I know,' he said, 'I know you'll never forgive me. But it is not because of what I've done to you. Why do you think Gail ever happened at all?'

'Don't you dare mention that bitch's name to me,' she shrieked.

'All right, I won't mention her name but it doesn't alter the truth. All this only happened because for years you have hated the sight of me. And you know that's true. You haven't wanted me physically: you haven't wanted me in any way. You've despised my ambitions: you've even resented my success.'

She glared at him, but made no reply.

'Tell me,' he asked, 'when are you going to see your lawyer?'

'I've already seen him . . . He says I've got an open and shut case. And he says you will have to pay me one third of your income.'

'What income?' asked Curtis.

'What do you mean "what income?"' she demanded.

'Exactly what I say. For if you divorce me and name a nineteen-year-old girl there will be no income. For I'll be sacked. And one third of nothing is nothing.'

'You should have thought of that before you began to sleep with a nineteen-year-old girl.'

He looked at her and realised not for the first time that money neither interested nor influenced Judith. It never had . . .

He tried another tack.

'Money may not matter to you. It doesn't matter all that much to me. But what about Sally?'

'Well what about Sally?' she countered.

'Just this. If you divorce me and drag Gail's name and picture across the front pages of every newspaper in London, it not only means that I lose my job. You don't care about that. It will give you a nice feeling of revenge. But how is Sally going to feel? It not only means that she will have to leave school. And believe me she will have to leave school. For it will be quite impossible to keep on paying £600 a year in school fees. But she will have to leave feeling utterly humiliated because every other kid in school will know exactly why she is leaving. Do you want her to go through all that?'

'You should have thought of all that before you started your adultery.'

'That's the second time you've said that in the last five minutes and it's a pretty trite pointless remark,' he retorted. 'For if Sally is humiliated and made to suffer, it will not be me to blame. It will be you. You may think you are taking your revenge on me but it is she you will be making suffer.'

He saw that despite the anger in her eyes, the point had registered.

'If you want to divorce me and name her, then bloody well get on with it. But don't wear your halo so tight that you give yourself a headache. You pretend you are a Christian. You go to church and expect to go to heaven. But what is the essence of Christianity? It's forgiveness. But how much forgiveness have you got in your soul? How much understanding of other people's weaknesses? None. None at all. I told you last night and I tell you again. To get your own back on me, you are prepared to crucify your own daughter.'

Once again he could see his deliberate taunt strike home.

'You bastard,' she spat. 'You absolute bastard.'

'Maybe I am,' he replied, 'but at least I don't want to see Sally suffer.'

Judith offers him a deal. He must get out of the house, but she won't start divorce proceedings until Sally has gone to boarding school at the end of the summer, in eight months' time, and if he promises not to see his 'floozie' again in that time, she will give him a quiet divorce. He meets Gail over dinner to tell her the news.

'What, not see you for eight months!' she cried. 'I couldn't face that.'

'We've got to face it,' he said. 'Listen to me. And I will be frank. I'm not only thinking of your mother or even of Sally. I'm thinking of you and me. If I get mixed up in a really smelly divorce then believe me I'm finished as an editor. And don't make any mistake about it, I would be. There is not a paper in town that would employ me. How could they after headlines, which would shriek "Daughter finds love letter in desk of forty-two-year-old father's nineteen-year-old mistress"?

'And the only other thing I want to do apart from newspapers is go into parliament. But can you see a Tory constituency accepting me with that record?

'. . . If I were to get a quiet divorce I might not be able to go into politics but at least I could stay where I am.'

She reflected on this for a moment.

'And at the end of eight months, we could then get married?' she asked.

'Of course we could,' he said. But if there was conviction in his voice, there was none in his heart.

For, even if there were no smutty divorce, he knew quite well what Lord Dalbeattie's reaction would be to his marrying a nineteen-year-old.

Pam must have kicked him out of the house too, because he wrote to me in my first term at boarding school to say he was staying in London for a while so that he could concentrate on writing a book, which was something he had always wanted to do, and how 'really kind and understanding Mummy is being to let me'.

Curtis continues to see Gail despite his bargain with Judith. 'He sent her red roses every morning. They made love every night.' But then Gail goes to Spain and while she is away she has an affair with a young, handsome Spaniard. She knows now that Curtis will never marry her and wants to find someone who will. On her return, Curtis guesses she has been unfaithful to him and wrings a confession out of her, but she begs forgiveness and promises him it was him she loved and not the Spaniard. Their affair continues, despite his jealousy, until one night he calls at her flat unannounced and finds photographs of the Spaniard all over her bedroom.

'I don't want to see or hear from you ever again,' he said. She was still sobbing pitifully as he slammed the flat door behind him.

He then goes to see Judith.

She answered the door and looked at him without emotion of any kind . . .

'I've come to ask if you will have me back,' he said.

'No,' she said flatly . . .

'I know I've treated you badly. But it isn't myself I'm thinking about. It's Sally . . . Oh I know I've been a complete bloody fool. But that's all finished a long time ago. I swear it is. All I long for is to come home to you and Sally.'

He pressed home his advantage.

'You must believe me,' he urged. 'What have I possibly got to gain by lying? You've already promised me a scandal-free divorce. If I wanted to be rid of you I would take it. But I don't. In fact I wouldn't even mind giving up the temptations of Fleet Street and becoming a quiet backbench MP, with you helping me in my constituency.'

She lit a cigarette. He could see that her hand was shaking.

'You're a bastard,' she said. 'An utter bastard.'

'I know,' he said.

She turned away for a full minute. Then she spun round. 'For Sally's sake you can come back. But I don't want you ever to touch me again. And if I ever find you even looking at another woman again I'll kill you.'

. . . He whistled happily on the way back to London. The road ahead was clear – and in every way . . .

He stopped whistling for a moment as he thought of sex. He knew damned well that it was beyond him to be faithful to Judith. He would just have to be bloody careful . . . someone in his own office would be the ideal answer. Someone he could be seen in public with without arousing suspicion. Someone who would not be too demanding.

In November of that year, my mother dropped the action, but they never slept in the same bed again and any residual warmth or affection that she may have felt for him vanished. He, perhaps because of the guilt, took every opportunity to belittle her and highlight her inadequacies, and, bit by bit, what little confidence she had by then evaporated entirely. He treated her with less consideration than he would have treated a housekeeper, and never failed to remind her that her car, her clothes, the house, everything she had belonged to him. For the next fifteen years they lived under the same roof in mutual contempt.

CHAPTER FIFTEEN

Home Truths

How many of us, I wonder, given the opportunity to revisit our past, would discover that the truths they accepted from their childhood as absolute, were in fact flawed? I have gone through my life with a set of unshakeable convictions about myself and my parents, which the novel of my father's, no less than the diaries I discovered, and the ageing letters and long-forgotten photographs, have blasted wide open. And suddenly at the age of fifty-two, I realise that some of my convictions have been quite wrong, and that the truth in any situation is never absolute.

Finding the novel in a faded, sealed brown envelope was a shattering experience. Not because I was shocked by the sex or the language, but because it told me more about my father than he ever revealed during his lifetime in person. He shows the most astonishing self-awareness between its covers, and he describes his own motivation, fears and feelings with such breathtaking honesty that all sorts of things fall into place about his general behaviour, his relationship with my mother and why she never went through with the divorce that she threatened when she found out about the affair.

I have spent the last forty years believing she didn't divorce him because of me; blaming myself for keeping them together to live in mutual misery. I thought that, if I had not been so upset when they told me about the plans to divorce, they would have parted company, and both might have been able to find a happier life elsewhere. They were young enough in 1962 to have started afresh, but at twelve I couldn't see that. All I could see in my selfish way, was that my world was about to disintegrate. I was about to lose my home, my security and one of my parents, and I was frightened. So I stopped them drawing a line under their marriage and condemned them to a loveless life of conflict and destruction.

But, as I turned the pages of his book, I realised that I had done nothing of the sort. The fictional version of events is far more credible than the tears of a twelve-year-old. JJ didn't want a divorce; he knew that the publicity of his adultery with a nineteen-year-old model would finish him, not just as Editor of the *Sunday Express*, the epitome of decent family values, but also in his fallback position as a Member of Parliament. He needed to save his bacon and, with characteristic cunning, I have no doubt he turned the tables on Pam and used my outburst to exert emotional blackmail on her, just as his fictional character Curtis turns the tables on his poor, hapless wife, and convinces her that if she goes ahead with a divorce, she will be the one responsible for destroying their daughter's happiness, not him.

Another misguided belief that was firmly planted in childhood was that my mother had always been repelled and revolted by the idea of physical intimacy with my father. But the diaries and the letters that I found proved that she had been hopelessly, desperately in love with him for ten years – or at least until 1951, when she was writing to him in the South of France. She never owned up to having ten good seconds with him. I don't think she tried to mislead me. I think she had simply been so hurt and disillusioned by what had happened later in her marriage that she rewrote the past in her mind; she refused to admit, even to herself, that she ever could have loved such a monster. And I in turn deduced that he had always been a monster. It was an extraordinary moment when I realised that he hadn't, and that she had loved him, and that my brother and I had been conceived by parents who at the time were very much in love.

It wasn't the affairs that killed her love for him. She had no idea he was being unfaithful until the affair with Zaza. What killed her love for him was the unkindness, the insults, the taunts, the unreasonable behaviour, the verbal battering – as he acknowledges in the novel, when Gail asks Curtis about his wife.

'What about your marriage?' she asked.

'I was a big flop even in that. And don't make any mistake about it, it was my fault . . .

'Judith loved me. But I killed her love.

'And I'll tell you how. I was so busy crawling up the Fleet Street ladder by being smarmy and pleasant to people by day that at night she got the backwash of how I really felt.

'She wasn't ambitious for herself and she didn't like the ruthlessness of my ambition.'

He was right. My mother didn't share his ambition. She liked people for what they were rather than who they were, and was totally unimpressed by titles, power or money. She saw through the people who sucked up to JJ, and cringed when he smarmed over them, as he often did. She liked one or two politicians, but, on the whole, the people she wanted to spend time with were friends from the past, and local families, people who had no pretensions; but as my father climbed ever upward, he outgrew those friends and dismissed them as bores. The social life that they once had, which I found documented in JJ's early diaries, along with the cinema-going, vanished and Pam became increasingly isolated at Wellpools. He didn't like her to go out to dinner with anyone when he was in London on Friday or Saturday nights, and during the week he was always working and demanded silence.

I wish I had seen some of the good years. I only saw the bad; and I am under no illusions about the nature of the man my father turned into in later life. But it's a huge relief and a joy to discover just how easy and likeable he was in those early days before the pain in his stomach, the power and the influence of Beaverbrook took a hold and distorted his personality.

Pam didn't tell me these stories about the past because she wanted to poison me against my father. In fact she did her best to shield me from her unhappiness. She would never write about him when I was away at boarding school – her letters were filled with trivia and news about the animals. But I didn't need verbatim accounts. I was a part of it, bound up in it. I could see and hear for myself what went on between them and I made my own judgements about

who was to blame. I could see that my mother irritated him, sometimes deliberately, but nothing she ever did to him deserved the
savagery with which he attacked her. And I could see her confidence
disintegrating day by day.

My mother committed very little to paper, apart from these odd
exchanges, which she feared she would forget if she didn't write
down. At some stage, however, she must have been asked to try
and explain what had happened in her marriage, maybe by the
divorce lawyer in 1962, and she had made a start.

It's very difficult to analyse the breakdown of a marriage.
Over so many years one forgets and becomes more immune to
insults. It was a wartime marriage of two completely different
backgrounds, which I was unaware of until I had married him.
He has always resented my affection for my family and made
unpleasant remarks to and about them – not that he saw them
that often as they emigrated to Kenya after we'd been married
five years.

Eccentricity and ridiculous behaviour over food I suppose I
originally accepted because of a stomach ulcer when he said he
couldn't eat this or that because it would upset his stomach.
His ulcer was cured years ago but his fetishes get worse. He
eats no vegetables except potato, toast must be burnt and cold,
butter must be hard and cold from the fridge and preferably in
its wrapper. He refuses to eat Sainsbury's sausages, says he
doesn't like them, yet eats cold leftovers from the fridge and
repeatedly asks me to make him Scotch eggs made from
Sainsbury's sausage meat. He can't eat sage he says, yet eats
butcher's sausages always made with sage. He refuses to eat
meat cooked with onions – we had a friend to dinner and had
braised steak and I forgot to camouflage the onions! 'I can't
eat this,' he said. 'I can't possibly eat this.' Two days later I
chopped up the remains and made a steak pie. 'Absolutely
delicious steak pie,' he said.

Verbal communication is practically nonexistent – not that I
have much to contribute – but he resents being asked who he's
lunched with, played golf with, or sailed with. He's finished his

dinner before I'm halfway through and invariably goes off to polish his shoes or says, 'Do you mind if I go and work?' I only discovered that our dentist, who is also a great friend, had retired and moved when I was writing his Christmas card list.

Each evening, because he refuses to work in his study, he sits in his armchair and works. I sit in another and read or draw. One evening I said I wanted to watch an arts programme on television. 'Oh shit,' he said. 'If you'd told me before I'd have stayed in town for the night.'

Many of the insults Pam kept over the years make a note of whether JJ was 'sober' or 'tight' at the time. '*Of course nobody tells you anything because you're incapable of comprehending anything.*' '*You're just so self-righteous and you're also such a bloody bore.*'

One entire sheet, ridiculous as it might sound, is devoted to the subject of pork.

(Sober) 21.6.65 because I have pork for lunch. 'You're one of the most evil women I have ever met, and selfish. I shall cut your allowance by £10. If I had a choice between you and cyanide I'd take the cyanide.'

Me: 'Why don't you then?'

'I'm hoping you will first.'

30.12.65 Had lunch with children and his choice from menu was pork! Also ate pork twice in Lech.

31.1.67 'I had minced pork and cabbage' – lunch with Cocky Dunbar.

6.4.67 Had minced pork at lunch with Pen, Howard French and me.

18.6.67 Ate cold pork and chicken for dinner here with George Green and Daddy.

Paris, 10.9.67 'I had pigs' feet.'

6.10.67 Had spare ribs of pork.

18.12.70 'I had asparagus, pork and cheese for lunch' – with George Gale.

22.12.70 'We had suckling pig and fresh raspberries' – with Penelope.

There were a few occasions during that time when Pam walked out on him. She went to stay with her sister, who had given up the water sports in Spain and lived in England briefly, but it was little more than a gesture. She knew she couldn't stay with her sister, or anyone, indefinitely. She had no money with which to find somewhere of her own to live, apart from a housekeeping allowance, which he gave her and could obviously stop, and no skills with which to earn a living. Leaving JJ was never a realistic option. She had missed the opportunity to divorce him and although technically I am sure she could have found other grounds on which to bring the marriage to an end, she didn't have sufficient strength for the fight – and he would have put up a very bloody fight.

On each occasion that Pam did pack her bags, JJ came after her on bended knee with abject apologies. He sent huge bouquets of flowers, and promised he loved and needed her and would never be beastly again; and she went home. The irony of it all is that I believe he meant it. I also think he bitterly regretted the sharpness of his tongue, but found himself quite incapable of curbing it.

Yet I don't think he regretted the affairs. As Alan Watkins says, 'He had no objection to infidelity or affairs provided it did not lead to marital break-up. Divorce, separation, big things happening, that was awful, but to get into bed with a girl was marvellous, this was what life was about. Slap a girl on the backside and say, "Come to bed, lassie." For him sex was carefree and happy, like the little children and the snowflakes and it did not lead to these consequences of awful splits and rows.'

CHAPTER SIXTEEN

Women

Amongst the unopened mail at my father's house after his death was a moving card simply signed 'Susie'. She had been trying to contact him, she said, but there was never any reply. She pleaded with him to ring; she missed him, longed to see him and loved him desperately. I guessed that this was the Susie who had been his secretary long ago, and whom I knew he had been seeing in recent years. She was a blonde, bubbly woman just a few years older than me, with rather more energy, or so he said, than he could cope with. I was pleased for him; he was lonely and she clearly adored him. So it was with reluctance that I rang the number on the card to make sure she knew that he was dead. A week later we met at his funeral, her pretty face stained and crumpled in grief. But I was quite unprepared for the story that followed when I went to see her, a year or so later, to talk about her memories; and not for the first time, I felt ashamed of the way my father had treated people, in this case a big-hearted, generous, gutsy girl.

Susie had started working for him at the age of nineteen – and had an affair with him, which began in 1964 and lasted thirty-two years. 'I arrived for the interview late and soaking wet. I was very young and sat on this low-slung sofa thing in his office, and the first thing I did was hit myself in the face with my brolly handle. But he was very sweet, we talked about religion and when I asked him why he gave me the job he said it was because I had been to convent schools and he always thought convent girls were nice, polite and well-mannered.'

He was flirtatious from the start and she soon succumbed. 'He was this all-powerful, dynamic man. He had an aura about him, a mystique ... I'd only been there two months when he said to me one day, "I've lost the button on the top of my shirt. Can you sew it back on, I'm going out to lunch?" And he pushed his chair back and there wasn't much room between the chair and his desk and I had to squeeze between his legs and my hands were shaking and he was enjoying every single second of it.'

It was several months before the flirtation turned into anything more. It happened on board the boat one Sunday, when he invited her sailing, along with Audrey, his back-up secretary. Audrey had been to an all-night party and was not feeling well on dry land, but by the time they had been across the Solent to the Isle of Wight she was completely green, and when JJ turned mischievously to her at lunchtime and said, 'Cold rice pudding, Audrey?' she was finished. She retreated, heaving and groaning, to a bunk in the after cabin, which JJ firmly locked behind her. 'You can't do that,' said Susie. 'Of course I can, she'll be dead for hours.' Left alone, JJ slipped an arm around her and, although they had no more than a quick snuggle that afternoon, it was the beginning of the affair.

They met secretly in the flat in Fetter Lane and sometimes he took her out to dinner, to the Hispaniola, a Spanish restaurant on the Thames, and occasionally to the Ivy or Rules. Once they went to The Compleat Angler, at Marlow, and on their way in met someone he knew coming out. 'He didn't introduce me, and he fretted for a while. He was very worried about people knowing about us, he didn't want people talking.

'In the early days it was just a wonderful flirtation for him and he didn't say he loved me, although he did when he was older.' But Susie knew she wasn't his only lover. He had a private telephone line into his office, which they rang him on, and when he was speaking on that line a light came on in her office next door. 'If the light was on I was not to go into his office – not even if the Queen had wanted him.' But it particularly upset her when he made a play for other girls in the office. 'There was a girl called Stephanie and I was convinced he was pursuing her, but he swore he was just lining her up for Roderick.'

I don't know whether he saw Zaza again, or whether she was one of the people he spoke to on his private line; but I do know he kept in touch with her mother for many years. Her name was on his Christmas card list, and through her I assume he learned news of Zaza.

When Susie and JJ embarked on their affair, Susie had plenty of boyfriends but she was not in any serious relationship. All that changed after her twenty-first birthday, however, when she fell in love with a charming young army officer called John Winter and became engaged to him. JJ was delighted. 'He said it would help enormously if I married John because it would stop the office talking.'

She and John were married in 1967 and JJ was amongst the guests. 'The night I got home from honeymoon he was on the phone, and again the next morning, saying, "I've got to see you, I've simply got to see you. Come to dinner."' When she asked where, he said Wellpools, and so she did. She and John collected him at Dorking station in their little two-seater sports car and she sat on JJ's lap all the way home, where Pam had cooked dinner for them. Shortly afterwards, John was conveniently posted to Hong Kong for nine months.

But their relationship had its ups and downs. 'One day he had some Admiral in his office and halfway through the interview, "Buzz, buzz," he hauled me in. "There's a spelling mistake in this letter," he said, in a frightfully abrupt manner, "Do it again." So I backed out and as soon as the Admiral left I marched in and thumped my fists down on the desk and said, "How dare you talk to me in front of someone else in that manner?" He was really taken aback. I was about twenty or twenty-one, and I was absolutely seething. It was power, control, a point for the Admiral to take in. He had done it deliberately. I think it was the only time I shouted back, but it wasn't the only time I seethed.'

After four years they had their first serious falling out. John was coming to the end of his stay in Hong Kong and wanted her to join him there for a holiday. JJ refused to let her go, saying she could only take holidays when he was on holiday, even though there was a permanent back-up secretary in the office. She protested that she might not get another opportunity to go to Hong Kong, he dismissed it, saying, 'Nonsense, you've got your whole life.' In the end it became a point of principle, and Susie announced she was going. 'Well it's your decision,' he countered, 'but if you leave you'll never work for the *Express* again. You'll never work for me ever again, you'll never be allowed in the Beaverbrook building again.'

'I stuck to my guns and at every stage I thought he might give in, but he never did, and I never did. I always regretted leaving. I loved the job. It was a stupid thing to leave over, but I couldn't understand why he wouldn't let me go. He was cross for years.'

She found another job in Fleet Street and they would pass one another in the street from time to time but he would never make eye contact. He didn't talk to Susie for about five years but they continued to send each other birthday and Christmas cards, and sometimes there would be a note inside suggesting lunch. She travelled with her husband to his postings abroad and it was always when she was away – in Berlin or West Germany – that the contact started. 'He'd ring and say, "How's my sunshine girl? What are you doing?" It was always when I was away. Once I came home, it would stop. The closer you got to him – it was fine for a few days, but then he got irritated.

'He could be wonderful at times, absolutely sweet and charming. He always brought me little presents back when he went away, like perfume or chocolates and he bought a cashmere twin set once when he went to Gleneagles, but he could be just wicked at times too. He always made me terribly nervous, even in my fifties. I was nervous of his tongue, he could be vicious with it, absolutely lethal, and he knew where to aim every time. Even the thought of having lunch with him, made me a nervous wreck much as I wanted to go. He was such a control freak. He once took me out to lunch at the Boulestin and I had bought a new knitted trouser suit that morning and had my hair cut, and felt I was the bee's knees, and he took one look and said, "You can't come in here dressed like that." When I asked why, he said, "Ladies in here can't wear trousers," so I stood up and a waiter said, "Gosh, that's a nice outfit," so I sat down again.

'I'd try to stand up to him but I'd just get abuse. That's when he could be really spiteful, but I would think, why should I be submissive? I could feel myself disintegrating in this relationship, but I couldn't cut him out of my life, I loved him to bits, and I thought he was so wonderful most of the time that I didn't ever want to upset him. How can one man make such a mark?'

Susie's relationship with my father followed an all too familiar pattern. The belittling, the petulance, the kindness then the cruelty, and the hot and cold nature of it – wanting contact when close intimacy was impossible, yet shying away from it when there was a chance of seeing one another. It was as though he couldn't cope with any kind of real closeness, as if he was afraid of it. He wanted her but on his own terms, wanted her to love him, but was compelled to hurt her, to spoil it, the way he spoilt every other relationship he ever had. I felt no animosity towards Susie, in fact quite the reverse; I felt sorry for her, just as I felt sorry for so many of the people who had suffered at the hands of my father.

Susie was not alone of course; she was not his first affair during his marriage to my mother and she was not the last. He used to tell Susie, 'I've had every woman I have ever wanted,' and she believed him. During the 1970s, there was a journalist on the *Sunday Express*, who was married with children. I am not naming her because she is still married, and her children know nothing of the past. The affair lasted some time – she was very smitten by him – and during the course of it she became pregnant. The baby, she knew, could not have been fathered by anyone else. He refused to believe it, and the row and the insults that ensued can only be guessed at, but she was a strong and determined character. She demanded a blood test, which would prove that he was the father of her child. The test was carried out by Sam Oram, a cardiac surgeon who was a friend of my father. It proved negative, and she suspects to this day that Sam Oram switched the blood sample with someone else's in order to produce the right result. If she is right, I have a much-loved half-sister who is the same age as my children.

If she's right, the question remains why did my father deny it? Was it simply to save his own neck or was it more pragmatic? If he had been identified as the father, it would have destroyed two marriages, two families and possibly his career as well. My brother and I were grown up and married, but her children were young and vulnerable. And for what? He would have had to pay for the child, certainly, but he would never have married her. However dishonourably he behaved, however angry she must have felt, I suspect she and her children, all of them, were better off the way they were.

There were rumours in the *Sunday Express* that JJ had fathered another child, but these were completely unfounded, as the mother is the first to admit. The timing is simply wrong. But he did have a brief affair with the girl. It began on the day the entire staff of the *Sunday Express* in London, plus the regional offices in Glasgow and Manchester, gave a lunch for JJ at the Press Club to celebrate his twenty-fifth anniversary as Editor. He feigned horror when told that a party had been organised, but stayed on after the lunch, drinking at the bar, talking to everyone. This was very unusual, but a colleague remembers it well. 'By 6.00 p.m. he was absolutely gone. I said goodbye to him and I could see he didn't know who I was. He was getting interested in the women around and a number were getting invitations to come back to Wellpools.'

The one that agreed was a secretary in her late twenties. First they went back to his office where their drunken fumblings were interrupted by the Sports Editor. By the time they reached Waterloo it was late, and the train they climbed aboard was empty. JJ was dying for a pee, and there was no loo on the train. By Clapham Junction he could hold it no longer and to his companion's amazement, he opened the door and relieved himself luxuriantly onto the track below. At Wellpools – my mother was not at home – he was beyond anything other than deep sleep, but awoke the next morning declaring that she would be the next Mrs Junor and they would 'make babies together'. It was the beginning of a brief affair, conducted thereafter in his flat in London on Friday nights, where his first priority seemed to be watching *I Love Lucy* with Lucille Ball on the television.

His heart was clearly not in this liaison, but she had high hopes. She burst into floods of tears in the office one day and confessed to a colleague that she was madly in love. Thinking this was a married reporter with whom she had been having an affair, he warned her there was no future in it, but she assured him there might be. After a while it became clear she wasn't talking about the reporter at all. He probed. 'It's someone very senior,' she said. 'Very, very senior.' His mind went back to the party, where he had seen her talking to JJ, and he tumbled. Excitedly, she told him what had happened.

But it didn't last. It was not many weeks before she was crying on her colleague's shoulder again. 'Something's happened,' she said miserably. 'I don't know what's going on; he's giving me the cold shoulder, I don't know what to do.' A little later JJ told her someone else was coming to stay at the flat and she wouldn't be able to go there. Gradually, she realised it was over.

My father's view of women was very black and white. They were either virgins or sluts. As his daughter, I had to remain a virgin, preferably forever. His son, however, should have as much sexual experience as possible – as should all men; it was in the nature of men to need variety. He saw nothing reprehensible or contradictory in this at all. Women were there to be plundered. They were adornments, playthings to be picked up and put down when they were no longer needed. Those who married were there to cook, keep house and bring up children. They were almost without exception intellectually inferior, and he liked them to keep their mouths shut and their opinions to themselves. He enjoyed being seen with glamorous women – it boosted his ego – but I think that secretly he rather despised them. He certainly relished any opportunity to belittle women; he made nasty remarks about them, and was quick to put women down. And there is no doubt that he much preferred the company of men.

Unsurprisingly, it followed that none of the women who worked for him on the *Sunday Express*, was in any position of authority. In the 1950s, when he became Editor, that was not so unusual – there were scarcely any women executives in the newspaper business – but over the following decades the picture elsewhere changed dramatically, yet still there were no female Department Editors on the *Sunday Express*. His attitude infuriated the women on the staff, but never more so than at the dinner to celebrate the newspaper's fiftieth anniversary in January 1969. It was a grand, star-studded, black-tie affair held at the Savoy Hotel, hosted by Sir Max Aitken, who succeeded his father as Chairman of Beaverbrook Newspapers – but not as Lord Beaverbrook. He disclaimed the barony on the grounds that there could only ever be one Lord Beaverbrook. The *Sunday Express* had attacked Harold Wilson relentlessly during the 1964 election when Wilson became Prime Minister, but he and my father were friends of old and, to JJ's delight, Wilson agreed to be guest of honour. And endeared himself to the room with a wicked parody of Cross-Bencher.

'As he lightly taps his golden brown breakfast egg this sunny Sunday morning what is *Sunday Express* Editor, John Junor, 50, expecting me to write? Be sure it is words to warm the heart of James Harold Wilson, 52, as he lightly taps his golden-brown Labrador, Paddy, 2, this sunny Sunday morning. For why? Assuredly because chubby Premier Wilson is to be a guest of Editor John Junor, 50, and Publisher Max Aitken, 48, at the star-studded *Sunday Express* 50th Anniversary Dinner.'

Star-studded it was, but it was studiously male. JJ had invited every man on the staff down to the office boys to that anniversary dinner, he had invited the Prime Minister, the President of the United States, President Nasser of Egypt, people from all over the world, but no women.

'I don't think he liked women,' said one reporter, echoing others. 'He fancied ostensibly beautiful ones, but he couldn't cope with women who weren't overly sexy.' When Jimmy Kinlay, the Features Editor, realised that no women had been invited – including big-name writers like Anne Edwards and Vernonica Papworth – he went to see JJ.

'Do you think this is a good idea to exclude these women writers, and reporters?' he asked.

'Oh yes, this is not for women. They've no business there.'

'But mightn't it cause resentment?'

'Well we can't help that,' said JJ, and arranged for cases of wine with notes from Sir Max Aitken inside to be sent to each of them instead.

The women were absolutely furious, also rather hurt, and in no way mollified to find the case of wine on each of their doorsteps with a note from Max saying, 'I'm sorry you couldn't go to the dinner. I hope this is some sort of compensation.'

JJ recognised, however, that women writers were important to the paper, yet he didn't take on anyone he thought unattractive, and could be scathing about anyone he thought plain. He once invited Jean Rook to lunch, intending to offer her a job. He was always on the lookout for new talent to bring to the *Sunday Express*, and had spotted Jean Rook's writing in the *Daily Sketch*, then in the *Daily Mail* and was keen to have her. So, in September 1971, he invited her to the Boulestin. As he told Richard Ingrams, Editor of *Private Eye*, 'She came in and, Christ, I caught sight of her, and I saw Reggie Maudling was lunching on his own and I said, "Reggie, come and join us." I couldn't have faced having lunch with that woman on my own. Reggie didn't know what on earth was going on but was perfectly happy to have me pay for his lunch.'

During lunch JJ said, 'Jean, I'm very impressed with your work. I'm going to have a word about you with Ian McColl on the *Daily Express*.' Afterwards he went straight back to his office and dictated a memo to Max Aitken. 'If I were running the *Daily Express* I would be searching like mad for a controversial woman columnist. I think that such a woman is Jean Rook ... I saw her today and I sensed from her conversation that her greatest ambition still is to work for the *Daily Express* ...' Next thing Jean Rook had been hired by the *Daily Express*, where she became a legendary figure, and inspiration for the satirical Glenda Slag column in *Private Eye*.

JJ hired pretty women without so much as bothering to read their cuttings, and even took on a secretary – Paula Bessell, nick-named Pooh – who was completely untrained. JJ was also very fond of Henrietta Mackay, the Cross-Bencher secretary known as Mac, and she of him. Once he became Editor of the *Sunday Express* they worked together for thirty years and their relationship was always rather special. Years later the big question vexing *Sunday Express* staff was whether or not they had had an affair. Mac always refused to say, but promised she would tell all when she retired. The staff awaited the day with bated breath. Come the day, in April 1984, when her husband's stroke forced her into early retirement, she coolly announced she had changed her mind. She confessed to me, however, that they had had a little romance but no affair. I am sure it was not for want of trying on my father's behalf.

Susan Barnes bluffed her way in. She wrote to JJ saying that she believed they had met at a *Spectator* party, which she knew she hadn't but easily could have done, and asking whether she could see him with a view to writing as an American living in London. 'I have never been to a *Spectator* party in my life,' came his reply, which was also untrue, 'but telephone my secretary and make an appointment to come and see me.'

'When I walked into his office, he grinned and I had the sense he was glad I didn't look like the back end of a horse.' Susan lied when he asked what experience she had, saying she had written occasionally for *Women's Journal*, *Vogue* and the *Baltimore Sun*, although she was, in fact, not long out of Vasser. 'As I was leaving he said, "Oh and could you just let me have two or three of your cuttings, not many, just two or three would do." I said, "Oh Mr Junor, it will take me some time to get them because I left them behind in Baltimore." I have never known whether he believed me.'

How he could tell I will never know, but my father had an unerring instinct for a lie or a half-truth, or even something you just didn't particularly want to tell him. And without fail he would ask the one question that was awkward to answer. Months could go by without him asking who I had lunch with, for example, but the one time I had a secret or had seen someone I didn't want him to know about, he would ask. He also had a way of looking at you, which implied that he didn't believe a word you said. A grin came over his face and he would nod knowingly, and the more you protested your innocence, the more he grinned and nodded. If Susan Barnes had had a cupboard full of cuttings in Baltimore, I am quite certain he wouldn't have asked to see a single one.

But, for all her sex appeal, it wasn't long before Susan experienced the rough side of his tongue. She wanted to go to France in the hope of interviewing Picasso. JJ agreed until, unaware that he would allow none of his staff to accept freebees, she told him that she had arranged for the French tourist agency to pay for her hotel. 'He absolutely hit the ceiling and said, if I was going to have them pay for me I would have to stop working for him.' The next problem was Picasso. 'I went to his house, there were great, barred security gates, a long drive, I couldn't even see the house and they wouldn't let me in. When I got back I had to tell John I had failed in this assignment and he went absolutely red in the face, and was very, very angry. "I know what you did," he said. "You went off there to be with your boyfriend." I was outraged. I can't remember whether I burst into tears, but I certainly made it clear that this was intolerable. First to be knocked back on an assignment, then to be told that I was in the South of France with my boyfriend being paid for by the *Sunday Express*. Then the row was over. It was all quite quick and he was pleasant before I left the office.'

The boyfriend was Anthony Crosland, the Labour MP, and in January 1964, Susan went to JJ to tell him that she was getting married and would therefore be leaving. 'He said, "I know why you're leaving the *Sunday Express* – because Tony Crosland doesn't want you to work for it." And because I didn't want a great vendetta to begin, I said, "No, no, it isn't that. I have to look for a house and have some time with my children [from a previous marriage] during these first months of marriage", and he didn't believe a word of it, but he wished me well. The truth is it would have been awkward for me to carry on, as the *Sunday Express* was so, so very anti-Labour, and Tony had been Hugh Gaitskell's right hand. You have a certain loyalty to your newspaper.'

Jimmy Kinlay remembers the occasion slightly differently. 'JJ reduced her to tears. She went in to tell him she was leaving the *Sunday Express* to marry Crosland and came back in floods of tears. He was terrible, horrible. The idea of her leaving was such a mark of ingratitude and going off to marry a Labour politician was just an insult.'

When Labour won the General Election that October, Harold Wilson became Prime Minister, and shortly afterwards Tony Crosland was appointed Secretary of State for Education. One evening there was a knock at the door and there stood a reporter and a photographer from the *Sunday Express*, two of Susan's former colleagues. They wanted to know how the new Secretary of State's stepchildren were being educated. Labour, of course, espoused the comprehensive system, and her children were then at a private school in London paid for by Susan's father. 'I didn't know what all this fuss was about comprehensives. I didn't know a comprehensive was simply like an American High School. I was ignorant of the whole British State system. It was a hopeless interview, absolutely hopeless and one in which I could only be seen to be the idiot about education that I was.' The interview took place on a Friday night. The next morning she rang my father and begged him not to use the piece. 'Of course I'll not run it, if that's what you'd like,' he said. Then added, 'Tony Crosland will never be referred to in the *Sunday Express* again.'

JJ regarded the people he worked with as his family and, although he was rough with them from time to time, he would have been astonished to discover that either they or their spouses harboured any ill will. And, in truth, not many of them did. As Michael Dove, who was Chief Reporter, says, 'I think I can speak for most of us. I worked for him for thirty years and, while we tell stories that may appear to be against him, we had this affection, sometimes grudging, but otherwise why did we stay? I think it developed rather like the Korean war captives or Patty Hearst: you fell in love with your captors. There was a respect and fondness for him. Peter McKay always said he loved the man.

'The *Sunday Express* was like a family. He was the great patriarch and, because there was no question of anyone superseding him, there was no backstabbing. When Ted Dickinson joined from the *Daily Express*, he said, "There are only really two elements in this office, JJ and the rest of us. Welcome to the *Sunday Express*." There was no empire building. A lot of us still socialise together, and did then – cricket, golf, parties. He could socialise very well. Some of those parties at Wellpools . . .'

The *Sunday Express* had a cricket team, which varied in degrees of ability, run by Michael Dove and Victor Patrick, JJ's deputy. One year JJ told them they must fix a match with his local village team in Charlwood, and come to lunch at Wellpools first. It was a blisteringly hot day, and everyone ate out on the lawn – the team plus wives, and other enthusiasts. Pam had prepared the food and, as usual there was plenty of wine, which the team made short work of. After lunch JJ produced his latest toy – a motor scooter – and urged everyone to have a go on it. 'Brendan,' he said, to Brendan Mulholland, a reporter, 'you look like a man who can ride a motor-bike.' So Brendan, who was on to his second if not third bottle of wine, jumped on to the scooter and careered dangerously around the garden, through a hedge and into some rose bushes before JJ managed to grab the scooter and suggest it was time for some cricket.

Just then, JJ spotted Dave Saunders, Deputy Features Editor and his wife, Kathleen, stuffing his pockets and her handbag with cheese from the table. He watched this and said to Victor Patrick, 'Victor, is Dave short of money?' 'No,' said Victor, 'I think they're just fond of cheese.'

The party moved down to the cricket pitch, where the drinks continued to flow, and JJ, incapable of staying in one place for long, kept finding excuses to leave the match. One of the wives was complaining of the heat, so he suggested she should come back to Wellpools and have a shower. After much badgering she agreed, drove back to the house with JJ, had a shower and came out of the shower to find JJ in his Y-fronts, ready for action. 'John,' she said, 'we've known each other a long time, don't let's spoil it.' And she quickly dried, dressed and dashed back to Charlwood.

After the match, the drinkers moved from the cricket pitch to the village pub. JJ disappeared for a few hours, to a cocktail party given by Ted Heath, but came back to find them still hard at it. And time had not dampened his ardour, although by now Michael Dove's wife, Marlene, was the object of his affection. 'Suddenly Marlene and Penny Hart disappeared,' says Michael, 'and we were all sitting, chatting and drinking, and it was like a Brian Rix farce. The door opened and there was Penny saying, "Have you seen JJ?" "He went that way." "Well don't tell him we're going out this way." Moments later JJ arrived. "Have you seen Marlene and Penny?" "I think they went out that way, John." They were running around and he was pinching bums and grabbing what he could. He disappeared breathless; then Marlene came in and sat down on a stool with her back to the door, and suddenly these hands slid under her arms and clamped over each breast, and without looking round she said, "Oh you're back, John." "How did you know it was me?" he said. "You must be fey, you must come back to the farm and discuss it."'

And so they all went back to Wellpools. 'We had three Australians playing for us that day who were overawed with the surroundings. "Do the Sunday Express do this every weekend with the Editor? Jeeze." By the fire was a little Queen Anne chair. Peter Vane was doing the maître d' job, making sure everyone had a pint of Scotch – we'd been drinking all day remember – and finally he lowered himself into this chair which promptly splintered. Pete was so embarrassed he didn't know where to put himself; and I thought the Aussies were going to die. One of them, a huge chap, was laughing so much he got a stitch, leapt up, threw himself back, missed the settee, and crashed into the central heating radiator which promptly bent. So JJ was looking at a bent radiator, a smashed Queen Anne chair – which he assured Peter didn't matter "Because it was old anyway" – and he turned to Victor and said, "Victor, next time I suggest you bring an axe."'

CHAPTER SEVENTEEN

Heavy Father

There is a scene in my father's novel where Curtis is sitting next to his fifteen-year-old daughter Sally at Midnight Mass.

> He looked at Sally sitting beside him in the pew – her eyes shining with the innocent love of Christmas . . . He knelt and began fiercely to pray.
>
> 'Dear God, please let me get through to you tonight just this once. I'm honestly sorry for all the things I've done wrong. Please God, don't let Sally inherit my weaknesses. Please may she stay pure and good. Please, too, may I not harm Gail. Please understand my weaknesses and forgive them. Please, too, may I not hurt Judith. But please don't ask me to be faithful because I know I can't be.'

If I never wholeheartedly trusted my father after the apple incident at the age of six, he never trusted me after my passion for horses gave way to an interest in boys. He was clearly terrified that the years of lecturing about the evils of sex and the importance of purity might not have sunk in, and this was when our relationship really began to fall apart. His decision to sell my pony while I was away at school, without either consulting or telling me, didn't help.

His interest in my schooling was minimal, and he never came to any school events or plays, but since these usually happened on a Saturday, when he was working, he had a cast-iron excuse. The only time he made an exception was the day I was confirmed, when my housemistress – I discover nearly forty years after the event – wrote to him suggesting that it was important for me that he should be there. So he drove down for the church service then whizzed off back to the office immediately afterwards.

This was a source of some relief to me. I was much happier to have him at arm's length and I certainly didn't feel neglected or unloved. Every week without fail he wrote to me, long newsy letters in his distinctive forward-sloping handwriting, in blue ink on blue notepaper, telling me what he had been doing: dinner parties he and Pam had been to or given, films they had seen, who he'd played golf or tennis with, and what the animals were up to. He was always thrilled if my pony had been friendly, although his dealings with her were almost exclusively from the safe side of the fence.

> *My darling, darling Tuppy,*
> *Perry got out last Thursday night and came nosing round the dustbin. I gave her a sugar lump and left her out with the gates closed. The next morning she was poking her head through the kitchen window looking for food. She is adorable.*

My mother found her less adorable:

> *Darling love,*
> *I'm absolutely furious with your b—— horse – she got into the kitchen garden this morning and has eaten all my beautiful cabbages 'cept three!! She then refused to be caught and went careering all over the garden – two hours later she made the mistake of coming to the kitchen window where I caught her and put her back!*

It was not surprising she kept trying to escape. She was bored and lonely in her field – the foal having long gone – and I scarcely rode her any more, so it was only sensible that she should go to a new home. But I never even had a chance to say goodbye, and never saw her again. I don't blame JJ, as I know he would never have done it if he had known how upset I would be. He simply didn't appreciate what she meant to me – and since we were never able to talk about anything that mattered, how could he have done?

After the boat came into our lives, we no longer spent our summer holidays together, but we did continue to go away as a family in the winter. Every year from 1962 onwards, Roderick and I were included in the skiing holiday, and we spent the two weeks between Christmas and the start of the school term in January staying in the Hotel Krone in the Tyrolean village of Lech.

I always rather dreaded the holiday because it was impossible to leave the house without a row. JJ suffered from the most terrible *Reiseangst* before every outing, but never so chronically, it seemed to me, as before our skiing trip: he flapped, he shouted, he went red in the face and threatened to cancel 'the whole goddamn thing'. He then drove to Folkestone, often through treacherous weather conditions, at top speed, with an atmosphere in the car that you could cut with a knife. We would leave the car at Folkestone and take a ferry across the Channel, and it was not until we were on board that he would cheer up. After making himself known to the Captain – as he did to every captain on every boat – we would sit down to a three-course lunch in the restaurant. For someone with my proclivities, December was not a good month to be crossing the English Channel, and I have never been able to look at a bowl of green pea soup since. At Calais, we would board a wagon-lit train and – this was the magical part – we would go to sleep in our bunks that night, in the drab surroundings of the noisy French station, and wake up next morning in a fairyland of mountains and bright, crisp, clean snow.

Lech was a pretty little village nestling in the valley, with a church spire in the shape of an onion. There was just one road in and out, which was blocked if there was a heavy fall of snow. It was glorious and despite the traumatic start, I loved it. I loved the skiing, I loved the bands and the dancing, I loved the rich hot chocolate and Sachertorte that I had for tea every afternoon when the temperature started to drop, and the horse-drawn sleigh rides through the fir trees. We had some wonderful holidays and, as usual, JJ – and his largesse – attracted people to him like a magnet. Every night he would preside over rather drunken gatherings, and flirt outrageously. One year he was very taken by a girl who couldn't pronounce her 'r's and for years he adopted an affectation of rolling his 'r's.

As with everything else, he was too impatient to learn to ski properly. So, although he was an enthusiastic skier in short bursts, he was never entirely in control of his skis. He was also a menace on the drag-lift, and many a skier, tipped off into the deep snow between the fir trees halfway up the mountain, lived to regret sharing a T-bar with my father. One year, however, JJ was schussing down a narrow, steep slope, travelling fast with skis parallel, when his skis fell into deep, icy ruts which took his legs in different directions with catastrophic results. A blood-wagon was summoned to return him and his broken ankle to base and he spent the rest of the holiday in plaster. For several days he was confined to bed, then he was up and about on crutches, and I don't remember a period when he was more bad-tempered and unpleasant to all of us. Under normal circumstances he would take it in turns to lash out at Roderick and me, thus ensuring that one of us was still speaking to him, but on this occasion he snapped and snarled at us all – whilst continuing to be the life and soul of the party amongst others. It was the last year Roderick came on a family holiday. He decided he had had enough, and the next year went skiing with a party from Cambridge, where he was now at university.

Back at the office, on JJ's return, the jokes came thick and fast. 'What's the ankle on this story?' someone might ask, or 'I think we need a new ankle here.' And Bill Martin, the cartoonist, produced a mock-up of the *Sunday Express* devoted to the ankle, with cartoons of JJ hurtling down the mountain, skis flapping wildly: 'Is it *Sputnik III*? STRANGE BODY FLASHES ACROSS SKY. AUSTRIAN WOMEN PANIC. Abominable Snow Man: "... I thought I was skiing things ..." There's a New Look on the Slopes. GIVE YOURSELF A BREAK IN THE "ALPS 1".' 'This childishness must stop,' said JJ testily, who was not fond of puns and not good at laughing at himself. But it went beyond the office. 'Ah, you've stubbed your toe once too often, John,' said Iain Macleod, on seeing him hobble into a restaurant one day.

It was two years after the broken ankle, when I was sixteen, that

I seriously fell in love for the first time. He was German, he was eighteen and his name was Philipp Solf. We met at a tea dance in the Hotel Post, where he was staying with his mother and younger brother, and for the next two weeks we were inseparable. We seemed to have so much in common, so much to talk about, and had such fun in each other's company. I had never been happier. He was a fantastic skier and every day we went up the mountain together. I abandoned ski school and following his lead, skied like I had never skied before, fast and fearlessly. He could have taken me over a precipice and I would have followed. He lived in Munich but was at boarding school in Switzerland and spoke English and French fluently. He was charming, he was polite and his manners were impeccable – JJ could not have hoped to see me fall for someone from a more respectable or cosmopolitan family.

At the end of the holiday we parted with great sadness but a determination to see each other again, and when I was back in England he sent me a gold ring, made out of a Deutschmark, which I still treasure. It is perfectly possible, of course, that this was nothing more than an adolescent holiday romance – but I didn't think so at the time and now, thirty-five years later, I still think it could have been more significant.

Back in our respective homes and schools, we wrote avidly. We sent each other books and music we thought the other might enjoy, and plotted how we might meet again. The perfect opportunity arose. There was to be a huge family gathering and party for his cousin's christening in Munich during the summer holidays. Could I come? His mother wrote to JJ formally inviting me, and saying that if he would give his consent, she would meet me at the airport, I would stay with her sister in a house full of girls and, he need have no fear, I would be closely chaperoned for my entire stay. JJ wrote back saying he would be only too pleased to allow me to visit Germany. There was just one condition. I could not travel on my own. If she were prepared to fly Philipp to England to collect me, and then travel back with me again on the return journey, then he would be happy for me to go. Otherwise, he was sorry but it was out of the question.

Not surprisingly, Baroness Solf found the conditions as bizarre as they were unreasonable. She replied politely that it would not be possible to fly Philipp back and forth twice, as the cost was more than she could afford – but reiterated that she would take the greatest possible care of me – she would look after me as though I were her own daughter. JJ stuck to his guns and, despite my pleas, and Pam's pleas on my behalf, I didn't go to Germany. I was furious with my father and embarrassed beyond words. Philipp and I continued to correspond but, after a year or so, it seemed rather pointless to pretend that our love for each other was going anywhere and we both moved on. Three years later he telephoned out of the blue and said he was coming to London. We met and had a wonderful day together, but by then I was engaged. It was too late.

My father had an antipathy towards the Germans, which I suppose was endemic in his generation, and he no doubt thought that, if I had the opportunity, I would sleep with Philipp, which he couldn't have borne. But I think the real reason why he effectively scuppered our relationship was because he was frightened that it might have been more than a holiday romance and that I might have married him and ended up living abroad; and that would have been the end of his world.

That October I was at school for my seventeenth birthday, and amongst my post was a bulky envelope with JJ's unmistakable handwriting on it. I ripped it open and a bunch of car keys fell onto the table. Inside the envelope was a Polaroid photograph of a shining white Fiat 500. On the back of the photo, he had written: 'Well, do you like it? I've just learned this morning that you've got a fabulous registration number – NPK 999D. In case you can't tell from the picture, she's white with a black sunshine roof and red upholstery and looks super. Love Daddy.'

It was the car he had promised me when I was three years old, the day he sold the Morris Minor. I was completely thrilled. I had always loved cars – the whole family did – and had been driving them off-road for years. As soon as I passed my test at the end of the Christmas holidays, I used to take my car out, just for the sheer thrill of driving. JJ let me drive the Aston Martin too, and he would very often bring home high-performance cars for the weekend that

Bobby Glenton, the *Sunday Express* motoring correspondent, was reviewing, and I drove them all.

The following summer I left school with three 'A' Levels and no burning desire to go to university. Benenden at that time was no great academic hothouse – more a safe haven for princesses. There were four during my time there: in addition to Princess Anne, there was Princess Basma, the King of Jordan's sister, and Princesses Mary and Sahine from Ethiopia. They were Emperor Haile Selassie's grandchildren and had grown up in a palace with lions roaming in the gardens. Although the school took 'A' Levels seriously, there was not much of a thrust towards university, or if there was it passed me by. I loved writing and had decided I wanted to be a journalist; I could see no good reason for delaying the process. What I needed was to learn shorthand and typing, so I planned to do a course at St James's Secretarial College in London.

JJ had never pushed me towards journalism; in fact we had never discussed what I might do with my life – those were the sort of discussions I suspect we both would have loved but which we could never have had together. I would never have felt safe telling him what was going on in my head, and he would have found some reason to become angry, and that would have been the end of it. So why did I choose it? Partly because I enjoyed writing, partly because it was in my blood, and partly I suppose because of him. I suppose, subconsciously, although I can hardly believe I am writing this, I wanted him to be pleased.

When he realised that I had not only missed the opportunity to apply for Oxbridge, but had failed to apply anywhere else as well, he hit the roof and forced me to sit down one evening and fill in a university entrance form. I sat across the room from him, seething with indignation. Of course he was right to have encouraged me to go to university, and I was idiotic to have decided against it but, as always, it was the manner in which it was done. He never held a rational conversation with me, wasn't interested in debate or bringing me to his way of thinking by persuasion or superior argument. He had to be the one calling the shots, he had to be in control of everything, and because he was the one who paid for everything, I had no choice but to do what he wanted. With the university handbook in front of me, I looked at the various options and picked the one that was furthest from home, and him. I chose St Andrews in Scotland. But first came nine months at secretarial college.

For the first term at secretarial college, I lived at home and commuted to London, but latterly JJ let me live in his flat in Clifford's Inn, which he only used – officially at least – on a Friday night, by which time I would be at home for the weekend. For the first time in my life I began to have a social life. I made lots of friends, most of whom lived in London, many sharing flats with other girls. In the evenings we used to go to cafés and pubs in the King's Road, like the Chelsea Potter and the Markham, to meet up with their friends, or we went to parties or films. Having lived in the depths of the country, and spent five years in a school in the depths of the country, this was a revelation. I didn't go wild; there were no drunken orgies, no drugs, but I had fun.

JJ became suspicious. I had taken a friend home that he took against. She wore very short skirts, black eye make-up – as we all did in 1968 – and had badly dyed blonde hair and dark shadows under her eyes. JJ decided she was a tart and probably a drug addict. She wasn't at all. She was quite a damaged girl, in fact, with cripplingly low self-esteem and a boyfriend who beat her up. JJ said he didn't like her and didn't like me hanging around pubs like the Chelsea Potter. Only cheap girls went to pubs, they were dangerous places, full of drugs and sex. He wouldn't listen to anything I had to say; he had made up his mind. I chose to ignore him. My friends were the sons and daughters of the affluent middle classes; there was neither a degenerate nor a drug addict amongst them.

One Friday night I was in the Chelsea Potter with a group of friends, not planning to stay long because I had to drive home to Surrey. Suddenly the doors flew open, Wild West style, and there stood JJ and Roderick dressed in dark suits and overcoats and looking as out of place as a pair of undertakers at a christening. They came across to our table and said, 'Get up, Penelope, you're leaving, you're coming home right now.' My humiliation and embarrassment was absolute. I protested vehemently, but they had their hands on my arms and I had no alternative but to get up, apologise pitifully to my astonished friends, and leave. Outside, JJ and I had the most terrible row during which he threatened to make me a ward of court if I continued to defy him and hang out in seedy pubs and mix with degenerates, drug addicts and sluts. Had he not seen the friends I had been sitting with? And Roderick, who had always been my ally against JJ, supported him.

It took me a long time to recover from the Chelsea Potter incident. My father and, tacitly, my brother, too, had accused and condemned me without listening to anything I had to say. I was not a child, I was eighteen. As it happened, I was a very sensible eighteen-year-old, not to say faintly puritanical – I was far too frightened by the years of lecturing to be anything else. My friends were upright, honest and law-abiding, I didn't sleep around, stay out all night, or get paralytically drunk, and I didn't take drugs. I had been given marijuana on holiday in Spain the summer before and would never touch it again. I hated the feeling of losing control – as I did if I had too much to drink. If we had ever been able to talk about such things rationally and unemotionally, I might have told JJ so – my mother knew – but he would never have heard what I said. I was condemned in his eyes whatever I did: damned if I did and damned if I didn't.

Of all the shock and indignation I felt that night, Roderick's betrayal was the worst. Throughout my life, he and I had shared everything together, all our innermost thoughts and feelings. We had commiserated on JJ's moods and temper, been at the receiving end of his boorish behaviour. How could he have stood shoulder to shoulder with him and manhandled me as though I was some kind of desperado in need of restraint? How could he stand by and listen while our father threatened to make me a ward of court? He knew I had done nothing to deserve any of this, nothing at all.

But what I realised that night was that something had happened to us. Our relationship had changed; we were no longer on the same side of the fence. Roderick was becoming as protective, or jealous, of my virtue as my father was. He was changing in other ways too. Three years before, he had fallen in love with a Swiss girl he met on the cross-Channel ferry, on his way home from a university skiing trip. Suzy Lüthi looked as though she had stepped from the pages of *Vogue* – whether she was strolling down Bond

Street or battling to keep her balance on the deck of *Outcast*. The blonde hair and the make-up were always perfect, whether it was eight in the morning or midnight, and everything she wore, from her underwear to her handbag, bore a designer label. Suzy was style personified and she looked wonderful on it; and as time passed, her fixation rubbed off on Roderick, who previously had taken no particular interest in labels, and who had been happy to be relaxed and scruffy, as I was.

Suzy was almost nineteen when they met and came from a wealthy family in Bern. Her father, Walter, was an eminent gynae-cologist, and Hanny, her mother, a talented naive painter. She her-self had been the Swiss Ladies' Golf Champion – the youngest ever – but was so sick of it she never wanted to look at a golf club again. She was on her way to London to work. Roderick was twenty and in his second year at Cambridge, reading history at Fitzwilliam.

Roderick loved Cambridge and was happier there than I had ever seen him. He made some good friends, punted on the river, won a half-blue playing tennis, spoke in debates, and spent much of his free time working as a reporter for *Varsity*, the university newspaper. Yet every week he would find time to write to Pam and JJ, and to me at school. Sometimes he would come with some friends to take me out on a Saturday afternoon, which sent my stock at school soaring, and after he met Suzy, he would occasionally bring her down too.

Initially she and I got on well together; and when he went off to America after graduating, to work on *Newsweek* in their Boston bureau for six months, we were almost like sisters. We both loved Roderick and we both had JJ to deal with. JJ and Suzy did not get on. I doubt that he would have liked any woman who planned to marry his son, but this was particularly tricky. Apart from their love of Roderick, they had nothing in common whatever, not even golf, because, having given it up, Suzy now detested the game. There was never any affection in their relationship at all. Perhaps in part it was a cultural difference. Perhaps it was simply a clash of person-ality. It was certainly a clash of style. And maybe JJ sensed, as I did, that Roderick was changing and Suzy was having a greater influence over him than he had. Having been brought up in the country surrounded by animals and muddy wellington boots, jeans and chaos, he became a designer-dressed, meticulous and rather serious, urban man.

They married in Switzerland in September 1968. I was a bridesmaid and I could not have been happier for them. Suzy looked sensational in her bridal gown against the backdrop of Bern Cathedral; and he looked immaculate beside her. They were a beautiful couple, and clearly both blissfully happy. It was a very jolly party with everyone on their best behaviour. Suzy's father, Walter, was a huge man, larger than life with a passion for hunting and dogs, and he and JJ struck up a great friendship – enhanced perhaps by the language barrier. Pam and Hanny, with their art in common – as well as difficult, domineering husbands – also became firm friends, and I got on famously with Suzy's younger brother Roland. But it was a false dawn. Our relationship was never the same again, and it was the beginning of years of difficulty between Roderick and JJ.

Roderick was working in Fleet Street by this time. He was fascinated by news, loved newspapers, and it would have been unthinkable for him to do anything else with his life. Although JJ may have kindled his interest in journalism, by quizzing him about the *Sunday Express* from a tender age, he went into the business entirely of his own accord. He returned from America with an impressive collection of cuttings, wrote letters to various newspaper editors and, after a spell on the *Daily Sketch*, was taken on by the *Daily Telegraph*, whose offices were next door to the *Express* building in Fleet Street.

JJ was delighted to have his son in the building next door, thrilled to have him following in his footsteps, and proud to be seen walking down Fleet Street with him. They talked news and newspapers with impunity, and Roderick continued to take a detailed interest in the *Sunday Express* each week.

It was in the family context that the relationship started to go awry. Roderick and Suzy moved into a modern flat in Barnes after they were married, which looked like the inside of the Palace of Versailles, and was about as cosy. It was furnished almost exclusively with Louis XV and Louis XVI antiques, which had been shipped over from Switzerland. JJ felt acutely uncomfortable there, in every sense of the word, and was dismayed to discover that his son, over whom he had always exercised such control, felt so at home.

CHAPTER EIGHTEEN

Battle Royal

My stomach was turning somersaults as I stood in the boardroom of a merchant bank in Piccadilly last summer, waiting for the chief executive. He was expecting me and would be with me in just a moment I was assured. I flicked through a copy of the *Financial Times* lying on a cabinet at the far end of the room, watched by half a dozen beady-eyed chairmen whose portraits hung from the walls, and wondered what he would look like, what he would be like. We had not met since 1968.

After what felt like an age, I heard his voice in the corridor outside – an unmistakable dark brown voice. My heart stopped. Then the big heavy door swung open, and thirty-odd years fell away. He came towards me with arms outstretched and a big grin on his face. His big brown eyes crinkled just as they always had done. Nothing had changed. He had not lost a hair from his head, not added a grey one to the dark curly tangle. He stood straight and tall in an immaculate pinstriped suit, and looked tanned and fit. The only sign that he was pushing sixty was a pair of glasses peeping out of his top pocket.

We had first met in January 1968 at a restaurant in the Fulham Road. One of my friends at secretarial college gave a cocktail party at her parents' house in Mayfair and afterwards a group of us went on to dinner. A couple of people I hadn't seen at the party joined our table. One stood out from the rest of the group and was slightly older. He was tall, dark and direct, with huge, dark brown eyes that crinkled engagingly when he smiled. Before I left he asked me for my telephone number. I was flattered but I didn't expect to hear from him again. The next day he was on the phone. Would I come out to lunch with him? He would pick me up from St James's Secretarial College in Exhibition Road at 1 o'clock. At 1 o'clock I stepped out of the college and there was a gleaming dark blue, Mark II Jaguar, with chrome wire wheels, sitting waiting at the curb. He opened the passenger door for me, strapped me into a full pilot's harness, and we set off towards South Ken pulling several Gs. I was impressed.

Colin Emson was twenty-seven, and one of the most energetic, enthusiastic, ambitious, exciting people I had ever been around. He was an amateur racing driver, he was a Cresta Run bobsleigher, he was a trumpet player. In short, he was part of the swinging Sixties, and had been out with most of the prettiest and aristocratic ladies in London. He worked hard and he played hard. He ran a small investment company by day and sold central heating by night. And having started with no privileges in life, except for some terrific parents in Maidstone, he was in the process of working his way up in the world with extraordinary success.

Over the course of the next few weeks I fell very seriously in love with him, and one Sunday, some months later, invited him home to meet my parents. I did so with some trepidation. Colin was not a forelock-tugging teenager who would call my father 'Sir' and listen to what he had to say without interruption. He was also nine years older than me, which at that time seemed a huge gap. There was every chance JJ would disapprove. Pam was not a worry; I knew she would like him. He had been at a house party in Sussex that weekend and the plan was he would have dinner with us, stay the night and drive us both to London on Monday morning. He arrived in good spirits. That morning his company, Emson and Dudley, had had a brilliant write-up in the *Sunday Times*. And, having just come from an extremely high-powered lunch, with characters like Hartley Shawcross, Harold Lever, James Callaghan and Harold Wilson sitting around the table, he was feeling pretty good – and in no way prepared for the onslaught that followed.

'I thought I was going to walk into a wonderful, open, smiling household that had produced this amazing daughter,' he recalls. 'I expected to be received as a young, reasonably intelligent, moderately well spoken, reasonably turned out, potentially extremely successful and currently not too unsuccessful, boyfriend. And I met this extraordinary man, unlike any father I had ever met before, who started prowling around me like a leopard. But it was very difficult to make me feel uncomfortable that day because I was absolutely on top of the world. Plus I knew that I could walk out and possibly take his daughter with me, so I wasn't there full of fear. He probably had more to fear than I did.'

Dinner was marginally uncomfortable, JJ was sizing him up, testing him, playing, but after dinner, he went for the kill. He savaged Colin in a way that I had never seen him do before to anyone. He had obviously seen the *Sunday Times* article, the brunt of which was that Colin's business was using a computer to analyse stock market movements – the first company to do so – and sending its clients a daily list of share tips, with phenomenal results. Where, JJ wanted to know, was he getting the information? Colin refused to say. It was in fact coming from a backroom computer analyst in an eminent firm of stockbrokers, who through a series of coincidences had developed a technique of analysing market movements that his firm wasn't interested in and wouldn't back. So Colin had offered to back him, but if the firm had known he was moonlighting, the analyst would have lost his job.

JJ wouldn't take no for an answer. As an investigative journalist he claimed he had a right to know, and if Colin wasn't prepared to tell him it was because he was a con man, a complete sham and a charlatan. The situation became very ugly. JJ was as vicious as I had ever seen him. 'I am going to crucify you,' he thundered. 'I am going to expose you for the charlatan you are. I am going to say that you are not willing to say where you're getting this information from. I am going to see you exposed and crucified.'

Colin's voice became suddenly very dangerous and steely; my father had met his match. 'Those are the words of a bully,' he said. 'You're using your newspaper as a weapon, you are standing with your newspaper behind you – which is owned by somebody else – and threatening me with it. You're nothing more than a bully and if you want to do that with your newspaper, you go ahead and do it.'

I had been standing beside them in horror throughout all of this, trying in vain to stop the vitriol, shouting at my father, begging him to stop, tears streaming down my face. Colin then turned to me and said he was sorry but he was leaving; he was not spending the night under the roof of a man who didn't trust him, who tried to bully him and treated a guest in his home so appallingly badly. At which JJ laughed and held his hands up in mock surrender, as if the whole thing had been a bit of sport, a joke. 'You can't go off at this time of night,' he said. 'Have another whisky. Stay. I want you to stay.' Needless to say, it was very late and they had both had a great deal of whisky already; and in the end Colin was persuaded.

We all went upstairs to bed and I remember my father lurching towards me with a big grin on his face, on the half landing. I hit him so hard he fell down a couple of steps. It is the only time I have ever hit anyone in my life, but I hated him that night. I was ashamed, shocked, and appalled. But miraculously he and Colin went to bed as friends.

Colin remembers the night as if it were yesterday. 'I wasn't at all afraid, and don't know quite why, because actually he could have completely slaughtered me. Any newspaper can. I had done nothing criminal, so I wouldn't have been seriously damaged, but I could have been badly discredited, and my man would have been sacked.

'I still think he was testing my metal to see if I was worthy of his daughter. It was almost like "You've passed the test, I don't want you to go." He'd had his sport and maybe it all had been a game that he'd taken a bit too far. He and I got on very well after that, and he never raised the question of where my information came from ever again, he just knew under great pressure and adversity I was not even bending let alone buckling or caving in. I think he and I respected each other.

'I was acting as though this whole family might one day be my family and this person is going to be very important to me for the future. So we got on well, but I never liked him. He was never dull, never boring, never without a very powerful opinion. Some of them I agreed with. You could not ignore him, you could never dismiss him, never second guess him, you could never anticipate what he was going to do, or think, or say, or who he was going to attack, or how foul he was going to be or how charming and nice he was going to be. He was just a wild creature driven by something that took him from Glasgow to running the *Sunday Express*. You've got to be a very tough guy to do that. And he was a driven man with all the power inside him.'

Colin and I saw a lot of each other over the next six months and I fell ever more deeply in love with him. We went to stay with his parents, we spent weekends with his friends in smart country houses, he came home to Wellpools, and we had evenings in London, and everywhere we went, we went in his big beast of a Jaguar with the pilot straps, at top speed, and never once was I frightened. I trusted him completely. But I was never certain that he felt quite so passionate about me. He had had dozens of beautiful and sophisticated girlfriends, all much older than me, and I suspected he still had a few of them. I was eighteen and knew nothing and no one. How could I compare? It troubled me. I couldn't work out what my appeal was – at one time I even wondered whether it might have been my father.

As if to confirm my insecurity, in the middle of the summer Colin started talking about my future. He said he thought I should go to university, knowing full well that I had decided to scrub St Andrews. Having not been keen to go in the first place, I was now desperate to stay in London with him. I didn't need a degree to be a journalist; and it seemed pointless to delay the process by four years. I argued my case, but he was persuasive, so persuasive that I came to the conclusion that he wanted to get rid of me, and packing me off to St Andrews more than four hundred miles away was the perfect solution. I thought my heart might break but he assured me that our love would survive, we would see each other – he would drive up to see me there, I could come to London for weekends.

And so in October 1968 I said a desperate goodbye to him and set off in my little Fiat 500 for Scotland. My nineteenth birthday was soon after the beginning of term and Colin drove up to see me. We went to stay at a little hotel called the Smuggler's Inn at Crail just down the coast from St Andrews, where the sea pounded the rocks, and had the most perfect weekend. He wrote long and loving letters each week, and I began to wonder whether he was regretting having sent me away.

St Andrews was a shock. Picturesque though it was, the town was small and parochial, and most of my fellow first-year students, or Bejantines as we were called, were a year younger and living away from home for the first time. We had precious little in common and, although physically in St Andrews, mentally and emotionally I was still very much in London.

And then one day I was in a pub with my Senior Man – a fourth-year student who takes a newcomer under his wing to show them around in their first few weeks – when I spotted someone across the room looking at me. He was very tall, very thin, with a mop of floppy brown hair, and better looking than anyone I had seen north of Watford. Our eyes met, and I felt in that brief moment, as though he had seen into my soul. My Senior Man, who had been very attentive in his duties and I suspect thoroughly frustrated by my loyalty to Colin, noticed and said I should steer clear of him. He was the local shark, fancied by every girl in St Andrews; he was South African, in his final year, and a leading light in the dramatic society. His name was James Leith. A couple of days later I ran into the infamous James Leith again. I was at a ball for first-year students. It was the end of the evening and I was looking for my coat when suddenly there he was, flanked by a couple of friends, none of them in dinner jackets and all looking slightly the worse for wear. He said he had climbed in through a window and gate-crashed the ball in order to find me. Would I have dinner with him the next night?

I was unaware that dinner happened in St Andrews. I thought a 'fish supper' from the chippy, taken away in a greasy paper packet and washed down with a pint of lager and lime, was about as sophisticated as the town got. It was certainly the best that anyone I had so far been out with of an evening had suggested. More often it was the pub and a packet of crisps. He had arranged to pick me up from my digs, where I lived in a terraced house at the bottom of the town with an academic and his wife and their two young children. I was in my room getting ready when James arrived. A moment later my landlady came charging upstairs to see what I was wearing. 'You can't wear that,' she said, looking at my jeans. 'He's taking you to Fernie Castle, the best restaurant in Fife.'

Fernie Castle was about twenty miles from St Andrews and very grand, so grand that James had to borrow a tie before they would let us in. We drove there in his car, a Mini Traveller with no carpets, and began with a glass of champagne. I had been warned that he was a fast mover, so I was well prepared to repel any advances, but none came. We sat and talked all night, so much so that our food became cold and we had to ask them to take it away and reheat it. James told me the story of his life: his upbringing in South Africa, his actress mother, his father's death from cancer when he was thirteen years old, and his escape from the army. While our food, still untouched, turned cold for the second time, he told me how just a year ago he had been involved in a horrifying car crash in South Africa. His girlfriend had died instantly and he had been left with a broken spine and the task of facing her parents, then giving evidence in a court of law. I knew this was not a story he told every girl he took out. Something special was happening. It was as though we had known one another all our lives but had a lot of catching up to do. His spine was more or less mended but the emotional wounds were still very raw and at various points in the story he brushed away tears. By the time we left the restaurant I think they were beginning to cook breakfast.

The next day he hijacked me as I was about to go in to a lecture and took me for a picnic lunch on the rocks at Crail, the village along the coast where I had spent the weekend with Colin just a few weeks before. This time the conversation was much more light-hearted. He had brought bread, cheese, pâté and a bottle of wine, but no corkscrew, so he improvised with his thumb. Again, we talked a lot and laughed a lot – he told wonderful stories and we argued ferociously about newspapers – and when the wine was finished and the seagulls had taken the last of our bread, we went for a walk along the beach. It was windy and cold and I started running to keep warm. He caught up with me, grabbed my arm and turned me round to face him. Before I knew what had happened I had kissed him. Suddenly the laughter was gone and he was very serious. 'Don't play games with me,' he said. I froze. I knew that I was already out of my depth. And I knew too that there was no way I could turn round and walk away.

We saw each other every day. We went to pubs with his friends, we played golf, we walked along the famous North Sands. We went to Ladybank, the only place you could get a drink on a Sunday night. I went to see him play the lead in the Samuel Beckett play, *Endgame*. We went to Pete's café for bacon butties before lectures in the morning, and Kate's for tea in the afternoon; and we went to the cinema, an ancient little flea pit called the New Cinema. One week we saw *Rosemary's Baby* and I was so distraught by the film he virtually had to carry me out; and the next week we saw *Cry the Beloved Country* about South Africa, and it was my turn to do the carrying.

I knew I had to make a choice. Three weeks later I went to London to see Colin. He had a little mews house in Hyde Park, where we stayed all weekend, seeing no one, listening to Simon and Garfunkel's new LP, *Bridge over Troubled Water*. He was more loving than ever, but I knew I had changed. He said he couldn't bear my being away; it had all been a big mistake; I should leave St Andrews and do a course in journalism in London; he had found one, he would fix it. Three weeks earlier his words would have had me packing my bags, my heart would have burst; the weekend would have been total paradise. Instead they were two of the most painful days of my life. He asked me to marry him and handed me a ring, set with three huge sparkling diamonds. It was the most beautiful ring I had ever seen, but I didn't even take it out of its box. I stood in front of him with tears rolling down my face. I had longed for him to ask me to marry him, for months I had dreamt and hoped and wished, and three weeks earlier I would have had the ring on my finger in seconds. But it was too late.

We were both in tears as he drove me to King's Cross to catch the night train back to St Andrews; and could barely speak to say goodbye. We just clung to each other. And as the train pulled out, he stood alone on the platform watching until I was out of sight. It was the last time I saw him until I walked into his office last year.

I had thought of him in the meantime, of course, and for a long time I felt sick with guilt about having hurt him so badly, but I had always believed that he only realised how much he loved me when I had gone away; that if he hadn't pushed me into going to Scotland, it would never have happened. I knew that the last time we saw each other I had broken his heart, but what I heard next broke mine.

Back in the summer of 1968, JJ invited Colin to lunch at the Boulestin, saying he wanted to discuss an important matter. The important matter was my decision not to go to St Andrews. 'A large part of the reason she doesn't want to go to university,' he said, 'is because she wants to stay here with you. And I know that I cannot force her to go, but I know you and I together could persuade her that it's in her best interests, and my purpose is to persuade you that it's in her best interests.' Colin assured him that he didn't need persuading. 'You don't have to say "Let my little girl go from your spell" because I'm not doing that.' 'Well, whether you know you're doing it or not, the effect is the same,' said JJ. 'She has a fine mind, tremendous ability, an enormous future, and for her to go into that untrained and untutored is a mistake. If what you have between you, which I am sure is fine, can't last out while she goes away for a period of time, maybe you haven't got anything that's so special anyway. But you owe it to her not to cripple her chances, diminish her potential and limit her life. You have it in your power to make her go and fulfil all that she's capable of, and all that I, as a father, want of her.' But the line that did it was: 'If you really love her you will want the best for her, and if she really loves you, she's a strong enough person to wait for you.'

As Colin now says, 'It was game, set and match before we started. What could I say? "No, I love her, I love holding her, I love being with her, feeling her, smelling her, listening to her, watching those big, blue eyes sparkle at me." He couldn't say any of that; instead he said, "Okay, I'll persuade her to go," which is just what he did. And that was it. 'That last weekend in London,' recalls Colin, 'you said with such wonderful honesty, "It's too late." And I didn't know whether it was a lament or a judgement. It was actually just a fact.'

CHAPTER NINETEEN

Gaining a Son

Had it not been for my father, I might very well have been Mrs Colin Emson, and who knows whether we would have lived happily ever after. As it was, on 1 September 2001, I was celebrating thirty-one years of being Mrs James Leith; and had it not been for my father, I might never have met him. We spent the evening in one of the best restaurants in Wiltshire. They didn't have to reheat our food this time, but I revel in his company as much, if not more than I did that night at Fernie Castle. And of all the things I regret most about my father, it was that JJ never did.

James and my father first met in St Andrews that November. JJ came up to visit the Glasgow office of the *Sunday Express* and then drove across to Fife to see me. He was staying in Russacks Hotel and took us both out to dinner. James was nervous, which was understandable. He was twenty-two and was meeting not just my father, but the Editor of a successful national newspaper. He was keen to please and JJ was charm personified. 'You're far too intelligent to be an actor,' he said when he heard of James's intention to go into the theatre. 'You must come and work for the *Sunday Express*. I'll give you a job any day.' We went back to Russacks for coffee and brandy and James knocked his teaspoon out of his saucer. 'It's funny,' said JJ grinning mischievously, 'how these things always happen when you've had a drink, isn't it?'

The next month James and I drove south in convoy at the end of term. It was a terrible journey: zero visibility, icy roads and driving snow. My windscreen washer froze solid. I had to drive with the window open so I could squirt water on to the windscreen from a washing-up liquid bottle in an effort to see through the filth. Home for James was Johannesburg, six thousand miles away, so he was going to stay with his older sister, Prue. She ran a small catering business from a little mews house in Paddington, from which grew Leith's, the phenomenally successful catering empire, restaurant, and cookery school.

James was close to Prue and wanted me to meet her. I understood why. She was in the midst of cooking for a big party when we arrived, and wonderful smells filled the house. There was salad in the bath, and every spare surface in the house was covered with bowls, baking trays and boxes. Amongst it all was Prue, a human dynamo, hands covered in pastry flour; and watching disdainfully from his lookout at the top of the stairs was Benny, her Abyssinian cat. She had obviously heard about me, as I had her, and she greeted me like a long-lost friend. I warmed to her immediately, and my affection and admiration for her has never wavered.

A couple of days later James came down to spend a few days at Wellpools. JJ said I should invite him; he seemed to like James and behaved as though he was pleased to see him – I should have known better. Pam thought he was wonderful, as I knew she would. That night they were going out so I cooked supper, and JJ found a particularly good bottle of wine for us to drink, which he presented to James with some ceremony, leaving him in no doubt about how expensive it was. Half an hour later we clinked glasses and took a mouthful of wine. Our faces puckered. It tasted disgusting and smelt worse. There was no way we could drink it, but what should we do? Lie and pour it away or leave it? We left it; and JJ's first question as he came through the door was 'James, how was the wine?' James confessed that it hadn't actually been all that good. He was no expert, but he suspected it might be corked. 'Really?' said JJ incredulously, with a slight smirk on his face. 'Let me taste.' He took a mouthful. 'What absolute balls,' he said. 'That's not corked; you must have a godawful sense of taste. That's a marvellous wine, great wine – it's the last time I waste a decent bottle of wine on you.' He was right; having been left open for three or four hours the wine now tasted entirely different – as JJ must have known it

199

would. But he wasn't going to say so, and he wouldn't listen to what we had to say. He had succeeding in humiliating James and he was enjoying it. How could I have guessed that this is what he would try and do for the next twenty-nine years?

James had grown up in a loving family in the affluent Northern suburbs of Johannesburg, the youngest of three children. His father had been a director of African Explosives, a subsidiary of ICI, his mother, Margaret Inglis, was the country's leading actress, with her own production company. It had been a healthy, happy household, marred only by his father's death. There was a big extended family too, with cousins, aunts, uncles and grandparents in different parts of the country, with whom James spent holidays – they all spoke to one another, all liked one another, were all supportive and kind to one another. My family, with its warring factions, and my father's gratuitous put-downs and point-scoring came as a shock.

James was sharing a farmhouse when I first met him, about fifteen miles outside St Andrews next to a remote little village called Brunton. There were no shops for miles around, but the butcher, the baker and the candlestick maker all came around selling their produce in vans. One day we had gone to wait for the bread van to arrive in the village. It was cold, dark and teeming with rain, and the bread van was late. We were soaked through, completely drenched and beginning to laugh rather hysterically. Suddenly a door opened and a voice with a strong Fife accent, said, 'Will you young people no come in and wait in the dry?' We accepted with alacrity and were soon warming ourselves around a coal fire with mugs of steaming tea, while a television burbled quietly to itself in the corner.

Our angel of mercy was an old lady called Agnes Dalrymple – the sort of person you meet once in a lifetime if you're lucky. She had never been further than Cupar – the local town about eight miles away – in her life, yet she was wise, witty, and could quote Rabbie Burns at length. She was also refreshingly frank, and within fifteen minutes of meeting us declared that she thought we should marry. It was the beginning of a remarkable friendship that lasted many years, and she went to her grave delighted by the belief that she had brought the two of us together. Her husband Roy was a crofter, although his son-in-law now ran the farm. I will never forget the cat sitting on the rug in front of the fire between us with one leg in the air like a ham-bone, licking its nether regions. 'I wish I could do that,' said Roy wistfully. 'Well, go ahead,' said his son-in-law, 'it's your ain cat.'

James went back to Scotland for Christmas and I went up for Hogmanay. His elder brother, David, and family were staying, plus a few university friends, and after midnight we all set off through deep, deep snow to first-foot the Dalrymples, bearing a bottle of Scotch and a lump of coal, as is the tradition. The small room with the TV still burbling in the corner was already full but everyone was delighted to see us, and Roy immediately began pouring drinks for us all. He handed both James and me a tumbler brimful of what we assumed was whisky and lemonade, as the Scots often serve it. 'Could we have ours without lemonade?' we asked tentatively. 'There isn'y lemonade there,' he said. Nor was there. It was neat whisky – and that was just the beginning. I don't remember much about the walk home, except that I think we crawled for the last bit, and along the way James and a friend got into an argument about me, which turned into a fight. Each of them swung wildly at the other, but missed, and the momentum of the punch sent them sprawling into the snow. The following morning I thought I had lost my hat along the way – a fox-fur, which tied under my chin, that JJ had bought me to ski in one year. I started to get very agitated until James noticed the hat was still on my head.

James asked me to marry him over breakfast on 15 January 1969. By coincidence it was my father's fiftieth birthday, James had left the farmhouse by this time and was living on his own in a flat in the little fishing village of Anstruther. We were discussing the merits of dogs versus cats, and he was so surprised by the question he had asked, which appeared to have popped out unbidden, that his thumb shot straight through the peach he was eating. He had intended to say that if I liked dogs then I couldn't marry him because he hated them, but it came out rather differently, and I had said 'Yes' before he could blink.

That evening we stood together in a public phone box on the harbour, pushing half crowns into the slot, and called home. JJ was in the middle of a dinner party and feeling jovial. I had sent him a ship's decanter from an antique shop in St Andrews for his birthday. It was the only present I ever gave him, apart from the Rupert Brooke poetry, that he really liked, but sadly it was taken in a burglary.

'I have two questions,' said James. 'One, may I give your name as a referee for the BBC Graduate training scheme?'

'Certainly. What's the other question?'

'May I marry your daughter?'

'When?'

'When she leaves university.'

'What does she say?'

'She says, "Yes".'

'She's mad. Put her on.'

That summer we bought ourselves a tiny two-man tent. The plan was to pack it into my microscopic Fiat 500 and drive to France to visit some South African friends of James's who had taken a house in Provence. We would then work our way down to Fuengirola to stay with Pam in Spain, and return via JJ in Barfleur.

When JJ heard the plan he went ballistic – and he didn't even know about the tent. He and Pam had fierce arguments about it. He said he wasn't prepared to pay for me to go away with James. 'But why not?' said Pam, the contretemps faithfully recorded on a scrap of paper. 'Just because I say not, that's why. I shall pay for her holiday if she goes away with you. I shall pay her airfare and £50 spending allowance, but not to go away with James. If she goes away with James, he can pay for it.' The problem was sex. He threatened that if I slept with James before we were married he would never speak to me again; and, as I wrote to Viki Ryde, my great friend from school, 'I had no idea it could be so easy'. I had long forgotten about this threat, but Viki still has my letter.

At the end of the summer I went back to St Andrews to a flat in Anstruther, where I lived by myself with a huge tabby cat called Christmas, and pined. Every day I wrote to James and every night I took a pile of coins down to the phone box by the harbour – the one from which we had phoned my father – and spoke to him until the coins ran out. He hadn't been given a place on the BBC trainee scheme, so had applied instead to the London Academy of Music and Dramatic Art, and had embarked on a three-year course. I grew more and more miserable with every week that passed.

When I went back to Scotland after the Christmas vacation, I knew that, if I wanted to keep my sanity, I had to leave. So I wrote to Hugh Cudlipp, Chairman of IPC. We had met a few times sailing at Cowes, and on one occasion he had told me that if ever I wanted a job in journalism I should get in touch. I reminded him of his rash promise and explained the situation. He wrote back saying that it just so happened that IPC Young Magazines had just advertised places on a trainee scheme, and although he couldn't influence their decision in any way, he gave me the name of the woman to write to. I wrote, was invited to London for an interview, and given a place. I don't know whether I was given the place because of Hugh Cudlipp, I would like to think not, but either way it was the greatest stroke of luck. This was a pilot training scheme, which, sadly, was never repeated. They took just six people, it lasted six months, and gave me a taste of everything there was to know about journalism. It began in February 1970. I went back to St Andrews, told the Rector I was leaving, packed my bags, put Christmas into a cat basket, said goodbye to my landlord, and rang JJ to tell him the news.

He hit the roof. I imagine he had fondly thought that if I spent another three years at St Andrews with James five hundred miles away in London, the chances of our ever actually marrying were zero. That was why he had given his consent so readily; he never thought it would happen. Now he realised there was a possibility. He told me that I was insane, that I would never earn a living in journalism, and that he washed his hands of me. For the first time in my life, he was not in control. The deed was done, and although he sulked, in time he came to terms with it. He even let me live in his flat in Clifford's Inn – knowing that the alternative would have been staying with James at his flat in Wandsworth. But still he had moments of childishness. When a magnificent fox-fur coat, which he had given me for Christmas two years before, was stolen from the IPC building, he refused to claim for it. He said that since I was going to marry James, it should be James's responsibility to insure my things. If I didn't live at Wellpools any more, why should he cover me? Pam told him he was being totally unreasonable. 'Why on earth should James insure her coat when she doesn't even live with him?' she shrilled. 'I've never heard of anything so absurd.' 'Don't shout at me,' he bellowed, which was his usual riposte when she attempted to challenge him. But he never claimed.

Once he got over his anger, he liked having me working round the corner in Farringdon Road. And there's no doubt he was pleased I had chosen to become a journalist. He now had both his children working within a stone's throw of his own office. Occasionally we would all meet for lunch and walk down Fleet Street, three abreast. I think he felt fiercely proud. I know I did.

For all the jokes about how nice it would be to have him never speak to me again, I was bound to him by an invisible length of tungsten and could never have walked away from him forever, however frightened, furious or ashamed he made me. Because, for all the anger in him and the viciousness, I knew without a shadow of doubt that he loved me, and I knew how desperate he was that I should love him. And I knew too that he regretted the way he behaved – in his maudlin, sentimental moments he would say so – but he couldn't stop himself. And because of all the hurt and the damage I had witnessed over the years, I couldn't let him get close; I loved him but I couldn't let him into my heart.

I had watched him destroy my mother, and now he was attempting to destroy James. James was not aggressive by nature and had never encountered a street fighter like my father. If JJ had only realised it, he could have had another son in James. James had lost his own father at the age of thirteen and missed him badly. He would have loved to spend time with my father, to go out on the golf course with him, to seek his advice and exchange jokes over a pint in the pub. They did play golf together and sail and go for the occasional pint, but it was never relaxed, never fun. JJ was constantly looking for an opportunity to put him down.

I imagine he was simply jealous. He couldn't bear to see me so happy, so much in love, so lit up, and so completely wrapped up in someone else. Maybe it reminded him of his own marriage that had turned so sour. Maybe he was just insecure and didn't trust me to love him too. Or perhaps he knew that I never had and never could love him as much as I loved James. But it was a vicious circle. The more he was unkind to James, the more I turned against him, which made him all the more unpleasant to James, and me to him, until our relationship was virtually in tatters. What we should have done, what JJ would have done under similar circumstances, was to walk away, to cut him out of our lives until he was prepared to behave decently. But we didn't. I couldn't walk away from him, and I couldn't leave Pam. I felt that Pam was alone, lonely and defenceless, and that if I was there as often as I could be, I could protect her or at least give her moral support. And such was the good nature of James – and his affection for Pam, who, in turn, simply adored him – that he put up with years of abuse and humiliation from my father.

Even my brother turned on James. One Friday night we were all staying at Wellpools for the weekend. Being Friday, JJ was in London, but Roderick more than made up for him. After supper and several glasses of wine and probably whisky too, he and James had an argument, which turned nasty. I happened to agree with James, and said so, whereupon Roderick suddenly launched into a vicious attack, accusing James of trying to turn me against my family. 'All you've ever wanted to do,' he said venomously, 'is break up this family.' Pam told him to stop talking such absolute nonsense, but he was warming to his theme and was not to be silenced. Finally Pam said that if he was not prepared to retract what he had said and apologise then she didn't want him in her house for a moment longer; and with much shock and distress all round, he and Suzy drove off into the night.

Of all the insults thrown at James in all our years together that was possibly the unkindest, because no one could have done more to keep my family together – nor suffered and sacrificed more in the process. The irony is that the people responsible for turning me against my family were Roderick and JJ. James was not a prickly character, not argumentative, not combative, and he didn't see my family as a threat in any way. He liked families and, with his own so far away, the last thing he wanted to do was break up mine.

But it never worked like that. James tried to make friends with Roderick but he never responded. James never saw the boy I had known as a child, the happy, silly, funny, kind boy that I had so adored. He saw the formal, rather pompous man that he had become, who like his father could be either a soppy or an ugly drunk. When James invited Suzy to supper with us one Saturday night, knowing that Roderick was working late and she would therefore be on her own, he had a call from Roderick wanting to know what was going on. 'Well, she can come,' he said, without a hint of humour, 'provided she is home in time to make my supper when I get home.'

James and I married in September 1970, in St Bride's church, Fleet Street. St Bride's, designed by Christopher Wren, was the most perfect place to be married, and the white-haired, white-bearded Reverend Dewi Morgan, whose love of God was matched only by his love of Fleet Street, was the perfect man for the job. In his pre-nuptial chat he had just one piece of advice, which served us well, 'Never go to sleep on an argument.'

It was a glorious day, although I was so excited nothing could have marred it for me. Suzy's parents came over from Switzerland, and JJ took us all to lunch at the Terrazza Est before the service. His generosity that day was extraordinary, and if he had any reservations about our marriage he didn't show them. He and I drove in his Aston Martin to the church, where there was a small crowd waiting, and he seemed nervous as we walked into that magnificent building together to the flourish of organ music, my arm linked through his. It was the first time we had held hands or linked arms in years, probably since I was a toddler. It was also the first time I had seen him nervous, but then he was playing host to an extraordinary roll call of guests, many of whom I had never even met. In addition to the great, the good and the super-rich, he had assembled most of the Cabinet and the ex-Prime Minister – it was not surprising crowds should have gathered outside. We had Harold Wilson, Enoch Powell, Quintin Hogg, Reginald Maudling, Duncan Sandys, and Tony Barber to name just a few. But the most important guest was Agnes Dalrymple, who had journeyed out of Fife for the first time in her seventy-odd years of life to see us marry. She travelled with a friend, and we sat them right at the front of the church. I wish I had been able to record the look on her face when she realised she was sitting ahead of Harold Wilson, Quintin Hogg, and the rest.

The reception afterwards was in the Stationers' Hall, another magnificent building, off Ludgate Hill. James and I were driven there in the Aston Martin, but most of the guests walked in the afternoon sunshine – security for senior politicians was not an issue in 1970. What was an issue, however, was protocol. Some of them wanted to get back to their offices after a quick glass of champagne, but didn't like to leave before the bride and groom. JJ began to agitate. I told him they should just go, we didn't care about the done thing, I wanted to talk to people, but he insisted we must leave first. He found James and told him he had to take me away – by this time he was angry – and James found me and told me to hurry up. I was deep in conversation with Agnes Dalrymple and told him to shut up. It was the first and last time I ever did, and he never let me forget it, but it was not the last time our relationship was put under strain by my father.

From the Stationers' Hall we went to the Savoy Hotel, where JJ had organised a suite for us for the night. The Savoy was simply sumptuous. The rooms were filled with flowers and a bottle of champagne was waiting for us on ice. The bed was about fourteen feet square with dozens of pillows in crisp white cases, and the bath like a small swimming pool with huge brass taps that would not have looked out of place at sea. We drank the champagne, had a pillow fight and a bath, then drank some wonderful wine with dinner, served in our room, and went to bed. By 3 a.m. we were wide awake with pounding heads and horrible hangovers, so we rang room service to see if they had any Alka-Seltzer – as much for a joke as anything. 'Certainly, sir,' came the reply and fifteen minutes later there was a knock on the door and in came an immaculately dressed waiter bearing a large jug of iced water and four Alka-Seltzer in little petit-four cases. There was not a hint of a smirk on his face; he looked for all the world as though this was the sort of request he had at 3 a.m. every night.

The next day we flew to Cyprus, again courtesy of JJ, to a hotel we had chosen in Kyrenia, a pretty harbour town in the north of the island. I now discover that Lewis de Fries, the *Sunday Express* travel writer, was charged with making the arrangements, and had to pull all sorts of strings to get us there. It explains rather late in the day, why the Minister for Tourism in Nicosia made such a fuss of us; we fondly thought this was how every visitor was treated.

The holiday was bliss, and by a stroke of luck, I had a bit of a journalistic coup. I had finished my training course and had just started working as a feature writer on *19 Magazine*, which I loved. One night we decided to have dinner in a restaurant by the harbour, and sitting across the terrace was a large and noisy party, amongst which were two very familiar faces – Raquel Welch and Richard Johnson, both in 1970 at the height of their fame. I sat for a moment and considered my options: sit romantically with my husband of two days or go over to their table and ask if I might interview them. No contest – although how I had the nerve, not to say bad manners, to walk up to them like that I shall never know; maybe I have more of my father in me than I care to admit. It turned out they were working on a film called *The Beloved* and were so astonished by my confession that I was interrupting them on the second day of my honeymoon that they invited us to join them. We not only ended up becoming rather good friends with them all, but I came home with two terrific interviews.

Six months later James had the sort of luck every young actor dreams of. He was spotted by a theatre director and taken from drama school in the middle of his second year to play a major role in a production in South Africa. The play was *Forty Carats*, about a forty-year-old woman who falls in love with a young man. He was the love interest, Glynis Johns, still very beautiful but stretching it slightly for forty, was the lead. It was a fantastic opportunity under any circumstances, but to be taken out to South Africa, where he had been brought up, was doubly exciting. He was going to be gone for three months in all – four weeks' rehearsing in Johannesburg, followed by a two-month run. It was the perfect opportunity to show me South Africa and one that, with our current income, was unlikely to come again. We could never have afforded two airfares, but could just scrape together enough for mine with Luxair,

Right: JJ at work, characteristically with his sleeves rolled up. You could tell who he had buzzed on the intercom by watching who jumped in the office.

Left: One of the perks of the job was meeting actresses, starlets and models. Several became regular companions. Archie Freedman, Editor of the Scottish *Sunday Express*, looks on amused.

Right: My father with Henrietta Mackay and Bernard Harris. Everyone suspected an affair – she could get away with murder – but she kept them on tenterhooks.

Above: With his team on the back bench on a Saturday night, checking the first editions. Afterwards they would go to the Press Club and play snooker.

Below: Twenty-odd years on, checking proofs with John Buchanan and Henry Macrory on the stone.

Above: Arriving with JJ at St Bride's church in September 1970. JJ had filled the church with the great and the good but Agnes Dalrymple, on her first trip out of Fife, had pride of place.

Below: Married and on our way to the Stationers' Hall. (*From left*) Pam, JJ, James's mother Margaret Inglis, James and me.

Left: Zandra Fisher. When Pam found out about her affair with my father, she began divorce proceedings.

Above: Susie Winter. Their affair began when she became his secretary in 1964 and lasted, on and off, for thirty-two years.

Above: Jane Crow. Friends for many years, and neighbours in Surrey and Barfleur, but she married another man.

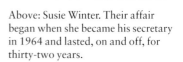

Right: With Selina Scott whom he discovered in Aberdeen in 1980. His adoration of her was legendary. After he wrote about her she was brought to London to front *News at Ten*.

Left: A masterly caricature by Trog, which accompanied a profile of JJ in the *Observer*. My father bought the cartoon – he loved to have photographs and cartoons of himself around the house.

Below: A snapshot of their weekly round of golf on Walton Heath, as seen by cartoonist Bill Martin. (*From left*) Bill is in the bunker, Monty Court in the heather, Curly carrying the clubs and JJ taking a divot out of the fairway.

Left: At the Ritz to celebrate twenty-five years as Editor, with Margaret Thatcher and Victor Matthews. He had just been told he could expect a knighthood in the New Year's Honours List.

Below: After his investiture at Buckingham Palace. The man who said he would never accept favours was utterly delighted.

Left: He wanted the motto: 'Look up and laugh and love and live'. It was too long and had to be abbreviated to 'Look up and laugh'. It was a curious motto for someone who seldom did.

Above: At Walton Heath. Ewen Murray (*left*), the young professional at the club, was like a son to him. To Ewen's left Sir Patrick Macrory.

Right: I handed him Sam. He beamed and I don't think stopped beaming at the sight of Sam, ever.

Left: Monsieur Jean in Barfleur, where he regularly won the yacht regatta until they banned the use of engines. Talking to Pierre Lamache, the one-legged fisherman. Edouard Boissard, in his wheelchair, is holding Sam.

The way he would have liked to be remembered.

the cheapest airline on the market. And so, with the blind confidence of youth, secure in the certainty that I would find a job when I came back, I handed in my notice to *19 Magazine*, the dream job I had had for just seven months.

My father once again hit the roof. It was the most idiotic thing to have done, I would never get another job in journalism, no employer would take me on with that kind of track record; I would be finished. And with his direst warnings still ringing in my ears, I set off for South Africa, a month after James, to stay with his mother in the northern suburbs of Johannesburg. I arrived just in time for his opening night.

In London, JJ was all too aware of James's opening night. He wanted to know what the reviews said, and charged Peter Vane, the Foreign Editor, with the task of getting hold of them. He failed. 'Surely to Christ there is some way we can find out how this play has done,' said JJ, and someone suggested trying the South African Embassy. Clive Hirschhorn, the theatre critic, who happened to be South African, was duly dispatched and came back victorious. He had found a review of the play, but it was not good. In fact it was disastrous. James wasn't singled out but the entire production was slated. With grave misgivings, Clive sent it in to JJ. A few minutes later he was summoned. 'Clive, if I ever thought you capable of writing poison like this about anyone striving to make it in the theatre, you'd be out of here in five minutes flat.'

CHAPTER TWENTY

The Column

Most people remember my father, not for having edited the *Sunday Express* but for the current events column he wrote. It was a brilliant blend of rage, indignation, prejudice and sentimentality, which became required reading for millions of people every Sunday. Whether you liked what he wrote or loathed it, agreed or disagreed, you couldn't ignore it. Every week it ran the gamut of human emotions. He would move from a fearsome attack on a politician, to an unkind jibe about a gay tennis player, to a whimsical thought about the bluetits in his garden, to fury over some bureaucratic blunder, to a humorous crack about the lassies in Auchermuchty, evoking in the reader astonishment, outrage, rage and laughter all within the space of a few column inches. Every week, without fail, he gave delight and offence in equal measure. The style of writing was unique. He wrote in a series of short sentences, peppered with question marks and, strangely for someone who was so punctilious about grammar in everyone else's writing, he broke all the accepted rules. It was written for his readers, whom he knew through and through.

He wrote about the issues that he knew they would be talking about, reflecting in his gut reaction their reaction – before they even knew they had it. He lashed out at anyone and everyone whom he thought greedy, stupid, self-serving, hypocritical, or corrupt – whether or not they were friends of his, and with no regard to any possible repercussions; and he revelled in the touching stories that demonstrated man's humanity to man. And yet even his most avid readers could never second guess him; just as you thought you knew his views on any subject, he would take a new line, come up with a surprising twist. When he was alive, I was often embarrassed by meeting someone whom he had mauled the previous week. Now that he is dead, people tell me how they miss him and how Sundays just aren't the same any more.

He inherited the column from John Gordon in December 1974. Gordon had not been well for the last two years of his life, and although he had struggled into the office and put his name to his much admired column, in truth JJ was virtually writing it himself. He would send Gordon a sheaf of memos, each one an idea for an item, and by altering the odd word here and there, Gordon was able to present them as his own. To begin with, JJ wrote these memos out of necessity, but he enjoyed writing them, and so when John Gordon died – not entirely unexpectedly – he had lined up no successor.

He did, in the end, make a half-hearted attempt to find a replacement. He suggested to Richard Ingrams, who was a regular lunching companion, that he and the campaigning journalist Paul Foot should take it over, but they thought it was a ludicrous suggestion, and never seriously meant. And so he carried on writing the column himself, ignoring the C. P. Snow dictum that he had once fondly quoted. 'Any man who writes for his own newspaper has a fool for an editor.'

The paper was now thirty-two pages and the strain of both editing and writing sharp, controversial comment was immeasurable – not just on him but on everyone who was around him. His column always read so fluently that no one would have guessed the hours he spent working on it, dictating into a little tape recorder, then writing and rewriting. He was a complete perfectionist, and each week struggled to find the right five or six items and to say something original in each. If ideas came, he would be buoyant, but if he had reached Friday night and the column was not yet finished, or he was not content with what he had written, he would be poisonous. But it added a new dimension to his life and the satisfaction when it all came right, as it eventually did every week, made it all worthwhile.

It was only when I started to write a weekly current events column myself, for the *Today* newspaper, when it was first launched in the mid-1980s, that I understood the agonies he went through each week. I lasted six months before I decided that there were less stressful ways of earning a living. He wrote a column for twenty-three years, and still managed to be unpredictable.

I also came to understand his need for praise. Every writer needs praise, but I found it quite surprising that, with his experience and apparent confidence in his own abilities, he should have needed it so badly. The answer I suppose is that he was just as insecure as the rest of us – only more aggressive about it. He would always ask what people thought of his column. If you said it was good he would either say, 'What do you mean? It was brilliant, absolutely brilliant.' Or he would say, 'No, I don't think it was awfully good this week.' The wise man did not take that as an invitation to agree with him, or his head would be lopped off his shoulders.

My brother telephoned JJ every Sunday morning to tell him what a brilliant column he had written, and he could set his clock by the call and was delighted by it. I didn't call. Frequently his column made my blood boil: his stance on most things was usually somewhere to the right of Attila the Hun, I found his attitude to gays obnoxious, I disliked the way he sneered at women, and the paragraphs about the bluetits made me cringe with embarrassment. I deemed it best to keep my mouth shut, but if he asked me what I thought of his column, and I felt particularly indignant, I might say, for instance, that I thought he'd been a bit unkind about gays this week. He would fix me with those pale blue eyes, his face would turn livid and he would say 'Oh do you just?' before launching into a damning and detailed diatribe about just what those sick, evil, perverted sodomites did to little boys – his voice growing louder and more menacing by the second, his finger stabbing the air in front of my face. 'You think that's all right, do you? Well, I don't.' If I felt brave enough to suggest that not all gays went after little boys, he would go ballistic. There was not even room for debate or discussion on less emotive topics. He had written what he had written and if I or anyone else failed to agree with it we were fools, intellectual pigmies, who didn't know anything.

Whatever I or anyone else thought of the views he expressed in it, the column was brilliant. It didn't matter whether people read it and raged, or read it and nodded in approval; the fact was they read it. It was parodied for many years in *Private Eye*; the expressions JJ used became common currency, and Auchtermuchty one of the best-known towns in the country. He considered using Ecclefechan, but he thought the name Auchtermuchty had a better ring to it. And so it became his Brigadoon, a place that had been bypassed by the modern world, in which old-fashioned virtues still persisted. He used to pass the little Fife town on his way to St Andrews, where he would go to play golf at the Royal and Ancient Golf Club, where he was a member, long after I had left, and used to love stopping there and buying fish and chips and walking through its streets without anyone knowing who he was. Every Christmas he would give us all cashmere jumpers made in Auchtermuchty; and every Christmas a woman who ran a bed and breakfast in the town sent him a tin of home-made shortbread – the best I've ever eaten anywhere.

She wasn't the only one who sent him presents, and some people sent him poetry, but mostly the column attracted letters, hundreds of them. Some people became regular correspondents over many years, pouring out their fears and worries to him – and he was painstaking in making sure that each letter, whether flattering or not, was answered promptly. He derived immense satisfaction in knowing that he had friends and admirers out there; that his column was giving comfort to people in straitened circumstances, most of whom he had never met and never would meet; he felt a real sense of responsibility towards them.

But no one can write with the savagery he did at times without making some enemies. Like most current affairs columnists, many of the items in his column were comments on stories he had read in other newspapers. In September 1976, when Prince Charles was going out with Davina Sheffield, and there was speculation that she might become the Princess of Wales, the *News of the World* had a scoop splashed over several pages: an exclusive interview with her ex-boyfriend, James Beard, with photographs of their 'love nest' in the country.

The next week, JJ wrote the following paragraph:

I don't know whether Prince Charles wants to marry Miss Davina Sheffield. Or, indeed, whether she wants to marry him.

But if she does have an ambition to wave a gracious hand to cheering crowds from the balcony at Buckingham Palace, then her ex-boyfriend Mr James Beard is doing nothing at all to help her achieve it.

Mr Beard, who never seems to have heard of the old rule that gentlemen don't talk about their conquests, has been telling us of the idyllic months when he and Davina shared a thatched cottage, and of how good a cook and how domesticated she was.

He adds: 'I think Prince Charles is a very impressive man and I am sure they will be very happy. I think she will make an extremely good Queen and a magnificent wife.'

How's that for generosity?

Even in this permissive age, might it not be just a little difficult having a Queen with a commoner ex-boyfriend going round the country saying what a marvellous hot-water bottle she used to be?

What JJ didn't know, and I only recently discovered, was that James Beard, who was an Old Harrovian powerboat racer, had been entirely misrepresented by a female reporter from the *News of the World*, who had sat next to him at a promotional lunch for the sporting press given by his sponsors. Amidst the talk about powerboats, championships and record speeds, she had slipped in the odd sly question about Davina. Off his guard when pressed, he had said she was a good cook, and that anyone who married her would be very lucky. That was about the strength of it, but with some creative writing and photographs of Beard's cottage in the country, it looked as though he had indeed ratted on his old girl-friend.

Without JJ, it might have been passed off as typical *News of the World* scandal, but he added credence to the story and presented it to a much wider audience. Davina was seen to have had a past, her relationship with the Prince of Wales came to an abrupt halt, and James Beard, who was in fact the most sensitive and caring of men – in every way a total gentleman – was never able to explain to Davina, whom he still adored, what had happened. He was wrongly accused and completely devastated.

James Beard happened to be a friend of my old boyfriend Colin Emson and, on Colin's advice, he went to see JJ to explain that he had been set up by the *News of the World*, and ask if he would put the record straight. James had been consoled to a degree by the fact his friends neither read the *News of the World*, nor took it seriously, but his friends did read the *Sunday Express*. JJ agreed to see him but he was unmoved. 'Life's tough, life's shit,' he said, 'and maybe you've had it a bit soft. Welcome to the real world.'

Colin then went to see JJ on his friend's behalf, but, try as he might, he was unable to persuade him of the injustice or the damage he had done; my father wasn't interested in the truth. 'If you're in the front line,' he said, 'you have to take it, and if you're not strong enough to take it, you shouldn't be there.' James was evidently not strong enough. He was broken by the experience and died of leukaemia a few years later.

Listening to this story from Colin, I felt hugely responsible for my father's behaviour, and it was not the only time I found myself gasping, apologising, willing there to be some way in which I could make amends for the past. But JJ had grown up on the maxim 'never apologise, never explain', and he was no more penitent when brought to account by the courts or the Press Council. He once wrote about the trial of a child specialist who had allowed a Down's syndrome baby to die, and found himself in contempt of court. 'The case is expected to go on for at least five weeks,' he wrote. 'Five weeks? If John Pearson had been allowed to live that long, might he not have found someone apart from God to love him?' He was fined £1000, but on leaving court told *The Times*, 'I very much regret inadvertently having been in contempt of court but what I said I believed then, I believe now and I will believe tomorrow.'

On another occasion he was reported to the Press Council for making racialist observations. This was the offending paragraph:

In my story last week of the old tramp who died from exposure after having been turned away from Hull Royal Infirmary in the early hours of a bitterly cold January morning, I did not give the name of the doctor who examined him.

It was Dr Falih Abed Ali Al-Fihan.

What was his nationality? I do not know. But I have a sneaking suspicion that he does not wear a kilt. And does not come from Auchtermuchty.

The Council held against him, and this is what he wrote the following Sunday:

Do I now bow my head in penitence? Like hell.

I would say exactly the same again.

But I tell you this. Even if Dr Falih Abed Ali Al-Fihan spends the rest of his life turning away dying tramps, I think I will still have more respect for him than I have for the po-faced, pompous, pinstriped, humourless twits who sit on the Press Council.

He was not a racist, and although he had a disconcerting habit of pointing out if someone was Jewish, I don't believe he was anti-Semitic either. But he was a lawyer's nightmare. He believed that the greatest protection against libel was the question mark, which was not strictly true. AN Wilson, who came to know him some years later, says, 'He believed you couldn't be done for libel if you posed a question. There is a bit of truth in that, and it's something he's taught to an entire generation including me. It might not be true in court, but it is as far as the libel lawyers on newspapers are concerned. If they ring up in an explosive rage and say "You can't say Mrs Thatcher's living on immoral earnings," you say, I didn't say she was. I ask the reader, "Does it not look as though she is?" And they often shut up. It's sort of Junor's Rule – one of his great legacies, the question mark.' Not every lawyer who read his column for libel agreed with Junor's Rule, however, and he gave those that didn't, hell. 'You know, Dorian?' he said to one barrister who had just stood his ground and prevented JJ from being in serious contempt of court over a paragraph he wanted to print, 'the *Express* employs fucking awful lawyers.'

And sometimes Junor's Rule landed him in more trouble than anyone could have foreseen. In 1981, Sidgwick & Jackson, owned by his friend Sir Charles Forte, later Lord Forte, published a compilation of his columns called *The Best of JJ*. Reviewing the book in the *Observer*, Alan Watkins commended JJ on his blunt and forthright approach.

> He is specially adroit at bringing a column-item to an end, as in the story of the headmaster who was acquitted of indecent assault after two previous cases of a similar nature: 'Having now proved his innocence thrice, might he not be wise to jack in a job which seems to carry such a high risk of false accusations?'

The headmaster, who had not seen the piece when it was first published in the *Sunday Express* two years before, recognised himself. He sued for libel and the books were impounded and finally pulped.

Some of JJ's most savage remarks were directed at the IRA, which brought him into far greater danger than the threat of libel. He was supposedly number two on the IRA hit list, but it didn't slow him up for a second. This was a typical paragraph.

> It was dark when I opened my door last Sunday evening to an unexpected knock. Outside were six strangers – four men and two women. All Irish.
>
> They had travelled more than 30 miles from London to protest to me about a remark I had made after the Brighton bombing about the IRA and those who supported them. 'With compatriots like these,' I had written, 'wouldn't you rather admit to being a pig than to being Irish?'
>
> The people on my doorstep could not have been more courteous or polite. But clearly they had been flicked to the raw by my comment.
>
> So let me make it clear that I think that the vast majority

of Irish people are decent and law-abiding and abhor violence just as much as I do.

And as for the yobbos who do support the IRA and rejoice in barbarities like the Brighton Bomb?

On that issue I also make an apology. To pigs.

So, when he found himself being chased at high speed by four large men in a car late one night, he automatically assumed it was the IRA. But it turned out to be something much more sinister. It all began with an incident in Fleet Street, which he wrote about in his column, as he often did about personal experiences.

At 7.30 p.m. a week last Friday I had just driven away from the office when I was stopped by two policemen less than 50 yards from the *Express* building and accused of having made an illegal right turn into Fleet Street.

I had in fact done nothing of the kind. But they refused even to listen to my protestations that I had just emerged from the *Express* building.

They swore they had seen me come out of an adjoining road.

Their attitude was as menacing as if they had just caught the Yorkshire Ripper.

One of them demanded to know if I had been drinking and asked to smell my breath.

He checked over his walkie-talkie with his control unit to see whether I was telling the truth about the ownership of my car. He spent a good deal of time checking the licence disc and my driving licence.

He apparently had difficulty in taking down my name and I had to spell it for him two or three times.

The next day I discovered that they had subsequently visited the *Express* building and found out that I had been telling the truth.

Yet they still went back to their police station and lodged the charge against me.

I know that only a tiny minority of police act unreasonably.

But what bothers me is that if I, who can defend myself, was handled in this way, how do you suppose inarticulate and equally innocent members of the public including blacks in Brixton and Toxteth are being treated?

Before he published the story, he detailed what had happened in a letter to the Commissioner of Police for the City of London, Peter Marshall, in which he identified the policemen. The letter ended:

> In the end they gave me a ticket for having committed the offence of turning right into Fleet Street – an offence which never happened and which witnesses, including the chauffeur who parked the car, will certainly testify could never have happened.
>
> I am addressing myself in the first instance to you. But I reserve the right to give the matter further publicity. For if this can happen to me, then what in God's name is happening to people equally innocent, who do not have a newspaper column behind them?

A superintendent came to see JJ to apologise and ask if he wanted to make an official complaint. Not wanting to harm the careers of the two officers, he declined, but on 18 October he did print the story.

Two weeks later, he was driving home late on a Saturday night, as he always did, when he became aware that he had attracted the attention of a car with four large, tough-looking men in it. They came alongside him gesturing angrily, as though he had driven badly or carved them up. He put his foot down, so did they, and when he turned left off the A3, in the direction of Dorking, they followed. He was convinced they were trying to push him off the road, and his only thought was to get to Dorking police station. On the Leatherhead bypass they overtook him on a roundabout, at the entrance to Cherkley, Beaverbrook's estate, and swung their car through forty-five degrees to block his exit. Knowing the area, he sped on round the roundabout and headed into the town. But they obviously knew the layout of the roads as well, and when he emerged at the next roundabout to rejoin the A24, they were waiting for him. He drove the next five miles, round the notorious Mickleham bends, at speeds of over a hundred miles per hour in blind panic and, as he swung into Dorking police station, the car drove off. JJ was given a police escort home, but there was no sign of the other car.

He was very, very shaken. We discussed it at lunch the next day – he came to lunch with us every Sunday. We discussed where, other than Dorking police station, he could have gone. He said he hadn't been able to see anything of the car's number plate in the dark, and it was all so fast and terrifying he wasn't even sure what make of car had been following him, save to say it was a saloon.

The next week the same thing happened. Once again he was picked up on the A3, once again there were four large, tough-looking men in the car, who made the same threatening gestures, and once again they followed him onto the A24, keeping close behind his bumper, at even higher speeds than the previous week. This time JJ decided to head for the police station in Leatherhead, but the layout had changed since the days when he knew it well, and in his panic he took a wrong turning and ended up in the entrance to a pedestrian precinct with a barrier across the road in front of him. He had no alternative but to stop. They stopped and two of the men got out of the car and came towards him. He locked the doors and put his hand on the air horn, but there was no one to hear it, the streets were deserted. But he also picked up the little tape recorder that he always had in the car with him, for recording ideas for his column, and held it to his mouth. It looked very much like a telephone or a walkie-talkie, he could have been summoning help, and as soon as the men saw it they turned round, went back to their car and drove off.

JJ's first thought was that it was the IRA. He spoke to Sir David McNee, the former Commissioner of the Metropolitan Police, who was on the board of Fleet Holdings, and he disagreed this was the work of the IRA. He thought it was Saturday night yobbos out for a bit of fun, but after hearing about the second incident, David took it rather more seriously. JJ also spoke to the Chief Constable of Surrey, Sir Peter Matthews, who sent a couple of unmarked

Surrey Police cars to follow him home for the next two Saturdays, and installed a series of sophisticated panic buttons at Wellpools with direct links to the police. For two more weeks Bill Martin, the cartoonist, who lived not far from Dorking, followed him home on Saturday nights; but it never happened again.

The landlord of the local pub was an ex-policeman, whom JJ rather liked and, although he was no huge fan of pubs, he did occasionally go in for a pint and would chat to him. When the landlord heard what had happened, he immediately said it sounded like the work of the police, and David McNee finally came round to that conclusion too. Although JJ didn't make a formal complaint, by writing about the incident he would have landed the officers who booked him in serious trouble. One of them was the son of a City of London policeman, and the theory was that some of his friends had got together to teach JJ a lesson.

After the hair-raising car chases, JJ was given a full-time driver and thereafter he was driven out to lunch each day and driven to and from the office. The regular man was Ray Cobb, of whom he became very fond. Ray, in turn, became very fond of my father, despite his eccentricities. 'You had to get used to him,' admits Ray, 'and it took a while.'

Ray used to pick him up at Wellpools every morning and drive him in JJ's own car. At 8.30 a.m. on the dot, JJ would come out of the house, clutching the day's newspapers, which he would read all the way to London, sitting in the front passenger seat. He insisted upon arriving in the office at 10.00 a.m. It couldn't be 9.50 a.m., or 10.10 a.m., which meant that if there was little traffic to slow them up, Ray had to crawl. 'I used to have motors flashing behind me; I used to sweat because I was trying to go so slowly. He could tell; he'd be reading, then suddenly he'd look up and say, "Where are we?" "Streatham." "We're running a little early." Then we'd get to Dulwich College, "No, we're about right." I'd have been doing 10 mph. That was the only thing he used to get annoyed about. I suggested leaving ten or fifteen minutes later, but no, he said 8.30 a.m. was the right time.' The return journey was completely different. He would be asleep by Vauxhall but, at the last roundabout before Dorking, he'd wake up.

JJ was generous to Ray as he was to everyone, but his presents always came with a catch. One night he gave him a bottle of wine in a box. 'Try this,' he said, 'and tell me what you think.' Since Ray never left Wellpools until after 8.00 p.m. and sometimes didn't get home until 1.00 a.m., he didn't have time to drink the wine that night. The next day, with his unerring ability to know when some-one was trying to hide something, JJ asked how it had been. 'It was very nice,' he lied. 'What did you think of the flavour?' 'Very nice.' 'Did you find it too sweet?' 'Well it was a little sweet.' 'That was a dry wine,' said JJ. Embarrassed, Ray confessed he hadn't actually drunk the wine the previous night. 'I was waiting until the weekend,' he said. 'I asked you to try that last night,' said JJ. 'I'm very sorry,' said Ray. 'I will in future do that.'

One night my father offered Ray some new potatoes from the garden. But he insisted Ray go and dig them out of the ground that very evening, despite the fact that it had been raining hard all day and that Ray, as usual, was dressed in a suit and smart shoes. 'It was like a mire, I was up to my ankles in mud, and what I got were potatoes the size of marbles. He made me get a couple of dozen of these and he got a bag and said I should take them home to my wife, Paul, and ask her to cook them. I rang her halfway home and said, "Have you got dinner on?" "Yes, a roast." "Well I'm bringing some potatoes home and you make sure you cook them and we eat them tonight because he's going to ask me in the morning what they were like." You had to make sure that what he said, you did, or you had to answer for it.'

On another evening, it was daffodils. Hundreds of daffodils grew in a wild part of the garden amidst long grass. Again it had been pouring with rain and the ground was sodden. 'Daffodils for Pauline tonight,' said my father. 'No, not tonight, I'll get them another time,' said Ray. 'No, she needs some daffodils, you get her a nice bunch.' Ray arrived home soaking wet. 'Paul looked at me and said, "The daffodils are lovely." Bloody daffodils – but you had to do it.'

CHAPTER TWENTY-ONE

Grandfather

I am known in my family as the Princess of Parking Spaces because, just when it looks as though there is nowhere left on the entire planet to put the car, a space appears as if by magic. I even found a space outside Harrods one Christmas Eve, when only idiots take their cars into central London. There's no doubt I do have the luck of the devil – and some day I have a ghastly feeling the devil's going to collect. Luck has been responsible for most things that have happened in my life; the rest have been determined by my father, and sometimes it has been a combination of the two.

Shortly before I left for South Africa to join James for the opening of *40 Carats*, JJ, Pam and I were all invited to lunch with the Chancellor of the Exchequer, Tony Barber, and his wife at Number 11 Downing Street. Pam hated most politicians, but Tony Barber, an extremely nice and unassuming man, was an exception. Before lunch their seventeen-year-old daughter, Josephine, popped in to say hello but didn't stay to have lunch with us because she was busy revising for exams. JJ was intrigued by the idea of a young girl studying in her bedroom in Downing Street, and suggested to me that it would make a terrific piece for the *Evening Standard*. He was absolutely right; Josephine made a wonderful interview. I sent it off to Charles Wintour, who was then Editor. He was delighted with it, gave the piece great prominence in his newspaper and said he would like to see anything else I wrote. JJ was thrilled, and I think would have traced my success in journalism back to that interview – which, of course, he had arranged.

A week later I arrived in South Africa and discovered, as luck would have it, that the British tennis champion, Virginia Wade, was playing in a tournament in Johannesburg. I caught her as she came off court and she agreed to an interview. She was another great subject, and I sent it off to Charles Wintour, who was again very pleased with what I had written. So when I came back to England a month later I wrote to him asking whether there was any chance of a job for me on the *Evening Standard*. He took me onto the Londoner's Diary as a temporary, and there I remained for the next three years until I left about a week before the birth of my first baby.

Nothing could have prepared me for the excitement of having a baby. But if I was in love all over again, so was my father. I have never seen a man – with the possible exception of James, of course – so smitten. Sam, named after James's father, was born on 1 January 1974 at St Mary's Hospital in Paddington. I had been in labour for the whole of the previous day and he arrived in the early hours of the New Year, a little shrimp with a shock of black hair and a very healthy appetite. He was perfect in every way, but slightly underweight at birth so he had to spend the first ten days of his life in the premature baby unit, where I went in to breastfeed him several times a day.

The day I brought him home, James had been to Covent Garden flower market before dawn, and the entire flat was filled with chrysanthemums. We were living in Westbourne Grove at the time, in a tiny top-floor flat with two Siamese cats called Damn and Blast. There were no antique shops in Westbourne Grove then, no designers; the brothel that we could see from our bedroom is now a smart, multimillion-pound house, and the laundrette where I took our washing is an upmarket estate agency. Pam and JJ never came to see us there – Pam seldom left the country any more, and JJ refused to go to London on his days off – but they did come there to see Sam. JJ was wearing golfing kit, a turquoise shirt and a pair of tartan trousers, and the image of him looking at his first grandchild is with me to this day. He stood and beamed and I don't think he stopped beaming at the sight of Sam, ever. He was terrified to hold the baby, although he was persuaded to let me place Sam in his lap. He was even terrified of letting Pam hold him, and terrified that one of the cats was going to sit on his face and suffocate him. He regarded him as the most precious, fragile, miraculous creature that had ever been born.

Three months later, James, Sam and I moved to the country. We had been looking as far afield as Wiltshire, but could afford nothing, and ended up in a dilapidated cottage with an outside loo that a friend of my mother's knew about in South Holmwood, just five miles from Wellpools. It cost £6,000 and we had to spend as much again making it habitable, but it was such a pleasure to be able to put the pram in the garden, to hang nappies on a line in the fresh air, and to be able to walk with Sam in woods and fields rather than along grimy pavements with buses belching fumes all over us.

But being so close to Wellpools was a mixed blessing. It was great to have Pam so close; she adored Sam and was no end of help. But my father was another matter. He drove us mad. He came to Grandon Cottage every single day – on most occasions, completely uninvited. He would 'look in' on his way home from the station in the evenings, and usually several times a day on his days off. The only exceptions were when he was away on holiday. He never knocked, he simply walked in as though it were his own house – at any time of the day or night, whether we had visitors or not. He would never accept any hospitality and nine times out of ten he was barely civil. Sometimes he would thrust a copy of the *Evening Standard*, or a bunch of flowers, gracelessly towards me, saying irritably, 'Here, take that from me,' or 'Put these in some water.' The person he had come to see was Sam.

Sam became his chum, his best friend. He showered him with presents, his weekly shopping trips now encompassed gifts for Sam: toys, teddy bears, pedal cars, tricycles, bicycles, train sets, peaches, nectarines, out-of-season strawberries, and sweets by the jar. I tried in vain to dissuade him. I didn't want my son to be spoilt, I didn't want him to eat sweets and ruin his teeth, but JJ was unstoppable.

Three months after Sam was born, Roderick and Suzy provided my father with a second grandson, Roderick Walter John, known throughout his childhood as Roddy. He was born in Switzerland, where Suzy's father still practised, and like Sam he also spent his first days of life in an incubator. But he was even smaller than Sam so it was many weeks before he and Suzy came home to England. Home by then was a lovely, old timbered house in the village of Leigh, near Tonbridge in Kent, which Suzy decorated beautifully. Kent was neither the quickest nor the easiest place to drive to from Wellpools. JJ didn't go without an invitation and didn't much care to be invited anyway; he was never good at sitting in one place for very long, and hated anyone else to be in charge. As a result he saw much less of Roddy than he did of Sam, and while he was fond of the child there was never the same bond.

The next few years were blissful for me, if impoverished. I had given up work to be a full-time mother, and James, being an actor, was often at home. Our cottage, tiny as it was, was in the most glorious position, with six hundred acres of National Trust land on the doorstep, and although the garden was small, the local village allotments were outside the back door. We took one over, bought books about growing vegetables, and became virtually self-sufficient. I baked bread, we brewed beer in plastic dustbins, made wine from kits – which tasted foul, we gardened and lived on home-grown produce and cheap breast of lamb.

Then, in the baking hot July of 1976, I had another baby, a boy whom we named Alexander, after my grandfather, although he was always known as Alex rather than Sandy. Sam, in the faltering speech of a toddler, had broken the news to JJ that I was pregnant, and he was lit up, not so much by the news itself as by the method in which it was conveyed. He made Sam repeat what he had said several times so he could record his voice on tape, and, for years afterwards, would talk about the moment he first heard that Alex was on the way.

During this second pregnancy I became vegetarian. It was triggered by an article in the *Guardian* by John Berger called 'Poor Cow', a beautifully written story about a peasant farmer regretfully taking his pregnant cow to be slaughtered. As he described the process, the tears rolled down my cheeks until I could no longer read the page. It certainly wasn't the first time I had been distressed by seeing or hearing what human beings did to animals, but it hit a nerve, possibly because I was pregnant and emotionally heightened. Suddenly I realised just how pathetic my tears were, how hypocritical and morally indefensible. I was crying because someone killed a cow, and yet day after day I was eating meat which I bought in neatly dissected, unidentifiable pieces, simply because someone else had done the dirty work of killing the animal for me. I knew that the time had come to shut up or put up, to decide between emotion and the Sunday roast. Unless I was prepared to kill the animal myself, I couldn't have both. And I haven't eaten meat or fish since.

My father insisted that the decision was entirely physical. This was evidence, he maintained, of a pregnant woman's body dictating what she should and should not eat, like the craving for chalk, strawberries or lumps of coal, and he would say so to anyone who would listen, usually in front of me. I identified, he said, with the pregnant cow, and thought the power of the mind and body to behave this way was extraordinary. He rejected out of hand my explanation that this was nothing to do with a craving of pregnancy. I still liked the taste of meat – in fact the smell from the leg of lamb that I roasted for James the night I made my monumental decision had never smelt so good. It would be a hardship to go without all the flavours and textures I loved. This was an intellectual decision, triggered maybe by my being pregnant, but born out of reason. It infuriated me that he dismissed my explanation, ridiculed the possibility that I might have thought the argument through and reached this decision on my own. His attitude diminished what I felt was one of the most important steps I had taken in my life and, although I was still vegetarian when he died more than twenty years later, he never revised his view. He maintained his theory was right. But then JJ seldom revised his views about anything.

I went back to St Mary's, Paddington, for Alex's birth and Sam stayed at Wellpools. Although JJ hated hospitals – even as a visitor – he came with Pam and Sam to see Alex the day after he was born. JJ always maintained thereafter that Sam, aged two and a half, had taken one look at his little brother and said, 'Can he play golf?' I have no such memory, but it pleased him to think that. JJ had already taught Sam the rudiments of the game. He had had some clubs specially cut down to size and the two of them would stand side by side in the garden at Wellpools, with Sam swinging wildly at golf balls.

I loved my role as earth mother, pushing swings and hanging nappies out to dry, but after a while I began to feel the need to establish my own identity once more. I had been asked once too often, on meeting someone new, what my husband did for a living, on the assumption that mothers had nothing interesting to talk about, and so I put a table and a typewriter in the cupboard under the stairs, which was the only spare space in the house and, when Sam and Alex were asleep, I wrote.

I wrote two children's books – yet to be published – and I wrote light-hearted pieces about motherhood, which I sent off to the *Daily Express*, where, from my days on the *Evening Standard*, I knew the Features Editor. One day I had a call from his deputy, Keith Turner, who had just been appointed Features Editor of the *Evening News* and wanted me to write for him on a regular basis. Not long afterwards, Richard Ingrams rang me up. He thought it might be an interesting idea to have a consumer column in *Private Eye*. Would I like to do it? Not long after that I had a call from *Business Traveller* magazine, then the *Guardian*, then the *Daily Mirror*, all wanting me to write for them. Finally I had a call from the BBC in Bristol. Would I be interested in television? And then a publisher rang to ask if I would like to write a consumer book about babies. I did it all and thoroughly enjoyed myself, and gradually, from being utterly impoverished, we began to have some money.

I was still writing in the cupboard under the stairs, and Sam and Alex, now aged five and three, were sharing a bedroom the size of a walk-in cupboard. With some money we were able to buy a new house and had some space at last. We moved half a mile down the road to an old orphanage in a glorious setting, with eight bedrooms and about twenty-four child-sized loos, and the same six hundred acres of common land on the doorstep. Room for a study, room for a playroom, and room for Pam. And so, in the summer of 1979, we invited her to come and live with us. I had always wanted to be able to rescue her, as she had known, and now at last we could. She came ostensibly to look after the children for us, while James and I rode a motorbike to the Dordogne for two weeks to stay in a villa owned by *Private Eye*, and she never left.

'You called me "mad" not so very long ago,' she said as a parting shot to JJ, recorded, like so many of her exchanges with him, on a scrap of paper. 'I would just like to let you know I am going to Nelson Cottage on the 17th, or whenever it is, and I'm staying.'

'Good.'

He was actually devastated, and I felt incredibly sorry for him. But I was torn, as I always had been, between anger and sympathy. He had driven her away. He had destroyed her love for him, destroyed her self-confidence, destroyed her self-esteem and he had hurt her, day in, day out, for as long as I could remember. The happy, laughing, joyous woman of my early childhood had disappeared years and years ago and he was responsible. He deserved to be hurt for a change, deserved to suffer, deserved to be left on his own. It was his fault. And yet, and yet. I felt terrible. I felt like a traitor, and I hated to see him so miserable and so alone. I didn't want to make him suffer; what I wanted, what I longed for, was for them both to be happy.

Pam didn't want to divorce JJ, she didn't even want an official separation, and she told no one that she had left. All she wanted was a sanctuary, which we were happy to provide. JJ at first responded childishly. He threatened to stop her allowance, telling James that if Pam was living with us then we could support her. He told a golfing friend that Pam had gone to stay with us because her eyesight was so poor she couldn't be on her own. He told someone else she had gone because, with him working in the evenings so much, it was unfair on her to have to sit in silence and not be able to watch television. But anyone who had seen the two of them together knew why Pam was no longer living at Wellpools.

I wrote him a long letter of commiseration – I found it easier to write than to talk face to face – saying that I loved him as much as ever, and the fact that Pam was now living with us changed nothing; he was as welcome in our house as he always had been. It wasn't long before he recovered his equilibrium and was once again calling in on the way home at night. But it was tough to watch him leave our house, warm and alive with the noise of children getting ready for bed, and the smells of supper cooking, knowing that he was going home to an empty house with no one to cook for him, no one to light a fire, and no one to ask him about his day – not that he ever told her if she asked.

Having their mother-in-law to stay is most men's idea of hell, and if you were to tell them she would be staying for twenty-three years you wouldn't see them for dust. But James and Pam adored each other, and he was as pleased to see her out of Wellpools as I was. He had always told me that he married me in the hope that I would turn out like Pam, and in twenty-three years I don't think she irritated him once. She settled into our household seamlessly. She never criticised, never complained, never suggested we do things her way. She was always the first to help with anything that needed to be done: cooking, cleaning, gardening, and as my workload increased she was there to help with Sam and Alex, to drive them to school, collect them and look after them if I was busy.

In 1981 I started to get really busy. Just after the Royal wedding, I had a call from Vicki Stace, a girl I had written about in the *Evening News* some months before. She was Publicity Director of Sidgwick & Jackson, and wanted to know whether I might like to write a biography of the Princess of Wales. It was the sort of phone call most journalists dream of; and turned out to be the first of many biographies and the beginning of my fascination with the Royal Family.

The following year I had another dream call. This was from Mary McAnally, a producer at Thames Television, who was making a consumer programme for the new Channel 4, which would begin broadcasting in the autumn of 1982. It was called *4 What It's Worth*, and despite a terrible screen test, I was given the job of investigative reporter, confronting villains on their doorsteps. After a few months, I became presenter too. It was a full-time job – we were on air for thirty weeks a year. I loved it, but I could never have done it without Pam.

For the next sixteen years, my book writing and television pre-senting careers ran parallel with one another. I wrote about Margaret Thatcher, John Major, and the Prince of Wales, to name but a few. I co-presented *The Afternoon Show* on BBC1 with the Scottish singer, Barbara Dickson, whom JJ quite rightly adored. And in 1987 I began a nine-year stint presenting *The Travel Show* on BBC2, which was perhaps the programme of mine he enjoyed best of all.

My father watched me religiously and, as the credits rolled at the end of every programme, he would telephone to say what he thought of it. He was by no means always complimentary, and one week was so incensed he wrote about *4 What It's Worth*, the consumer programme, in his column. 'I switched on Channel 4 last Monday night and thought I was watching a party political broadcast on behalf of the Labour Party . . .' My colleagues found it hard to believe that the first I knew of it was when I read Sunday's paper. But, generally, how I looked on screen seemed to be more of a preoccupation for him than what I said. 'That outfit you were wearing tonight looked awful,' he would say. 'You must never wear that colour again.' Or he'd give me some jewellery and say, 'That would look marvellous on the box.'

I only once remember him praising me for something I said. One day on *The Afternoon Show* I interviewed Jimmy Boyle, the rehabilitated Glaswegian gangster who had served a life sentence for murder. We talked about the work he was currently doing with drug addicts, and I then asked him if he felt any remorse for what he had done in the past. It was quite clear he had none. That night JJ rang to say what a brilliant question I had asked and how riveting Boyle's reply had been. It was rare praise and I glowed.

He was obviously pleased by my success and proud of me, but he would always tell me that Roderick was the best journalist in the family. Nor did he ever tell me that he had enjoyed a book I'd written, not even when I wrote about Margaret Thatcher, who was a great heroine of his and the prime minister who gave him a knighthood. He knew her well, they lunched together periodically, he went to Downing Street to talk to her from time to time, and on several occasions he was a guest at Chequers. I don't pretend I knew her better, although during the course of my research, I did spend a year talking to her friends and family, and excavating details about her life. Yet never once did he ask my opinion on any aspect of her or anyone else I had ever written about. On the contrary, he would say, 'If I could just explain something to you about

Margaret,' or John Major or the Prince of Wales or whoever ...
the implication being that his knowledge and understanding of them
was always greater than mine. However, after he died, I discovered
that he had kept all the books I had written on a bookshelf tucked
behind his chair in the sitting room, with all his favourite books.

What he loved was fame, his fame and my fame. For years, when
I met people, they would ask whether I was John Junor's daughter.
Occasionally my fame, such as it was, turned the tables slightly,
and it tickled him. As he wrote in his column:

> I had a raging toothache and had stopped at a chemist in
> London's Camberwell to have a prescription dispensed.
> The chemist was a black African, possibly Nigerian, young-
> ish, good-looking and friendly.
> As he handed me my tablets he looked at me inquiringly.
> 'You wouldn't happen to be, would you,' he began. I pre-
> ened myself expectantly, 'the father of Penny Junor?'
> Isn't it just bloody marvellous to be famous in Camberwell?

JJ was right, Roderick was a better journalist than I was and he
looked as though he had a dazzling career ahead of him on the
Daily Telegraph; he was also writing speeches for Mrs Thatcher.
But something went disastrously wrong. And as my career began
to take off, his life began to fall apart. Suzy's mother, Hanny,
developed cancer. Suzy was exceptionally close to her mother, they
spoke daily, and she spent much of the summer of 1982 in Switzerland by her side.

That August, while she was away, Roderick took Roddy to stay
with JJ in Barfleur, intending to go on to Switzerland afterwards.
He was very fond of Suzy's parents – as we all were, JJ included –
so when Suzy rang to say things were not looking good and he
ought to come right away, he didn't hesitate to start packing. JJ
was miffed and probably jealous; he might even have thought it
was a ploy on Suzy's part to get Roderick away. Roderick and Suzy
were always very secretive and he may not have been told the
complete truth about Hanny's illness. Whatever his thoughts, when
Roderick told him that he would have to cut short his holiday and

go to Bern because Hanny was so desperately ill, JJ dismissed it, said he was dramatizing the whole thing, insisted there was nothing seriously wrong with Hanny, it was ridiculous to give up his holiday. Roderick, his emotions presumably heightened by Hanny's condition, took serious objection to JJ's remarks and an ugly, blazing, knockdown row ensued. They were both, I suspect, very, very drunk; and in the early hours of the morning, Roderick packed his suitcase and walked out, taking eight-year-old Roddy with him. The pair of them set off on foot for Cherbourg, a forty-five minute drive away.

Suzy's mother died in September at the family home in Bern, and her father, who had been looking after Hanny during the final stages of her illness, committed suicide the same day. Words can't describe the shock and the horror. Suzy was in England when it happened; it was her younger brother, Roland, who discovered the bodies, but she and Roderick flew out straightaway. None of them ever truly recovered from the experience. And at the time, when my brother badly needed support to help cope with a distraught, traumatized wife and all the horrors that were unfolding in Switzerland – where suicide was still considered illegal and, to compound matters, her father had died intestate – he and JJ were hardly speaking.

Drink helped him cope, and who could blame him? He was already quite a heavy drinker, and on the occasions I saw him – over lunch at Wellpools for example – he was not very good at holding it. He would get drunker much faster than anyone else seemed to and become either belligerent or amorous, and either way difficult to deal with. And there was an occasion in Fleet Street in the late 1970s, when he came to a Christmas party at the *Evening News* and was so drunk he could barely stand up. I was always rather disapproving, and could be distinctly humourless about it. Drink frightened me; I hated what it did to people, hated the loss of control – in myself as much as in anyone else – and hated the sickening sentimentality or the hurtful words that always seemed to follow.

Then, shortly after JJ's terrifying high-speed car chase, Roderick was found by the police slumped at the bottom of some steps outside Waterloo station in the early evening, with a gash on his head,

smelling strongly of whisky. They took him down to the local police
station, charged him with being drunk and disorderly, and kept him
in a cell for most of the night. He had been on his way home, and
although he admitted he had had a drink in Fleet Street after leaving
the office, he insisted he had not been remotely drunk, and was
filled with righteous indignation. He thought he had been attacked,
but the puzzling thing was he had not been robbed; he still had his
wallet, none of his money or valuables had gone, and he still had
his briefcase. Someone, he maintained, must have hit him over the
head and poured whisky down him – someone who wanted to
discredit him. He had the answer; this was revenge. JJ had discredited the policeman's son, and so the police had gone for his
son. He managed to convince JJ of this too, and sought his support
in fighting the charge in court.

Roderick compiled a stack of affidavits from people who were
with him in Fleet Street and could confirm that he had not been
drunk when he left for Waterloo, he gathered character references,
and had a team of people standing by to give evidence in court;
and JJ sent one of his staff off to buy a steel-topped bowler hat to
prevent any further assaults. But sadly, as anyone who had seen
Roderick in recent years knew, the conspiracy theory was far-
fetched. Far more probable was that he had gone into a pub when
he arrived at Waterloo, which the landlord confirmed, had had too
much to drink and had fallen over and hit his head. The magistrate
agreed, found him guilty as charged and fined him some minimal
amount. His defence cost JJ more than a thousand pounds.

Roderick continued to believe it had been a police stitch-up; and
he became convinced that the police were out to get him. He and
Suzy were living in London again by this time, they had bought a
house in East Sheen, and he became so certain that the police were
following him that he stopped using his car and took taxis. And
when Suzy was arrested in a dawn raid on the house and taken
down to the police station for partially obstructing a neighbour's
driveway he felt he was vindicated.

I no longer saw Roderick very often but we spoke on the phone
and it was becoming increasingly difficult to hold any kind of sensible conversation with him. I knew in an instant that he had been

drinking. His voice would be slow and deliberate, he talked non-sense, he veered between fantasy and paranoia, and it was imposs-ible to get him off the phone. I came to dread the sound of the telephone. At first it was only in the evenings but, as time went by, he began to call in the afternoons too and those calls were no better; eventually it made no difference what time of day it was.

Despite the history of alcoholism in the family, JJ refused to believe there was anything wrong with Roderick. Admittedly, in the climate of Fleet Street, where he was surrounded by very heavy drinkers – many of them in his own office – it can't have been easy to recognise that his own son was in trouble. But essentially he denied it because he didn't want to believe it – and what father would? Pam was the same. She and I had always been able to talk about any subject under the sun – we had no secrets from one another – but this was the one exception; she didn't want to discuss it. They both closed their eyes to what was happening, both pre-tended that the telephone calls were perfectly normal, and were both indignant at any suggestion that he was in need of help – even after he lost his job.

He was sacked from the *Daily Telegraph* by Max Hastings, who became Editor in 1986, and was one of many to go. He believed it was because of his involvement with the Institute of Journalists, but he was seldom in the office, and seldom sober when he was. It was a crushing blow. A year or so later he sold his house, and he and Suzy began living in rented properties in the Kingston area, where Roddy went to school.

The previous year we had also moved house – half a mile back down the road, to within fifty yards of where we'd lived originally. This time we were in the big house, to which the little cottage had once belonged. James was running a restaurant in Battersea at that time called The Punter's Pie, which we had bought with the proceeds of one of my books. He had given up the stage. He was a talented actor and he had done some good work – he had spent a year at the National Theatre, he'd played some great parts in rep all over the country, he had been in a number of films and a couple of television series, but, like 99.9 per cent of actors, he hadn't hit the big time. The jobs he enjoyed paid next to nothing, and those that paid well he didn't enjoy. So at the age of thirty-four, after ten years, he decided he had had enough. He did a postgraduate course in business management, took his sister's food and wine course at Leith's, and went into the restaurant business, working initially for a franchise of Pizza Express.

Many were the times I wondered why, on each occasion we moved house, we stayed so close to JJ. He was the principal cause of friction in our lives. James resented the daily intrusion, resented the bad manners and the way he was spoken to in his own home, resented having to rush Sunday lunch each week so that JJ could have his first cigarette of the day, and resented the expectation that he should drop everything whenever my father appeared, in order to do his bidding. He tried writing to JJ, suggesting, in a calm and reasonable fashion, that he might limit his visits to Sunday lunch. JJ took offence on each occasion, stayed away for a few weeks, cut off all phone calls, but then, without any reference to what had gone before, was back to normal. Occasionally the letters were sparked off by rows, when suddenly James could take no more.

One such row happened over Sunday lunch when we had just heard the news that Sam had won a full scholarship to Eton. JJ's immediate reaction was to calculate how many thousands of pounds it would save us over five years. James was appalled; and, for once, I think my father was genuinely puzzled that his remark could have been taken as anything other than a genuine expression of pleasure.

I presented JJ with his fourth grandchild in January 1985, two days after his sixty-sixth birthday. He was another boy, again born in St Mary's, Paddington. We called him Jack, after James's uncle, and from an early age he and JJ took a shine to one another. Then, three years later, on New Year's Eve 1987, I had my fourth and final child, a daughter called Peta. She was named after the theatre director, Peter Coe, a close friend who was killed in a car crash while I was pregnant. JJ was delighted with Peta. He adored all of them, and they adored him in return. It was fascinating to watch the relationships between them develop. They were always pleased to see him when he came through the door, knowing he never came empty-handed, and while they were young they were totally uncritical, and happy to listen to what he wanted to tell them and do what he wanted. But as each child grew older and started to have views of their own, they began to challenge his, which he didn't enjoy, and I think he was pleased to have a younger model to turn to. Whatever their age, he seldom if ever asked them about themselves, about their lives, their friends, their schools, what they thought or felt or hoped for – except in the material sense, like what they wanted for Christmas.

When Sam went to Eton in the autumn of 1987, Alex became the focus of my father's attention, as Jack and Peta were too young. He would take Alex golfing and treat him to Coca-Cola and crisps, and every Monday afternoon, his day off, he would collect Alex from school and take him shopping. And every Monday afternoon, without fail, he would return with some expensive toy or gadget. Sam had not been particularly interested – all he cared about was having a good book to read. But Alex was an insatiable consumer like his grandfather. I was watching my second son become hopelessly spoilt and I was powerless to stop it. When Alex went away to Eton, two years after Sam, Jack and Peta became the objects of JJ's relentless giving. I tried to stop him, to suggest it wasn't good for them to expect a present every time they saw him, and for a while he would stop. He would arrive and say, 'I'm sorry I haven't brought you anything because your mother won't let me.' But he was soon back to arriving with something, even if it was only sweets and comics.

I suppose it was another manifestation of his insecurity. He didn't trust my children to love him for himself; he wasn't confident enough to arrive empty-handed for fear that, without a bribe, they might not be so pleased to see him. So, at Christmas and on birthdays, everything he gave them was bigger and better than their presents from us; just as in my childhood, his presents to me had put my mother's offerings in the shade. He was the one who gave them tricycles and bicycles, golf clubs, archery sets, train sets, the most expensive boxes of Lego, and the biggest teddy bears. It was as though there was some kind of competition, and maybe I shouldn't have minded, but I did.

CHAPTER TWENTY-TWO

Time for Change

My father never doubted he was going to be a success in life, but the young boy who pressed his nose against the window of the Turnberry Hotel and dreamt about one day joining the smart people inside, could never in his wildest dreams have imagined that, nearly fifty years later, he would be seated between the first woman Prime Minister of Great Britain and the Lord Chancellor at a dinner in his honour at the Ritz Hotel in London.

The occasion was his twenty-fifth anniversary as Editor of the *Sunday Express* in November 1979. It was a truly magnificent affair, graced by many of the most influential people in the country, and must rank as the most triumphant evening of his life. Furthermore, he had just had a letter from the Principal Private Secretary at 10 Downing Street, confidentially informing him that he could expect a knighthood in the New Year's Honours List. He had come a long way from the tenements of Glasgow.

The *Sunday Express* had played a very significant part in Margaret Thatcher's election victory six months before. Having at one time been dismissive of Mrs Thatcher's ability – just as he was dismissive of most women's ability – JJ had become a complete and dedicated convert. They had first met in 1974, shortly after Ted Heath had lost the General Election, and shortly before she challenged him for the Leadership of the Tory Party. Gordon Reece, who had once been a reporter on the *Sunday Express*, was then acting as her personal adviser and introduced them over lunch at the Boulestin. JJ's first impression had not been favourable. He thought her unattractive, asexual and intellectually second-rate. But they lunched again and Mrs Thatcher no doubt turned on the charm and the sex appeal – which she had in abundance. My father revised his opinion. It was rare for him to revise his opinion about anything, but the power, the flattery and the sex appeal were a heady combination and he became a devoted and loyal fan – some would say too loyal. And she rewarded him.

His speech that night at the Ritz was superb. He proclaimed Mrs Thatcher to be, 'Our best and maybe last hope,' and suggested ways in which she might remain Prime Minister as long as he had been Editor of the *Sunday Express*. He drew parallels between the two jobs – though 'the parallels between running a country and running a newspaper are not obvious'. He talked about the need to be surrounded by good men, to be motivated by a greater purpose than profit, the need to be sincere, to fight for what you believe and to stand for unchanging values – because 'essentially the British public is unchanged and unchanging. The wild young ravers of yesterday became the staid, sober, fifteen per cent mortgage payers of today.

'For their children, they – as their own fathers and mothers did – want the decent things in life. And they will buy and keep on buying a newspaper that stands for these unchanging values.

'There is not the slightest doubt in my mind that it is this that explains the extraordinary and continuing success of the *Sunday Express*.'

His philosophy had served him very well for twenty-five years, he had been right to resist every passing trend in an attempt to attract new readers, right to keep the paper true to its principles for family reading. But Fleet Street was changing. Newspapers were bigger and more expensive than they had ever been, so people were buying fewer of them. The start of commercial television meant greater competition for advertising revenue, production costs were soaring, the industry was vastly overmanned and the all-powerful print unions had the management in a stranglehold, nowhere more so than at the *Express*, where weak management under Max Aitken had more or less brought them to their knees. What the *Sunday Express* needed as it embarked on the 1980s was someone at the helm who would embrace change, take measures to attract younger readers and see off the competition. JJ at the age of sixty was not that man.

New technology was looming, which would revolutionise the industry, change everyone's working practice and make hundreds of print workers redundant. The unions were determined to fight for their jobs. They were so powerful at that time that if they disapproved of an editorial stance or even the political message of a cartoon, they could stop production of the entire newspaper. Phantom workers with names like Mickey Mouse and Donald Duck were on the payroll. It was cheaper for management to pay these fraudulent salaries than risk a walkout. Every job was strictly delineated and, if someone from the wrong union did something or touched something that fell into another union's province, the workforce could call a strike.

JJ deliberately courted the unions. He used to go down to the machine room with Mike Murphy, the General Manager, on a Saturday night during the print run and chat to the men, which was unusual for an Editor; and he was friendly with several of the Fathers of the Chapel. He played golf with them, they addressed him by his first name and came to drinks in his office at Christmas with senior executives. As a result, if there was a problem with editorial content, the Fathers of the Chapel would bypass the General Manager and go straight to JJ. Mike could see the pros and cons to this; Andrew Cameron, who succeeded Mike as General Manager, thought it was dangerous. 'What JJ never really figured out was that they could drink together, go to each other's functions, but they had different agendas. The mandate of a union official is hours, money, not the profit of the company. No matter how well you got on with the lads, they would stuff you as soon as look at you.'

The company's profits were disastrous; the *Sunday Express* was the only newspaper in the group that was making money – partly because it was a successful formula, partly because JJ kept a tight control on editorial spending – and it was propping up the other titles. They were difficult times, but the real problem was management. Max Aitken was simply not up to the job; he was fundamentally a weak man, who had no real feel for newspapers and none of the passion for them that his father had.

Max surrounded himself with cronies like John Coote, a sailing friend who left the Navy to become Chief Executive and was immortalised by *Private Eye* as Captain John Coote RN (submerged). He was a charming man, as most of Max's friends were, but well out of his depth. In the early 1970s he introduced a redundancy scheme to try and reduce costs, with an unrestricted offer of a month's salary for every year served. Unsurprisingly, there was a mass exodus of all the best journalists who had been with the *Express* for twenty years or so, who pocketed nearly two years' salary and went straight across the road to join the *Daily Mail*.

Jocelyn Stevens was another crony; a flamboyant, hugely wealthy Old Etonian, famous for editing the fashion magazine *Queen*, which he also owned. His grandfather had once owned the *Evening Standard*, and legend had it that he had been swindled out of its ownership on his deathbed by a young and ruthless Beaverbrook. Legend also had it that Jocelyn, who had a fearsome temper, had occasionally chewed the carpet in rage and hurled a filing cabinet out of a fourth-floor window. My father was deeply contemptuous of him – and the feeling was reciprocated. He thought Jocelyn was nothing more than a society dandy who had worked his way into Max's confidence. According to Peter McKay, my father used to suspect there was something homoerotic about Max and the way in which he surrounded himself with men like Jocelyn. He seemed to need them. Not long after the Arab-Israeli Six-Day War in 1967, when the victorious Israeli General Moshe Dayan was about the most famous man in the world, he came to a lunch hosted by Max in the boardroom at the *Express*. It was the most incredible coup. Every newspaper in Fleet Street would have stopped the presses to secure an interview with Dayan, a dashing figure with a black patch over one eye. He was visiting London on a two-day Jewish fundraising trip and Stewart Steven, who was then Diplomatic Correspondent on the *Daily Express*, had been asked by the Israeli Embassy for his advice on how to handle the visit, and had secured the lunch as part of the package.

That morning, Stewart hired a huge limousine to collect the

General from the Israeli embassy, drove down Fleet Street, which was packed with photographers and reporters hoping to get a glimpse of the great man, fought their way into the *Express* building, and arrived on the fourth floor on the dot of one o'clock. The boardroom was empty and Stewart thought for one terrible moment he had told everyone to come on the wrong day. After a minute, JJ arrived with the Editor of the *Daily Express*, Derek Marks. At a quarter past one, fifteen minutes late for his celebrated guest, Max Aitken swept in, flanked by a collection of good-looking men, all of them young, muscular and bronzed. After the introductions, which shed no light on who or why these men were there, Max said, 'We'd better get a move on,' and organised the seating. He put himself at one end of the table and Moshe Dayan at the other, surrounded on both sides by the mysterious young men, with Derek Marks and my father opposite one another in the middle.

The conversation quickly turned to sailing, and it became apparent that the people Max had chosen to meet this incredible figure were members of his Admiral Cup racing team – sailors, who talked about nothing else for most of the lunch. JJ kept trying to interrupt to let the General speak but it was impossible. Finally, when they were on their coffee, he could take it no more. 'We've got Moshe Dayan here,' he said pointedly, 'General, I wonder if you would like to give us your impression of what is going on in the Middle East and how you see things working out?' 'Yes, yes,' said Max, 'absolutely right.' So Moshe Dayan spoke for about five minutes, and JJ and Derek Marks asked him some questions for no more than another five or ten minutes, before Max looked at his watch. 'Well, boys,' he said, 'I think we'd all better go back and do some work. Very nice to meet you, General,' and he was gone.

Stewart Steven was left to take Dayan down in the lift, and back to the Israeli Embassy. They drove in silence; Stewart entirely lost for words. Eventually at Trafalgar Square he said, 'I suppose I owe you an apology?' 'I suppose you do,' said the General. Embarrassed and humiliated, Stewart walked into Derek Marks's office when he got back to the office and said, 'I just can't take this organisation, I'm going, I've got to resign.' And Marks said, 'Oh, John Junor said you would say that, but don't. Come on, for heaven's sake, don't be so silly. I know. We all know. Just grow up.'

In January 1977, at the age of sixty-six, Max had a serious stroke and, although he eventually came back to the office, he never fully recovered. A year later, the ailing empire he had inherited from his father was sold to Trafalgar House for £12 million. On the night of his anniversary dinner at the Ritz, therefore, which Max attended in a wheelchair, JJ had a new proprietor, Victor Matthews – better known to readers of *Private Eye* as Chips and Four Forks.

There is no doubt my father was keen to like his proprietors, for self-preservation if nothing else, but I think he genuinely did like and admire Victor Matthews. Matthews was a self-made builder from North London, whose only previous experience of newspapers had been delivering them as a teenage paperboy. JJ would tell with admiration the story of how Victor made his fortune. Having worked his way up through the trade, he finally started a small building firm of his own, and won the tender for a job on which there was a misunderstanding about quantities, which worked in his favour. While he had estimated the job in square yards, the client had thought the estimate was for square feet. Victor never looked back; his company was taken over in 1968 by Trafalgar House, a property and construction group run by Nigel Broakes, and the two men made a powerful team and – with the acquisition of companies like Cementation, Cunard and the Ritz – a rich team.

Matthews and JJ worked well together, largely because the Chairman didn't interfere in either the content or direction of the *Sunday Express* – except once. Victor had long hankered after an honour, and was extremely miffed when JJ was given a knighthood and he had nothing. His behaviour entirely changed and he started trying to throw his weight around editorially. JJ spoke to Mrs Thatcher and shortly afterwards had a call from Gordon Reece, indicating that Victor could expect something more than a knighthood in the Birthday Honours. JJ let Victor know and the relationship returned to an even keel.

JJ was completely thrilled to have a knighthood and all his well-held beliefs about journalistic independence, being beholden to no one, and accepting no favours went by the wayside as he designed his coat of arms, incorporating a jay in memory of the orphaned birds that Roderick had rescued as a child, and the motto 'Look up and laugh'.

After his knighthood, the name at the head of the spoof column in *Private Eye* changed to Sir Jonah Junor and, when Matthews was given his peerage, he was referred to as Lord Whelks. The cover that week depicted him with his head up someone's body, with the headline, 'The Real Burke's Peerage'. Matthews was mortified, he thought everyone was laughing and sniggering at him, and called JJ in to see him. 'I think you should give up *Private Eye*,' he said. My father assumed he was talking about his lunches with Richard Ingrams. 'He's very well informed,' he protested. 'No, no, not that,' said Matthews; 'the column you write. I know you've changed the name, but I know it's you.'

Four years later, Trafalgar floated the newspaper group as a public company called Fleet Holdings. JJ was brought on to the board – the only Editor who was – and given share options valued at 22p per share. A year later the share price fell briefly to 16p and, such was his confidence in Victor Matthews and the direction in which the company was going, that he advised all his friends and colleagues to buy Fleet shares. Some took his advice and when, three years later, they were worth 368p, lived to thank him. Others who had had one duff tip too many from JJ in the past, kicked themselves.

The year of the flotation, the *Sunday Express*, which for years had reigned supreme in the middle market, faced competition. Associated Newspapers launched the *Mail on Sunday* in May 1982 as a direct challenge to the *Sunday Express*. Everyone on the paper was worried; the *Sunday Express* was looking tired, its readership was ageing, it needed to attract younger readers. But if JJ was concerned that the new paper was going to take circulation from the *Sunday Express*, he didn't show it. He made not one single change. The first edition of the *Mail on Sunday* was disastrous. JJ declared it 'Piss poor', as it was, and as it continued to be for the next three weeks. But after four weeks the Editor was sacked and David English was sent in with a team from the *Daily Mail* to start again. It swiftly became a very good newspaper and, as the circulation of the *Mail on Sunday* started to soar, the *Sunday Express*'s went into freefall. Stewart Steven was appointed Editor of the *Mail on Sunday* in November and is convinced that, if JJ had not been so complacent about the *Sunday Express*, he could have killed the *Mail on Sunday* stone dead. Instead he gave it breathing space.

It was not that JJ was short of ideas. He repeatedly asked the younger members of staff for suggestions about what could be done to attract a younger readership and they provided him with plenty. Graham Lord, the Literary Editor, was not the only one to suggest a proper television page – until 1982 there had been nothing more than a programme listing. What about an interview or two and a guide to next week's viewing? 'You're obsessed by television,' JJ told him scornfully.

'John, I hardly ever watch TV,' protested Graham, 'but ninety-five per cent of the population of Britain does, and we should have it.' 'Only morons watch television,' retorted my father, and ignored that and every other idea that was put to him. The staff concluded he wasn't really interested.

The News Editor, Henry Macrory, suggested a new typeface on the leader page, and changing the long page leads. 'I'm not asking how the paper could be changed,' said JJ, 'I'm asking for additional things to make it better; the paper itself is fine.' Henry admits that he probably said, 'Yes I agree, it's a wonderful newspaper,' and that he is as culpable as everyone else in the office, who used to say 'Yes' for fear of having their heads bitten off or being told 'You must be completely naïve if you think that.'

I think JJ was frightened of change, frightened of getting it wrong and losing those readers who had been loyally buying the *Sunday Express* for decades. The paper may have lost circulation but it was still making a lot of money and it was supporting the rest of the group; he sat on the board, he knew the figures, and knew that, if he lost circulation, the whole group could go. Beaverbrook had been passionate about newspapers; the men who took over his titles were not, they were businessmen and financiers. And in the absence of a strong proprietor, constantly writing memos, criticising the newspaper and keeping his Editors on their toes – something my father had not had since Beaverbrook's death nearly twenty years before – he had been allowed to stick belligerently to the formula he was comfortable with. But he was obviously aware of the problem because he was hugely defensive about the paper, and lashed out at any kind of dissenting voice, however well intentioned.

In the mid-1960s, the Finance Director had written a memo to Max Aitken, copied to JJ, flagging up his concern for the future and arguing that, although the circulation of the *Sunday Express* was currently 4.25 million, unless they attracted a younger readership the existing readership would eventually die off with obvious consequences. JJ's reaction to the memo was one of absolute fury, he insisted it be withdrawn, and he all but demanded the culprit's resignation.

Nearly twenty years later, Peter Walker, then Secretary of State for Energy, endeavoured to compliment his host at JJ's annual Boat Show lunch. He told JJ how he had picked up a copy of the *Sunday Express* and was reading and enjoying it when he suddenly spotted that the date at the top of the paper was 1949 and he had failed to notice. JJ was furious and instructed Cross-Bencher to write a paragraph saying that Peter Walker had not changed since he was a schoolboy in 1949.

Part of the problem was my father's inability to get rid of people who were past their best. Some of the writers on the *Sunday Express* had actually been there since 1949, but he had always been loyal to his staff and liked to be surrounded by people he knew and could count on, even if they were no longer as effective as before. Jimmy Kinlay had tackled him about this; he wanted to lose Roderick Mann, the show-business writer, who in the 1980s was working for the *LA Times* in America, and sending very inferior copy to the *Sunday Express*. One day even JJ lost patience with him. 'What are we going to do about Roddy Mann?' he said, pacing up and down his office. 'This is intolerable.' But when Jimmy said he should be sacked and Clive Hirschhorn, his deputy, be given the job, JJ prevaricated. Jimmy was disappointed. 'This was someone who had preached to us, and virtually made it an act of faith to us, that the *Sunday Express* came first, it was providing our livelihood, it was a great newspaper, and we had an obligation to it. I thought this was a betrayal.'

There is no doubt that JJ stayed where he was for too long. He didn't choose to go – probably because he was afraid of losing the routine he relied upon; and no proprietor dared make the choice for him for fear of unbalancing the milch cow. For years he had hinted to a chosen few on the staff that they would be the next Editor of the *Sunday Express*, and whenever he was feeling particularly sorry for himself he would tell me that he was going to 'chuck it all in and go and live in Barfleur'. But it was bravado. He was terrified of retirement and having no desk to go to.

Yet, in 1985, at the age of sixty-six, it looked as though he might actually do it. He took Graham Lord, one of the chosen few, to lunch to talk about the paper. Graham had met JJ through Roderick when they were at Cambridge together, had been on the *Sunday Express* ever since and was one of my father's favourites. JJ told Graham that he would soon be stepping down as Editor, and there were only two people on the paper that he could trust to keep it going in the right direction, Graham or Henry Macrory, who was then the News Editor. Graham had never wanted the job, as JJ knew, because he was a novelist in his spare time and as Editor would have no time to write. 'Mike Murphy and Victor Matthews don't want Henry to succeed me. That leaves you.' Graham protested but eventually, after a bottle of wine and a couple of glasses of Calvados, agreed to apply for the job, wrote to Matthews and was called in for a lengthy interview. 'I like you, Graham,' said Matthews, 'I like you a lot.' And at the end of a second interview, a few days later, announced, 'You've got the job, you will succeed John Junor. You will be Editor within a couple of months.'

Graham went back to his desk feeling sick. A moment later the buzzer went, and JJ called him into his office. 'Victor's fallen in love with you,' he said.

'Yes, that's great isn't it?' said Graham.

'No, it's not great at all. He wants to announce that you'll be the next Editor in this week's paper.'

'Well, that's what you wanted, isn't it?' said Graham.

'No, no, no, not now, he hasn't even interviewed Max Davidson yet.'

He then told Victor not to make an announcement, and told

Jimmy Kinlay, by now JJ's deputy – Victor Patrick having been tragically killed by a car in Spain some years before – Max Davidson, the Features Editor, Henry Macrory and one or two others to get an application in to Victor Matthews immediately. Graham never forgave him, quite understandably. But Henry Macrory thinks JJ suddenly realised that if Graham's appointment had been announced, without Matthews having seen anyone else, the other people JJ had hinted to over the years would have been justifiably upset.

Victor Matthews was completely baffled. He thought he'd done what JJ wanted. 'I don't really know what JJ's up to,' he told Henry. 'He says one thing one day and another the next. I don't even know that he's resigning now.'

The reason JJ changed his mind about leaving was because it had become apparent that Fleet Holdings was facing a hostile takeover bid from United Newspapers, and helping Victor fend it off became the priority. But they were unsuccessful. The climax came on 14 October. JJ had been playing golf at Walton Heath and found an urgent message waiting for him in the clubhouse. His presence was needed at a Fleet board meeting right away. At the end of the meeting, Victor Matthews packed his bags and JJ had yet another new proprietor.

David Stevens, now Lord Stevens, was a very different character from Victor Matthews, with a very different background and field of expertise. He was a public school educated, economics graduate from Cambridge, and a very substantial figure in the City. But, like Victor, he was no newspaperman. JJ was nevertheless optimistic at their first meeting. He had high hopes that Stevens might turn out to be another Beaverbrook, and initially he was enthusiastic about him. Peter McKay thinks JJ had a 'Hudson complex' – named after the butler in the TV series *Upstairs Downstairs*. Whoever was master of the house deserved his complete support and he wouldn't allow the under staff to rebel against him. Initially, Stevens claims to have liked my father but, after three years, the relationship had become poisonous, and there was not a hint of warmth in Stevens's voice or demeanour when he spoke to me about him.

My father offered his resignation as soon as United took over

Fleet, and although Stevens persuaded him to stay for a few months to see how things went, it was clear he wanted out. Stevens had set a target of two thousand job losses from the offices in London, Manchester and Glasgow. It was inevitable: the newspapers were losing ten million pounds a year but, for someone who had done so much to nurture his staff and protect them from the ravages of management, it was more than my father could stomach. Anyone over the age of sixty-five was automatically retired, and Les Vanter was one of the casualties. JJ was mortified. He had always told Les that, as long as he was Editor, Les would be Sports Editor, and had promised to double his salary six months before he retired, to boost his pension. Les was sixty-five, so he was out. 'John went berserk,' says Les. 'He was terribly upset that I hadn't had this big increase – he felt he'd let me down. He wrote me a remarkable letter; and after I'd gone he'd ring every three or four months to fix lunch.'

My father's successor was Robin Esser, who had been on the *Daily Express* as Executive Editor. JJ wasn't consulted about the appointment, which irked him, and, when he heard who it was, called it 'absolutely laughable – it's a man I once gave a job to on Saturdays and he was so bad I couldn't keep him on'. But, according to Robin Esser, who feared the relationship might be very difficult, my father behaved impeccably. He gave up the Editor's seat immediately and was given an office owned by United Newspapers in Tudor Street, five minutes' walk away, where he continued writing his column, and never once tried to interfere in what Esser was doing to the paper or its staffing. 'Stevens was keen to bestow a title on JJ like Editor-in-Chief,' says Robin. 'I didn't want that, neither did he. I said, "I think I have the title for John – John Junor, it's the best by-line in Fleet Street." John said, "Absolutely," and that was that.'

By way of farewell, the staff gave a party for him on board a barge on the River Thames, at which he was presented with a decanter, and a special mock-up edition of the *Sunday Express*. 'Will ye nae come back again?' asked the headline; Giles drew a special cartoon and Mrs Thatcher wrote a tribute. 'Is it the end of civilisation?' asked another headline:

It is said that at the impressionable age of two, when he was not quite yet Editor of the *Sunday Express*, John Junor was frightened by a queer wearing Hush Puppies and sipping white wine. If this is indeed the case, then he has certainly had his revenge.

For he has dedicated himself with spectacular success to the task of terrifying pooves, pipe-smokers, Lefties, prelates, politicians, pederasts, lesbians, the Irish, bearded men (and bearded ladies), ponces, poseurs, perverts, mugs and muggers, wimps and wallies, morons, bunglers, cretins, toy-boys, clowns and the Royal Family . . .

JJ was delighted, but he was still no good at laughing at himself, and the leg-pull would have amused the assembled crowd far more than my father.

And so he moved out of the office on the fifth floor that had been his kingdom for thirty-two years. He took down the photograph of me, aged eighteen, taken by Colin Emson, that hung on his wall, and the pictures of him aboard *Outcast*, and with President Lyndon Johnson in the Oval Office, and entered the lift, which had been the scene for so many priceless conversations as he searched for small-talk, for the last time. It was a sad moment, but JJ never allowed himself to wallow for long. He moved into his new office and began work on next week's column. David Stevens was happy for him to carry on with it. 'I liked his column, it was good, it was sparky, he'd take people out to lunch on Friday and slam them on Sunday. I quite liked that.'

His column became his life and, far from easing off, relaxing the routine, and enjoying a slower pace, which at the age of sixty-seven might have held some appeal, he drove himself harder than ever. He allowed the column to fill as much time as he had previously taken to write it and edit a thirty-two-page newspaper as well. The pressure on him seemed to be more rather than less, and his temper was as fearsome as ever, as those who continued to work with him knew.

Robin Esser did not turn out to be a success. He survived for three years, but the circulation was continuing to drop, while the

Mail on Sunday's was climbing ever upward. David Stevens, by now Lord Stevens of Ludgate, decided Esser would have to go and started to look around for a successor. In retrospect, Stevens says he should never have allowed JJ to continue writing the column; the continued presence of such a dominant personality made it difficult for Esser to succeed. But Ian Irvine, the Chief Executive, who left Fleet Holdings with Matthews, believes the real problem was not editors but money. 'David never invested in the newspapers and if you don't keep the marketing and promotional spend up, and keep yourself in front of the public, they forget you. It's never any one person's fault; it's a whole series of happenings. David had paid a lot of money for Fleet so he had to make it pay, and he squeezed it. He inherited several of our investments, which he sold – he was taking money from wherever he could, to make up for the price he had paid. And they had to re-equip, so they had to move from Fleet Street, and all of that took money away from the newspapers.'

They moved from the old building, affectionately known as the Black Lubyanka, to a smart new block on the south side of Black-friars Bridge, where JJ had an office on the eighth floor. Stevens asked my father if he had any suggestions about who might replace Robin Esser. He put forward two names as possible candidates; the one that interested Stevens was Charles Wilson, Editor of *The Times*, a fellow Glaswegian with whom JJ had become friendly during a press trip to Moscow six months before. A lunch was duly arranged in Stevens's office in the City, but, although the lunch went well, the questions he asked were cursory and there was no offer of a job. It was not surprising, because, by the time they sat down to lunch, someone else had already been given the job – his appointment was announced a few hours later. My father was furious; he had been ignored and humiliated and it was the end of any kind of friendship or admiration for Stevens. He felt nothing but contempt for him.

Robin Morgan had previously been Features Editor of *The Sunday Times*, and his appointment as Editor of the *Sunday Express* must have surprised him as much as it surprised everyone else. He had applied for a job as Editor of the *Yorkshire Post*, a regional paper owner by United, and been given the *Express* instead. JJ took against him – quite unreasonably, he confessed – but as he pointed out with some pride, during the thirty-two years he had been Editor of the newspaper he had always been totally unreasonable.

Meanwhile, over at the *Mail on Sunday*, the *Sunday Express*'s archrival, the Editor there, Stewart Steven, had a phone call out of the blue from JJ. 'I don't think much of that Julie Burchill columnist you've got,' he said. 'What you need is a proper political columnist.'

'What, like you, John?' said Stewart.

'That's not why I telephoned you. I phoned to say I didn't think much of your Julie Burchill.'

My father had scarcely spoken to Stewart Steven for twenty years, and Stewart couldn't decide whether this was an approach or just JJ mischief-making. If it was an approach, he knew he would be mad not to take the column – it had an incredible readership and a huge following. But if he got it wrong, he could see JJ tagging his column 'The one the *Mail on Sunday* wanted but couldn't get'. The reality was a combination of the two. JJ wanted to move, and he wanted to make mischief – but not for Associated Newspapers. His intention was to take his column, defect to the enemy, and give Lord Stevens and Robin Morgan a two-fingered salute in passing.

Not only had Stevens snubbed him, but Morgan had done the unforgivable. In an interview with *UK Press Gazette*, the journalists' trade paper, he had said of the *Sunday Express* that 'One of the world's great newspapers under Sir John Junor had, in the 1980s, become one of the poorest newspapers in Britain.' JJ had been Editor until 1986, and for him this was the final straw. That August he went off on holiday to Barfleur, leaving a characteristic tailpiece – but with one intriguing sting in it that only a few recognised.

When you read this I will once again be walking barefoot on the wet sand of a Normandy beach.

Watching the fishing boats come back to harbour. Taking care to keep clear of men with moustaches and sideburns, wearing braces and sunglasses, and clutching purses tightly in their hands.

And humming all the while that wonderful love song of Robert Burns:

'Ae fond kiss, and then we sever'.

Anyone know the next line?

The missing line is 'Ae fareweel, alas, for ever!'

On his first day back from holiday, he sent Stevens a letter of resignation. They had a tempestuous last meeting and JJ was out of the building within hours. 'I felt sorry that he'd gone,' says Stevens. 'One always regrets the passing of an era, so one was sorry he felt he had to go, but it was his wish to go, not mine. You could still have a column like that in a paper that was changing, but I don't think he liked the changes. Then he went to work for someone he had spent the whole of his life denigrating.'

Murdoch MacLennan was a fellow member of the Express board, who joined as Production Director after the takeover, and became one of my father's closest friends in the last years of his life. His memory is that my father went seconds before he was pushed. 'JJ did the unthinkable in moving to the *Mail on Sunday* – unless you knew some of the background to the unhappiness. It was all being done behind closed doors. They were ganging up on him. He was going to be asked to leave because he was quite vocal about his unhappiness with Morgan, and he decided to make the move just ahead of the posse.'

JJ said he was given virtually twenty-four hours to clear his desk and take all his possessions with him, and that was the story, which was reported in the following day's newspapers. Andrew Cameron, who was General Manager, says this was not so. He was asked when he wanted to go – 'one week, two weeks? He chose to go straight away.'

There were many tributes to him that week. Peter McKay, then writing a column in the *Evening Standard*, seemed to say it all.

I saw no mention of Sir John Junor in my edition of the *Sunday Express* yesterday. You would have thought they might have found space to mention the departure of a man who spent half of his seventy years, most of them as Editor, at the paper.

His predecessor, John Gordon, was given a large dinner in Whitehall by the then proprietor Sir Max Aitken. There was a new Rolls-Royce waiting for him at the door. And that was for his eightieth birthday. The Aitkens may have made a mess of things in the end, but few who worked for Sir Max, or his father Lord Beaverbrook, fail to treasure rich memories.

I do not know the present businessman who runs the *Express* group, Lord Stevens. Neither do I have the faintest idea why he was ennobled by Margaret Thatcher. But I feel sure it won't have been for journalistic flair, style or the type of decency which, when an eminent employee who has made millions for your company leaves after thirty-five years, insists on honouring the man.

I have an axe to grind on the subject of John Junor. He was my first Fleet Street Editor twenty-five years ago. He advanced me £10 to buy three nylon shirts which, he said, 'will stop you sending your washing to your poor old mother in Banffshire'.

I have never been blind to his faults – impatience, cynicism and a tyrannical intellectual style – but for me they are chickenfeed when put alongside his huge virtues, which include a fantastic zest for life and journalism, the courage of a lion, and charm that owes nothing to posh public schools and everything to his vast experience of life and people. Shame on you, Lord Stevens.

CHAPTER TWENTY-THREE

Selina

When he gave up being Editor of the *Sunday Express*, a number of people that JJ thought were friends – politicians, business leaders, the great and the good – people he believed lunched with him because of who, rather than what, he was, started to fall away. It was inevitable, and happens as much to politicians and captains of industry when they retire, as it does to Editors of national newspapers. They lose their value; there's a new person in the hot seat, and no time in busy people's lives to keep up with everyone.

But, to his great joy, amongst those who continued to lunch with my father, and be pleased to do so, was Selina Scott. My father's passion for her was legendary; he had been raving about her in his column for seventeen years, and what everyone wanted to know was did he ever sleep with her? She was his discovery, the gorgeous young television presenter he found hidden in Scotland. After he wrote about her she was brought to London to front the *News at Ten* and became one of the best known, best loved faces in Britain. She went on to host *Breakfast Time* and *The Clothes Show*, and interview people like the Prince of Wales and Donald Trump.

My great fear was that she would refuse to talk to me. Speculation about whether they had been lovers had been rife for years, and I don't deny that I was as interested as anyone to know the truth. I knew they met for lunch regularly, and I found letters and photographs amongst my father's things. I also knew she was an intensely private person, who as a rule said nothing about her personal life, and, when after several weeks there was still no reply to my letter, I began to think I had fallen under that rule.

But Selina had been abroad, and eventually did reply, saying she would be very happy to talk to me. Lunch seemed the appropriate way to discuss my father, so we met at the Groucho Club. It turned out to be an emotional meeting. We sat down as strangers – having only ever met briefly at his funeral when she had been in tears – but left as friends. I felt an extraordinary affinity towards this woman who had so enchanted him; there seemed to be so much to talk about, so much in common – it was as though we had shared and now lost a difficult but doting father. We compared notes, we cried, we laughed, we analysed. I understood exactly what he had loved about her, and I understood, without even having to ask, the nature of their relationship. He called her his friend – gorgeous, delicious, warm, compassionate and unaffected. She was all of those things. But she was more. She was successful, famous, intelligent without being overweening, pretty and feminine, quiet, gentle, non-confrontational, well-informed, prepared to listen and take his advice, and best of all she was always pleased to see him. I have no doubt he fancied her rotten, but I think more than that, she was the daughter he would have liked to have.

As I sat and listened to her talk, I envied her relationship with him. She came to it with none of the history; she hadn't heard the things he'd said to my mother, hadn't seen the hurt and could take him at face value. What she saw was the charming, generous, endlessly inquisitive man, who knew everyone and everything – and if he didn't, bluffed. She found him exciting to be with, interesting, powerful, mischievous, and even faintly dangerous – the man that I saw glimpses of but couldn't allow myself to embrace. They could talk – although she learnt there were topics to avoid – and she could enjoy his company, his support and the interest he took in her life and her welfare. I knew why she missed him.

They first met in 1980 when she was a presenter on Grampian Television in Aberdeen and she interviewed him for a series called *The Reporters* about expatriate Scots who had reached great heights in journalism. Selina had written to him to ask if he would take part, and was surprised when he agreed. It was a terrific interview and there was a lot of feedback from viewers, many of whom remembered his family in Easter Ross. But she admits that if she had known then what she knew about him later she would never have had the courage to write to him. That evening she took him to dinner in Aberdeen and, at the end of the night, his parting shot was that when she next came to London she should ring him so he could repay her with lunch.

In his column that week he said he would remember the blue eyes of the beautiful lassie, Selina Scott, who made Angela Rippon and Anna Ford look like a couple of sock-knitting crones.

Is there a TV boss reading?

Why should the whole country be denied a sight which the people in the Grampian Region enjoy almost every evening?

Shortly afterwards Selina was approached by ITN and asked to present the *News at Ten* in place of Anna Ford. Since he had written about her, she telephoned him to let him know. He repeated the invitation made in Aberdeen, and when she arrived in London to start work she phoned and they lunched at the Terrazza Est.

'JJ always claimed the credit, and I didn't admit it for years,' says Selina. 'But when Anna Ford decided to leave ITN, the fact that he had written about me, did help. They had a policy of looking at the regions so they might have found me anyway, but it did help. So I rang when I arrived in London and he took me to lunch, and that's when he started giving me advice. Then it became a regular thing, every two months or so he would ring and say, "Let's have lunch."'

He wrote about her repeatedly. Sometimes whole paragraphs were devoted to her, sometimes her name was a throwaway line. 'How do the French do it? I do not know,' he wrote after a piece about yet another cheap and delicious meal he'd had in Normandy and his reluctance to come home. 'It was only the thought of Selina awaiting on the quay with haggis and chips that kept me going.' He had been lost for words, he wrote on another occasion, at a lunch to mark the publication of *The Best of JJ*, where the glittering guests had given him a standing ovation.

After all that, what can there possibly be left for me to look forward to for the rest of the year?

Except, perhaps, the chance of having the last waltz with Selina?

Nothing delighted him more than the speculation that they were lovers; he fuelled it himself. He arrived in the office one Saturday morning in such a good mood – unheard of on a Saturday – that everyone remarked upon it. They decided he must have had a good night, and each member of staff homed in on a separate clue. Peter Vane saw he was writing a letter to 'Darling' someone, Henrietta Mackay was given a letter addressed to Selina Scott to post when she went out at lunchtime, which he could perfectly easily have posted himself, and, over lunch, he confided to Henry Macrory that he had had dinner with Selina the night before, saying, 'Marvellous. Everyone was watching and they were all wondering who the lucky man was.' They pieced their bits of the story together, as he no doubt knew they would, and deduced an affair. At JJ's Boat Show lunch a month or two later, where Selina was a guest, as was Margaret Thatcher, everyone was watching like hawks. 'They seemed very close,' was the consensus. The evidence was compelling, but no one was certain one way or the other.

The truth is there was no affair, and there was no dinner either. 'He was a father figure to me, a friend, an ally, and always a supporter, instinctively,' Selina told me. She talked about their lunches and their conversations, and yet again it all had a familiar ring to it. He'd be complimentary when they met, but he never told her he liked what she was wearing or even that he liked her TV work. She would find out what he thought of it by what he wrote in his column. He didn't want to know about her work or the people she'd met and inter-viewed. He wasn't interested in people like Gore Vidal, and if she said she had talked to Tony Blair, all he would want to know were details about what he was wearing, what shoes he had on – and then what did she think of men who wore grey shoes. He wanted her to gossip about her co-presenters and tell him how much money she was earn-ing and what she was spending on her flat and on living in London. And he told her what she ought to be doing with her career.

She gave him a number of presents during the course of their friendship, little things at Christmas or as a thank you after a spate of lunches, because he would never let her pay. 'He made me think what I had given him was the best gift in the entire world and would write me a little note.

'I was always delighted to see him, always felt happy when he rang to say "Come and have lunch," but lunch used to be a bit of a trial. I would go away and think, "What have I said that he could use – not against me but someone else?" You had to be on guard with him all the time.'

When Selina moved to *Breakfast Time*, her co-presenter was Frank Bough, and the question of her salary was raised on the floor of the House of Commons by Teddy Taylor MP who said, 'Is this woman worth £50,000?' No one evidently thought of asking whether Frank Bough was worth more than that. JJ was on the phone immediately to Selina, suggesting lunch. 'I knew immediately what it was all about. I said, "You can save yourself lunch. I am not earning £50,000." He never once said they're not paying you enough, it was always the other way around. "Aren't you? How much are you earning?" "I'm not telling you how much I'm earning, it's not as much as that, and what do you think about Teddy Taylor?" But he wasn't interested in him at all. I had to go and have lunch and go through the whole thing again. "Well is it near £50,000? Or over £50,000?" I said, "I am not getting involved in this. It is not enough. I have to get up every morning at 3 o'clock . . ." But he wasn't a bit interested, all he wanted to know was how much I was being paid.'

The other thing that fascinated him was her private life, but she wouldn't play on that subject either. 'He kept saying, "There's someone in Scotland isn't there?" I'd say, "I don't know who you're talking about," and he'd say, "They say there is," and I'd say, "Well there isn't." '

During Robin Esser's editorship, his deputy wanted to run a story that Selina was gay and told Henry Macrory to have her doorstepped. JJ got to hear about this and rang Henry. 'Is it true that you've got reporters watching Selina?' he asked. Henry explained the story they were checking out. 'What an absolute hoot,' he said contemptuously. 'Anybody who thinks that must be so naïve.'

He would warn Selina about these kind of stories. He would ring her up and say in an ominous tone of voice, 'Something's going to appear about you in the *Mirror* or the *News of the World*. I've been hearing about it, I'll try and find out more.' Selina admits, 'I didn't really want to know, because it made it worse.' But he never warned her when he was writing about her himself. It wasn't always a lunch that triggered a paragraph in his column, but very often what he said instinctively reflected what she was thinking herself – even if articulating her thoughts wasn't always helpful. In 1992, for instance, he asked in his column why Esther Rantzen, 'whose *That's Life* audience figures have slumped from 15 million to 8.4 million and who many feel is long since past her sell-by date, is awarded a new four-year contract worth £1.2 million,' while Selina Scott, 'is shunted into inconsequential programmes. I do not pretend to know,' he wrote, 'but I sure as hell hope that the Chairman of the BBC, Mr Marmaduke Hussey, is going to tell us.'

'I could always depend on him to pick up my mood, my particular predicament. He could instinctively do it, even when I hadn't seen him for a couple of months. When I went from Sky to ITV in 1995, he wrote that I had been like a duchess in a whorehouse reading the news at Sky.'

'It was the same with Diana. He kept an eye on her and what she was doing with her life. If I started to defend Charles, if I dared, there was no question we were going anywhere with that line – he'd made up his mind.'

The Princess of Wales was another of my father's heroines and, although he did stick the knife into her from time to time – as he did occasionally to Selina, he wouldn't countenance criticism from anyone else. She had wooed him, and he had fallen under her spell. I remember him coming home from their first meeting in November 1984. He had been invited to lunch at Kensington Palace to find he was the only guest. The Prince of Wales was trying to persuade Editors to understand her need for some privacy, and she had sat on a settee and motioned him to take an armchair beside her. He was enraptured and entranced, and came away with the conviction that Charles was a serious man obsessed with the idea of serving the nation, and in danger of both overwhelming and boring his wife.

He turned on her savagely, however, when Andrew Morton's book came out, calling it 'an act of the basest treachery . . . not just against her husband but against the whole institution of Monarchy', but his anger didn't last for long. He was turning out of the *Mail on Sunday* in his Range Rover one night, when a woman driving a car leaned out of her window and said, 'Sir John, how lovely to see you. I do like your column, even when you have a go at me.' He looked down to find the Princess of Wales twinkling at him, and, from that moment on, he was once more her greatest supporter, and chided Charles for trying to foist his mistress on the country.

'I can't figure out why he was so absolutely black and white,' says Selina. 'You couldn't change his mind, even if you'd wanted to have a real argument with him. I gave that up very early on. If you argued he would just keep very quiet, say nothing and then come back in his column the next week and say exactly what he felt about whatever it was.

'Whenever I left the restaurant, we'd get to the corner, I'd get into a cab or, if it was Arcadia in Kensington, I'd walk back to my flat, which was nearby and he'd stand on the corner and watch me. He waited until I was out of sight, or he'd watch the cab pull away. He had a look of vulnerability, but I thought it was part of him, rather like a little spaniel pup. He was very secretive about so much: he kept a ring around him, which didn't allow penetration but I always thought he was lonely, I felt that very strongly. He missed having a family around him.'

He wrote about her for the very last time on 27 April 1997, in the very last column he wrote, six days before he died.

Selina Scott must be bitterly regretting her decision ever to leave ITN to join Sky TV. Since the move, her audiences have become smaller and smaller – and through no fault of her own. Simply because viewers are not turning on to Sky talk-shows. It is said that her new weekly talk-show on Sky One has an audience of only 45,000 viewers. There are occasions when it has plummeted to 6,000.

For my own part I think this is a cruel waste of talent. As well as being a vision of beauty on the screen, Selina Scott has a wonderfully warm TV personality and a voice which makes even strong men feel weak at the knees.

Why doesn't ITN invite her back to front their *News at Ten?*

She would be a far better presenter and attract a bigger audience than both the unctuous Trevor McDonald and the po-faced Julia Somerville put together.

What he didn't know was that Selina had already quit the programme and decided to back away from television for a while. 'To my real sadness, his last column was a valediction to me in a way. I just thought how can anyone do that, know that about someone? After all these years, from the beginning to the end, he wrapped up my career. He was right in some ways. I think I took on too many challenges, perhaps I pushed myself too hard for too long. When he wrote that I felt television hadn't fulfilled my expectations and I wanted to back away from it, he was partly right. He instinctively knew, even though I hadn't seen him for a long time. It was uncanny, almost like putting a marker down in your life. I miss him in lots of ways.'

CHAPTER TWENTY-FOUR

Relative Values

If I could go back in time and change just one day in my life it would be a summer's afternoon in 1986 when I sat down in the sunshine to talk about JJ for a magazine article. One of my father's favourite quotations was from the Rabbie Burns poem, *To a Louse*:

> *O wad some Power the giftie gie us*
> *To see oursels as ithers see us!*

It's not often we get to know how other people see us, but that afternoon he and I did and I wish it had never happened.

I had had a call from an American journalist living in London called Danny Danziger. He was writing a series for *The Sunday Times Magazine* called 'Relative Values', in which two members of a family talk about one another, separately. My father had agreed to be interviewed about me, would I agree to talk about him? It sounded harmless enough and since my father had agreed, I said yes.

Danny arrived from London, bearing a bag of sugar mice for my children, and a tape recorder. He was charming, unfazed by the chaos at the door of dogs, cats and wellington boots, and I warmed to him immediately. One of my colleagues on *4 What It's Worth* was his cousin, he told me, so we had something in common, and plenty to talk about while I made us some tea. By the time he switched on his tape recorder my guard was down, and I spoke as I might have spoken to a friend. My father, by contrast, saw Danny briefly in his office, and gave him a conventional interview. That was where we posed together for a photograph to go with the article, sitting back to back, smiling lovingly at one another. This is what appeared, one verbatim interview following the other in the style of the series.

Sir John Junor. I like her looks very much indeed, she's smashing. I don't think she takes after me at all. I look on myself as being singularly unattractive, but I think she is a pippin.

My very first memories are her crying out 'Mummy, Mummy,' from her bed at night and wanting absolutely nothing. But when I went up she would say 'No, no I want Mummy.' The only occasion in my life in which I have raised my hand to her was when she had cried 'Mummy' one night perhaps 100 times, merely to attract attention. I took this three-year-old and smacked her once gently on the bottom. I don't think she or I have ever forgotten that traumatic moment.

We're very like each other, very close to each other in temperament, and we have the same sort of nature. Of course I never dreamed of her becoming a writer or a journalist because the journalistic talent in our family is my son, who I suspect is a much better journalist than Penelope and me put together.

I did argue with her, counsel her, advise her to get a university degree. I'm a Presbyterian Scot with this belief in education. If you have got the basic insecurity of early poverty – early Scottish poverty – then the great thing to do is to get a degree on which to fall back if all else fails. If you have a university degree you can always teach, if nothing else, so I wanted my children to have degrees – simple as that.

I pressurised Penelope into going to university. I pushed her to St Andrews, where she met her husband. James graduated while she was still in the middle of her course and as she didn't want to stay there without him she came to London and without my knowledge saw Hugh Cudlipp. And I was very angry with him about this. Hugh gave her a job as a trainee at IPC Magazines.

I simply wanted her to get married happily and to have

children much more than I wanted her to get a job or have a career. I suppose once again that's part of the Scottish ethos that a woman's place is as the mother figure and the greatest happiness that can come to anyone, the only wealth in the world, is children; the only hope of immortality is in children, and that people who put anything above children, including prime ministers or chairmen of great companies, should realise that if they lose the affection of their children then they've lost everything.

I admire her compassion and the fact that she hasn't become hard and tough. She is essentially a mother figure because, when the chips are down, the one thing that matters more than anything else in the whole world to Penelope is her own family, her own children and her own marriage; and fame or even money and glamour don't mean a thing compared with these.

She may give the impression of being a career person, but if there arose any form of conflict between career and children, or career and marriage, I haven't the slightest doubt that she'd go for her family. It's not a subject I've discussed with her – I take it entirely for granted.

I would like to think that I've been more of a friend than a father because I've always taken the view, right from the beginning, that no matter who came to our house I regarded the children as being intellectual equals. I've never believed in saying there's a place for children and that children should keep their mouths closed and shouldn't interfere with or interrupt grown-up conversation.

I suppose I was reasonably strict about boyfriends. I simply regarded a young girl, particularly an attractive young girl, as always being prey to young men, perhaps because of my own time as a young man. So naturally I was protective. I suppose I have always been anxious about the possibility of her marrying someone from another country and going to live in that country, because I do care for her a great deal and I'd hate to see her separated from me by even the English Channel. It may be selfish, but who isn't selfish?

She was seven months pregnant with her second child when she read an article in the *Guardian* about an Indian farmer who sold a cow, which was seven months pregnant because he could get a bigger price because it weighed more. I expect like most *Guardian* articles it was absolute bullshit, but she read it and from that day she has remained a vegetarian. I have nothing but respect for that. But I have an eighteen-acre wood and I have two shotguns, and it used to be my pleasure to go and shoot the odd rabbit or pheasant or pigeon. But I found her influence on me was so strong, and even though she wasn't pressurising me – she never said she was against shooting – I not only abandoned shooting, but I now won't allow anyone else to shoot on my land. I haven't become a vegetarian because I don't believe in extremes of any kind.

I think the most terrible thing in life is to be bored and that is something I won't allow myself to be. It's the one price I'm not prepared to pay for anyone. Now if you exact that price in others, you must expect them to adopt the same criteria towards you, and one has to be aware that some old men become boring. And so the day may come, perhaps it already has, when one has become a bore, and it might be that young Alex and Sam might look on me as a bore. I don't think it's happened yet.

Penny Junor. We don't actually talk a lot. I find him in some ways quite hard to talk to and I think I probably always have. When I was young he had a habit of lecturing me and I suppose when I was a child I sometimes didn't want to be alone with him because he unnerved me. I think he was really terrified of the real world. I mean, he knew too many horror stories. Being at the centre of news, he was always very protective about his children, particularly his daughter, and I don't think he would ever have let me go abroad. In fact I wanted to go to McGill at one stage. I thought it would be fun to get away. He was fiercely against that. I didn't originally want to go to university, but he virtually forced me. He sat me down with an UCCA form and told me to fill it in. I remember very clearly one night, I looked through all the universities and thought, now which is the farthest away, and I plumped for St Andrews and got a place there. I did what he wanted but then left it.

He's a very dominating man, he would like to have everybody jump when he presses the button. But I'm very like him in many ways and I rebel almost just because I've been told to do something.

He doesn't have much of a sense of humour about himself, I don't think, but he has a very lavatorial sense of humour, a very basic schoolboy's sense of humour. He loves stories about people slipping on banana skins. Other people's misfortunes are a pure delight to him.

He has a very Protestant ethic. He's Scots Presbyterian, and is filled with enthusiasm for everything. Every day is the best day; wonderful weather – even if it's pouring with rain; great day for a game of golf; let's go and play tennis although it's freezing. Everything that he does is the very best, everybody he meets is the greatest, if he likes them.

He hates bores. He has a very low boredom threshold and therefore he's lost a lot of friends throughout his life simply because he's outgrown them. They've come to bore him. He's in constant need of stimulation and this is a key factor in his personality. He can't sit still. His days off are spent running between one thing and the next. He's always about to do something. I mean, he comes here a lot but he never sits down and relaxes, and he never relaxes in his own home. He's always on his feet. He wants to play golf, sail, play tennis, go shopping. He has to be stimulated, and he even breaks people off in the middle of their conversation if it tires him.

The whole of his life is his work. He lives and breathes the *Sunday Express* twenty-four hours a day. And it totally impinges on his home life. Another childhood memory is that he used to bring proofs home at night. He was never there to play with at all, he was always working. Even his hobbies are enforced, he doesn't really enjoy exercise for exercise's sake, he does it because it's good to do on one's day off.

I think he is the only way he could ever have been. He

has worked enormously hard throughout his life; he's pulled himself up from fairly humble beginnings in Glasgow with very few opportunities apart from his brain, and he does have the most extraordinary brain and capacity for very hard work. And, like every self-made man, the ambition and the need.

He chooses his time to talk. He's not the sort of person who will come home and tell you his troubles instantly, and if he doesn't feel like talking, he'll snap your head off. At times he's angry, sharp; at other times he's very loving and enormously sentimental. He's very sentimental with my children, maudlin sometimes if he drinks a lot, very soppy.

He attacks people. He makes very personal, virulent attacks on people, and every time I have actually ceased talking to him for a while, it's been because he has attacked somebody in my presence who I felt couldn't stick up for themselves, and I have weighed into him. He attacks people in social situations as well. It's not really an out-and-out attack, it's not sarcastic, it's just personal – it's quite unique. I've not really come across anybody like him. He says things he bitterly regrets afterwards. In his office he will really lay into somebody and be unkind to them and attack their integrity, attack their ability to write, attack everything, but then later that night he'll ring them and he'll make it up to them, or ring their wives. He must be enormously difficult to work for.

His passion has been being at the top, being powerful, being in charge of everything, his family, his friends, his colleagues. I think he's as content as anyone with that kind of make-up ever could be. But I don't think he's happy. I fear for him in retirement.

My mother is very gentle, a complete contrast to my father. She's not ambitious in the way he is and in fact when I was a child I was convinced she was a saint. So she was a great moderating influence and I'm terrifically close to her.

I think he needs somebody to answer back to him. I think this is one reason why he and I do actually get on well, because I think he does respect that I am as tough a character in some ways as he is, and I think he needs that and should have had that a lot earlier. He's had it too much his own way. But because he's been Editor, people have not really been able to stand up to him – you do what your Editor tells you or you don't do it for him any more. Perhaps he'd have been a very different person if he'd had a wife who stood up to him, but then he probably wouldn't have chosen such a wife.

When the article came out, I felt completely devastated. Of course I had said what was quoted, and I meant what I had said, but on the page it looked excessively harsh, and beside his warm and loving words, downright cruel. Sunday lunch that day was appalling. I have never felt so ashamed. To have said some of these things to his face, in private, was one thing. To have them published in *The Sunday Times* for all his friends and colleagues to see – bearing in mind that journalists read all the newspapers – was quite another.

I apologised, I tried to explain that it had been a long interview and that Danny had been selective in the quotes he had used, but he didn't want to hear, and what good was it anyway? The fact was I had said these things. I had hurt him in a way that no one had ever done before. I, the daughter that he loved and adored, the daughter he liked to show off, the daughter he was so proud of, had thrust a dagger into his heart. After that lunch, neither of us ever referred to it again, but it was a seminal moment in our relationship. According to someone he did speak to about it, he was astounded that I felt the way I did. 'Does Penny really think that?' he said. 'Am I really like that?'

The following Christmas he gave me a copy of the photograph that had accompanied the article – the photograph on the front cover of this book. It was in a shining silver frame. Attached was a note that made my blood curdle. 'You may not like what's inside it, but you may at least like the frame.'

But if this was a moment of self-awakening, a moment when he truly saw himself, 'as ithers see us', and saw in the mirror what I saw when I looked at him, he didn't show it. I often used to wonder whether he ever had moments of remorse, or at least doubt, whether, when he was alone at night and the wind howled, he felt ashamed of the way he trampled over people, whether deep down he was as satisfied with himself as he appeared.

Five years later, Lynn Barber wrote a searing profile of him in the *Independent on Sunday* and, to my horror, used my words from the 'Relative Values' piece to reinforce her conclusions.

It is his hatred, his rage, that give his column its appalling fascination. His daughter, the journalist and TV presenter Penny Junor, describes his rage as 'quite unique. He makes very personal, virulent, attacks on people.' . . . I saw the rage in action at lunch with him in Dorking when I tried to argue that his view of Aids as appropriate punishment for sodomy was wrong-headed and cruel. Immediately the eyes bulged, the skin mantled – it was as if someone had shot purple dye into his veins – the voice curdled into a snarl. His first assumption was that, if I were defending gays, I must be a lesbian. 'You seem to have an extrrrrrrrrra-ordinary sexual attitude yourself if I may say so, Miss Barber. No doubt you approve of lesbianism yourself?' I found myself gabbling that I was happily married, with children. But why did he hate homosexuals so much? 'Unhappily,' he intoned, 'some men are born in a certain way and with those people I have great sympathy. It's the proselytisers I object to; the people who flaunt their homosexualism and try to subvert and convert other people to it. These are the people I have an utter hatred for, because I think they are spreading filth.'

By now the voice was booming round the walls of the genteel Dorking restaurant, the face was deep indigo, and an unfortunate waiter who had come to collect our plates stood paralysed like a rabbit in a car's headlights. 'Filth, Miss Barber. I regard buggery' – he paused to savour the word – 'buggery as the putting of a penis into shit. Don't you, Miss Barber? Don't you?'

Had he suffered, I asked, some personal assault by a homosexual, a childhood fumbling from a scoutmaster, perhaps? 'Absolutely not. Absolutely not. Absolutely not. Absolutely not. But it may of course have something to do with my generation. Homosexualism was virtually unknown in Scotland.' A long pause. 'Anyway, what would you do with the problem, Miss Barber? Stick it under the carpet, never mention it?'

'Oh no. I have several gay friends. We talk about Aids.'

'Gay friends! Where do you meet them?'

'Well, at home.'

'And do you tell your dinner guests, "This is John. He's homosexual"?'

'Well, not like that. I might say, "This is John, and this is his boyfriend, Hugh."' JJ goggled at me, completely purple, eyes popping, but silent. Eventually he managed to croak, find that idea most . . . unusual. It does not happen in Auchtermuchty.'

. . . When I tried to ask him about Penny's interview, he cut me off sharply.

'I'm not really responsible for what my daughter says. All I can say is that when the children were young I never had people to dinner, no matter how important, without the children being there too. They were always treated as equals.' A good father, then? 'I think so, yes.' But later he rang me especially to say, 'Of course, if Penelope says I was not a good father, she must be the judge.'

My blood froze when I read Lynn Barber's piece; JJ was desperately hurt by it. He rang me at once and said, 'She's quoted you, we must complain.' I said I thought it better just to ignore it. 'No, no, because if we leave it uncorrected, it will get into the cuttings and people will be quoting it for ever more.' And with the heaviest of hearts, I had to say, 'But, JJ I can't complain. It's what I said.' He hung up, I was no longer the ally he had hoped I would be. I had never met or spoken to Lynn Barber, but in his eyes I had handed her the knife with which she had eviscerated him.

I held the silent telephone in my hand, my stomach knotted tight, and wished things had been different, wished I could have helped him. Why were we constantly at war? I would love to have had a really close relationship with my father, to have been able to share thoughts and ideas with him, confide fears and failings, and talk openly without constantly being on my guard. We were alike in so many ways, we laughed at the same things, we were in the same business, and could have had fun together.

I am tempted to think he would have liked that relationship too, but I am not sure he would have understood the concept.

CHAPTER TWENTY-FIVE

Golf

Hanging in my garage at home are golf bags, lots of them, and as often as not I hit my head on one, getting out of my car, and curse. They have short cut-down clubs in them, which JJ had specially made for my children when they were young, and more full-size clubs than you see in the average pro's shop, which he collected over the years for himself. He had carbon fibre clubs, Callaway Big Berthas, Ping putters, hickory-shafted putters – you name it, he had it. His collection of golf clubs was second only to his collection of lawn mowers, all bought in the hope of miraculously improving his game.

Golf was probably my father's greatest passion, but I don't believe he enjoyed it for its own sake. He went out on to the golf course, at least once, virtually every week of his life with the compulsion of a zealot. It could be blowing a hurricane, lashing with rain, hail could be bouncing off the fairway, and JJ would be out there, usually saying "Isn't this marvellous? Isn't this the greatest?" But his golf was rather like his swimming in the icy sea in Barfleur. The having done it seemed to be more pleasurable than the activity itself.

He was a member of Walton Heath, the championship course at Tadworth in Surrey, and even when there was a deep layer of snow on the course he would take his car up the notoriously steep and hazardous Pebblecombe Hill to get there. It was a compulsion, another aspect of the routine that ruled his life, and a destination – somewhere he needed to be on the way to, which provided escape from the last activity – even if that was sitting at home with a cup of coffee and the newspapers. And, for ten years, the excuse he used to make the journey on those days when no sensible person ventured out was a destitute Irish caddie called Curly.

Curly was the most disreputable-looking character for miles around. He slept rough out on the heath, he was unwashed and unshaven, and lived in a shabby, full-length railway coat that he wore done up to the chin with a hat pulled down low, exposing only his mouth and a wild beard. My father called him 'a fiercely independent wisp of a man'. Most people who knew him describe him as an evil-smelling bundle of rags that swore at you if you tried to say 'Good morning'. No one knew where he had come from, and no one cared. Most people found him deeply repugnant but JJ befriended him, and from the early 1970s until Curly's death in 1982, he carried my father's clubs. JJ paid him £10 every time – a fortune for a caddie at that time and as often as not, he gave him a bottle of whisky too. And if there was snow on the ground and the course was closed, he would drive up to the club nevertheless – a good twenty minutes from Wellpools – and fleetingly knock a red ball around on the heath, as an excuse to give Curly some money. And every Christmas morning, without fail, he would take Curly some lunch – turkey, Christmas pudding, mince pies and a couple of bottles of wine or whisky.

Time and again Ewen Murray, the young professional at Walton Heath, would say, 'I don't know why you bother with Curly. He's rude, he's filthy . . .'

'In my world,' said JJ, 'I mix with the most successful people. There are other people who are not so fortunate. You will have to learn,' he said accusingly, as if it was Ewen's fault, 'that you have to be kind to everyone, not just people who are important.' In the last months of his life JJ spoke to the Club, and managed to get Curly shelter in a room at the back of the caddie shed but there was no bed or running water; the first bed he had was in Epsom hospital where JJ, who hated hospitals, was his only visitor. 'Last Friday night Curly died,' he wrote in his column, whilst praising his treatment by the NHS, 'and I mourn his going.'

I think he truly did mourn his going. His relationship with Curly was one he could handle. Curly was beholden and, because he was beholden, JJ could legitimately be the one who called the shots and be as difficult as the mood took him. Curly did what he was told, he was grateful for the patronage, especially the whisky, and he was as reliable as the weather. Every Sunday and/or Monday he would be waiting at the clubhouse, at ten to ten ready for the off.

Golf was no leisure activity for my father and although there were several people JJ played with regularly for many years, no one found the experience relaxing. He wanted the game to be over in 2 hours 41 minutes, which left no time to stop, linger, chat or admire the scenery. He would arrive at the clubhouse, change his shoes and go straight out onto the course. Curly would be ready with his clubs. 'Right, come on now,' he would say, 'we've got to go.' He would have no practice swing on the first tee, he would just tee up the ball, whack it and walk as fast as he could to his second shot, and if he had not completed 18 holes by a certain time, he would abandon the game and go back to the clubhouse, saying to his partners, 'It might be all right for you, but I don't have time to play golf all day.' He would then shoot off into Dorking to do some shopping, drop some offering in to me on his way past, saying 'Quick, take this, I'm off', then hurry home for lunch. Because after lunch came that magical moment in his day when he could have his first cigarette.

As a result he never played golf very well, and any attempts by Ewen Murray to improve his game fell on deaf ears. 'You couldn't show him what he was doing wrong because that would mean you were in control. You could pass on a couple of tips on the walk but you had to keep walking, because that would just be a piece of information, but if he allowed you to stop and show him, that would be a sign of weakness.'

Ewen Murray went to Walton Heath as the Assistant Pro in the early 1970s at the age of eighteen. He was from Edinburgh, a good-looking boy with tremendous talent, but he had just left school and had scarcely been out of Scotland in his life. JJ took an immediate shine to Ewen and took him under his wing. He treated him like a son, and Ewen regarded him as a second father. Every week they played golf together and tennis, they went sailing and shopping, and Wellpools became a second home, Pam a second mother. Ewen was his protégé and he talked excitedly about what a great golfer he was and how one day he would be a champion. He talked to him for hours about his golf, about what he should be doing and how important it was to have the right mental attitude; he talked about the friends he was making at the Club, about the problems of growing up, and he advised him about buying his first house and getting a mortgage. 'His advice wasn't just about my career, it was about life, and I listened to every single word that John had to say, and when I look back ninety-five per cent of what he said was true.'

Once again, it was the sort of relationship JJ could handle. Ewen looked up to him, adored him, and relished his company. He was happy to sit at his feet and listen to the lectures and learn. JJ liked nothing more than disciples on whom he could exercise his generosity – and his control. The difficulty arose when the disciples were no longer so compliant, and when they started to have ideas of their own and started to demonstrate their independence.

One of his regular golfing chums was Sir Adam Thomson, the Glaswegian Chairman of British Caledonian. B Cal was Ewen's main sponsor and it was he who introduced JJ and Adam to one another. They became good friends, and when B Cal started an annual pro-am tournament in The Gambia in 1977, JJ became a regular participant. Nigeria was the airline's most profitable route and golf was an important device in cementing good relations; the African heads of state would then come to play at Gleneagles in Scotland. JJ loved these tournaments, loved being surrounded by young professional golfers and golf-playing celebrities like the astronauts Alan Shepard and Neil Armstrong. And he loved his trips to The Gambia, where he became pally with the President, Sir Dawda Jawara, who was a fellow alumnus of Glasgow University. He wrote regularly about it all in his column.

While the rest of you were shivering last week, I was playing golf under the scorching sun in that West African paradise The Gambia.

The white sand on the beaches swept by Atlantic surf, the friendliness of the natives and of the expatriate whites will long linger in my mind.

But the memory that will stay longest of all?

The chagrin on the face of that golfing legend and former Ryder Cup captain, Eric Brown, when he discovered, on closer inspection, that the biggest topless boobs around the hotel pool belonged to a businessman from Bootle.

Peter McKay used to tease him. 'You're going to be found out one day about these freebies,' he said. 'Freebies?' said JJ indignantly. 'Freebies? I went up to Lillywhite's the other day and bought Dawda a whole set of golf clubs in the Lillywhite's sale.'

JJ didn't enjoy being in anyone's debt, and maintaining his independence was a matter of principle, which he carried throughout the newspaper – although as he grew older he did go on press trips, which amounted to little more than freebies. But he always paid for his B Cal flights on these golfing holidays. Ewen asked him why, when Adam was paying for everyone else's ticket. 'If I accept a free ticket I can never be critical about B Cal in my column, and I never want that freedom to be taken away from me.'

The twelve young professional golfers who went to The Gambia each year flocked around JJ and relished his company. They queued up to play golf with him each morning, even though he played as he did at Walton Heath – teeing off at 8.20 a.m. – he seldom used the quarter-hour markers that everyone else uses – and smacking his way round the course at top speed, abandoning the game before the end if it took too long. After the game they would have a quick drink in the clubhouse, then he'd take them all off to lunch. He had discovered a restaurant of sorts on the beach where a local couple with three young children scratched to earn a living by cooking fish on a wood fire. He insisted they all eat there every day, keen to give the family his business. Ewen protested. The fish was usually half raw, as were the chips, and while it might have been fresh from the Atlantic, there was no running water on the beach, no toilets and the standards of hygiene were zero. To cap it all, the only drink on offer was a can of warm 7 Up. 'Isn't this marvellous?' JJ would say, sitting in the sand. 'One of the very best restaurants I've ever been in.' And Ewen and the others would think longingly of the smart hotels they could have been comfortably settling into;

but such was JJ's influence over them all, that year after year they risked typhoid on the beach rather than go against his wishes.

But then it was very difficult to go against his wishes. He was so forceful that most people found it easier just to comply. He was as much of a bully on the golf course as off it, and what he lacked in golfing technique he made up for in gamesmanship. Max Davidson, the Features Editor, was once about to play a shot with a number seven iron. 'If you play a seven iron you'll be far too short,' said JJ. 'I'm going to play a five.'

'But I'd rather play a seven,' said Max.

'Well I've played this course before and you haven't and I'm telling you to play a five.' So Max did as he was told and his ball went straight over the green and into a bunker at the back. He turned to my father busy lining up his shot beside him and said, 'What club are you playing?'

'A seven,' said JJ with a malevolent grin.

Another of his occasional golfing partners was Sir Patrick Macrory, a director of Unilever, who was a fellow member of the club and lived in a house right by the course. They were all square one day as they reached the eighteenth hole. Pat was lining up his shot and was just about to strike the ball when JJ suddenly said, 'Has it ever occurred to you, Pat, that the earth could be a giant spaceship?' Pat was completely thrown, his ball shot straight into a bush and JJ unashamedly pocketed the winnings.

Pat was the father of Henry Macrory, the News Editor, and one of those JJ hoped might succeed him. Pat had mentioned on the golf course one day that one of his sons wanted to go into journalism, and, in 1972, Henry joined the *Sunday Express*. He remembers the first editorial conference he attended. He was acting Foreign Editor, and had been told everyone had to put up ideas. When JJ asked what he had, he said, 'I've just worked out that this week President Kennedy would have been sixty years old, and it might be quite interesting to think what President Kennedy would be doing now if he was still alive.' 'I'll tell you what President Kennedy would be doing if he was still alive,' said JJ. 'He'd be rogering Marilyn Monroe if she was still alive.' The conference erupted.

When Pat Macrory died in 1993, the family held a memorial

service for him at Walton church. Although JJ hadn't known Pat that well, his widow was keen that he should give the address. Henry rang to ask if he would, and at first my father said he'd rather not, but finally agreed, provided Henry sent him some material on his father, which he duly did. The service was on a Saturday afternoon, the church was packed and JJ arrived in the nick of time, with golf clubs in the back of his Range Rover. The notes Henry had sent were lying on the front seat, indicating he had only just read them. 'Thank you very much for the notes,' he said, 'they were very good,' and he left them in the car. 'Oh God,' thought Henry, 'he's not even going to take them into the church.' But Henry's fear was unfounded: 'JJ got up and spoke for ten minutes without notes; he never faltered once and was absolutely brilliant. My mother was so thrilled. It's these things that made him great. He had obviously just memorised all the stuff I had sent him and added his own little detail and one anecdote of his own, which I didn't know about, and it was fantastic. Everybody was mesmerised because he was a wonderful speaker. And that's why, whatever else, whatever brutalities he might have inflicted, I for one will say, "He was my boy" in the end, because he was brilliant like that.'

I hadn't seen Ewen Murray for years – other than fleetingly at JJ's funeral, when he was distraught. At one time I had known him quite well. He had lived close to us, and during the 1970s, when he was at Wellpools so much, I had seen quite a bit of him. But he had married, his marriage broke up, he moved away and I lost touch.

What I hadn't known was that my father had also lost touch. He hadn't spoken to Ewen for the last two years of his life. Having at one time been like a son, Ewen was dropped like a burning brick – and as he showed me around the house that JJ visited just once, it was clear that he is puzzled and still very deeply hurt.

The story of JJ's visit filled me with shame, and a futile wish yet again that I could in some way make amends. Ewen doesn't know for certain what he did to lose my father's affection, but he began to sense JJ was cooling towards him from the time of his divorce. His first marriage was a mistake. He realised it the day before the wedding and told JJ but JJ said it was just nerves; his own father agreed and so, against his better judgement, Ewen went ahead. Two months later he found he had married not just his wife but her family too and couldn't handle it. JJ had no sympathy. He didn't believe in divorce and told Ewen over and over again not to be so stupid; she was a marvellous girl. But by this time Ewen had grown up sufficiently to be able to answer back. 'I could never have done so for the first ten years I knew him because he was the boss, but you reach a stage in your adulthood where you can turn round and say "I disagree with you" or "You're wrong." That's when I enjoyed our relationship more than ever – but he didn't like it.

'He thought I was a fool to get divorced. "That's not what you get married for" he said, and I know he hated me for doing it; he kept telling me I was a failure. I didn't like it either, I felt a failure; but I couldn't deal with the situation and I know he wouldn't have been able to deal with it if he'd been in the same position.' But what galled Ewen most was that JJ was in no position to take the moral high ground. 'For him to tell me all about my mistakes, and there was Pam, and all his womanising.'

The divorce cleaned him out, but he eventually managed to get back onto his feet, and he and his girlfriend Nicky, who had worked for B Cal and therefore knew JJ well, bought a bungalow together in Sussex. Soon after they moved, they invited JJ for dinner. 'I knew he wouldn't eat much or stay until 10.30 p.m. drinking coffee and reminiscing about old times, but I just wanted him to come to my house as a small way of saying "Thank you for all the times I've been eating and drinking and laughing at your house, the good fun and the tennis." And to show him that there was life after Newdigate and the divorce. I wanted to show him that I had survived.' He told Nicky to make sure dinner was ready at 7 o'clock, knowing that my father wouldn't sit and have a drink because he'd be driving, and would want to go straight in to dinner. Ewen knew him well, he knew all his faults and foibles and loved him nonetheless. But JJ exceeded all expectation.

He arrived at 6.55 p.m. and was gone precisely one hour and fifteen minutes later, having bolted his way through a three-course meal. Ewen offered him a drink when he arrived. 'No, I'll go straight in to dinner. Is dinner ready?' They sat down, he had one glass of wine, and left. 'We had the house all nicely cleaned for him, everything polished up, table nicely set, all the best cutlery, crystal glasses, and he was out the door at 8.10 p.m. I said did he want to look round the house? He had a quick look. "It's very modern." I said, "It's new, it was built last year." "Oh, I don't like modern houses. I like the charm of old places like Wellpools. You live such a long way away now, I must be going."'

He never visited again, and, whenever Ewen rang, he'd say it was too far to go. 'That was almost a way of saying, "I don't really want to see you again." He didn't like the fact I'd moved. It was handy to have me nearby; if he got lonely, he could ring and say "Come up and have a drink," or "I'll be at your house in three minutes, I've got a bag of apples for you so could you please be at the gate because I'm in a hurry," as he always was.'

Having taken such an interest in Ewen's career when he first knew him, JJ no longer wanted to know. He no longer plays championship golf – he does golfing commentary for Sky Television instead and when he started in 1990, he used to ask JJ what he thought of his performance, and what he should do to improve. 'Oh I never watch that rubbish,' said JJ. 'I watch the BBC.' He was not good at enjoying other people's success, and was no doubt galled that Ewen had got the Sky job by himself. 'I kept ringing him up and leaving messages on his answering machine saying, "Let's have a drink, let's meet," but he'd never ring me back. One night I got him, and he said there'd been something wrong with the answering machine and he was a bit busy this week, he'd got this and this on. It was a definite "Don't bother." He didn't want to know.'

But Ewen suspects the major reason for the falling out was over a car. He wanted a cheap second car that he could take his two dogs out in. JJ was on the point of buying Pam a new car, which he did every three or four years, and suggested that Ewen should buy the old one for the trade-in price he had been offered from the garage, which was £4,400. It was a Ford Escort convertible, which turned out to be completely unsuitable. The first time he took the dogs out in it with the roof off, a cat crossed the road and one of the dogs jumped out of the car and was nearly run over; so Ewen put four new tyres on it, a new exhaust, touched up the paintwork, had it steam cleaned, put an ad in the local paper – which cost him a total of £800 – and sold it for £5,400 – a thousand more than he had paid for it. JJ discovered when the buyer rang him to check the mileage was genuine, and was furious. 'You made a big profit on the car,' he said accusingly, and wouldn't listen to any explanation. 'After that he changed. I thought it would pass but he never became friendly again.'

Not long afterwards Bill Martin, the *Sunday Express* cartoonist, a lovely, gentle Australian, who had played golf with JJ most weeks for nearly thirty years, died of cancer. Ewen loved him – we all did – and was sitting at the back of the church for his funeral when JJ arrived, halfway through the service, dressed in pale blue golfing trousers, and sat down beside him. The church was charged with emotion and James Mossop, a *Sunday Express* sports writer and another golfing companion, was in the midst of an impassioned address. 'God they don't half go on,' said JJ after about fifteen minutes, and then, as James broke down and had to be taken from the pulpit, hissed 'What a bloody carry on.' Ewen rounded on him in disgust then turned away; when he turned back, JJ was gone.

On another occasion they were lunching at Arcadia, a restaurant around the corner from the *Mail on Sunday* in Kensington, which became a favourite. Ewen was about to film an advertisement for some golf clubs called Rogue and hadn't shaved for four days because they wanted him to look the part. 'Good God,' said JJ, and ignoring all attempts at an explanation, 'you look bloody awful, you've gone to the dogs.' Then he berated him for having ordered a bottle of Rioja. 'I'm not drinking that rubbish,' he said and made the waiter take it back and bring some French wine. He then ordered lunch, and had finished his main course when Ewen was still halfway through his and was on to his first cigarette of the day. 'Gosh you're a slow eater,' he said and left before he had finished, saying he had to get back to the office. 'And have a shave when you get out the door,' he said as a parting shot.

The next and last time they met was at the dentist in Dorking. 'He was limping badly and I tapped him on the shoulder and said, "JJ, how are you doing?" I hadn't seen him for six or eight months, maybe a year, and he turned round and said, "Gosh, you're fat."

And I said, "Well never mind that, I haven't seen you for a year." And he said, "I can't believe how fat you are and how old you look." I thought, he's losing his marbles a bit because I wasn't any fatter than I had been, but those were his first words, and then he said, "When's your appointment? Oh mine's before yours." When he came out he said, "Nothing wrong with my teeth, but I suspect there'll be a lot wrong with yours." And that was it, that was the last time I saw him, and I thought after all the time and all the places we'd been . . .'

It is probably quicker to list the number of friendships that JJ did not destroy during the course of his life than those he did. He so desperately craved love, so desperately wanted to be fêted and admired, and yet, whenever anyone came close, he cut them off. There was not one friendship from his youth that he carried into old age. All the family friends from my childhood had long gone. Some of them kept up with my mother, but JJ would have nothing to do with them; he said they were 'bores' or 'old men'. He had fallen out with Bill Martin before his death. Because of his illness, Bill could no longer play golf as early as JJ wanted to and, rather than accommodate his pal of thirty years bravely battling with cancer, and alter his Monday morning routine, JJ stopped playing with him. Adam Thomson started slowing up on the course. He had Alzheimer's Disease. Ewen played with them both. 'I remember Adam when he finished a golf hole would say, "How many was that I had, John?"

'"You're running a bloody airline and you don't know how many shots you took. Can't you count?"

'Then he found out about the Alzheimer's. Adam couldn't add up because he couldn't remember what happened twenty seconds ago. JJ felt very bad about it because he had given him a really tough time. He showed a lot of grief when he realised Adam was about to go into a home, felt very guilty, but I doubt if he ever visited him. John wouldn't do anything that took time.'

And yet Ewen can't bring himself to condemn my father. 'I learned to put up with all of that because I enjoyed his company, I enjoyed his energy, he had tremendous energy, he had a wonderful outlook on life, he looked forward to every single day, he looked forward to everything he did, and if he didn't fancy doing something he wouldn't do it. He would never do something he didn't want to do.

'I'd love him to come back for a week, and say, "Look, I'm going to spend the whole week with you and we'll take *Outcast* and go to Cowes like we used to, and we're going to go and play golf at Walton Heath, and we're going to play a set of tennis, and open some wine and chat about Tony Blair and what a pillock he is, and how wonderful Maggie was." I'd like to spend a week at the age I am now rather than the young boy who used to play golf with him.'

My heart bleeds for Ewen, still wondering to this day what it was he did that turned my father against him and still mourning his loss. Ewen's only crime was growing up, having a mind of his own, a life of his own, being unafraid to say what he thought and no longer being dependent upon JJ's patronage, his gifts or his advice. The irony is that JJ was his role model; it was JJ's guidance in the first ten years of their relationship that helped him become so competent and capable on his own – which surely is what any parent hopes for a child, that one day their charge will be able to fly unassisted. It is the measure of their success as a parent. But JJ couldn't cope with that, didn't want to meet Ewen as an equal, didn't want him challenging, answering back or ignoring his advice. He wanted the child who worshipped him.

CHAPTER TWENTY-SIX

A New Start

Graham Lord, the Literary Editor who so nearly became the next Editor of the *Sunday Express*, now divides his time between the South of France and the Caribbean. He stayed on at the *Sunday Express* for several years – and three more Editors – after my father's departure, before a run-in with one released him to a life of writing books in sunny climes. He and I have been friends for over thirty years – he is one of the few people who worked for my father that I ever really got to know well. But he and JJ fell out so spectacularly by the end that Graham refused to come to his memorial service; not because JJ had scuppered his chances of becoming Editor, but because he knew that my father would not have wanted him there. He was probably right, but it seemed sad after all the years they had known and liked one another on the *Sunday Express*, for things to have come to such a disastrous end. Graham had been one of his favourites, but I suppose it was precisely because they were so close at one time that Graham's sin could not be forgiven.

His sin was a review he wrote of JJ's memoirs. Throughout his years at the *Sunday Express*, my father had kept notes about the conversations he had had over lunch. Every afternoon he would return to his office and dictate snippets into a little tape recorder, which his secretary would type up, waiting for the day when he would write about his life. It was an impressive roll call: princesses, prime ministers, film stars, sporting heroes, captains of industry – everyone who was anyone. And in the autumn of 1989, with his future at the *Mail on Sunday* secured, JJ set about the task of writing a book.

He asked whether I would help. I was flattered; I thought it might be fun to work on a book together, and it might be a way of saying thank you for everything. I don't know what possessed me. I should have known it would be impossible from the moment he unceremoniously dumped the notes from thirty-two years of lunches on the floor of my office. There were some wonderful stories amongst them, fascinating insights, and wicked observations; but when we tried to talk about how the book might work or what kind of book it should be, I realised I had made a big mistake. This was another subject we were going to be unable to discuss calmly. When I said I thought he must talk about himself in the book, his childhood, his family, his feelings and emotions, his face reddened in anger, his pale eyes fixed me with an unblinking stare and he told me I didn't know the first goddamned thing about what sold books. Anecdotes were what people wanted to read. The problem with my books was they didn't have anecdotes, which is why they were all so goddamned dull. So I gave him back his piles of notes, and he enlisted, instead, the help of Jimmy Kinlay, who had taken early retirement from the *Sunday Express* when Robin Esser became Editor.

I was not alone in what I wanted him to write. His publisher, Ian Chapman, said he should write about himself and his family – but JJ refused. First he said it was insulting, then he said he couldn't write about his family because his wife had left him, she was an alcoholic and round the bend. Ian Chapman ran his own imprint with his wife Marjory, and in all their years in publishing I doubt if they ever came across a more difficult author. When they told him he needed to be careful about libel, he responded angrily. "Ian, if I say I'm telling the truth, are you going to say I'm a liar?" And when he was finally persuaded he had to talk to the libel lawyer, he saw him for forty-five minutes and then threw him out of his office.

'I have never been clear myself about whether his irascibility was genuine or an affectation,' says Ian Chapman, 'and whether his bad manners and rudeness were a reflection of his insecurity. He was extremely insecure, yet almost went out of his way to pick a fight.'

The book was called *Listening for a Midnight Tram*. He was hugely excited about its publication, as if writing a book, which might sell a few thousand copies over a year, was in some way a greater accomplishment than editing a national newspaper that had once sold over four million copies every week. But this was all his own work, with his name and photograph on it, it was his life, his story, his achievement, and he was proud of what he had done. He was a remarkably vain man: he filled his house with photographs of himself, scanned the index of every book written by people he knew, looking for his own name, and kept tape recordings of radio interviews, videos of TV appearances and everything anyone had ever written about him. And for all his bullying and bravado, if anyone turned the tables on him, he was very easily hurt. The most wounding review of his book was Graham's in the *Sunday Express*, entitled, 'Few Friends Aboard Junor's Empty Tram':

> When *Sunday Express* ex-Editor and columnist Sir John Junor first sought a publisher for his memoirs he was told he needed a ghostwriter. Instead he has relied heavily on the assistance of his loyal one-time Deputy Editor, James Kinlay.
>
> Yet in the main text he makes no mention of Mr Kinlay or of others who helped him so much with his column for so long. Nor is there a word about *Sunday Express* stars like Danny Blanchflower, Denis Compton, Anne Edwards, Alan Hoby, Roderick Mann, Veronica Papworth. Even Dick Francis rates only a caption and Sir John's other invaluable deputy Editor, the colourful Victor Patrick, is dismissed in four sentences about cricket.
>
> Instead JJ serves up a gauche goulash of lunch table tittle-tattle, mainly about politicians, in a smug style that is disloyal, bitchy and hypercritical. His book is very readable, but it will sadden his friends and strengthen his enemies.

'I thought I had been comparatively gentle,' says Graham, 'but he went through the roof.' The next week JJ responded in his *Mail on Sunday* column:

When you publish a controversial book, as I did last week, you expect to get a few knocks from reviewers.

Especially those working for newspapers which might have a few past scores to settle with you.

Fair enough.

If you dish it out, you also have to learn to take it.

But there was one review of my book which saddened me. It appeared in a newspaper which I myself edited for more than thirty years, the *Sunday Express*.

It was written by a man to whom many years ago I had given his first chance in journalism.

It suggested that my book had not been written by myself, but had been ghosted. It even hinted that my columns were not all my own work.

The man who wrote it must have known that what he wrote was utterly untrue.

He must have known that nothing that has ever appeared in print under my name has ever been written by anyone except myself. Yet he still wrote as he did.

Why? Anger because I now write for the *Mail on Sunday*? I neither know, nor care.

What I do deplore is that a once great newspaper should have sunk so low as to be so mean and spiteful.

The *Sunday Express* once bore the proud legend: Founded by Lord Beaverbrook.

Is its epitaph going to be: Killed by Lord Stevens?

Graham wrote in reply:

JJ accuses me of being disloyal to him on the grounds that he gave me my first job in Fleet Street. Is he really saying that I should evade the truth when reviewing books by old friends or colleagues? I have been no more disloyal to him than he was in his autobiography to his predecessor John Gordon.

Stewart Steven refused to publish this, and Graham and my father never spoke again.

Jimmy Kinlay was equally indignant at Graham's review. 'I remember saying to him, "It is as if you had gone through your years at the *Sunday Express* with your eyes firmly closed. Can you imagine John Junor allowing me to write his book for him or for that matter his column? You know very well he didn't operate like that, and wouldn't operate like that, and any suggestion of it would drive him bananas, and it did." I felt so annoyed about it myself and wrote a long letter to Robin Morgan, part of which was published in the *Sunday Express*. I sent a copy to JJ and he said, "I would have sued them if they hadn't published your letter."'

Meanwhile, in the *Spectator*, Alan Watkins, who over twenty-five years previously had committed the unforgivable sin of leaving the *Sunday Express*, had penned an even more damning review. Under the headline, 'Not a Nasty Man Exactly', he wrote:

However hard he may try to be nice ... what comes out at the end is almost always nasty ... he finds it difficult to deal with anyone on a footing of equality ... He is either a bully or a sycophant ... He is also, I now discover, something of a humbug ... Sir John is somewhat misleading about both his own and his colleagues' attitude to Max, who, he tells us, 'not only had great personal charisma, he was genuinely liked, respected and indeed almost worshipped'. Steady on a bit. Max was respected for his gallantry in war and envied for his gallantry with women ... Certainly Sir John regarded him as a bit of a booby, and would sometimes indicate as much when he lunched with his leader-writing colleagues on a Saturday in the Cheshire Cheese. If Sir John's book has a theme, it is lunch. The title could well have been *All My Lunches* ... Unhappily there is little new information ... in these memoirs. They are mostly tittle-tattle, becoming less and less interesting as they approach the present. They do not do Sir John justice. Or perhaps they do him all too much.

In the following week's *Spectator*, Alan wrote again, saying he had received the following anonymous letter:

In your *Spectator* review you traduce the memory of a better man, Sir Max Aitken. When he was alive, you were happy enough to fawn over him and accept his money. When he is no longer able to defend himself, you are pleased to sneer at him. You might have told your usual small audience why you got the push from his papers. Was it not because of drunken afternoons slumbering on Cross-Bencher's chaise longue while decent people, including Max Aitken, were working?

It was signed 'Junius'. Watkins, in reply, observed:

Odd. I would occasionally have a nap, not on any 'chaise longue' but on a narrow, meagrely padded bench in Cross-Bencher's tiny office. This practice of mine was noticed by only a few people, most of whom are now unhappily dead. The surviving possible suspects would know perfectly well that I happily handed in my notice in summer 1964, having been offered the job of political correspondent of the *Spectator* by Iain Macleod – and that, far from 'fawning' over Max, we did not exchange a single word in five years, apart from 'good morning'. From the parodic element, I think I know who the culprit is. Rum.

He also knew from JJ's blue-black ink and distinctive handwriting. 'It just showed I had hurt him very much.' In the same edition was a letter JJ had signed:

Sir

Poor old Alan Watkins. Until I read his review of my book *Listening for a Midnight Tram*, I had no idea of what a slave-driver I had been or of how I had made him work such cruelly long hours on the *Sunday Express*. Could this perhaps explain why, after his two-hour lunch break, he was so often found, mouth open, fast asleep on the office sofa snoring his little head off?

John Junor
Wellpools Farm.

They never spoke again.

Peter McKay, predictably, enjoyed the book. He wrote in the *Evening Standard*:

> This is the most astounding volume of memoirs I have ever read. It breaks the genteel English literary convention about only writing ill of the dead by telling hair-raisingly indiscreet stories about public men and women who are still alive. Sir John Junor spares no one he has known, from his own mother to the Queen.

There was one particularly indiscreet story, which infuriated not only the subject of the story, but also most of his former colleagues on the *Sunday Express*.

> In the early 1980s, I may have played a part in the removal of Sir Maurice Oldfield from his job as head of security in Northern Ireland. He had been head of MI6 and had been called out of retirement at Margaret Thatcher's personal request.
>
> He had been in Ulster for only a few months when Sir David McNee, the Commissioner of the Metropolitan Police, telephoned me to ask if I had read a paragraph in Auberon Waugh's Diary in *Private Eye*. McNee thought that Waugh was hinting that Oldfield was homosexual. And in fact McNee was absolutely convinced that he was. He had evidence, he told me, from a Special Branch officer who had been guarding Marsham Court, where Oldfield lived, of the tremendous number of young men who visited Oldfield's flat. He indicated to me that the hall porter, if interviewed, would sing like a bird.

McNee had wanted Mrs Thatcher to be made aware of the situation and asked for help. It was the sort of story every journalist longed for, a fantastic scoop by any standards, handed to him on a plate. But JJ did not give it to the *Sunday Express* – a fact he fails to mention in his memoirs, which suggests he didn't even consider it.

Instead he arranged for the information to be passed directly to Mrs Thatcher in a private letter. Two days later he had a visit from her official private secretary, who wanted proof of the allegations. He said he had none – ensuring David McNee's name would be kept out of it – but told him how to get proof. Within weeks Maurice Oldfield was gone.

The first any of his staff knew about this story was when they read it in the book and they were flabbergasted – and also incensed. He had obviously allowed his friendship with the Prime Minister and allegiance to the Government to come before his loyalty to the *Sunday Express* and his most basic instincts as a journalist. Andrew Cameron, the General Manager, thinks it goes with the territory. 'When you make someone an Editor you give them a crown of laurels which sends them crackers. You introduce them to showbiz personalities, politicians, there are invitations to No 10, it's all very grand and they become very grand. And when a story like that comes across their desk they forget who their paymasters are.'

But it was not just colleagues; David McNee was also incensed when he read this story in the book, and he and JJ, who up to that point had been very good friends, had a major falling out. McNee had given my father the story on the understanding that it was strictly non-attributable, and believed that that was how it should have remained for ever. JJ kept his word at the time, but by the time it came to writing his book thought it was so long ago it wouldn't matter. 'David was absolutely furious,' recalls Ian Irvine. 'They both acted like children. I said to John often, "Pick up the phone speak to him, you're a bloody grown man, don't mess around with people like that."

'"No, if he wants to speak to me, he can call me." And David was the same, they were both stubborn as hell.'

The book sold a healthy 13,000 copies, and was brought out a year later in paperback by Ian Chapman, junior, at Macmillan. 'I introduced them,' says Ian, senior, 'and he and I had many a laugh together since about some of the conversations we've both had with JJ. There were occasions when I would come away from him and think "He's an impossible man, an absolutely impossible man." There were times when he made me angry, when I strongly disagreed with him in many of his views, but I used to quite enjoy jousting with him and, although he'd get cross and angry with me, we'd always finish up with him putting his arm round my shoulder.'

JJ was now firmly ensconced at the *Mail on Sunday*, housed, since its move from Fleet Street, in an impressive modern building in Kensington High Street with an atrium that he raved about. His arrival on the paper had been heralded by some striking television advertising, which he found enormously flattering. Two typewriters facing each other, with a roll of paper running from one to the other: 'What happens when two columnists take diametrically opposite views?' The paper rips.

'He could see more clearly than a lot of people in the office,' says Stewart Steven, 'the value of Julie Burchill to him and to the paper. Having them head-to-head was incredible. He was in his seventies, Julie Burchill was in her crazy twenties, and sometimes what she wrote was drivel, but one of her greatest supporters in the office was JJ. He said to me once that having Julie Burchill on the next page sharpened him up. There is no doubt it was one of the single most important things I ever did on that paper. The great thing about JJ as a columnist – why he was the prince of columnists – is although he was right-wing you could never predict what he was going to say. JJ was the very first writer in a mainstream newspaper who began writing critical stuff about the Royal Family; it caused quite a lot of shock at the time, and in the *Sunday Express* of all places. Also the police. After the incident in Fleet Street he was very suspicious of the police, there was some quite important stuff he wrote about them in that column which made others think, well, if JJ is writing this . . . Again, the police had been sacrosanct. His weakness was he could be easily flattered, so if anyone thought they were going to be under attack they would take him out to lunch and suddenly he would become a friend for life.'

He had left the *Sunday Express*, thanks to his share options and payoff, a rich man; and negotiated a deal with Associated Newspapers by which he earned more money for his column than he had ever earned on the *Sunday Express* as Editor and columnist put together. But he had disappointed most of his former colleagues. They could scarcely believe that he would go to the competition, knowing the damage it would inflict on the newspaper that had been his life for thirty-five years. And his defection did damage the *Sunday Express* – to the tune of more than 80,000 copies lost to the *Mail on Sunday*. Most people think JJ chose the *Mail* to spite Stevens. I don't. He originally put feelers out to Rupert Murdoch and they had lunch together but JJ didn't like the idea of being buried along with dozens of other columnists in the vast and multi-sectioned *Sunday Times*. The *Mail on Sunday* promised him prominence, it was a middle-market newspaper with a high AB readership; it was the natural home for his column. He also enjoyed Lord Rothermere's flattery. After they lunched together, Lord Rothermere wrote:

> *Dear Sir John*
>
> *A mutual admiration society has developed. Your sentiments are exactly mine toward you and have been so ever since I started reading your column and newspaper.*
>
> *I have instructed the management to make an office available for you when you should be here. I hope you will feel free to visit me whenever you wish.*
>
> *I look forward with excitement to a joint future for us.*
> *Yours sincerely*
> *Vere Rothermere*

'I certainly didn't feel betrayed,' says Lord Stevens, 'although I know a lot of people did. I thought it was rather interesting and rather sad. The only times he'd mentioned Lord Rothermere to me he had slagged him off, and then he goes and works for him and says he's the most brilliant publisher he's ever come across in his life. So I just shrugged my shoulders and hoped he was happy, and I think he was quite happy.'

He was. He had landed in clover, and was very well looked after by the *Mail on Sunday*; they provided him with an office, a secretary and a brand new Range Rover – and treated him and his column with kid gloves. He could not have been happier, but he was keen to establish early on that he was no ordinary contributor. Before he began, Stewart Steven took him out to lunch at Le Gavroche, one of the most expensive restaurants in London, to put to JJ his idea of placing his column opposite Julie Burchill's. 'I know you don't like her, and she writes a lot of rubbish sometimes, which I don't particularly like, but I do know she has an incredible following and really stirs up controversy, as you stir up controversy. And I think it would be fantastic if both of you were to follow on from each other.'

'I think that's a very good idea,' he said. 'What makes you think I don't like Julie Burchill?'

'Well, you indicated to me earlier . . .'

'No, I didn't. I said to you she was not a political columnist and so she isn't. I didn't say she was not a good columnist. I seldom agree with her, but that doesn't mean I don't think she's a very good writer.'

At the end of the meal he said, 'Do you mind me asking, Stewart, how much this meal cost?'

'£60,' said Stewart quickly deducting about £40.

'£60? And how much, as a matter of interest, did that bottle of wine cost?'

'That was a bit extra, that was £20.'

'£20? So the whole meal cost £80? Do you think that is a sensible way of dispensing with *Mail on Sunday* money?'

Three months later, Stewart took him out again, this time to an ordinary Italian trattoria and at the end JJ said, "Tell me one thing, Stewart. Is this the place where you take your Cabinet minister friends?"

But, for all his bravado, JJ had been secretly quite anxious about starting afresh in a new organisation, and was delighted when Peter McKay and Nigel Dempster who were both writing columns for the *Mail* took him to lunch on his first day. 'He was feeling vulnerable,' says Peter, 'and made a point of saying how pleased he was that we had taken him out. Years later he would say, "I can't tell you how grateful I was, it was such a joyous lunch, I felt I had come home."'

Two years later there was a major shuffle at Associated Newspapers and he found himself with a new Editor. Jonathan Holborow took Stewart Steven's place at the *Mail on Sunday*. Steven moved to the *Evening Standard*, and Paul Dacre, who had been editing the *Standard*, was given the *Daily Mail* to prevent him taking up a generous offer from Rupert Murdoch to edit *The Times*. And in the shuffle, David English became Editor-in-Chief of the whole lot.

Jonathan Holborow and my father did not get off to a good start. 'JJ was very pissed off with me,' says Jonathan. 'The first person I saw when I arrived was Julie Burchill. She was completely mad, very awkward, and I didn't want to lose her, so saw her first. I suddenly realised I'd made a terrific gaffe, so asked JJ for lunch on the Thursday, at Arcadia; he paid. "I hear you've seen Julie," he said. "She's wonderful isn't she?" We got back to the office after a very good, long lunch. He had this habit after a good lunch of wandering around the news room with his hands in his pockets looking evil. "Jonathan Holborow's a very nice chap, very nice chap," he said. "I think he'll last a week."' But a couple of days later Jonathan heard that his wife had cancer and had six months to live. JJ somehow found out and wrote expressing his sympathy, and thereafter he was Jonathan's staunchest supporter. 'After that he wouldn't hear a word against me in the office. He was great, and would go out of his way to make sure no one was being nasty.'

Since his move to Kensington, Arcadia, formally the Ark, had become JJ's favourite restaurant. He could walk to it from the office and had established ownership of a table, to the left of the door by the window. He ate there several times a week, insisting his guests travel to him, no matter how far it meant they had to travel. Peter McKay and Nigel Dempster were regular lunching companions, also Peter Tory, a columnist on the *Express*, who had been given his first job in journalism by JJ. They had all been lunching together for years in Fleet Street, but a new and unlikely addition was Andrew Wilson, then Literary Editor of the *Evening Standard*. AN Wilson, as he's better known, is an intellectual and serious literary figure, thirty years my father's junior, with a public school and Oxford education. Andrew and JJ should have been poles apart, but JJ always spoke about him with a great deal of affection and admiration.

JJ revelled in his friendship with people like Andrew, Peter and

Nigel – all young enough to be his sons – and in his years at the *Mail on Sunday*, with fewer Cabinet ministers to lunch, they became his lifeline. He would come home and tell me what marvellous company they were, what great chums, and what great journalists – he was flattered and, I think, in a way surprised that they liked him. But like him they did, and the affection and indeed the admiration that JJ held for them was reciprocated. Andrew had joined the party seven years before my father died.

'I knew him mostly over lunch in the Arcadia, expressing the view that the Chilean red – long before it was any good – was delicious. It was quite disgusting; that was parsimony, I like that. I did look forward to lunches with him. I was fond of him. I didn't regard him as a monster to be approached through the bars. He was a monster, but I think, in his way, he was rather a great man.

'He had a very strong sense of what mattered in life, as well as in newspapers. He knew the Fourth Estate was very important in a democracy, but realised newspapers couldn't do much more than nudge – they couldn't rule the universe. Yes, he had his little weaknesses and liked to be flattered, but it wasn't just that he was sucking up to prime ministers, they were sucking up to him, they wanted his support, they knew his support meant something.'

JJ, once converted, gave Mrs Thatcher loyal and devoted support – some would say too loyal – but, when she was ousted from Number 10 in the leadership contest in November 1990 and started to snipe at her successor from the back benches, JJ laid into her with ferocity. 'Can there be anything much sadder than the conduct of Margaret Thatcher?' he wrote in one of many attacks.

When she was Prime Minister there are people who would have followed her to hell. I was one of them.

But isn't it, to say the least, distasteful that she is now doing to John Major what the venomously spiteful Ted Heath did to her?

Who signed the Single European Act which led us into Europe?

Margaret Thatcher did.

Who was it who turned her face against a referendum when she was Prime Minister?

Why, Margaret Thatcher did.

Doesn't she feel the slightest bit of shame that she should now be spitting at everything in which she once believed?

As for her claim that she does not want to harm Mr Major, just who does she think she is kidding?

Wouldn't she cut a more dignified figure if she were honestly to admit that only one thing motivates her? The fact that she just cannot abide being out of office?

When John Major succeeded Margaret Thatcher as Prime Minister in November 1990, he enjoyed my father's support every bit as much as his predecessor. They had first met at Chequers with Mrs Thatcher in 1986, and the two of them periodically lunched together thereafter. On the first occasion, JJ grilled him about his background. John Major recalls, 'He wanted to find out what it was really like in Brixton, what my father was like. In some ways he reminded me of my father, he had the same capacity when he was speaking to you, to look directly at you, so if you had had a guilty secret I think you would have probably quailed. He was fascinated, he didn't let it go; he went on and on as if trying to uncover what really lay beneath the exterior. It was a friendly but thorough investigation, and at the end of it I thought I had an ally, and subsequently it proved to be so; he was a pretty firm ally.'

After Major became Prime Minister, JJ was one of the few allies he had. Most of the media sneered at him. 'He had a capacity to side with the underdog, and I think he thought people had behaved badly as far as I was concerned and he wasn't going to join that particular crowd. So he probably gave me more support than he actually felt was merited from time to time. From my point of view he was a good man to go into the jungle with – we might even have got out the other end.'

Andrew Wilson admired his ability to go against the grain. 'He wasn't a stuff-pot journalist at all. He loved Richard Ingrams, and *Private Eye*, because he liked undermining things – although he was a little bit thrown by the fact that he'd become a *Private Eye* character. He had no strong desire to be part of the Establishment. Although he loved mixing with the great and adored being flattered by them, in the last resort, I still believe there was a dagger stuck under his coat, and, if necessary, he would have stabbed them in the chest.

'Another thing I think was very touching about him – if you consider how eminent he was – Sir John Junor, Editor of a great paper and, in his declining years, a great columnist. He never believed from one day to the next that he was going to keep that column. He was perpetually afraid people were going to steal it from him, that the moment he went away on a golfing holiday we were going to run upstairs and ask the Editor of the *Mail on Sunday* for his column. He was obsessed by that; totally obsessed.

'When he went through all the other columnists, as he did endlessly every week, in the last analysis they were always "Piss poor". He might see some merit but it was only that "Bernard Levin once was brilliant," and none of the women were ever any good. He delighted in the awfulness of people like Alison Pearson; he loved the thought that successive generations of *Evening Standard* Editors were clearly off the rails if they were employing piss poor material like that. "It would never have appeared in the *Sunday Express*."

'You'd have expected him to quite like Julie Burchill because she didn't pull her punches. On the other hand, if we were to say we quite liked Julie Burchill because she didn't pull her punches, he was quite capable of suddenly becoming extremely Presbyterian and prim and saying he would not, ever, have wanted anyone in his paper who had admitted to promiscuous behaviour, who took drugs and who abandoned her wee bairn. He would look rather solemn and sad and you'd feel as though you'd offended an Elder of the Church. He was also contrary, saying one thing one day and the complete opposite the next; but I think all journalists have to do that. They need to be organic and alive; if they don't they turn into pillars of stone.'

JJ took Jimmy Kinlay to lunch at Arcadia one day, saying to him, 'Jimmy, your problem is you live in the past. I live in the future, you live in the past. By the way, do you ever hear from Leslie Vanter?'

'Oh, that person from the past, do you mean, John?'

My father very seldom let anyone else pay for lunch, and very seldom went anywhere as anyone's guest. He liked to be in control of where they ate, how they ate, and what they ate – as well as what they talked about. Some people fretted about it more than others; Eric Sykes, the comedian, was one of them. He had been a firm lunching and golfing friend for many years and JJ had always foiled any attempt by Eric to pay. One day Eric was determined. They were lunching at Arcadia, he arrived early and handed his credit card to the maître d'hôtel and instructed him to use it to pay the bill, however much JJ protested. They had a very enjoyable lunch as ever and, after coffee, the waiter brought Eric the bill with a credit card slip, which he quickly signed. Eric Sykes has been deaf for many years, but his eyesight is also very poor, and he had scarcely looked at what he was signing. JJ asked whether he might see the bill, to check that everything was in order. He discovered a mistake: Eric had been overcharged. He said nothing to the manager, gave him no chance to apologise or explain; he decided arbitrarily that the mistake had been deliberate, and never set foot inside the restaurant again.

He missed it. From his table by the window he could watch the world walk by, and in summer he would sit at a table on the pavement and enjoy the short skirts and skimpy tops that the sun brought out. 'Whether he completely knew, when he talked about women, that they were the same species, I'm not sure,' says Andrew Wilson, who sat with him on the pavement many a time. 'I always got the impression he detested women. It seemed to be very odd to be sitting there, three or four of us, or maybe just two, both falling to bits and no beauties, and his making these comments about women walking past or sitting in the restaurant, as though he were the absolute arbiter of human taste. "Oh she's let herself go," about a woman who was perfectly well-groomed and rather beautiful, aged about forty-five, and there was he with his droopy red eyes. What would she think of him? But that was all par for the course. I loved his fantasies about women. He used to believe that the premises opposite Arcadia was a brothel – there was a door in the corner to some flats or something. He did it in the way he wrote his column with questions. "Do you suppose that young woman is going in there with an honest purpose?"

' "I can't honestly tell."

' "Have you not noticed that she's been in before, every time we've been eating here, she's been going into the corner? I think you'd find if you went upstairs, it's a knocking shop. There's another of them." And another perfectly innocent woman, of forty perhaps, would be walking past. He had built up this story, but it wasn't a joke. I said, "Surely if it's a knocking shop, you wouldn't see a lot of women going into it, you'd see a lot of men going into it, and the women would be going up the back stairs."

' "Not necessarily," he said.

'Germaine Greer is right, a lot of men hate women. It doesn't mean you love your own sex, it just means you're an insecure, unhappy person, which a lot of men are, and JJ was. He was a vulnerable person. I never suspected he had real friends. I think he sort of knew he couldn't conduct normal human relationships and was haunted by it, which was why he liked journalism and male friendships and sitting in restaurants and giving opinions about what was going on in the world because it's much easier doing all of that. He had a great feel for the camaraderie of Fleet Street. You could just go to the bar and there they all were. There's nothing very unusual about that; most men are like that, which is why they form themselves into gangs. They don't trust themselves to form such friendships and therefore go to clubs, unions, the local pub, where nothing's too challenging.

'He knew in his own life that a lot of things had gone hideously wrong and there was a lot of darkness there, and he knew that was part of the human nature and human character and the human scene in society and any politician who pretended it wasn't there was a humbug. To that extent, that is why he liked Thatcher because she recognised the dark side of the human soul, and didn't pretend it wasn't there. He never talked to me about his marriage but he always hinted that it had gone disastrously wrong and he regretted it. He used to say, his old eyes becoming all watery, that he had made a terrible mess out of life and he regretted it.'

CHAPTER TWENTY-SEVEN

What Ye Sow . . .

I don't know what my father's theory of hell was. I doubt that he believed in the eternal damnation of the Bible – his God was an understanding, forgiving God; but towards the end of his life he must have begun to think that there was some kind of reckoning and that sentence was meted out right here on earth. Because although he found a new lease of life at the *Mail on Sunday*, his last years were one long trial of guilt, worry, pain and loneliness.

The principal worry was Roderick, whose drinking continued unabated. The subject of Roderick's drinking had always been very difficult between JJ and me – as so many subjects were – because for so long he had denied there was any real problem. When he could deny it no longer, he laid the blame at Suzy's feet. Suzy, being blindly loyal to Roderick, also denied there was a problem, as did Pam; yet day after day Roderick's phone calls to us all were incoherent ramblings about far-fetched conspiracies and, when we met, his skin would be clammy to the touch and he reeked of alcohol at all hours of the day, as though it was seeping through his pores. One Christmas I gave him a big, illustrated book about wildlife in London – he was living in a house that backed onto Richmond Park at the time and told me how he liked to feed the deer – and he rang me up when he got back home to say that he had burnt the book – there were scribbles inside it, it was clearly not new.

It was his son, Roddy, who finally broke the cycle of denial. It was Roderick's birthday and Pam and JJ had gone together, as they often did on special occasions, to have lunch with them all. By this time they were renting a house in Kingston. At the end of the meal, Roddy, then aged eighteen, handed his father a letter he had written, which he asked him to read aloud. It was a plea for him to stop drinking, pointing out that if he didn't stop, this could be the last birthday he would be alive to celebrate. The reaction around the table was shock, outrage and condemnation and when JJ brought Pam home that afternoon he was still livid. 'How dare he spoil lunch like that? How dare he speak like that to his father? How dare he make him read it out in front of everyone? It was the most appalling thing anyone could have done. He's a little shit that boy.' How he dared I don't know, because it must have taken an enormous amount of courage; I suppose it was desperation. I said what Roddy had done was the bravest thing I had ever heard of. It was the absolute truth, and it was about time JJ and Pam and everyone else woke up to what was happening before it was too late. JJ shouted at me a bit more, then drove off in a sulk and we didn't talk for a while, but the day left an impression on him. And he started to talk about it.

One of the people he talked to was Stanley Miller, a fellow Scot and the latest in a long line of doctor friends. Stanley was a general surgeon who worked locally; they had met on the golf course and played golf together, dined together and occasionally even went on holiday together for the last ten years of my father's life. He would bring his ailments, both imagined and real, to Stanley and also seek advice about Roderick, who one Christmas was admitted to hospital in Kingston. He was jaundiced and swollen like a balloon, and for a while afterwards stopped drinking, but still there was no discussion about it, no admission that what he had was liver disease and that his drinking was slowly killing him.

I knew Stanley only slightly. My father used to rave about his surgical skills, and tell the story time and again about how Stanley had saved the life of a neighbour who appeared to have had a heart attack in bed. His GP had refused to come to the house, telling his wife to send him to hospital but, after the ambulance had gone, Stanley spotted a dead wasp on the bedding and realised it was not a coronary the man was suffering from but anaphylactic shock.

Stanley and his wife Kathleen lived on a smart estate called The

Warren – my father's idea of suburban hell. There was a similar estate at Mickleham, and, although we had friends who lived in houses on the estate, JJ could never get over the mentality of wanting to live so close to one's neighbours. I was always slightly surprised by his friendship with Stanley, suspecting it was born more of convenience than a meeting of minds, but there is no doubt JJ relied upon it. 'It was a very peculiar type of friendship,' admits Stanley. 'We had a rapport, in as much as it was possible to with John. We had the common heritage of the Scot, but at times we would fight like cat and dog. He would raise family matters and I would say, "You do understand these matters are privy between you and me." But I didn't confide in him because, to be honest, I didn't feel I could trust him. He was never very good at giving you advice. He wouldn't get involved in your problem. He'd stand back; he wasn't interested. He was interested in problems he could relate to: ill health, death and disaster, things he could possibly fit into a column. But if you gave him some other sort of problem he might say something fairly banal, but you never felt he was getting involved. He was not the sort of chap who would phone you up later in the day and say, "I've thought about this, I think you should do the following."'

In 1993, Roderick hit the buffers. He had run out of money, he had no job and was soon going to lose the roof over his head. He turned to JJ for help; not for help with his drinking, which he still denied – even after the birthday lunch – but for help financially. JJ was at his wit's end, he didn't know what to do, and almost for the first time we were able to talk. I contacted my cousin, Muir, Tom's son, for advice. He and I had spoken many times in the previous few years about Roderick. He was an alcoholic who had come through the worst. It had cost him his marriage, but he was an active member of Alcoholics Anonymous, he had been dry for some years, and was only too keen to help now. His advice was unequivocal: JJ must do nothing. It is what the text books call 'tough love'. Roderick would only be cured by wanting to be cured, which first meant admitting he was an alcoholic. Brutal though it sounds, what he needed was to wake up in the gutter one morning, alone, and realise that if he ever wanted to get out of it he would have to take charge of his life and stop drinking.

'Alcoholism is no respecter of persons or of intellect or of status or wealth, or of sex or of sexual proclivity,' wrote Muir in a long letter to JJ, which summed up the disease to perfection.

Very often intellect, status and wealth are the major stumbling blocks which pride uses to deny or diminish the problem and to inhibit the natural instinct for survival and to ask for and accept help. It is a cunning, powerful and baffling illness, which maims and kills just as surely as an untreated diabetes. It is no more the fault of the human being who succumbs to it than it would be if he were to develop an allergy to penicillin or shellfish or have defective islets of Langerhans. But in addition to having an allergy to alcohol, of course, the alcoholic tends to destroy all his close relationships by his appalling behaviour; always promising that 'it' will never happen again and always failing in his resolve. Eventually nobody wants to know and he is left on his own. Doctors, ministers, counsellors in this, that or the other, wash their hands of this hopeless pest. Even mothers and fathers get to the stage where they know in their hearts that all their love and reasoning, all their threats, all their scolding will not deliver their child from the grip of this relentless and progressive disease. Only they know what their pain is just as only an alcoholic knows the terrible fear and loneliness of being caught inside that empty husk of a person with nowhere left to go – physical, mental and spiritual bankruptcy.

This is the point, the rock bottom, at which the alcoholic is most likely to reach for help. And all you can do is to disengage or detach with love until that time comes. You and I are as powerless over Roderick's alcoholism as he is. In our experience, relatives are very often the last person who can help and in many cases, albeit with the best will in the world, they can enable the problem to continue by bailing them out of financial and other scrapes and by not carrying out threats. If you have no intention of carrying out a threat – don't make it in the first place. The corollary of course also applies.

There is one last thing I would like to pass on which may help you and this is the apportionment of 'blame' in all this. I blamed people, places and events for my drinking. I blamed my mother for dying; I blamed father for dying and for years of threatening to take his own life; I blamed my wife because she wasn't the way I wanted her to be and I couldn't change her – anything that would give me a reason for being the way I was. And I could convince most people that I had a pretty good case. But of course it amounted to no more than a frightened little boy whistling in the wind. It turned out that it was nobody's 'fault' – not even mine – because from that night in the bistro in Carolle Plage when I discovered that alcohol could dissolve all my grief and fear and uncertainty, the curtains opened on life, the lights came on and the play started in earnest with me in the lead role. But it turned out that my body could not tolerate alcohol. I have a disease and all I have to do is not to pick up that first drink and I can't possibly get drunk.

JJ listened to Muir, and he listened to me, and he listened to others. Intellectually he knew that he ought to stand back but JJ couldn't go through with it. Intellectually he knew that this was a disease and no one's fault, but emotionally he felt that somehow he must have been responsible for Roderick's drinking, and had to help; and the only way in which he knew how to give help, or express love, was with money. He bailed him out. He bought him a cottage to live in, and set up a Trust Fund, with sufficient income for him, Suzy and Roddy to live on for the rest of their lives. The cottage was about three miles from Wellpools, not the place where Roderick or Suzy would have chosen for themselves I am sure – but JJ wanted to exercise control, and he never left them alone. Every evening on his way home he drove first to me, then on to see them. He took them the day's newspapers, and he took them food supplies. He gave Roderick a job, clearing the undergrowth in the woods at Wellpools and thinning out the trees. For a while it seemed to be working; he took pride in what he was doing, but the drinking continued.

Then one Sunday morning, not long after they had moved, I had a telephone call. It was JJ ringing from Walton Heath, where he had just had a message from the police that Roderick was in a bad way in his car on the forecourt of our local petrol station. The manager had alerted them. JJ was on his way but he wanted me to go and see what was going on. James and I went together, and sure enough Roderick's distinctive cream Land Rover was parked just short of the forecourt, and he was slumped over the wheel. The manager said he had called the police, because he hadn't been able to rouse the driver, and was worried that he might be ill. Roderick looked as though he might have had a heart attack, but when we opened the door, it was all too apparent what the problem was: he was in an alcoholic stupor, with several empty bottles of wine in a plastic carrier bag beside him. Moments later the police arrived, the more senior of whom was an extremely kind and sympathetic character, to whom I explained the situation. They endeavoured to get Roderick to blow into a Breathalyzer without success, and took him away in their panda car to the police station. We were all agreed that a charge of drink-driving might be just the thing to make Roderick face facts and, given the state he was in, his reading would clearly be off the Richter scale. Shortly afterwards, JJ arrived and I think he was very glad to have been so far away when he got the call. For the first time in my life I could see that my father was out of his depth, and frightened.

I had friends who worked at Farm Place, the addiction unit frequented by celebrities and the sons of the aristocracy, which by good chance was in Ockley, a village four miles away. I rang to find out more, and then talked to JJ. He was prepared to pay what it took to get Roderick sorted out – and what it was going to take was around £2000 per week. In the days that followed, Roderick seemed a changed man. He was penitent, he drank nothing and he seemed to be ready to accept help, and so not long afterwards, I drove him to check in to Farm Place.

Farm Place is a seventeenth-century manor house, set in lovely gardens, with tennis courts and a gym. It could be a luxury hotel, but the regime, devised by American psychologists Joyce and Jim Ditzler, is extremely tough. The idea, as it was explained to me, is that when a patient arrives he joins a group in front of whom he confesses all. Each member of the group describes the mayhem they have caused by their drinking or drug use, the friends they have lost, the harm and embarrassment they have caused their families and, in the process of confessing and being judged by their peers, they are stripped of their confidence and self-respect. Once they have reached rock bottom, and recognise the need to change, they are then buoyed up by the knowledge that recovery is within their power and, bit by bit, they are made whole again. By the time they leave at the end of six weeks, their self-esteem is restored and they are healthy, confident and capable people once more.

Roderick, sadly, had no real interest in being cured. What he cunningly realised was that if he turned up in court to answer his drink-driving charge as a patient at Farm Place – someone who recognised he had a problem and had taken steps to prevent it ever happening again – the magistrates might be lenient. They were. When his case came to court he was fined and banned from driving for six months. But Roderick put on a good show of wanting to be cured. He wrote to JJ after a few days thanking him for his support, understanding and kindness, and saying that he was exactly where he ought to be and that with the treatment on offer, with the counselling and medical attention, it would be possible for him to make a full recovery and never pick up even so much as a spoonful of sherry trifle again.

In practice he was less convinced. His counsellor rang me to say that Roderick was still in denial, he was not prepared to say anything about himself in group sessions, and didn't believe that he had anything in common with the others, who clearly had serious problems. Could I help? Could I get together examples from members of the family of how and when Roderick's drinking had led to his behaviour being disruptive, embarrassing or unacceptable? Without these, he had no hope of helping my brother; it was absolutely essential that we provide the means of confronting him with his past. He also wanted the family to come to the clinic so we could have a private group session.

Suzy was not in a position to help, and it was not a matter I could have spoken to her about. I spoke to JJ. He had a catalogue of incidents, I knew, and had been with his driver to rescue Roderick on a number of occasions. He had had just as many phone calls as

I had, and had seen far more of Roderick in recent years than I had. He refused point blank to help. He was not prepared to say a word against Roderick, not even if it was a means of helping him, and he was damned if he was going to go and talk to any counsellor. I could count him out. Pam was not much better, she said she couldn't remember any occasions when Roderick's drinking had been a problem – she was still in denial. And so I did it alone. I wrote out a long list of the times, going back many years, when I had found my brother's drunkenness offensive, including the *Evening News* Christmas party. I also said that, when drunk, he had a tendency to grope me, and blow cigar smoke in my face.

The result was catastrophic. The counsellor confronted Roderick with this catalogue of memories, citing me as the author, and he was apparently made to feel so humiliated in front of his therapy group that he walked out. He signed himself out of Farm Place, where they had no power to hold him, took a taxi home and rang JJ to tell him why he had left. JJ immediately came to see me. He took me into the children's playroom, closed the door, as he did when he wanted to have a private talk with me – another thing which used to drive James mad – and launched into the most ferocious attack on me for telling lies.

I didn't know what had happened at that stage, I didn't know Roderick had walked out of Farm Place. But I had never, ever seen my father so angry, and for a good three minutes he screamed at me. He said I was wicked and evil to have made up such lies about Roderick, and I had wrecked his chances of ever getting better. I was selfish, stupid, and ignorant, and if Roderick drank himself to death it would be my fault. I hadn't the first idea what he was talking about, until he finally said, 'And how dare you accuse Roderick of groping you? Do you have any idea what that word means?' Suddenly I realised he must have seen the list I sent the counsellor. 'Yes, I bloody well do know what grope means, it means grabbing bits of my body.' 'That is a wicked and complete and utter lie. He has never done that in his life.'

'He's been doing it for years,' I screamed, 'and if you don't believe me, ask Pam, because he's been doing it to her too.'

309

The real tragedy was that Roderick left before the treatment was complete. He attended AA meetings and stayed off alcohol for a while, but in time he secretly went back to it, although denying it the while. My mother found him drunk one day and discovered bottles hidden under the grill and in other places around his cottage, and only then did she really face up to the fact that he was an alcoholic. But my relationship with him was destroyed forever. I thought I was helping, I thought I had done the right thing, and maybe, if he had not reacted so violently, what I did might have helped. But it was not to be.

That night after our row JJ went home to Wellpools on his own and drank heavily. In the middle of the night he rang Jane Crow, a widow living in a neighbouring village to whom he had become very close. 'I could tell he was drunk on the phone, he was distraught about Roderick. I went there the next morning and the little lacquered cabinet on the hall table, which I'd given him as a Christmas present, was smashed all over the floor and the table was upside down and everything was everywhere. It was quite frightening because he never allowed himself to get out of control – it was his horror. He told me he'd attacked you for telling lies. He was furious you had gone to a session at Farm Place and that they had wanted him to go. I tried to explain this was part of repairing Roderick but he wouldn't get emotionally involved. He couldn't cope with it.'

Jane Crow had known JJ since the early 1970s. Her husband, Maurice, had been an estate agent in Dorking whom JJ had known for years. He had brought his young wife to dinner at Wellpools. 'I remember I was wearing a pair of Rayne brown patent leather boots, which his eyes kept returning to. "Where did you buy those gorgeous boots? How much did they cost?" I was riveted by his powerful personality and charm, the force and penetration of his non-stop questioning, the insistence that he know everything about me, and my background, searching into my very soul. He was fascinated that my father had been shot down during the war five weeks before I was born.' They became close – there were dinner parties, tennis, sailing; Jane and her husband helped my father buy his house in Barfleur and she and Maurice bought one of their own a couple of streets away – and when Maurice died suddenly and unexpectedly, in 1984, leaving her at the age of forty-one with four young children, JJ was there.

They had supper together most weeks, he encouraged her with her business, their holidays in Barfleur coincided, she went to The Gambia with him on a couple of occasions, and on other trips. Roderick was suspicious of the relationship. He disliked every woman that JJ saw – he thought they were all after his money. I didn't care one way or the other; I just couldn't bear him being so lonely and if someone could make him happy I was all for it, but I was astonished that she put up with him being so rude to her.

Jane says she had no interest in marrying my father, and is now happily remarried to someone else, but admits she loved him very much. 'He wasn't a part of my family life. He never came for Sunday lunch, didn't want to sit round the kitchen table with my children, he didn't want to get involved at all. At Christmas he'd be totally alone, and wouldn't come to lunch. I'd ask why. "Oh, I'm such a loner," he'd say. "I don't need people." But if he had come, it would have been so unrelaxed. Suppose lunch was ten minutes late, or we didn't eat fast enough, or someone talked for too long about something that didn't interest him, or the children started telling silly jokes, or lunch took three hours instead of half an hour?'

Throughout his friendship with Jane, my father was also seeing Susie Winter, his old secretary, as and when he got in touch and her travels allowed it. On one brief trip to England for a minor operation, she went to stay at Wellpools for a while, and accompanied JJ on his visits to drop things off to Roderick two or three times a day. 'Why are you doing that?' she said. 'Leave them alone, let them get on with it. Why are you buying their Sunday lunch, that's Suzy's job?' He didn't like being questioned, but sometimes he told her to get out of the car, and smell Roderick's breath, to see if he'd been drinking. 'Once when I dropped off the newspapers, Roderick said to me, "How kind of my father to pay for your little operation." He thought he'd paid for it because I went to a private hospital.

'"No, Roderick, you've got it very wrong," I said. "I have BUPA, I don't need your father to pay for things like that." I think he

311

thought I was some blood-sucking female who was trying to take his inheritance.'

One night, when Susie had gone away to stay with her mother, Roderick broke into Wellpools in the middle of the night and appeared at JJ's bedside. He said he had come to check all was well because he had seen JJ and Susie dancing naked on his lawn. 'Johnny didn't think it was funny at all. I screamed with laughter. A couple of weeks later, I said to Roderick, "I loved the story about me dancing on your lawn," and he didn't say a word, there was a long, long silence, then Suzy came to the door, took one long cold look at me and walked off. I said to Roderick, "I'm sorry, I wasn't even there that night."

'I felt sorry for Roderick. We took him and Suzy out to supper in a restaurant and Johnny was horrid to him. Bicker, bicker, bicker until I told him to stop it. Suzy said nothing and opted out. Whatever Roderick was saying, he wasn't making sense, and I wished he would just be quiet. He was trying to tell a story and Johnny was shouting at him, saying "That's rubbish, you don't know what you're talking about." It was all rather embarrassing and other diners were staring at us.'

JJ adored Susie. She was very different from Jane: Susie was bubbly, energetic, and sexy while Jane was cool, calm and tough; but he was equally beastly to them both. And yet both women loved him, and I believe would have married him. He told me one day, grinning all over his face, that he simply didn't know what he was going to do, both women wanted him, both women made such demands on him, and he didn't think he could cope. If only he had been able to curb his vicious tongue, he could have had either of them and been loved and looked after in the last years of his life. Instead he managed to destroy both relationships.

Disillusion began to set in with Jane when her daughter, Sara, collapsed in Oxford and was taken into the John Radcliffe Hospital with what was thought to be a flu virus. Jane and JJ were due to leave on a golfing holiday in America five days later but, when the hospital were unable to stabilise Sara's heart and didn't know why, Jane warned him that she might not be able to go. 'Oh, it's nothing,' said JJ, 'she's just got flu.' Forty-eight hours later, she discovered

Sara was desperately ill and was going to need open-heart surgery. 'Oh, that's nothing,' he said, 'you'll still be able to come.' It was just like the night on which Roderick and he had such a blazing row in Barfleur, when Roderick said he had to go to Switzerland because Hanny was so ill. He couldn't see beyond his own needs; all he felt was irritation that he was going to be inconvenienced. 'It was unbelievable. I had to sit through eight hours of open-heart surgery and he told me I was neurotic and overreacting.'

It was the beginning of the end. For the first time since Maurice died, Jane felt she couldn't cope, so she went away to stay with a friend in Zimbabwe and came back with plans to marry a man she had known for some years, who lived in South Africa. 'I had to look after myself and my future. The incident with Sara had a huge impact on me. Something started to go, but it didn't mean I loved him any the less. I was very torn. The day I told him I wanted to get married again, he gave me a whole lot of emotional and financial blackmail. He begged me to stay, said he would pay me to stay. "If you marry Colin," he said, "I'll never see you again, never want to see you again." When he saw that I really meant it, he called in to see me, backed his Range Rover into the drive and just sat there playing 'Ae Fond Kiss', and sobbing over the steering wheel, with his cheque book, wanting to give me anything not to go to Africa. It was heartrending.'

JJ had always said he would never divorce Pam, but that July he asked Susie Winter to marry him. She laughed, and asked, 'Is this a joke? One of your little fantasies?' But he said, no, he was deadly serious. And when she arrived to stay with him in Barfleur a month later, he took her straight off in the car to a neighbouring town, saying it was a nice place, she would like it, and without a word of explanation, marched in a determined fashion down one street after another until he found what he was looking for: a jeweller's shop.

'I was so flummoxed, I stood there thinking this can't be real, this must be a joke. We tried several rings and I chose the simplest I could find, I thought it was so crazy.' When they got back into the Range Rover, JJ tossed the box across to Susie saying, 'There. That's what you wanted, isn't it? Put it on.' And in a single gesture spoilt everything – just as he always did.

313

Back in Barfleur, they went into the church. He said he loved me and would like to marry me – but I knew it was a game. 'He said he was old and lonely and didn't want to spend his last days being alone – he was frightened of being alone. Maybe that's what triggered his being nice to me and asking me to marry him. I don't know what he wanted. Maybe he thought I'd move in and look after him.'

Susie's husband had often asked why she wanted to go on holiday with JJ – was she having an affair with him? She had always replied that they were just old friends and he wanted someone to go on holiday with. 'I adored the old bastard, I really did, and it was wonderful to be back together again. I knew about Jane Crow through Bill Martin. "What am I doing here?" I said, "Where's your friend Jane Crow? Why didn't you marry her?" "Oh, I didn't love her," he said. That was it, end of conversation never to be mentioned again.'

There were good times and bad times thereafter. 'Whenever I went to lunch with him, he was wonderful, there was always a glass of champagne on the table for me.' Sometimes she would go down to Wellpools with him for the night, and he once asked Peter McKay and Jak, the cartoonist, to look after her while he went back to the office for another hour. As usual, she had her instructions to meet him at a quarter to four in the foyer, for the drive home. 'We got stuck into more champagne and, by the time I met Johnny, I was very jolly. That didn't go down well at all.' After supper JJ would go into the sitting room and start on his work, which he insisted on doing in total silence. He said Susie was fidgety and that she unsettled him, but he wanted her with him, not watching TV in the kitchen. And so she sat quietly until he had finished. 'Often I would just sit at his feet while he worked, then we'd chat and laugh and watch a bit of the news. On those occasions it was very easy. He'd mellow with a few whiskies – or he'd drink too much and get plain nasty – but sometimes he was absolutely perfect and you'd think this is really nice, really cosy.

'Then we'd fall out. The rows were over such petty things. I was talking about our ambassador in Moscow, for example, and he said, "Oh they're all rubbish, they're not intellectuals," and I said,

"How do you know? You don't even know the guy," and he'd go off at a terrible tangent, decrying the whole system. I would then get on my high horse, which was a waste of time because he'd just get nasty, and I'd disintegrate. I'd think I'm too old and too wise, what am I doing sitting in a restaurant being shouted at by this man, there's no point? He always had to be right, he was always best, he knew best, and if I said, "Not always," he'd just get snarly.'

Once, during a row in Barfleur, Susie was so incensed she got up and walked out of the house. They had been out to dinner and had gone home for a nightcap. She left without her shoes, purse, or even a cigarette, and spent two hours wandering around. Finally she went back to the house and sat down on the kerb outside wondering what to do next, when the door opened. JJ gathered her into his arms and said, 'Don't do that again, I've been so worried.' Susie recalls, 'He was hugely contrite, big hugs, but he'd do exactly the same again the next night.'

His image with her was diminishing. Her wonderful knight in shining armour, the man she had always adored, had turned into a bitter and twisted old man. 'I'd try to stand up to him but I'd just get abuse. That's when he could be really spiteful, but I'd think, why should I be submissive? But I couldn't cut him out of my life.'

It seemed that the sorrier he felt for himself, the nastier he was to those who tried to love him. And by this time my father was feeling very sorry for himself. He was plagued by the knowledge that he had done the wrong thing with Roderick. He knew that, so long as he was supporting him, Roderick would never face and fight the problem of his alcoholism, but there was Suzy to think of, and Roddy; he couldn't abandon them. He was also worried about his own health and what might become of Roderick if he were to die – there would be no one to look after him.

He had already had intimations of mortality. He and Charles Wilson, the Glaswegian Editor of *The Times*, had just sat down to lunch in Arcadia one day in 1993 when his speech suddenly became momentarily jumbled and his body slumped to one side. Immediately sensing something seriously amiss, Charles asked the proprietor to call an ambulance and, within minutes, the two of them were on their way to the Kensington and Chelsea Hospital. He had suffered a mini stroke, better known as a transient ischaemic attack, a TIA, which was quickly over and left no lasting symptoms.

I was in Hampshire when I heard he had had a stroke. I was visiting a mushroom farm belonging to the John Lewis Partnership, at Leckford. I had been appointed General Editor of the company – broadly speaking, the director responsible for communications – just a few weeks before and was still visiting the various parts of the business in the course of my induction programme. James phoned me with the news, having been alerted by Charles, and he in turn phoned Roderick. Roderick set off from Surrey, and I went straight to London from Hampshire, stopping only to buy a large bunch of daffodils on the way, which were one of JJ's favourite flowers. We met outside the hospital.

I knew he was in no immediate danger but a lot went through my mind as I hurtled up the M3. JJ was an indestructible figure in my mind; he had tummy problems, yes, and he was an incorrigible hypochondriac, but it had never seriously crossed my mind that he might die. James and I had always joked that he would outlive us all just for spite. He kept telling me how healthy he was, he wore a watch which doubled up as a blood-pressure gauge, and he'd boast about what amazing blood pressure he had for a man of his age – which was now seventy-five – how much better it was than mine. He had discovered some years before that he had 'atrial fibrillation' – he loved the medical terms – but otherwise his heart was as strong as the heart of a thirty-year-old. He had himself checked by 'the great Sam Oram, who was the best doctor since Dan Davies'. And although he smoked and drank and was clearly overweight, and lived largely on beef and boiled sweets, he was so forceful about his good health, and the impossibility of any part of him ever giving out, that I believed him.

But if I thought I was about to see evidence of frailty I was much mistaken. As Roderick and I walked into the room where he was sitting up in bed, he took one look at the flowers I was carrying, and said, 'You can take those bloody things away for a start.' The following morning he discharged himself and, by Tuesday, he was back in the office.

As soon as JJ had arrived at the hospital, he had called for Iain

Murray-Lyon, a Scottish consultant who had treated him for a huge stomach ulcer eight years before. Thereafter, Iain became a regular lunching companion. He found it reassuring to have doctor friends on tap. Ian Clarke, his GP in Dorking, whom he used to consult over Monday morning coffee, had long since retired, and had insisted that JJ sign up with his successor, Pip Young. Pip was a very different character, and did not take kindly to consultations out of his surgery no matter how many cases of wine JJ was prepared to drop in by way of recompense. And so JJ relied on his friendships with Stanley Miller and, to a lesser extent, Iain Murray-Lyon, and since Iain was a liver expert, some of his questions inevitably involved his concerns about Roderick.

JJ, having refused to talk about it, now often discussed Roderick's drinking, but only with people that he felt had the right credentials. Charles Wilson was one. He had firsthand knowledge of the problem, having been married to Anne Robinson, who was an alcoholic. After his stroke, JJ was very grateful to Charles for looking after him, and this was an additional bond between them. Murdoch MacLennan, his friend from the *Express* board, who moved to Associated Newspapers shortly after JJ, was another. His father was an alcoholic and, since his death in 1991, Murdoch had regarded JJ as a replacement, a mentor; and, as father and son might, they shared confidences.

'JJ never stopped promoting me and I was eternally grateful to him. At every twist and turn, if I had a problem, JJ was there. He was immensely worried about Roderick. He blamed himself; he knew he wasn't handling it properly. He paid the money, but it was only buying a quick fix; longer term he knew he was making a rod for his own back. This was a regular talking point, not something we talked about in a blue moon. "He's sick," he would say. "I've got to do something about it, I know I'm not doing the right thing."'

In the summer of 1995 – a year after JJ had given her the ring – Susie was back in Barfleur. She arrived on the Saturday and he met her off the ferry at Cherbourg. He had fallen over and hurt his shin, and his first words were not 'How are you?' or 'How nice to see you,' but 'Look at my cut, and I've come all this way to meet you and it hurts to drive.' It wasn't the most auspicious start and, although his humour had returned when they went out to supper that evening, by Tuesday she was planning to leave.

'I did something to irritate him and he had me in tears in a restaurant. I thought I'll go now, this is really stupid, it's not worth staying. Then I thought I'd eke it out and I lasted until the Friday when, over dinner, we had a spitting match in another restaurant. He stormed out and left me sitting there. I sat for some time wondering if he would come back. Then he backed the car up to the window and sat there revving, so I made my apologies to the waiters and left.'

Earlier that day, Jane Crow's daughter had dropped in – and Susie had been deposited on a beach for two hours. By 4 p.m., his mood was thunderous, and by dinner he was being so unpleasant that Susie asked him what was going on? Wasn't she supposed to be the person he loved and wanted to marry and be with? He then denied, several times, that he had ever asked her to marry him and when she asked what the ring was all about, he said it was only symbolic. That was the point at which he stormed out of the restaurant.

They drove back to the house in silence, and Susie went straight upstairs and packed her bags and banged them down by the front door, and said, 'Would you mind calling me a taxi, I think I'd better go now?' 'JJ started throwing things. "You've left this and this," bang, bang. And he said, "It would be the greatest pleasure to drive you to Cherbourg in the morning, and I'm taking the car keys to bed with me so you don't even think of driving the car there." Then he stormed up the stairs and I remember calling up after him, "I hope your conscience allows you to sleep." I thought he was going to hit me. I'd never seen him so angry in my life. He was so horrid. So I took off the little ring and put it in its little box and left it on the mantelpiece with a note inside saying "It's cruel to play with people's emotions". I sat downstairs for a few hours, then thought I'd better go to bed as well. I got up early the next morning, dressed and was downstairs by the time he got up. He didn't say a word to me; he got his breakfast, picked up the car keys and said, "Right, let's go." So I got in, thinking he might have changed his mind by then, but no. And we hadn't even got out of Barfleur when he said, "By the way, this is for you," and handed me a little box. I'd really gone to Barfleur for my birthday, and I said, "Are you really sure you want to give it to me?" And he said, "Yes," and I said, "Well thank you, I'll open it on my birthday." We got to the port in Cherbourg, he stomped into the departure lounge, bought me a ticket and said, "There you are. Go." We went outside to get my bags, and he put his arms around me and said, "I'll always love you." Then he got into the car and drove off. That was the Saturday. I got home to my mother and took to my bed for three days with a raging headache. He rang on the Thursday and said, "Happy Birthday." I said, "You've missed it by three days, but thank you for the bracelet." Then I said, "I know you're coming back overnight on Saturday. I'm staying with a friend in Guildford that night, if you like I'll meet you for breakfast in Guildford, and he said no, he was having lunch with Roderick. And that was the end of it until the next year.

'By September I was getting worried, he hadn't made any contact at all, so I rang and I said, "I'm taking a friend to Gatwick," which was a lie, "I could look in, I'd like to see you, see how you are?" He said, "Fine, come on down," but there was no conversation, there was nothing. He was obviously still terribly angry. He gave me a bottle of perfume and said, "Here, I bought you this," and I said "Thank you, I've got a pot of honey for you." I was there for about twenty minutes and he said, "If there's no conversation, you might as well go." Then he just put his arms round me and said "Farewell." That was September 1996, and that was the last I saw him. We didn't even speak again. I kept ringing Wellpools, but he was never there.'

CHAPTER TWENTY-EIGHT

Shit-Scared

On the bookcase beside me as I write sits a turquoise quill pen encased in a Perspex block. My father's name is inscribed on the base. It is the *What The Papers Say* award for a lifetime's achievement in journalism, which he won in 1996. He was not pleased. He professed to have no interest in awards, but what he secretly wanted was the award for Best Columnist. He would insist, without a trace of modesty, that his column was brilliant and there wasn't another columnist to touch him. But I suspect that, deep down, he was as uncertain about his column as he was about everything else in his life. The aggression was nothing more than a symptom of insecurity.

His column was what kept him going. Four days a week a driver would arrive to collect him from Wellpools and take him into the office. He was given a driver after he fell asleep at the wheel one morning, wrote off his Range Rover and demolished half of Hammersmith Bridge. He said it was because he took a sleeping pill at 5 a.m. after a sleepless night, but his doctor suspects it was another TIA. He worked on the column every day of the week and would often still be fiddling around with it, perfecting it, on a Friday night or even Saturday morning. And his mood and the column were still inextricably linked.

By 1996 it had become almost all that was left in his life. The yacht had gone some years before, an arthritic hip meant that he could no longer play golf, and he had driven away most of the people that cared about him – including me. As he grew older and more crippled by the pain in his hip, he became more and more cantankerous and impossible. So, when James and I started to run out of money in the early Nineties, we decided to move out of Surrey, which was an expensive area, and go and live near James's sister Prue and her husband, Rayne Kruger, whom we both adore, in Gloucestershire. Her children, Daniel and Li-Da, and ours were good friends, and property, we hoped, would be cheaper. I knew JJ would be completely devastated if we moved and took his grand-children away from him, but I had to make a choice. We had lived on JJ's doorstep for twenty years, and for twenty years James had put up with my father invading his home, and being rude and unpleasant. It was time his happiness came before my father's. He deserved a break.

I had had ten very successful years with plenty of television. I had written lots of books that had done very well, and, on the strength of it, we had bought The Punter's Pie restaurant in Batter-sea, which James ran. We were living relatively high on the hog but, by the time recession hit, I was down to one programme – *The Travel Show*. We had sold the restaurant and become involved in a new venture with two restaurants, which were struggling to stay alive; we had a mortgage and four children in private education. Something had to give.

JJ was always trying to find out how much money we had, how much I earned for my television work, how much I was paid for each book, and I would never tell him. So he guessed at wild figures, which were hugely inflated. But then he started to realise that maybe I wasn't as rich as he had assumed, and kept asking if we were all right, whether we needed any help, and made me promise that if ever we did need money we would come to him. I thanked him and said of course I would, but I would rather have moved into a garden shed than accepted help from my father. If we had borrowed so much as one five pence piece, he would have used it as a means of humiliating James.

And so we put the house on the market. We had always viewed it as an insurance for leaner times, and these were leaner times. But there was one small complication – we didn't own the freehold to the entire property. When we had bought the house we were vastly overstretched and Iain Stewart, a mutual friend at the Bank of Scotland, persuaded my father to buy the cottage my mother was to live in. At the time it was a godsend but, in trying to sell, if JJ decided to be awkward and refused to sell Pam's cottage, he would have us over a barrel. The property would be worth a fraction of its real value and we wouldn't be able to afford to move.

But JJ didn't do what we expected; he seldom did. When we told him we were planning to sell the house, his first shot was, 'I'm not surprised, I don't know what you ever saw in that house anyway.' Then when we said Pam would be coming with us he said, 'That's marvellous, couldn't be better, suits me fine,' and, as he quickly calculated in his head how much money he had made on his investment, a big grin came over his face. In ten years the value of the property had quadrupled. 'Of course, if you are taking Pam with you, then you realise that's her finished with me. I'm not buying her another house. In the future, you can pay for her, she's your responsibility, I want nothing more to do with her.'

James calmly and quietly said, 'Fine, JJ,' but the fact was that, without a contribution from him we could never have afforded the house we had found, which was perfect with a two-bedroom annex for Pam. But Iain Stewart once again came to our aid, and persuaded my father that it was hardly fair to expect us to buy a house for his wife.

And so we moved in August 1994, to a very pretty, seventeenth-century, Cotswold-stone farmhouse in North Wiltshire. We were a hundred miles away from my father, and the relief was palpable. I realised that for the last twenty years I had been living with a permanent knot in my stomach, waiting for the rumble of his Range Rover in the drive, waiting for the atmosphere in the house to freeze, never knowing whether he would be in a good mood or bad, never knowing whether an innocent remark might spark a livid response, never knowing whether he would be spoiling for a fight or, just occasionally, would be cheerful and good company. He often used to say to me, 'Why are you so tense? What's the matter? Is everything all right between you and James?' The irony was that the only time James and I ever argued was because of my father. When we woke up in Wiltshire, James looked as though he had been given a new lease of life and so did my mother. For the first time since she left JJ, she was free of his bullying. We all felt as though lead weights had been lifted from our shoulders.

But of course I was racked with guilt. JJ's reaction when we finally left was to sulk. He said he didn't want to come and see the house, had no interest in going to Wiltshire, didn't want to come and spend Christmas with us. It didn't matter if we didn't see each other again. We had moved to be close to Prue, he said, so we would be all right, we would see her instead. He took no interest in how we lived, or where we shopped, or where the children went to school, he even stopped telephoning for a while. I knew he was desperately hurt that we'd left him, and desperately lonely; he was worried sick about Roderick, and frightened by his own intimations of mortality. Although I knew that he had brought just about all of it on himself, I felt as though I had betrayed him.

But there was an unexpected bonus in our move to Wiltshire. My job at John Lewis meant I was in London three days a week and JJ and I started lunching together. Away from James and Pam, on neutral ground, our relationship was as good as it had ever been. Sometimes he would ring and invite me, other times I would ring him to see if he was free and, even if he wasn't, he would almost always invite me to join his other guest, and would send his driver with the Range Rover to collect me.

He loved showing me off to people, and, in introducing me, piled on the praise and the accolades in a way that I found excruciatingly embarrassing. But then he did that with everyone. He never knew a plain ordinary actress, she was always 'the greatest talent on the British stage'; a cartoonist was always 'a genius'; a doctor always 'the best' – everyone he knew was described with a string of superlatives – they could even be a bore, but they were 'the biggest, goddamned bore this side of the English Channel'.

My father came to see our new house in Wiltshire once. He invited Alex, who was then nineteen, on a trip to Madeira with him, eight months after we moved, and they were due back at Gatwick on an evening flight. I suggested to JJ that he should keep Alex for the night at Wellpools, which was close to Gatwick, and then drive him home to us the following day and come and have lunch. He agreed, and I set about killing the fatted calf. I cooked all his favourite things, cleaned the house and filled it with flowers. I was really looking forward to showing it off and, having spent a week with Alex, I thought there was a good chance he would be in a good mood. Jack and Peta were looking forward to seeing him. At about 12.30 p.m. the phone rang. It was JJ calling from the car. 'I'll be there in sixteen minutes. I am not going to stay for lunch. I'm going straight home and I want you to get a sandwich ready for me for when I arrive.'

Sixteen minutes later his Range Rover scrunched up the drive: 'Right, got my sandwich for me? I'm in a hurry, it's a bloody long way to drive, it's taken hours.' He said no hellos, no apologies and volunteered nothing about the house or the holiday. He came inside in search of his sandwich, and still said nothing. He didn't even look around him. I was stunned. 'Look, I don't mind if you don't want the lunch I've cooked you,' I said, 'but you're going to bloody well look round the house.' I took him no further than the ground floor and he showed no interest.

'Marvellous,' he said flatly. 'Have you got my sandwich?' He wouldn't have a drink or even a cup of coffee, and as I took him back out to his car he looked at the barn conversion that had once been part of the farm and shared our drive and said, 'How splendid to have such close neighbours.' With no other neighbours for nearly half a mile in either direction, this barn was the single drawback to our new house – and probably the only thing that made it affordable. He made the one comment that he knew would hurt.

As Sam and Alex grew older, their relationship with him became much more difficult. What JJ liked to do, increasingly with age, was to pontificate. His favourite expression was, 'If I could just explain something to you.' He didn't want debate; he wanted an audience, and an uncritical one at that. Sam was a combative character and didn't like being preached at, particularly on subjects that he knew about; and couldn't resist challenging some of my father's more extreme and prejudiced attitudes. He was brave. JJ, his face puce, would turn the full force of his invective against Sam, but Sam held his ground and said precisely what he thought, calmly but forcibly. It made for some very tense moments and, as his mother, I was afraid that the boundary between justifiable self-defence frequently crossed into bad manners, but my sympathies were with Sam. I remember the Sunday lunch when Sam, aged sixteen, was just back from a Russian exchange trip. He was learning Russian at school and had spent two weeks living with a family in Moscow, where the women spent their days queuing for food. It was before Glasnost and the most fascinating experience. But JJ couldn't sit down at the lunch table and say, 'Tell me about your trip.' He had to tell us about Russia, although at that point he had never even been there. It was the same when, after Eton, Sam spent part of a gap year travelling in China, India and Pakistan. JJ didn't want to hear about it, he wanted to explain to us all about the Chinese.

But when Sam left Oxford, in the summer of 1996, everything changed. He went to work for Peter McKay, who was about to re-launch *Punch* magazine. It was JJ's suggestion. Knowing that Peter was recruiting a team, he told Sam to write and ask for a job. Sam made no reference to either JJ or me when he wrote, but Peter immediately realised who he was when he arrived for the interview, and gave him a job as his assistant, and general office dogsbody. It wasn't complete nepotism; Sam already had some experience outside school and university. Before travelling, he had spent six months working for Auberon Waugh on the *Literary Review* and working shifts on the Londoner's Diary of the *Evening Standard*; I don't imagine the First in English that he came away from Oxford with did him any harm either. JJ could not have been more delighted, not only that Sam was going into journalism, but that he had been given his first job by Peter, his friend and the protégé to whom he gave his first job in Fleet Street more than thirty years ago. He was able to take them both to lunch and he loved it.

The dynamics of their relationship changed. Sam had everything to learn about journalism, and about the people, the personalities, and the gossip, and there was no better, more experienced teacher to show him the way. They continued to spar however. 'You'll never make a journalist,' JJ would say in his most didactic way, 'if you don't learn to keep quiet and listen. That's what makes a good

journalist, not talking, listening. Now shut up and listen to me.'
The irony was entirely lost on him.

I would sometimes join them for lunch, and was appalled by the
way my father poured drink down Sam's throat. He would keep
topping his glass up and, if Sam wasn't drinking fast enough, say,
'Come on, Sam, you're not drinking.' He had done it to members
of his staff on the *Sunday Express*, and he had done it to guests at
Wellpools – still delighting in watching people lose control – but I
couldn't understand the desire to force alcohol on his own grandson,
particularly given the family history. Besides, the culture of Fleet
Street had changed. Fleet Street itself had gone and so too had much
of the heavy drinking. Sam was in his first job. To swagger into the
office after a long lunch and more than half a bottle of wine seemed
to me to be completely idiotic. I used to try and intervene, but Sam
was grown up and it was really none of my business. As it happens,
Sam could handle it, but I still didn't understand what JJ thought
he was doing.

Three months after the re-launch of *Punch*, Peter McKay moved
to the *Daily Mail* to write a new gossip column called Ephraim
Hardcastle. Within weeks he had invited Sam to join him as his
deputy. So, for the last six months of my father's life, Sam was
working in the same business, for the same people, in the same
building. Nothing made my father prouder than being able to walk
in and out of the office with his grandson, to take him to lunch and
to show him off to his friends and colleagues. And nothing pleased
him more than to see Sam enjoying Peter's company as much as he
did.

There was a glorious symmetry to the situation. Not only was
Sam employed by JJ's protégé, Peter McKay, the name of the column
he was working on, Ephraim Hardcastle, had originally been a
column in the *Sunday Express*, which in the 1950s, under JJ's editorship, Peter Dacre had written. And it was Peter Dacre's son, Paul
Dacre, who was now Sam's Editor at the *Daily Mail*.

One day over lunch with Sam, JJ became very melancholy. The
pain in his hip had suddenly become chronic. He even found walking
to and from the car an effort. He was virtually crippled and he
knew that if he wanted to walk properly again he would have to

have the hip replaced. The idea of going into hospital for an operation terrified him. He pulled out a poem he had written and passed it to Sam. 'What do you think? It's crap isn't it?'

I dreamed that I was young again.
Alone, shit-scared and lost at night
In the cockpit of a Fairey Battle.
Into the black, starless night
The plane's exhaust spat out flames,
Blue-green flames, I knew that soon would cease.
The flickering fuel gauge showed close, so close to empty.
Dear God, I prayed, don't let me die.
Just let me live and I will pledge my life to you.
I'll do Thy will. I'll serve Thy purpose.
In his mercy, my prayer was answered.
Now I am old, unloved, unwanted, a life of sin behind me.
And once again I pray.
Dear God, let me be young again.
Alone, shit-scared and lost at night in the cockpit of a Fairey
    Battle.

JJ sought advice about the hip from all sorts of people, but it was a trip to Barfleur in December 1996 that tipped the balance. He took Stanley Miller and his wife Kathleen over to do some Christmas shopping. 'I didn't think he was fit enough to go on his own so I drove the car for him,' says Stanley. 'There was no heating in the house, he came in, took off his jacket and said, "I'll not bother lighting the fire, it's lovely and warm in here." I kept my coat on all weekend, but Kathleen and I didn't stay in the house, couldn't stand it, it was far too cold.

'He was in agony and had been in agony for many months. He just couldn't move. His condition was a bit of a medical nightmare. He had caned himself for years with cigarettes and alcohol and the fast life, then he developed this hip problem, and he was overweight. He had all the stigmata of impending disaster, probably cardio-vascular, because he still smoked quite heavily.

'We used to discuss this many a time. I said it was his life, he had to make the decision about the quality of it. A bad hip is like having a monumental toothache in your hip, it doesn't go away and you can't rub whisky into it. His stomach wasn't of the best, so if he tried to take aspirins he'd get into tummy problems, it was a vicious circle. So he made the decision to have it done.'

Iain Murray-Lyon had lunch with JJ shortly beforehand. 'He could hardly get out of the car or walk into the restaurant, so the hip had to be done but was a high risk strategy – at his age, with his weight, and he was on anticoagulants. I didn't try and persuade him not to, but I had a bad feeling that the whole thing might not go terribly well. He wanted to take the risk.'

JJ talked it over with me too, although not as calmly as we might have done. The pain was making him very short-tempered and, in retrospect, was probably the cause of quite a lot of his irascible behaviour in the last few years. He was frightened, he thought he might not survive the operation, there would be complications because of the Warfarin, he hated hospitals, he didn't trust doctors. The truth is he was terrified of dying. On the other hand, the pain was intolerable, and if he were unable to walk, there would be no pleasure to life at all. There seemed to be no alternative to having the operation; besides, there were countless examples of people who had successfully had hips replaced, including the Queen Mother when she was a good twenty years older than JJ.

And so he went into Epsom Hospital under the care of Mr Andrew Cobb, who was recommended by Stanley Miller. JJ liked him and Andrew Cobb very swiftly became 'The very best orthopaedic surgeon in the country' and he trusted him entirely. It was a few days before they could operate, while a haematologist took him off the Warfarin and adjusted his blood clotting levels, and during that time I went to see him and take him out to lunch.

I took Alex with me, who was at home for the Easter holidays. He was studying History of Art at Edinburgh University. JJ loved Alex. Just to be perverse, he called him 'Eck' which is a Scottish abbreviation for Alexander – although his father was always known as Sandy. Alex was very different from Sam, much less sure of himself, much more compliant, and his relationship with JJ was entirely different. He was less easily provoked than his brother, and hated rows with JJ, so tended to be much less confrontational. During their holidays in Barfleur – which had latterly included Jack, who was now twelve, Alex was often caught in the middle of the crossfire between Sam and JJ and would spend much of his time calming stormy waters and looking after Jack.

JJ was in a filthy mood when we arrived to collect him from the hospital. Again, I am sure it was the pain. He grumbled about my car being too low, and then as we drove out of the town, I suggested a restaurant I knew about a mile away. 'I'm not having lunch there,' he barked. 'I've been shut up all week in that goddamned hospital, I don't want to go and sit in some bloody awful restaurant in Ashtead. I want to get into the countryside. Just drive on.' We ended up at a pub called The Running Horses in Mickleham, opposite the church, which we used to walk to sometimes on Sunday mornings from Garden Cottage. Then he was bristling with energy and drive, he was young, charismatic and heady with the power of his position; he was at the start of one of the most extraordinary careers in Fleet Street. That day, more than forty years later, he was a sad, frail old man, who had to be helped out of the car, and walked with a stick, slowly and painfully. Once we were sitting down, he complained about the food, and the wine wasn't right, but otherwise he was strangely subdued; and when I insisted on paying for the lunch, for the first time in my life, he let me.

The operation was a success. He insisted he didn't want any visitors, but I ignored him and went to see him a couple of days later. He was already up and a physiotherapist had been helping him walk with a frame. He was in good spirits – he even accepted the flowers I brought him with reasonably good grace, also the chocolates. He was working on his column. The only problem, he said, was that he had a very upset tummy. A few days later he discharged himself from the hospital, against the doctor's advice, and went home.

For many years he had had a husband and wife team look after the house and garden at Wellpools, Les and Hazel White, who lived in the village and came on a Saturday when JJ was in London. When they moved away, Les continued to drive back to do the garden, and their daughter Sandra, who still lived in the village, cleaned the house. After his operation, JJ's plan was that Sandra should live in the house for a bit to look after him until he was back on his feet, and his bed would be moved downstairs to the sitting room, so he didn't have any climbing to do. I suggested that I should find a nurse to look after him, but JJ wanted none of it, and angrily told me I could forget it. So I did, and the day he arrived home he went into the garden, where the sun was shining, sat down on a garden chair that was too low, dislocated the new hip and was taken straight back to hospital.

By the time he next came out I had organised some professional care for him, via a nursing agency. Sandra was much relieved, and I think that, secretly, JJ was too, although he grumbled about some of the older nurses he was sent and snapped and snarled at them all. I went to see him. He still complained of an upset tummy, and terrible pain in his stomach. He thought maybe it was his old ulcer playing up and started to take the Tagamet tablets again that had once been his staple diet, but they made no difference. It was beginning to get him down. Then one night he got out of bed to go to the loo, which was down the corridor, and lost his balance. He crashed into the doorframe and gashed his bad hip. The wound bled profusely, an ambulance was called and he was taken back into Epsom Hospital.

The pain was not the only thing that was getting him down. Roderick, probably because he was worried about our father, became a menace. He got it into his head that JJ was having an affair with Sandra, which was of course complete nonsense, and spread the story around the village. Sandra knew all about Roderick, she and her parents had dealt with him many times when he had turned up at Wellpools, but it was nevertheless acutely embarrassing for her, particularly since she lived with a partner.

JJ was explosive when he heard and, when he discovered that Roderick had also telephoned the hospital and told the sister on duty that his father was having an affair with his cleaning lady, he hit the roof. He phoned me in despair. 'I can't cope with him any more,' he said. 'I haven't got the strength. I need all my energy to get myself better. Please, please, please keep Roderick away from me. Just let me get better. Please.' I promised I would keep him away, and Stanley Miller spoke to the hospital, 'I told them that if they got any calls from Roderick, he had been under terrible stress and to ignore it.'

I went to see JJ again, and he looked worn out, the fight had gone out of him, and for the first time there was a closeness between us, almost a softness. I felt that our roles were at last reversed, that he was looking to me for strength and help. When I left to drive back to Wiltshire, I told him I loved him. I hadn't often done that before and meant it.

JJ went home once more, but the pain in his stomach continued until he could take it no more. He rang Stanley's wife Kathleen, she got hold of Stanley, and he was admitted to the BUPA hospital in Ashtead. 'He was in severe distress with an acute abdomen, he was tender, rigid, no bowel sounds and was obviously unwell. It was perfectly apparent to me what he had done: he had thrown up a blood clot into the vessels that supply the gut. This was my theory but when I went in – when you do that you get a bit of gangrenous gut which is usually only about a foot long, and you can take the damaged bit out and sew it up, and Bob can damn nearly be your Uncle if you're lucky. I opened him up and the whole gut had gone black. The reason for this was the main artery to the gut had become totally narrowed. If you kill the artery to the gut, it has no alternative blood supply, and you're in big trouble. He also had an aortic aneurysm, the main artery of his body had swollen up and, in addition to that, his liver, which should be nearly as big as a rugby ball, was the size of my shut fist, it was seriously cirrhotic. I reckon he would have been in liver failure within two to three years maximum if everything else had been all right. So that was the nature of his pathology, he had a stacked deck against him. But what killed him was gangrene of the gut.'

JJ phoned me to say he had gone into Ashtead, and that Stanley thought he had a blockage in his gut and was going to operate. I said I would come and see him straight away. He said no; he didn't want me to. 'Please, Darling,' he said, 'I would rather you didn't. I don't feel like seeing anyone – not even you. Please, please.' Something made me respect his wishes.

It was 1 May 1997, the day of the General Election. He was

convinced the Tories were going to win. 'He was so unwell that night,' recalls Stanley. 'I had a very good Scots anaesthetist. I told JJ what the problem was, I said you've got a black loop of gut, there's no need to do any investigations, the only thing to do is open it up and deal with it. This is serious, you've got to have it dealt with, you can't just ignore it and he said, "Well, you'll just need to do whatever you can do." I said, "I'm a travelling optimist, I've done lots of these." You tend to tell white lies just before the anaesthetic – even though you're not allowed to do it any more.'

I was at a party that night. I had told Stanley how to contact me if he needed to. At about 10.30 p.m. he called. The news was bad. He had opened up my father and found gangrene in his bowel, which he had tried to patch up, but the damage was too extensive. He was not going to survive. It might be two or three days at the most, he was unconscious and peaceful, what did I want him to do? To bring him to the surface so that we could all say our farewells, or to leave him sedated? I was totally unprepared for this. It had never crossed my mind that his tummy-ache and diarrhoea could kill him. The noise of the party was going on behind me, the results were coming in, it looked as though John Major, whom JJ had championed in his column just four days before, was on his way out, and Tony Blair might be the next Prime Minister. Time stood still, I had to make a decision, but there was no real choice to make. I said, 'Keep him under.' I thought it was the kindest thing to do.

The next day I rang Roderick and told him that JJ was in Epsom Hospital, in intensive care on a life support machine, and if he wanted to see him he should be quick. He said I didn't know what I was talking about, it was nonsense, anyway, JJ hadn't been answering his phone calls, so he was not going to go. I don't know whether he ever did or not. I phoned Alex in Edinburgh and told him to get on a plane, and then James and I took Pam, Jack and Peta to see him. Sam came down from London on a train and we met him at the station and all went together. It was a harrowing half-hour, each of us with our private memories. The monster who had dominated our lives, each in our own separate way, was stilled, was tamed, was defeated.

I met Alex's plane early the next morning, on the Saturday, and we dashed to Epsom but we were too late. He was dead. We clung to each other and cried for a long time, then we sat with his body, each with our thoughts. The tubes and the machinery were gone and so too was the man. All that remained was an empty shell. I cried bitterly for days, mostly out of regret. Regret that I hadn't been able to show him the love I felt, regret that our relationship had been so tortured, and regret that, as a result, he had been so lonely and frightened at the end.

Unknown to me, he had appointed me as an executor of his will, along with Ian Irvine and, when I looked amongst his papers, I found another poem.

So very soon for me the last waltz will be playing.
Thank you dear God for having asked me to the ball.
Thank you for all the fun, the fear, the tiny successes, the
    failures too.
For the scent of roses, for friendship, the taste of wine and
    women's lips,
The touch of thighs in hot surrender, for love won for a
    moment and for love lost for ever.

Thank you for Pam and Pooh, and Anne and Jane and Sue
    and Zaza.
For Rod and Alex, Tink and Tup.
May they all go on dancing yet awhile.
But thank you most of all for little Sam.
May the party for him go on forever.

The news of his death was on all the television and radio news broadcasts that night, and the Sunday papers were full of lengthy obituaries. The *Mail on Sunday* carried his last column, written that week, and dictated to his lovely and long-suffering young secretary, Harriet Arkell. Throughout all the operations and pain, he hadn't missed one week.

We buried him in the churchyard at Mickleham. It seemed to me to be the place where he had been happiest, and the Reverend Gary

Bradley, a friend from London, came to conduct the service. I was touched by the number of people who came, most of them from far afield. Alex read the poem JJ had read out to Sam, Sam read 1 Corinthians 13, and Peter McKay gave a very funny address, mostly about the quirkiness of JJ's lunching habits, which was perfect. And, at the end, Roderick climbed unsteadily into the pulpit, while everyone held their breath, and very slowly but touchingly, said what a great man his father had been and thanked every one for coming.

Afterwards, James, Sam, Alex, Jack, Rod and I all lowered his coffin into the grave. I had written him a long letter, which went inside the coffin, telling him all the things I was never able to say to him when he was alive. My faith, like his, is very simple, and I believe that wherever he is, we have made our peace. Then we all went to have lunch in the Running Horses where we had been not three weeks before.

In September, there was a memorial service in St Bride's, Fleet Street, organised by Associated Newspapers, whose generosity, support and kindness throughout what – because of my brother's condition – was a nightmare period, could only be marvelled at. Lord Rothermere gave the address, Roderick read a poem, Peter McKay and I read a few classic columns, and once again my sons did readings. Sam read 1 Corinthians 13, which I had chosen for both services not really knowing why. When he heard my choice, Canon John Oates at St Bride's, said, 'How strange. I once heard your father read 1 Corinthians 13, and it was incredibly powerful. I have never heard anyone read it better.'

The church in which JJ had walked me up the aisle twenty-seven years before was once more filled with friends, journalists, politicians, and the serried ranks of the great and good. And the choir sang 'Ae fond kiss, and then we sever!' But the best part of the service was my brother's idea. As Ephraim Hardcastle concurred:

The star was Fettes College's Niall Rowantree, 15, a gamekeeper's son from Sutherland, who played the bagpipe lament, Highland Cathedral. He's at Fettes on a piping scholarship from Sutherland's Golspie High School. Sentimental Sir John

– famously canny with his bawbees – would have approved. Not only is Niall a bagpiper so subtle he can reduce grown men to tears, but his other speciality is mathematics.

Epilogue

It is nearly five years now since my father died yet his memory is as vivid today as if I had just said goodbye to him at the lunch table. Alex did a painting of him, from a photograph taken about ten years before he died, which hangs in my office. He is in belligerent mode, his head is down and cocked at a slight angle, one big clumsy hand with its winner's thumb that bends right back to form a hook – which I inherited – is jabbing the air and his hooded eyes fix me with ferocity. He is wearing a yellow and white striped golfing shirt and his jet-black hair sits starkly against the red background of the painting; hair, which in reality had turned snowy white – like every member of the Junor family over the age of fifty. For years he dyed it amateurishly in his bathroom at home, his one gesture of defiance towards the ageing process, and the older he grew the harsher and more ridiculous it looked against his florid skin. But no one ever dared say a word – not even when he had the audacity to criticise Ronald Reagan in his column for 'getting at the Cherry Blossom boot black'. He looks down at me from the wall, and I wish we could have another chance.

I still talk about him, and I still think about him; his influence on my life and the lives of my family was all-pervading. We use his phrases all the time. 'Don't you know I've got a column to write?' he would say irritably when invited to do anything he didn't want to do. 'Just you sink your teeth into that,' he would say when handing over a bag of ageing fruit that he had bought at a knock-down price. And 'If I could just explain something to you.'

His superstitions live on too. We may not throw spilt salt over our shoulders, and we always, always put shoes on the table, and go out of our way to walk under ladders, but we do it knowing JJ would have had a fit if he was there to see us do it. The difference between now and then is that the knot in my stomach has gone and, when I hear some of the more outrageous stories, I can laugh. The astonishing thing is that so many of the people who used to know him in Fleet Street still talk about him and laugh uproariously at his idiosyncrasies too, just as they did when he was alive and they were working for him. They never stopped swapping anecdotes, each one of them lapsing into their own hopeless impersonation of his accent and, so long as there is breath in them to make it to the lunch table, I doubt they ever will. Alan Watkins once had plans to create a JJ Luncheon Club, specifically for exchanging JJ stories, and the only person who would be barred from membership would be JJ himself. But they didn't really need a club; they talked about him anyway.

The father I knew when I was a child was a much more likeable character than the volatile, didactic man he grew into. The intolerance of age obviously contributed to that, but I think the power he wielded as Editor of the *Sunday Express* for all those years changed him, and my mother was never an aggressive enough character to remind him of who he was.

Paul Dacre, as a powerful Editor himself, agrees it's a danger that goes with the territory. 'JJ was a very, very powerful Editor. He had huge political power, and huge respect and reverence by his own company and by politicians. That's a dangerous, heady mix. You have a job to which you devote a hundred hours a week, and you're used to everyone dropping everything for you, doing everything at your beck and call, never questioning your judgement – and people didn't question JJ's judgement, he didn't like it if they did. Going home after that can be very difficult.'

JJ turned into a monster, and he left some serious casualties in his wake; my mother was the one I find least forgivable, also James – two thoroughly good people who did nothing to deserve such cruelty. Yet most of the people who knew him talk about him with a kind of gritty affection and some with genuine love. Besides, someone who can keep his staff for twenty or thirty years, can't be all bad. He wasn't all bad. He had some great qualities, and an enthusiasm for life that I have seldom seen matched. He had passion, which I admire in anyone; and he had compassion. He was not boring, he was not dull and, for all the rigidity of his routine, he was never wholly predictable. He was dangerous.

But, for all his bravado, for all his protestations, I don't think he was a happy man. He longed for love – the one thing that eluded him – particularly the love of his children and grandchildren. It eluded him because he didn't know how to love himself. He didn't understand that love is about giving – not money and presents – but giving selflessly and unconditionally, giving time and interest; love is about making yourself vulnerable, exposing your soul, sharing your thoughts and dreams and fears, and trusting those you love to keep those aspects of yourself safe. JJ was too insecure to trust anyone with his innermost feelings. He was afraid of exposing his emotions and weaknesses, and his defence in any situation where he felt himself becoming vulnerable was to attack. He killed my mother's love for him entirely.

There are all sorts of things I wish about him. I wish I had been able to trust and confide in him, I wish I had been able to ask his advice and talk to him calmly about any and every subject, I wish I had been able to relax in his company and laugh with him more. I wish I hadn't been frightened of him, I wish we had really known each other, and I wish he had been a happier man. But I would not have swapped him. For all his monstrous behaviour, I was enormously proud of him, proud to have a father who had achieved so much from so little, proud that he never conformed, and proud that he had the courage to write what he thought, and be different from the crowd. He was rude and offensive, bigoted, intolerant and impatient – in his writing no less than in his dealings with family, colleagues and friends – but he could also be brilliant company, he was a good storyteller, a delicious gossip, he could be charming and witty, and his enthusiasm for newspapers, politics and personalities was as keen and infectious at the age of seventy-eight as it had been when he first came into Fleet Street.

The blessing is that he died when he did, still writing, with an office to go to and interesting people to lunch with. Retirement, infirmity and old age would have been purgatory for him – and pure, unadulterated hell for anyone who had the task of looking after him. I greatly fear that task would have been mine.

Postscript

After my father's death, Roderick and I, sadly, scarcely spoke again. JJ divided his estate between the two of us, with Wellpools going to Roderick if he had wanted it. If not, it was to be sold and the proceeds divided between us both. He didn't want it, and the house was sold. But, to ensure that my brother didn't squander his inheritance on drink, and that Roddy, now known as Rod, would be provided for in the future, JJ left Roderick's share of his estate in Trust and appointed me a Trustee.

It was not a happy situation. Roderick, five years my senior, was bitterly resentful. He wanted to challenge the legality of my being an executor of the will and a beneficiary. He became convinced that I was stealing from him – as, on the advice of Ian Irvine, my fellow Trustee, I had taken papers, a few valuables and some guns from the empty house for safekeeping. Ian also suggested we appoint a professional executor, who worked for JJ's legal firm in the City. Roderick didn't trust them either and appointed his own lawyers to look after his interests, and it all became extremely unpleasant.

Roderick didn't speak to me at the memorial service, he pushed me away when I went to try and kiss him, and he didn't come to the reception laid on by Associated Newspapers at the Howard Hotel afterwards. Instead, he hosted a rival party at the Cheshire Cheese. Two months later, he collapsed in the house that JJ had bought for him, and was rushed to East Surrey Hospital where he remained for the next two months. I took Pam to see him twice, but he was unconscious on both occasions, and he died there on

341

Christmas Eve 1997, at the age of fifty-three. The sweet, loving, talented brother I grew up with deserved better – but that person had gone years ago.

My mother didn't cry when Roderick died. I don't think she had any more tears left; as if the years of grief and pain had left her emotionally bankrupt. But she went downhill after his death. A series of mini strokes have left her immobile, and dementia has mercifully released her from most of her memories. But she still has the kindest, most selfless nature of anyone I've ever known. It's not surprising he loved her so much; it's just a tragedy for them both that he couldn't show it.

With my share of the inheritance, I bought the barn at the back of our house. I wonder if JJ would have appreciated the irony?

Index